Dreamweaver® CS4 For Dummies®

The Property Inspector in HTML Mode

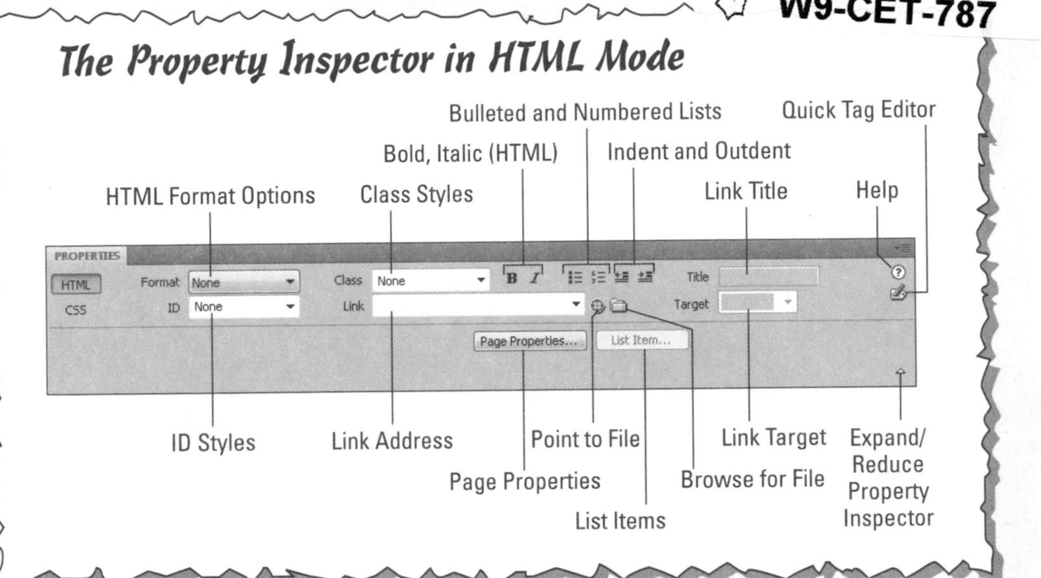

The Property Inspector in CSS Mode

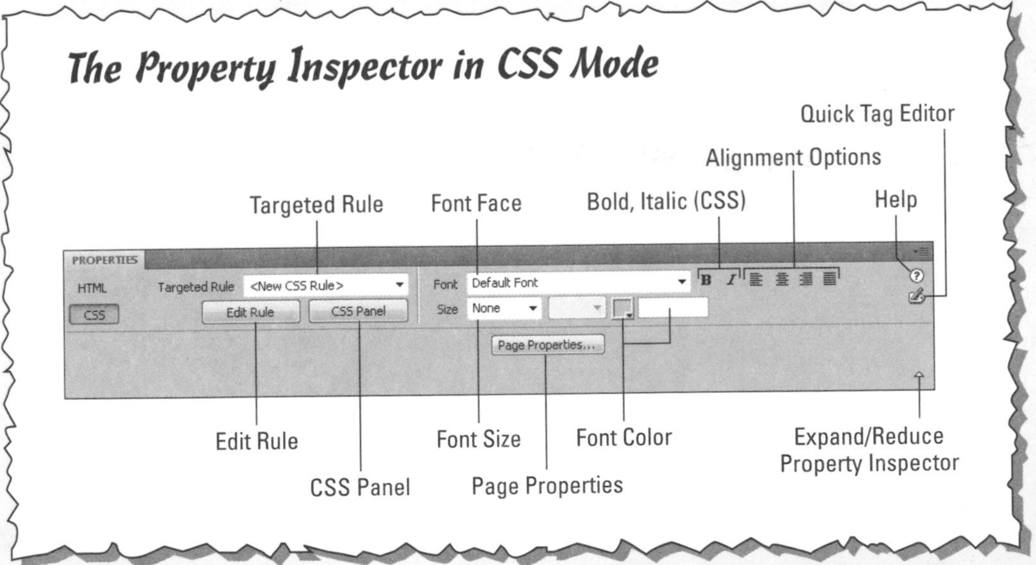

For Dummies: Bestselling Book Series for Beginners

Dreamweaver® CS4 For Dummies®

The Panel Group

INSERT

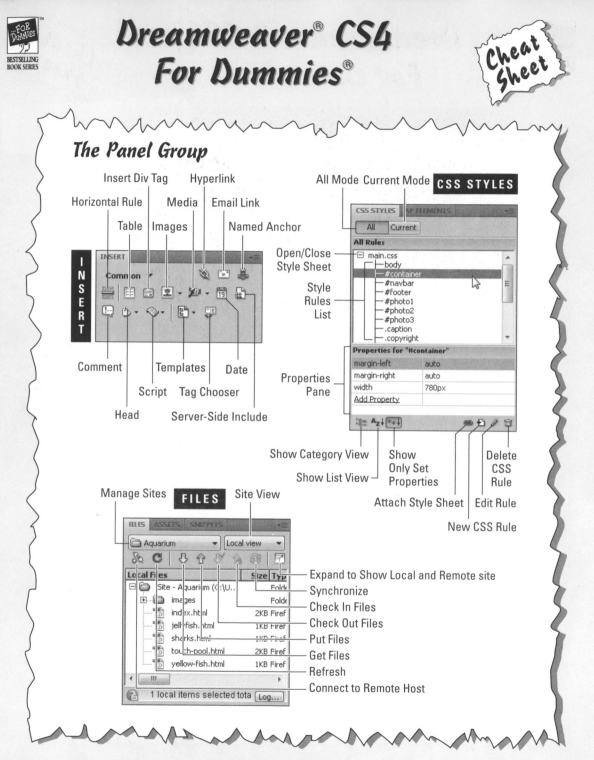

Insert Div Tag
Hyperlink
Horizontal Rule
Media
Email Link
Table
Images
Named Anchor
INSERT
Common
Comment
Templates
Date
Script
Tag Chooser
Head
Server-Side Include

CSS STYLES

All Mode
Current Mode
CSS STYLES
AP ELEMENTS
All
Current
All Rules
Open/Close Style Sheet
main.css
body
#container
#navbar
#footer
#photo1
#photo2
#photo3
.caption
.copyright
Style Rules List
Properties for "#container"

margin-left	auto
margin-right	auto
width	780px
Add Property	

Properties Pane
Show Category View
Show List View
Show Only Set Properties
Attach Style Sheet
New CSS Rule
Edit Rule
Delete CSS Rule

FILES

Manage Sites
Site View
FILES
ASSETS
SNIPPETS
Aquarium
Local view
Local Files
Size
Type
Site - Aquarium (C:\U..
images
index.html 2KB Firef
jellyfish.html 1KB Firef
sharks.html 1KB Firef
touch-pool.html 2KB Firef
yellow-fish.html 1KB Firef
1 local items selected tota
Log...
Expand to Show Local and Remote site
Synchronize
Check In Files
Check Out Files
Put Files
Get Files
Refresh
Connect to Remote Host

For more information about Wiley Publishing, call 1-800-762-2974.

For Dummies: Bestselling Book Series for Beginners

Dreamweaver® CS4 FOR DUMMIES®

Dreamweaver® CS4 FOR DUMMIES®

By Janine Warner

Wiley Publishing, Inc.

Dreamweaver® CS4 For Dummies®

Published by
Wiley Publishing, Inc.
111 River Street
Hoboken, NJ 07030-5774
www.wiley.com

Published by Wiley Publishing, Inc., Indianapolis, Indiana

Published simultaneously in Canada

For general information on our other products and services, please contact our Customer Care Department within the U.S. at 800-762-2974, outside the U.S. at 317-572-3993, or fax 317-572-4002.

For technical support, please visit www.wiley.com/techsupport.

Wiley also publishes its books in a variety of electronic formats. Some content that appears in print may not be available in electronic books.

Library of Congress Control Number: 2008935811

ISBN: 978-0-470-34502-3

Manufactured in the United States of America

10 9 8 7 6 5 4 3 2

About the Author

Janine Warner is a bestselling author, speaker, and Internet consultant.

Since 1995, she's written and coauthored more than a dozen books about the Internet, including *Web Sites Do-It-Yourself For Dummies* and *Teach Yourself Dreamweaver Visually*.

She's also the host of a series of training videos on Dreamweaver and Web design for Total Training. Her first video on Dreamweaver has won two industry awards, and excerpts of her videos are features at both Microsoft.com and Adobe.com.

An award-winning journalist, her articles and columns have appeared in a variety of publications, including *The Miami Herald*, *Shape Magazine*, and the Pulitzer Prize-winning *Point Reyes Light* newspaper. She also writes a regular column about Dreamweaver for *Layers Magazine*.

Janine is a popular speaker at conferences and events throughout the United States and abroad, and she's taught online journalism courses at the University of Southern California Annenberg School for Communication and the University of Miami.

Warner has extensive Internet experience working on large and small Web sites. From 1994 to 1998, she ran Visiontec Communications, a Web design business in Northern California, where she worked for a diverse group of clients including Levi Strauss & Co., AirTouch International, and many other small and medium-size businesses.

In 1998, she joined *The Miami Herald* as their Online Managing Editor. A year later, she was promoted to Director of New Media and managed a team of designers, programmers, journalists, and sales staff. She left that position to serve as Director of Latin American Operations for CNET Networks, an international technology media company. Warner earned a degree in journalism and Spanish from the University of Massachusetts, Amherst, and spent the first several years of her career in Northern California as a reporter and editor.

Since 2001, Janine has run her own business as a writer, speaker, and consultant. She now lives and works with her husband in Los Angeles. To read more, visit `www.JCWarner.com` or `www.DigitalFamily.com`.

Dedication

To all those who dare to dream about the possibilities of the Web: May all your dreams come true.

Author's Acknowledgments

I love teaching Web design because it's so much fun to see what everyone creates on the Internet. Most of all, I want to thank all the people who have read my books or watched my videos over the years and gone on to create Web sites. You are my greatest inspiration. Thank you, thank you, thank you.

Thanks to my love, David LaFontaine, whose patience and support have kept me fed, loved, and entertained. You are the greatest researcher I've ever known and a constant source of inspiration.

Thanks to photographers and Web designers Mariana Davi Cheng (DaviDesign.com), Jasper Johal (Jasper-Art.com), Pamela Kerr (LouiseGreen.com), Anissa Thompson (Anissat.com), and Stephanie Kjos Warner who designed many of the Web sites and took the photographs featured in the examples in this book.

Thanks to the entire editorial team: Mark Justice Hinton for his superb tech editing; Becky Huehls for catching the details and improving the prose; and Bob Woerner for shepherding this book through the development and publishing process.

Over the years, I've thanked many people in my books — family, friends, teachers, and mentors — but I have been graced by so many wonderful people now that no publisher will give me enough pages to thank them all. So let me conclude by thanking everyone who has ever helped me with a Web site, a book, or any other aspect of writing and Internet research, just so I can go to sleep tonight and know I haven't forgotten anyone.

Publisher's Acknowledgments

We're proud of this book; please send us your comments through our online registration form located at www.dummies.com/register/.

Some of the people who helped bring this book to market include the following:

Acquisitions and Editorial

Project Editor: Rebecca Huehls

Executive Editor: Bob Woerner

Copy Editor: Jennifer Riggs

Technical Editor: Mark Justice Hinton

Editorial Manager: Leah P. Cameron

Editorial Assistant: Amanda Foxworth

Sr. Editorial Assistant: Cherie Case

Cartoons: Rich Tennant (www.the5thwave.com)

Composition Services

Project Coordinator: Patrick Redmond

Layout and Graphics: Reuben W. Davis, Stephanie D. Jumper, Christin Swinford, Ronald Terry, Christine Williams, Erin Zeltner

Proofreaders: Broccoli Information Management, Melissa Bronnenberg, Amanda Steiner

Indexer: Broccoli Information Management

Publishing and Editorial for Technology Dummies

Richard Swadley, Vice President and Executive Group Publisher

Andy Cummings, Vice President and Publisher

Mary Bednarek, Executive Acquisitions Director

Mary C. Corder, Editorial Director

Publishing for Consumer Dummies

Diane Graves Steele, Vice President and Publisher

Composition Services

Gerry Fahey, Vice President of Production Services

Debbie Stailey, Director of Composition Services

Contents at a Glance

Table of Contents

Introduction

In the ten-plus years that I've been writing about Web design, I've seen many changes — from the early days (before Dreamweaver even existed) when you could create only simple pages with HTML 1.0, to the elaborate designs you can create with Dreamweaver today using XHTML, CSS, AJAX, multimedia, and more.

If you're not sure what those acronyms mean yet, don't worry. I remember what it was like to figure out all this stuff, too, so I designed this book to introduce you to the basic concepts. I also want to prepare you for the ever-changing world of Web design, so I show you how to use Dreamweaver to create Web sites that take advantage of the latest advances in Web technologies, such as CSS and AJAX.

One of the challenges of Web design today is that Web pages are not only being displayed on different kinds of computers, but are also being downloaded to computers with monitors that are as big as widescreen televisions and as small as cell phones. As a result, creating Web sites that look good to all visitors is a lot more complex than it used to be, and standards have become a lot more important. That's why in this book, you find out not only how to use all the great features in Dreamweaver but also how to determine which of those features best serve your goals and your audience.

About This Book

I designed Dreamweaver CS4 For Dummies to help you find the answers you need when you need them. You don't have to read this book cover to cover, and you certainly don't have to memorize it. Consider this a quick study guide and a reference you can return to. Each section stands alone, giving you easy answers to specific questions and step-by-step instructions for common tasks.

Want to find out how to change the background color in page properties, design styles to align images, or add an interactive photo gallery with the Swap Image behavior? Jump right in and go directly to the section that most interests you. Don't worry about getting sand on this book at the beach or coffee spilled on the pages at breakfast — I promise it won't complain!

What's New in Dreamweaver CS4?

Dreamweaver's high-end features make it the preferred choice for professional Web designers, and its easy-to-use graphical interface makes it popular among novices and hobbyists as well. With each new version, Dreamweaver's become more powerful and feature-rich, but this upgrade is arguably the most dramatic, with the following new features:

- **Gray interface:** The first change you notice when you launch Dreamweaver CS4 is that it's all shades of gray. This change to the interface wasn't intended to make the program look dull — it's designed to help you work better with color in your own designs. If you miss all the colorful icons, don't fret. When you roll your cursor over the icons, their colorful designs reappear, making it easier to recognize and select them.
- **Customizable interface:** Dreamweaver now comes with more preset layout options. Dreamweaver CS3 offered three choices, but when you choose Workspace⇨Layout in CS4, you find eight preset layout options, each optimized for a specific profile, including Designer, Coder, and Programmer. If you miss the Insert panel being positioned at the top of the screen instead of at the top right where it's positioned in CS4, choose Classic from the Layout menu to get your old favorite back. All the panels, palettes, and toolbars can be repositioned on the screen with click-and-drag ease, and you can save multiple layout options by choosing Workspace⇨Layout⇨Manage Workspaces.
- **Enhanced CSS support:** Among the most dramatic (and welcome!) changes to Dreamweaver CS4 are better CSS (Cascading Style Sheets) support and a new host of CSS features. Creating and editing styles is now better integrated throughout Dreamweaver, especially in the Property inspector. Creating Web sites with CSS is by far the best option today. That's why so many of the improvements to Dreamweaver are related to CSS, and why I've dedicated more of this book than ever to the best strategies for creating styles and CSS layouts. Chapters 5 and 6 explain what you need to know in detail.
- **Property inspector:** The Property inspector has been split in two in Dreamweaver CS4 to better separate HTML (HyperText Markup Language) options from CSS. You can also create and edit styles as you specify settings in the Property inspector — a welcome addition that makes working with styles much faster and more intuitive (after you get the hang of it). See Chapter 5 for more.
- **Better integration with Photoshop, Flash, and other design programs:** Some of the coolest improvements to Dreamweaver CS4 include greater integration among Adobe's suite of programs. If you're a former GoLive user, you'll be pleased to find that Adobe added Smart Objects to CS4 (the lack of this feature was a big complaint among former GoLive users who tried Dreamweaver CS3). Smart Objects makes it possible to drag and

drop a Photoshop (PSD) file into a Web page in Dreamweaver and then use the Image Preview dialog box to optimize and resize the PSD file on the fly. Another great benefit — if you update the original PSD file later, Dreamweaver adds a little, red arrow to the optimized version in your Web page. Click the Update from Original button, and the changes are applied automatically. Working with graphics is the focus on Chapter 3, and multimedia with Flash is covered in Chapter 11.

- **Spry features for AJAX:** If you want to create drop-down menus, collapsible panels, and other interactive AJAX features, you'll appreciate the Spry menu in the Insert panel and all the ways you can use Spry to save time (and coding) with AJAX. See Chapter 13.
- **Live View:** CS4's new Live View makes it possible to render a page as it'd be displayed in a browser so you can see AJAX and other interactive features in action without leaving Dreamweaver. Live View uses the *WebKit* rendering engine (the same open source option used in Safari). Not only does the new Live View feature save you from launching a browser to test these kinds of features, but you can disable JavaScript while you use Live View to do things, such as freeze a drop-down list in action so you can more easily edit the CSS that controls the drop-down list display.
- **Code Navigator:** The new Code Navigator is a handy way to keep an eye on the CSS code for your pages. Anywhere in a Web page, you can right-click (Windows) or Control-click (Mac) and choose Code Navigator to open a small window that details the CSS on the page. Roll your cursor over any of the listed styles and you see a little pop-up with details of the style rule. Double-click a style name, and Dreamweaver takes you to the style in the CSS code, which makes editing styles quick and easy while you work in design view.
- **Related Files bar:** Just above the workspace, you find a handy list of associated files and scripts for any open document in the new Related Files bar. The files you find listed include external CSS files, JavaScript files (such as those created with the Dreamweaver Spry feature), and other programming files. Not only is the Related Files bar a handy reference that can help you keep track of all the files in your site, but it's also a shortcut. Click any filename to open it, and you can edit and apply the changes automatically to the HTML page you're working on.

Using Dreamweaver on a Mac or PC

Dreamweaver works almost identically on Macintosh or Windows computers. To keep screenshots consistent throughout this book, I've used a computer running Windows Vista. However, I've tested the program on both platforms, and whenever there is a difference in how a feature works, I indicate that difference in the instructions.

Conventions Used in This Book

Keeping things consistent makes them easier to understand. In this book, those consistent elements are *conventions.* Notice how the word *conventions* is in italics? I frequently put new terms in italics and then define them so that you know what they mean.

When I type *URLs* (Web addresses) or e-mail addresses within regular paragraph text, they look like this: `www.digitalfamily.com`. Sometimes, however, I set URLs off on their own line, like this:

```
www.digitalfamily.com
```

That's so you can easily spot them on a page if you want to type them into your browser to visit a site. I also assume that your Web browser doesn't require the introductory `http://` for Web addresses. If you use an older browser, remember to type this before the address (also make sure you include that part of the address when you're creating links in Dreamweaver).

Even though Dreamweaver makes knowing HTML code unnecessary, you may want to wade into HTML waters occasionally. I include HTML code in this book when I think it can help you better understand how things work in design view. Sometimes it's easier to remove or edit a tag in code view than design view. When I do provide examples, such as the following code which links a URL to a Web page, I set off the HTML in the same monospaced type as URLs:

```
<A HREF="http://www.digitalfamily.com">Janine's Digital
          Family Web Site</A>
```

When I introduce you to a new set of features, such as options in a dialog box, I set these items apart with bullet lists so you can see that they're all related. When I want you to follow instructions, I use numbered step lists to walk you through the process.

What You're Not to Read

If you're like most of the Web designers I know, you don't have time to wade through a thick book before you start working on your Web site. That's why I wrote *Dreamweaver CS4 For Dummies* in a way that makes it easy for you to find the answers you need quickly. You don't have to read this book cover to cover. If you're in a hurry, go right to the information you need most and then get back to work. If you're new to Web design or you want to know the intricacies of Dreamweaver, skim through the chapters to get an overview and then go back and read what's most relevant to your project in greater detail. Whether you're building a simple site for the first time or working to redesign a complex site for the umpteenth time, you'll find everything you need in these pages.

Foolish Assumptions

Although Dreamweaver is designed for *professional* developers, I don't assume you're a pro — at least not yet. In keeping with the philosophy behind the *For Dummies* series, this book is an easy-to-use guide designed for readers with a wide range of experience. Being interested in Web design and wanting to create a Web site is key, but that desire is all that I expect from you.

If you're an experienced Web designer, *Dreamweaver CS4 For Dummies* is an ideal reference for you because it gets you working quickly with this program, starting with basic Web page design features and progressing to more advanced options. If you're new to Web design, this book walks you through all you need to know to create a Web site, from creating a new page to publishing your finished project on the Web.

How This Book Is Organized

To ease you through the learning curve associated with any new program, I organized *Dreamweaver CS4 For Dummies* as a complete reference. This section provides a breakdown of the five parts of the book and what you can find in each one. Each chapter walks you through the features of Dreamweaver step by step, providing tips and helping you understand the vocabulary of Web design as you go along.

Part I: Creating Great Web Sites

Part I introduces you to the basic concepts of Web design as well as the main features of Dreamweaver. In Chapter 1, I give you an overview of the many approaches to Web design, so you can best determine how you want to build your Web site before you get into the details of which features in Dreamweaver are best suited to any particular design approach. In Chapter 2, I start you on the road to your first Web site, including creating a new site, importing an existing site, creating new Web pages, applying basic formatting, and setting links. To make this chapter more interesting and help you see how all these features come together, I walk you through creating a real Web page as I show you how the features work.

In Chapter 3, I move onto graphics, with an introduction to creating graphics for the Web, an overview of the differences in formats (GIFs, JPEGs, and PNG files), and detailed instructions for adding and positioning graphics in your pages. In Chapter 4, you discover Dreamweaver's testing and publishing features, so you can start uploading pages to the Internet as soon as you're ready. If you work with a team of designers, you may be especially interested in the Check In/Check Out feature, which makes it easier to manage a site when several people are working together. You'll also find instructions for using integrated e-mail for communicating with other team members.

Part II: Appreciating Web Design Options

Chapter 5 provides an overview of how Cascading Style Sheets work and how they can save you time. CSS has become *the* way to create page designs and manage formatting on Web pages, and these features have been nicely improved in Dreamweaver CS4. In this chapter, you find descriptions of the style definition options available in Dreamweaver as well as instructions for creating and applying styles. In Chapter 6, I take you further into CSS, introducing you to the power of `<div>` tags and how to create CSS layouts. Here you'll find instructions for working with Dreamweaver's Layers features, as well as how to create centered CSS designs and fluid layouts.

In Chapter 7, you discover how to use HTML table features (and when they're still recommended on the Web). In Chapter 8, you find all you need to know about designing a site with frames and iframes. (This chapter also includes tips about when frames are useful and why they should generally be avoided.)

In Chapter 9, I introduce you to some of my favorite Dreamweaver features, including sophisticated template capabilities, that enable you to create more consistent designs and make global updates across many pages at once. I also cover Dreamweaver's Library items, which can be used to place and update commonly used elements, such as navigation bars or copyright tags.

Part III: Making It Cool with Multimedia and JavaScript

In Part III, you discover how cool your site can look when you add interactive image features, audio, video, and Flash. In Chapter 10, you find instructions for creating an interactive photo gallery with the Swap Image behavior, as well as how to use other features in Dreamweaver's Behaviors panel, including the Open New Browser behavior. In Chapter 11, you find out what it takes to add multimedia to your Web pages, including how to insert and create links to a variety of file types — from Flash to video and audio files. In Chapter 12, I cover Dreamweaver's HTML form options, which you can use to add feedback forms, surveys, and much more. In Chapter 13, you discover how great the Spry features are for adding AJAX interactivity to your site. In this chapter, you find instructions for creating and customizing drop-down lists, collapsible panels, and more.

Part IV: Working with Dynamic Content

Part IV features three chapters that cover the most advanced features in Dreamweaver CS4. Chapter 14 is designed to help you understand how database-driven Web sites work and why they're so important on the Web. In Chapter 15, you discover how to add dynamic content to your pages, define data sources, display recordsets, and take advantage of Dreamweaver CS4's new Spry features.

Part V: The Part of Tens

Part V features three quick references to help you develop the best Web sites possible. Chapter 16 provides a collection of online resources where you can register domain names and find hosting services, as well as a few services that can help you take care of more advanced challenges, such as setting up an e-commerce system. In Chapter 17, you find ten design tips to help you get the most out of Dreamweaver.

Icons Used in This Book

When I want to point you toward something you can download for your use, I use this icon.

This icon points you toward valuable resources on the Web.

This icon reminds you of an important concept or procedure that you'll want to store away in your memory banks for future use.

This icon signals technical stuff that you may find informative and interesting but that isn't essential for using Dreamweaver. Feel free to skip over this information.

This icon indicates a tip or technique that can save you time and money — and a headache — later.

This icon warns you of any potential pitfalls — and gives you the all-important information on how to avoid them.

Where to Go from Here

If you want to get familiar with the latest in Web design strategies and options, don't skip Chapter 1, which is designed to help guide you through the many ways to create Web sites today. If you're ready to dive in and build a basic Web site right away, jump ahead to Chapter 2. If you want to find out about a specific trick or technique, consult the Table of Contents or the index; you won't miss a beat as you work to make those impossible Web design deadlines. Most of all, I wish you great success in all your Web projects!

Part I

Creating Great Web Sites

"Just how accurately should my Web site reflect my place of business?"

In this part . . .

In Part I, you find an introduction to Web design and an overview of the many ways you can create a Web site in Dreamweaver. Chapter 1 compares different layout techniques and provides an introduction to the toolbars, menus, and panels that make up Dreamweaver's interface.

In Chapter 2, you dive right into setting up a Web site, creating a Web page, and adding text, images, and links. In Chapter 3, you find an introduction to Web graphics and tips for using Photoshop to optimize images in GIF, PNG, and JPEG formats. Chapter 4 covers testing and publishing features, so you can make sure that everything works before you put your site online.

Chapter 1

The Many Ways to Design a Web Page

In This Chapter

- Comparing Web design options
- Knowing about browser differences
- Developing a Web site
- Customizing your workspace

In the early days, Web design was relatively easy — and vanilla boring. You could combine images and text, but that's about it; no complex layouts, no fancy fonts, and certainly no multimedia or animation.

Over the years, Web design has evolved into an increasingly complex field, and Dreamweaver has evolved with it, adding new features that go way beyond the basics of combining a few words and images.

When I first started learning to create Web sites in the mid 1990s, it was easy to learn and easy to teach others how to do it. More than ten years and a dozen books later, it's a lot more complex, and I've come to realize that one of the first things you have to understand about Web design is that there isn't just one way to create a Web site anymore.

Today, you can learn how to design simple Web sites with HTML (HyperText Markup Language) in a matter of hours or you can spend years developing the advanced programming skills it takes to create complex Web sites like the ones you see at Amazon.com or MSNBC.

For everything in between, Dreamweaver is the clear choice among professional Web designers as well as among a growing number of people who want to build sites for their hobbies, clubs, families, and small businesses.

Before I dive into the details of creating a Web page in Dreamweaver, I think it's helpful to start by introducing the many ways you can create a Web site. The more you understand about the various approaches to Web design, the better you can appreciate your options.

Developing a New Site

In a nutshell, building a Web site involves creating individual pages and linking them to other pages. You need to have a *home page*, the first page visitors see when they arrive at your Web address, (also known as your URL), and that page needs to bring them into the rest of the pages of the site, usually with links to each of the main sections of the site. Those pages, in turn, link to subsections that can then lead to deeper subsections.

A big part of planning a Web site is determining how to divide the pages of your site into sections and how those sections should link to one another. Dreamweaver makes creating pages and setting links easy, but how you organize the pages is up to you.

If you're new to this, you may think you don't need to worry much about how your Web site will grow and develop. Think again. All good Web sites grow, and the bigger they get, the harder they are to manage. Planning the path of growth for your Web site before you begin can make a tremendous difference later. Neglecting to think about growth is probably one of the most common mistakes among new designers. This becomes even more serious when more than one person is working on the same site. Without a clearly established site organization and some common conventions for tasks like naming files, confusion reigns.

Managing your site's structure

Managing the structure of a Web site has two sides: the side that users see, which depends on how you set up links, and the side that's behind-the-scenes, which depends on how you organize files and folders.

What the user sees

The side that the user sees is all about navigation. When users arrive at your home page, where do you direct them? How do they move from one page to another in your site? A good Web site is designed so that users navigate easily and intuitively and can make a beeline to the information most relevant to them. As you plan, make sure that users can

- Access key information easily from more than one place in the site
- Move back and forth easily between pages and sections
- Return to main pages and subsections in one step

Setting links is easy in Dreamweaver; the challenge is to make sure that those links are easy for visitors to follow. One of the best ways to ensure that visitors can easily move around your site is to create a navigation or menu bar to include links to the main pages of your site on every page of your site. You find instructions in Chapter 6 for creating a menu bar with CSS. In Chapter 13, you find out how to use Dreamweaver's Spry features to create a drop-down list using AJAX. And in Chapter 9, you find instructions for using Dreamweaver's template and library features, which make including menus on your pages faster and easier to update.

What's behind the scenes

The second side to managing your Web site structure happens behind the scenes (where your users can't see the information, but you want some kind of organizational system to remember what's what). You'll have files for all the images, HTML pages, animations, sound files, and anything else you put in your Web site. Before you begin building your site with Dreamweaver, think about how to keep track of all these files. At minimum, consider the following:

- **A file naming system:** For example, naming image files consistently can make them easier to find if you need to edit them later. Similarly, giving the pages the same name for the main sections of your site that you use in the text of the links on your pages, can make it easier to set the links.
- **A folder structure:** When your Web site grows past a handful of pages, organizing them in separate folders or directories can help you keep track. Fortunately, Dreamweaver makes this easy by providing a Files panel where you can see all the files of your site and even move and rename files and folders. (You find detailed instructions for organizing the files and folders in a Web site in Chapters 2 and 4.)

Understanding the basics of XHTML

Hypertext Markup Language (HTML) is the formatting language used to create Web pages. When you open a Web page in a Web browser, the HTML code tells the Web browser how to display the text, images, and other content on the page. By default, Dreamweaver CS4 writes XHTML instead of HTML because XHTML is a stricter version of HTML that's designed to comply with contemporary Web standards. Among the requirements, XHTML must be written in lowercase letters.

The basic unit of XHTML is a *tag.* You can recognize XHTML tags by their angle brackets. You can format text and other elements on your page by placing them inside the XHTML tags. When you use the formatting tools in Dreamweaver, the program automatically inserts tags in the code. You can view the code behind any Web page by choosing View⇨Source in most Web browsers or by choosing the Split or Code view options in Dreamweaver. When you use split view, you can see the code and design views simultaneously, and when you select text or an image in one view, it's automatically highlighted in the other view.

Although at first glance, the code can look like hieroglyphics, basic HTML is not that complex. Most XHTML tags work in pairs and include an open tag as well as a close tag that surround content. For example, the `<b>` tag tells a browser to begin making text bold and the closing `</b>` tag tells the browser to end the bold formatting. Other tags can stand alone, such as the `<br />` tag, which adds a line break. XHTML tags must have a closing tag, even if there's only one tag, and closing tags always contain a forward slash (/). As a result, the line break tag in XHTML looks like this: `<br />`.

```
<h1>Format headlines with heading tags like this</h1>
<p>Paragraph tags add a line break and a line space
        between elements. <b>This tag makes text
        bold.</b> This text will not be bold.</p>
```

One of the great advantages of using Dreamweaver is that you can specify formatting by clicking buttons or using menu commands, and Dreamweaver takes care of writing the underlying XHTML code for you.

In the old days, many Web designers created sites entirely in HMTL, using tags such as HTML tables to create page layouts. These days, the best Web designs are created by combining HTML tags, such as the Heading tags, which include `<h1>` through `<h6>`, the `<div>` tag, which *divides* sections of a page, and many other tags, with CSS rules, covered in the next section.

Comparing Web Designs

Throughout this book, you find chapters covering a variety of aspects of Web design, from the basics of creating a page and adding images and links to more complex concepts such as Cascading Style Sheets (CSS) and one of the newest options in Web design AJAX (Asynchronous JavaScript and XML). You can even use these different technologies in combination. The next few sections are designed to help you understand the differences in the many approaches to creating page designs to help you decide which one is best for your Web site, whether you're building a new site or updating an existing one.

Appreciating the advantages of CSS

A Web site designed with CSS separates content from design. Keeping the content of a site (such as the text and images) separate from the instructions that tell a browser how the page should look has many benefits:

- **CSS simplifies design changes.** For example, instead of formatting every headline in your site as 24-point Arial bold, you can create a style for the `<h1>` tag and use that tag to format all your headlines. Then if you decide later that you want all your headlines to use the Garamond font instead of Arial, change the style for the <h1> tag only once in the style sheet and it's automatically applied everywhere you've used that style.

- **CSS enables you to create different style sheets for different audiences and devices.** In the future, this is likely to become even more important as a growing number of people view Web pages on everything from giant, flat-screen monitors to tiny, cell-phone screens.

  As you get more advanced with CSS, you can create multiple style sheets for the same Web page. For example, you can create one that's ideally suited to a small screen like the one shown in Figure 1-1, another one that works best when the page is printed, and yet another designed with a larger font size for anyone who may have trouble reading the small print that is so common on Web pages.

  In Figure 1-1, you see one of the coolest preview features in Dreamweaver — *Device Central* — where you can preview your page designs in a variety of cell phone models to see just how different they can look when displayed on these small screens.

- **Using CSS makes your site comply with the current standards.** Today, the *W3C,* which sets standards for the Internet, recommends CSS because the best CSS designs are accessible, flexible, and adaptable. Following standards has become increasingly important as Web design has become more complex over the years.

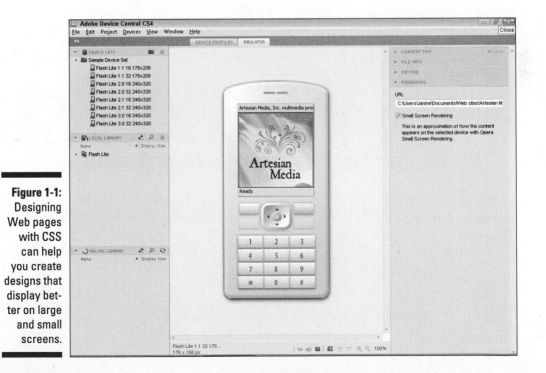

Figure 1-1: Designing Web pages with CSS can help you create designs that display better on large and small screens.

- **Web sites designed in CSS are accessible to more visitors.** When Web designers talk about *accessibility,* they mean creating a site that can be accessed by anyone who might ever visit your pages — that includes people with limited vision who use special browsers (often called *screen readers*) that *read* Web pages aloud, as well as many others who use specialized browsers for a variety of other reasons.

  If you work for a university, a nonprofit, a government agency, or a similar organization, you may be *required* to create accessible designs. Even if you're not required to use CSS or to design for accessibility, it's still good practice. That's why Dreamweaver includes so many CSS features and a collection of predesigned CSS layouts like the one I used to create the site design shown in Figure 1-2. You find instructions for creating CSS layouts like this one in Chapter 6.

Reviewing old-school designs

Although CSS is by far the best option for creating Web designs today, many sites on the Web were created with tables to control the layout, like the one shown in Figure 1-3. Old-school sites like this one were created with the HTML table tag. To help you appreciate how this page was created, I altered the original design to display the table borders, although most designers turn off table borders when using Tables to create layouts like this.

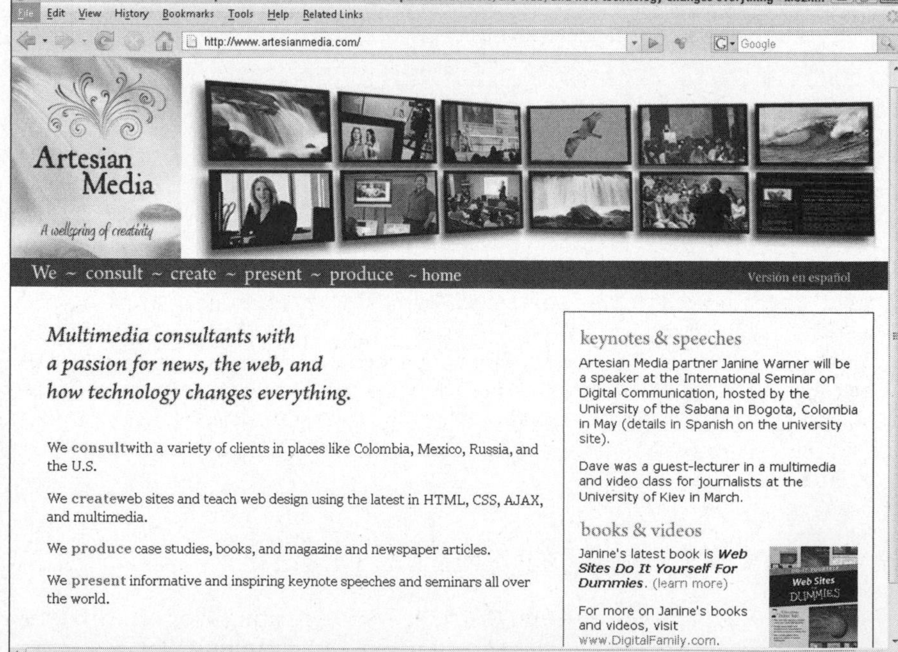

Figure 1-2: This site was designed with one of Dreamweaver's CSS layouts.

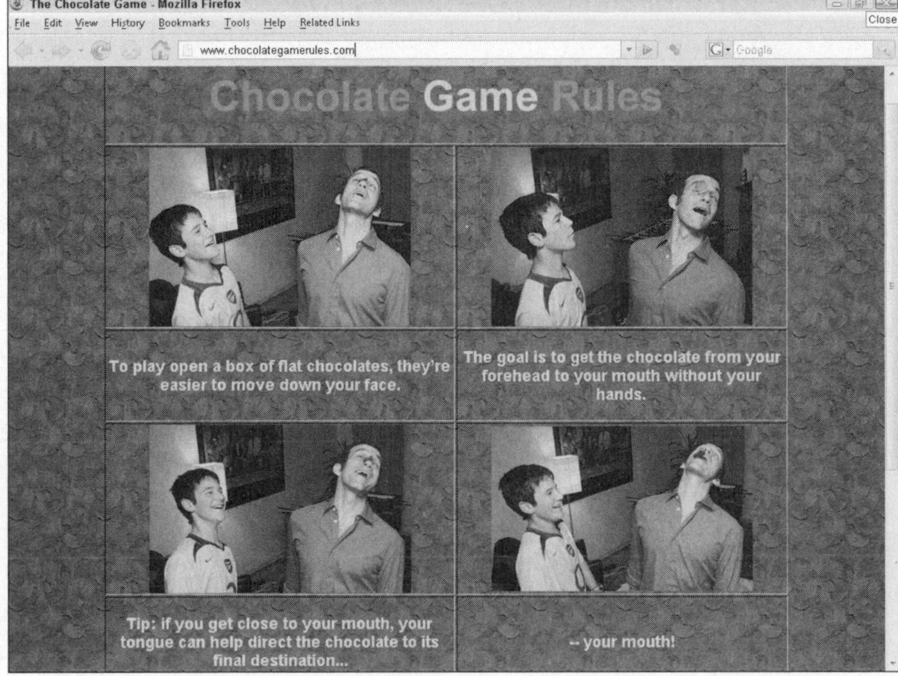

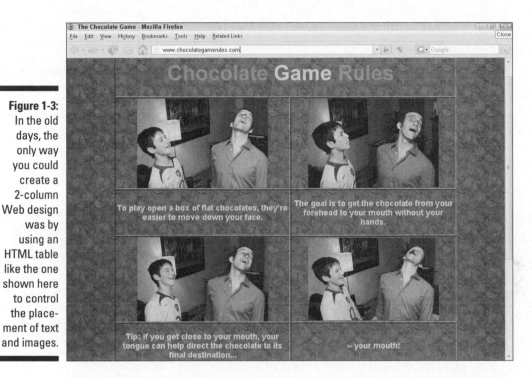

Figure 1-3: In the old days, the only way you could create a 2-column Web design was by using an HTML table like the one shown here to control the placement of text and images.

Because you can merge and split table cells, you can use them to control the layout of a page, positioning text and images more or less where you want them. If you set the table border to 0 (instead of 2 as I did here to show you the borders), you can hide the table so that it doesn't interfere with the design.

Although I recommend that you redesign sites like the one shown in Figure 1-3 with CSS and `<div>` tags (covered in Chapter 6), I do understand that some designers still find it easier to create layouts with tables, and not everyone has time to redesign existing Web sites.

Tables are still considered the best way to format tabular data like the columns and rows that might make up a list of winners from the chocolate game with their photos, and scores. In Chapter 7, you find an introduction to Dreamweaver's Table features and tips for creating accessible table designs by including the table header tag in all your tables. You can even combine CSS with tables to create more streamlined designs.

Considering frame options

In Chapter 8, you find instructions for creating Web sites that use frames, like the Flamingo site shown in Figure 1-4. Among Web designers, frames are a little like the plastic Pink Flamingos stuck in the front yards of so many homes in South Florida; some people love how kitsch they are, others just think they're tacky. Although frames still have a place on the Web, many designers don't like them because they can make navigation confusing for visitors and make it difficult to link to pages within a site.

If you want to create pages like the one in Figure 1-4 that display multiple Web pages in one browser window, you'll find everything you need in Chapter 8.

Creating dynamic Web sites

When you use Dreamweaver's most advanced features, you can create Web sites (like the one shown in Figure 1-5) that connect to a database and display content dynamically on a Web page.

What's happening behind the scenes of a site like the one at `www.TotalTraining.com` gets complicated fast, but one of the advantages of using this kind of technology is that you can create a Web page like the one in Figure 1-5 that displays a collection of products and then display product information for each product individually, drawing the product photos and other details from a database as a user requests the information. When a site grows bigger than about 100 pages, graduating to a database-driven model like this is far more efficient than creating individual static pages for every product description or other content in your site. Dreamweaver supports many technologies for this kind of site development, including PHP, JSP, ASP.NET, and ASP.

In addition to drawing content from a database, you can also create interactive features that display content created by visitors to your site, such as an online discussion board or any other system that collects data in one page and then uses that data to determine what's displayed on another page.

That's how the most advanced sites on the Web do things like remind you of the last book you searched for or keep track of your order as you select products in an online shopping cart. Although I can't cover all these advanced features in this book, you find an introduction to creating database-driven Web sites in Chapters 14 and 15.

One other thing I feel compelled to mention at this point is that most of the big, complicated Web sites in the world were created by a team of developers, not just one person. In the case of the Total Training site, a great team of people was involved in the many elements of the site, from the design, to the videos, to the programming. If you're working with a team of developers, you may appreciate Dreamweaver's site management features, such as the ability to check pages in and out so that no one overwrites anyone else's work. You find information about these features in Chapter 4.

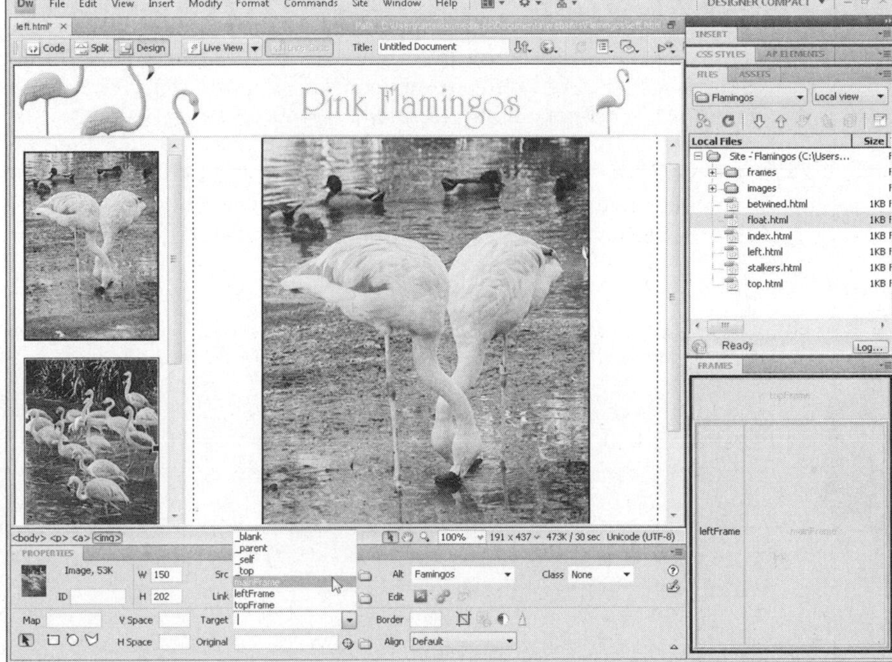

Figure 1-4: Frames enable you to display multiple Web pages in one browser window.

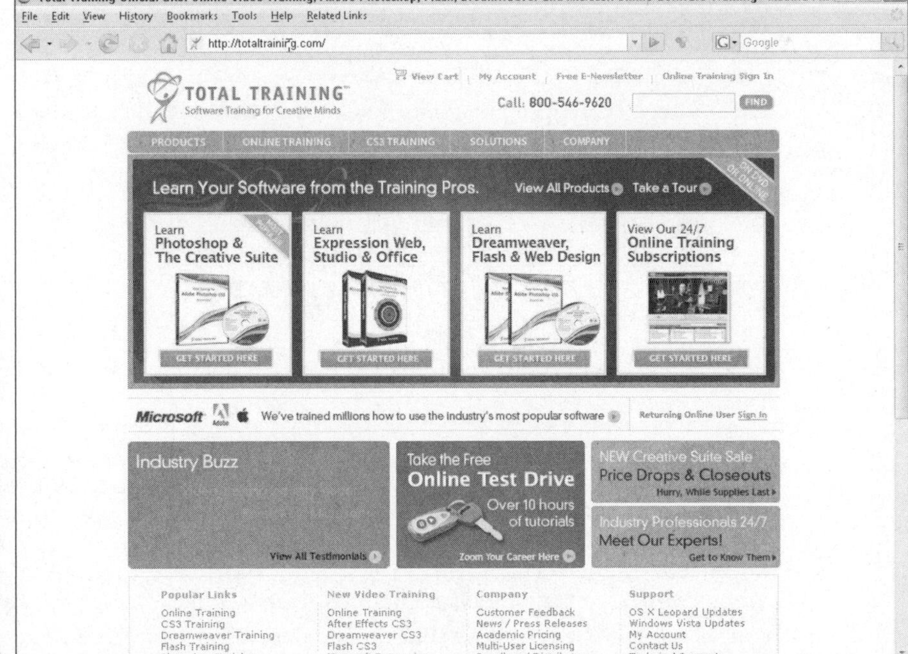

Figure 1-5: Total Training.com is a dynamic Web site that displays content from a database using PHP.

Understanding Browser Differences

Before you start creating Web pages, know that no matter how carefully you create your designs, your pages will never look exactly the same to every possible visitor to your site. That's because one of the greatest advantages of the Web is also one of the biggest challenges. HTML was created to share information in a way that could be displayed on every computer on the planet. Unfortunately, not all those computers use the same browsers, the same fonts, or the same-sized monitors. On top of that, a lot of older Web browsers are still in use out there, and they can't display the latest Web features. Even all the newer browsers don't display the latest Web design options the same way.

Because of these browser differences, you have more design control today than ever before and the capability to create more interesting Web sites, but you also have more challenges if you want your pages to look good to everyone who might visit your site. My best advice is to test, test, test, and then ask your friends to test your pages some more. If you want to play it safe, the simpler your page design, the more likely it will look the same, or at least similar, to all your visitors.

If you want to create more interesting designs and you want to reach the broadest possible audience, pay special attention to Dreamweaver's browser preview and compatibility features and be prepared to look for more advanced books and training programs when you finish with this book. Entire books and Web sites are dedicated to creating highly complex CSS layouts that display well on a variety of computers and browsers.

In Chapter 4, you find more information about Web browser differences, as well as Dreamweaver's testing and compatibility features, which can help ensure your pages work well for a broad audience.

Introducing the Workspace in Dreamweaver CS4

Dreamweaver can seem a bit overwhelming at first — it has so many features, spread among so many panels, toolbars, and dialog boxes that you can easily get lost. If you prefer to understand by poking around, have at it (and feel free to skip ahead to Chapter 2, where you start building your first Web page right away). If you want a tour before you get started, the last few sections of this chapter introduce you to the interface and are designed to give you a quick overview of the features in this powerful program.

Here's a bird's-eye view of getting started in the Dreamweaver interface:

1. When you launch Dreamweaver, the Welcome screen appears in the main area of the program (and reappears anytime you don't have a file open, unless you close it by selecting the Don't Show Again option).
2. From the Welcome screen, you can choose to create a new page from one of the many Dreamweaver predesigned sample files, or you can create a new blank page by selecting HTML from the Create New options in the middle column.
3. When you select HTML and you choose None from the Layout list, Dreamweaver creates a new blank HTML page in the main *workspace,* as shown in Figure 1-6.

   The workspace consists of a Document window, which displays the page you're working on and is where you add text, images, and other elements that will appear on your Web pages. The Document window is surrounded by a collection of panels, toolbars, and menus that provide easy access to Dreamweaver's many features. More detailed descriptions of each of these follows.

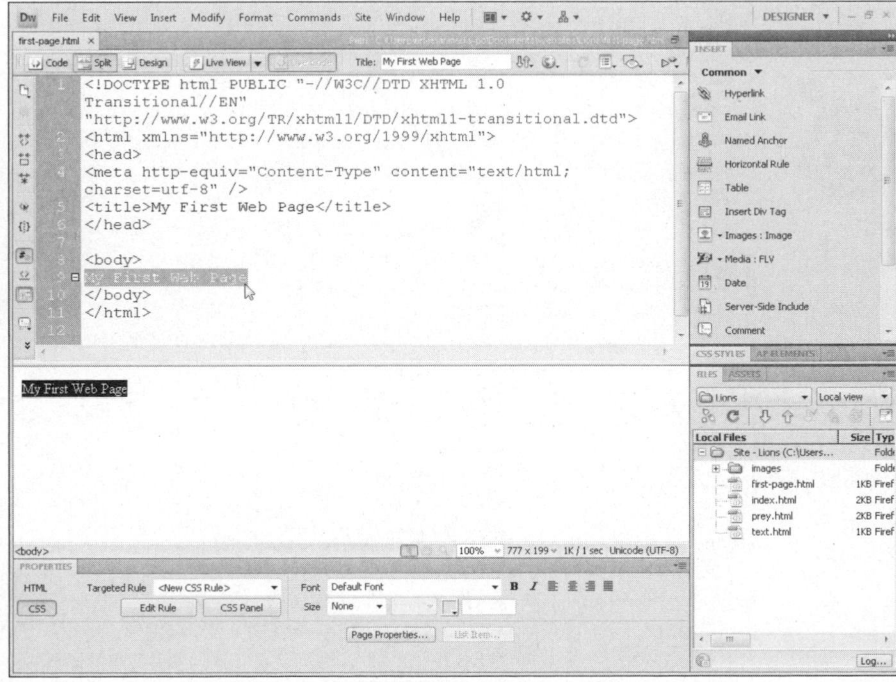

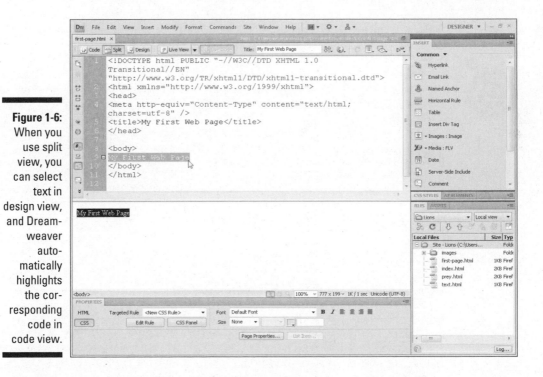

Figure 1-6: When you use split view, you can select text in design view, and Dreamweaver automatically highlights the corresponding code in code view.

Changing workspace layouts

Dreamweaver CS4 has eight preset workspace layouts to choose from. These layouts arrange the many toolbars, panels, and other features in popular configurations. You can change layouts by choosing Window⇨Workspace Layout and then choosing from any of the listed layouts, such as Designer, as shown in Figure 1-6, or App Developer, as shown in Figure 1-7. You can also access the list of layouts by clicking the arrow next to the layout button, as shown open in Figure 1-7.

As the names imply, the Designer layouts were created for people who have a design background, whereas the App and Coder layouts were created for programmers who are likely to prefer working in the code view more than in design view.

In addition to the preset workspace layouts, you can create your own by opening, closing, or moving any of the panels, inspectors, or other features, as described in the following sections. You can even save your own layouts by choosing Window⇨Workspace Layout⇨New Workspace and giving each new workspace layout its own name, which is then added to the menu so you can easily reset it. If you move a panel or inspector and then want to return it to its original location, choose Reset Workspace to restore any of the preset layouts.

Create a collection of workspace layouts optimized for common tasks, such as creating and applying CSS, or working with database content, and save them so that you can easily arrange the program to best suit your preferences.

The menu bar

Like most programs you've used, the menu at the top of the screen provides easy access to most program features, including the options you find in the Insert bar, Property inspector, and panels, as well as a few others that are available only from the menu.

The Document toolbar

Across the top of the workspace, just under the menu bar and above the workspace, is the Document toolbar, as shown in Figure 1-6. Here you find the Code, Split, and Design view buttons, which make it easy to change from displaying only the code or design in the workspace, or both the code and the design (using split view, which is shown in Figure 1-6). You also find the Live View button, which provides a preview of the page, complete with working links and dynamic content so that the page works in Dreamweaver much as it would when previewed in a Web browser. The Title field displays the *page title,* which is the text that appears at the top of a browser window when a page is displayed. This is also the text that's saved when a visitor bookmarks a page. Other features in the toolbar, include the Preview in Browser button, which launches the page in a Web browser; the View Options button, which provides access to additional display features, such as the ruler and guides; and the Visual Aids button, which makes it easy to turn on special display features, such as CSS Layout Outlines, which add a thin, dotted line around otherwise invisible elements, such as `<div>` tags.

The Document window

The big, open section in the main area of the workspace is the Document window, which is where you work on new and existing pages. If you use the Designer workspace layout, as shown in Figure 1-6, the Document window is displayed in split view, showing the code at the top of the window and the design at the bottom. If you want to hide the code, which makes it easier to focus on your designs, click the Design view button in the Document toolbar. Click the Code view button to see only the HTML code and click Split view button to divide the window.

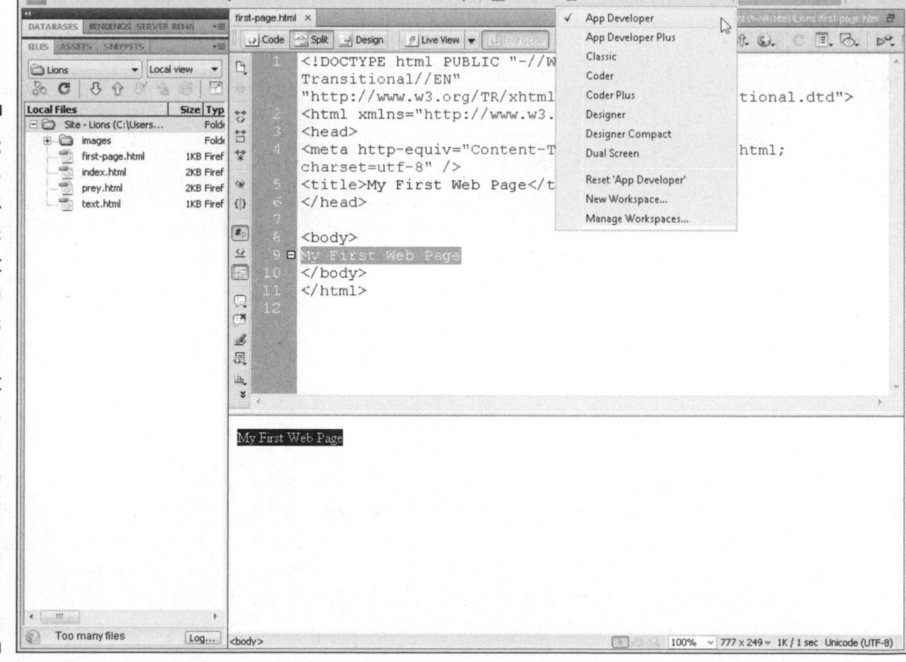

Figure 1-7: Dreamweaver CS4 includes eight workspace layouts optimized for different work styles, such as App Developer, which is optimized for working on dynamic Web sites.

The docking panels

The docking panels are located to the right of the work area when you choose any of the designer layouts, such as the one shown in Figure 1-6, or on the left when you choose any of the developer layouts, such as the one shown in Figure 1-7.

The docking panels display a variety of important features in Dreamweaver, including the Insert panel (described in detail in the following section), the Files panel, which displays all the files and folders in a site, and the CSS Styles panel, which displays a list of all the Cascading Style Sheets available to the document.

- **To open and close panels,** click the gray bar at the top of any panel next to the panel's name or double-click the name in the tab at the top of the panel.
- **To move panels anywhere on the screen,** click the dark gray bar at the top of the panel and drag it to the desired location.
- **To display more panels,** select the panel name from the Window menu.
- **To expand or collapse all the visible panels at once,** click the double arrow at the top-right corner of the top most panel.
- **To expand or collapse a single panel when the panel collection is collapsed,** click the name of the panel, as shown in Figure 1-8.

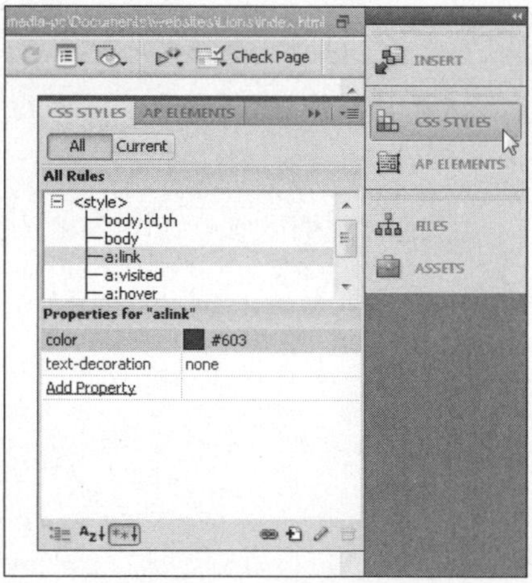

Figure 1-8: When the panel group is collapsed, you can click any panel name to expand only that panel.

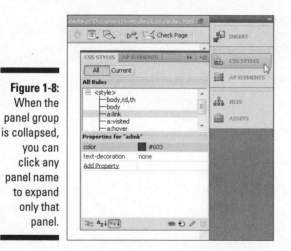

The Insert panel

The Insert panel, located at the top of the panel section, includes seven *subcategories,* each with a different set of icons representing common features. Click the small arrow to the right of the name to access the drop-down list and switch from the buttons of one subcategory to the buttons for another. The options are

- **Common Insert panel:** Displays icons for many of the most common features, including links, tables, and images.
- **Layout Insert panel:** Displays div, table, and frame options essential for creating page layouts.
- **Forms Insert panel:** Features the most common form elements, such as radio buttons and boxes.
- **Data Insert panel:** Displays options for building dynamic Web pages powered by database material.
- **Spry Insert panel:** Features a collection of widgets that combines HTML, CSS, and JavaScript to create interactive page elements, such as drop-down lists and collapsible panels.
- **InContext Editing Insert panel:** Displays features that are handy for creating Repeating and Editable Regions, as well as managing CSS classes, when working with dynamic content.
- **Text Insert panel:** Displays common text-formatting features, including paragraphs, breaks, and lists.
- **Favorites Insert panel:** Enables you to right-click (Windows) or Control-click (Mac) to add any of the icons from any of the other Insert bar options to create your own collection of favorite features.

At the end of the drop-down list are the two options that control the display of the list of options in the Insert panels. Color Icons restores the color to the icons. Hide Labels/Show Labels enables you to display the names of the Insert panel features next to each icon, or to remove the names.

The Property inspector

The Property inspector is docked at the bottom of the workspace in Dreamweaver. If you prefer, you can click the gray bar at the top of the inspector and drag it to detach it so that it floats in the workspace. You can move the inspector anywhere on the screen or you can drag it into the panel group and dock it there. When you dock the inspector with the other panels, you can expand and collapse it just as you would any other panels. To restore the inspector to its original location, choose Window⇨Workspace Layout⇨Reset. I rather like that the Property inspector is handy, yet out of the way, at the bottom of the screen.

The Property inspector displays the *properties,* or options, for any selected element on a page, and it changes based on what's selected. For example, if you click an image, the Property inspector displays image properties. If you click a Flash file, the Property inspector displays Flash properties.

In Dreamweaver CS4, Adobe split the Property inspector into two sections for many elements, one for HTML features and the other for CSS. Use the CSS and HTML buttons on the left side of the Property inspector, as shown in Figure 1-9, to switch from one to the other. (You find detailed instructions for how to use these two modes of the Property inspector in Chapters 5 and 6.)

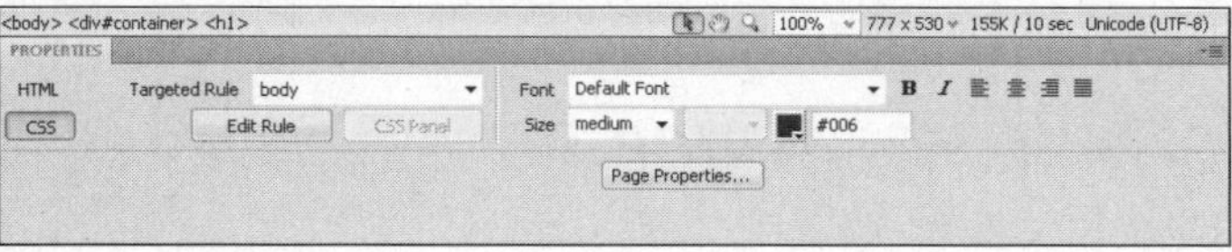

Figure 1-9: The Status bar and the Property inspector in CSS mode.

At the bottom-right corner of the Property inspector, you see a small arrow. Click this arrow to reduce the inspector. Click it again to expand the inspector to reveal additional attributes that let you control more advanced features, such as the image map options when a graphic is selected. Click the gray bar at the top of the inspector to close and open the inspector.

The status bar

The status bar is located at the bottom of the Document window and just above the Property inspector, as shown in Figure 1-9. The status bar includes access to a number of features that control the display of a page in Dreamweaver's workspace, such as the magnifying glass, which enlarges the view of the open page.

On the far left of the status bar, as shown in the top of Figure 1-9, you find the tag selector, which displays the HTML tags and CSS rules that apply to any selected element on the page. In Figure 1-9, the cursor is inside a text block that's formatted with the `<h1>` tag, which is inside a `<div>` tag with a `#container` ID, which is inside the `<body>` tag. Clicking any tag in the tag selector selects the tag and all its contents in the workspace. Right-clicking (Control-clicking on a Mac) a tag opens a pop-up menu with formatting options that make it easy to add or remove tags and CSS rules.

Toward the middle of the status bar, you find the select tool, hand tool, zoom tool, and magnification pop-up menu, which you can use to move, enlarge, or reduce the display of a page in the workspace.

On the far right side of the status bar is the download size/download time tool, which displays the total size of the Web page, including all images and other elements on the page and the estimated time it will take the page to download, based on the connection speed specified in Dreamweaver's preferences. By default, the connection speed is set to estimate the download time of a page over a 56K modem, but you can change it to a faster or slower speed by changing the preferences, as shown in the following section.

Changing preference settings

The more you use Dreamweaver, the more you're likely to appreciate the capability to customize its features. Remember that you can always change the workspace to better suit the way you like to work, and you can easily alter Dreamweaver's preference settings using the Preferences dialog box.

To open the Preferences dialog box, choose Edit⇨Preferences on a Windows computer, or Dreamweaver⇨Preferences on a Mac. Dreamweaver includes 19 different categories in the Preferences dialog box and makes it possible to change the appearance, default settings, and many other options throughout the program.

Chapter 2

Opening and Creating Sites

In This Chapter

- Opening an existing Web site
- Creating a new Web site
- Making new pages
- Inserting and formatting text
- Creating links

If you're ready to dive in and start building a Web site, you've come to the right place. If you're working on an existing site and need to make changes, this is also the place to start because in this chapter, you discover an important preliminary step — the *site definition process,* which enables Dreamweaver to keep track of the images and links in your site. After you've completed the site definition process, you're ready to create Web pages, insert text and images, set links, and more. (You discover how to do all those things later in this chapter, too.) But whatever you do, don't skip the first step of defining a site — it only takes a minute or two.

Although you can use Dreamweaver without doing this initial site definition, you run the risk of breaking links when you upload your site, and then many of Dreamweaver's features, such as automated link checking and the Library, won't work at all.

Setting Up a New or Existing Site

The first thing to understand about the site definition process is that you need to store all your site's resources in one local root folder on your hard drive and identify the folder in Dreamweaver. That's because all the elements of your site must remain in the same relative location on your hard drive as they are on your Web server in order for your links, images, and other elements to work properly.

As you go through the site definition process, you can create a new folder on your hard drive and designate that as your local root folder or you can identify an existing folder.

The Site Definition dialog box also contains a category where you can set up your site to use Dreamweaver's file transfer features, including its FTP (File Transfer Protocol) capabilities. (*FTP* is a common method of copying files to and from computers connected across a network, such as the Internet.) To keep things simple for now, you can skip those file transfer feature settings (as well as Dreamweaver's other publishing and site management features in the Site Definition dialog box). In Chapter 4, you find detailed instructions for using Dreamweaver's publishing features as well as instructions for downloading an existing Web site hosted on a remote server.

As a general rule, you first create a Web site on your computer's hard drive, where you use Dreamweaver's preview options to test the site before it's visible on the Internet. Then when you're ready to publish the completed site, transfer it to a Web server. A *Web server* is a computer with a permanent connection to the Internet and special software that enables it to communicate with Web browsers, such as Internet Explorer and Firefox. Find detailed instructions for publishing a Web site in Chapter 4.

Defining a Web site in Dreamweaver

If the site definition process seems a little confusing at first, don't worry; it's a quick, relatively painless process that you have to do only once for each site.

Whether you're creating a new site or working on an existing site, the following steps walk you through the process of defining a root site folder.

1. **Choose Site⇨New Site.**

   The Site Definition dialog box appears.

2. **Click the Advanced tab.**

   The Advanced window appears, as shown in Figure 2-1. If you prefer, you can use the Basic Wizard that steps you through the setup process, but I find it faster and easier to view all the options at once with the advanced option.

3. **In the Category box on the left, make sure that the Local Info category is selected.**

4. **In the Site Name text box, type a name for your site.**

   You can call your site whatever you like; this name is used only to help you keep track of your sites in Dreamweaver. Many people work on more than one Web site, and the name you enter here is the name also listed in the Files panel. To switch from working on one site in Dreamweaver to another, you select the site's name from the drop-down list in the Files panel. Similarly, to edit any of the Site Definition settings for a site, you select its name from the Manage Sites dialog box, which you can open by choosing Site➪Manage Sites. In the example shown in Figure 2-1, Lions is the name of the new site.

5. **Click the Browse icon (hint: it looks like a file folder) next to the Local Root Folder text box and browse your hard drive to locate the folder you want to serve as the main folder for all the files in your Web site.**

   If you're working on an existing site, select the folder that contains the files for that site. If you're creating a new site, you can create a new folder as you go through this process by using the Create New Folder icon at the top of the dialog box in Windows or the New Folder button at the bottom of the dialog if you're using a Mac.

   The point is to simply select the folder so that Dreamweaver can identify where all the files and folders for your site will be stored.

6. **Specify the Default Images folder by entering the location or by using the Browse icon to locate it.**

   This works just like the previous step, you simply want to browse to the images folder and select it so that Dreamweaver can identify the location.

   Although you don't have to identify an images folder, this is another way Dreamweaver helps keep track of things for you. You can store images in more than one folder in your site, but I still recommend that you identify a main image folder. If you're setting up a new site, you can create a new folder inside your site folder and identify that as your images folder, even if it's empty.

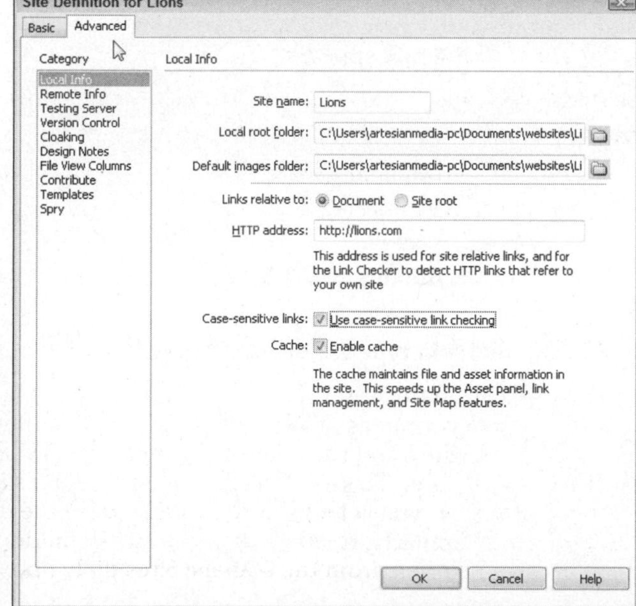

Figure 2-1: Use the Site Definition dialog box to set up a new or existing Web site in Dreamweaver.

7. **For Links Relative To, leave the Document option selected unless you know that you want your links to be set up relative to the root of your site.**

   This setting controls how the path is set in links. If you're working on a site with other developers and you're not sure, check with your colleagues. If you're working alone on your own site, Links Relative to Document is the simplest option to manage. (You can read more about relative versus root links in the section "Setting Links," later in this chapter.)

8. **In the HTTP Address text box, type the URL of your Web site.**

   The HTTP address is the *URL,* or Web address, that your site will have when published on a Web server. If you don't yet know your site's Web address or don't plan to publish the site on a Web server, you can leave this box blank. Include the `http://` at the beginning.

9. **Select the Use Case-Sensitive Link Checking box.**

   Unless you know for sure that you don't have to worry about the case of your filenames, checking this box means Dreamweaver ensures that the case matches for all your site's links (which many Web hosting services require).

10. **Select the Enable Cache option.**

    Dreamweaver creates a local cache of your site to quickly reference the location of files in your site. The local cache speeds up many site management features of the program and takes only a few seconds to create.

11. **Click OK to close the Site Definition dialog box and save your settings.**

    If the folder you selected as your local site folder already contains files or folders, they're automatically cached and all the files and folders in your site are displayed in the Files panel. As you see in Figure 2-2, my newly-created Lions site contains only an empty images folder.

    If you haven't checked the Enable Cache option, a message box appears asking whether you want to create a cache for the site. Choose Yes to speed up Dreamweaver's site management features.

Editing and managing multiple sites

You can define as many sites as you like in Dreamweaver and change from one site to another by selecting the site name in the Files panel. To load a different site into the Files panel, use the drop-down arrow next to the site name and choose the name of the site you want to display.

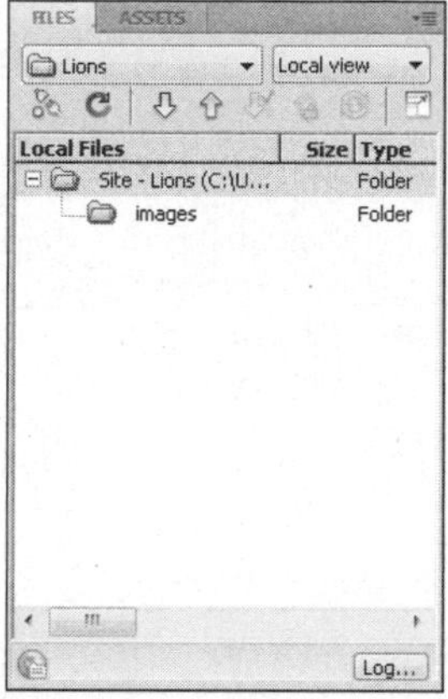

Figure 2-2: When site setup is complete, the files and folders in an existing site are displayed in the Files panel.

In Figure 2-3, I'm selecting the DigitalFamily.com site from a list of defined sites. Having the site you're working on selected in the Files panel is always best.

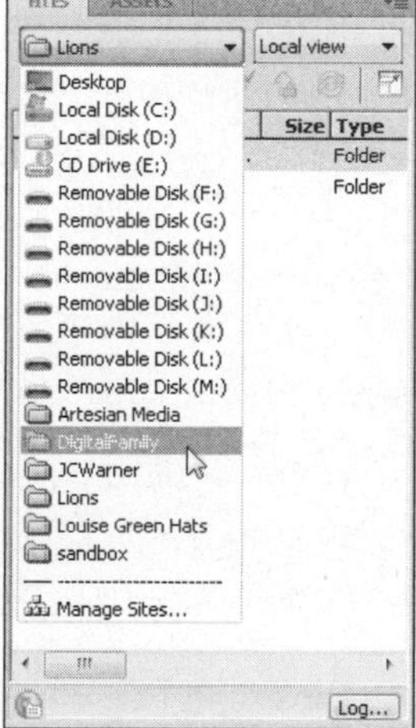

Figure 2-3: You can define multiple sites and change the active site by selecting its name in the Files panel.

After you complete the site definition process covered in the preceding exercise, you can make changes and additions to a site definition by choosing Site⇨Manage Sites, selecting the name of the site in the Manage Sites dialog box, and then clicking the Edit button. The defined site is then opened in the Site Definition dialog box, where you can make changes to any of the settings.

In Figure 2-4, I selected the DigitalFamily.com site to edit. You can use this dialog box to define a new site, remove an existing site, duplicate a site, and import or export a site. Note that when you remove a site from the Manage Sites dialog box, you don't delete the site's files or folders from your hard drive; you simply remove the site definition in Dreamweaver.

Figure 2-4: You can edit any site definition by selecting it in the Manage Sites dialog box and clicking the Edit button to open the Site Definition dialog box.

Creating New Pages

Every Web site begins with a single page. Visitors are first greeted by the front page — or *home page* — of your site, and that's usually a good place to start building. Dreamweaver makes creating new pages easy: You can work from the Welcome screen or use the New Document window. The following sections explain both methods, and you find details about naming those new pages, too.

Starting from the Welcome screen

When the program opens, you're greeted by a Welcome screen with shortcuts to many handy features for creating new pages in a variety of formats:

- **If you want to create a simple, blank Web page,** choose HTML from the Create New list in the middle column (see Figure 2-5).
- **If you're creating a dynamic site,** choose ColdFusion, PHP, or one of the other dynamic site options. (If you don't even know what those options mean, you probably won't need to use them yet, but you can find some information about these advanced options in Part IV.)

If you prefer not to use the Welcome screen, you can turn it off by selecting the Don't Show Again box in the bottom-left corner.

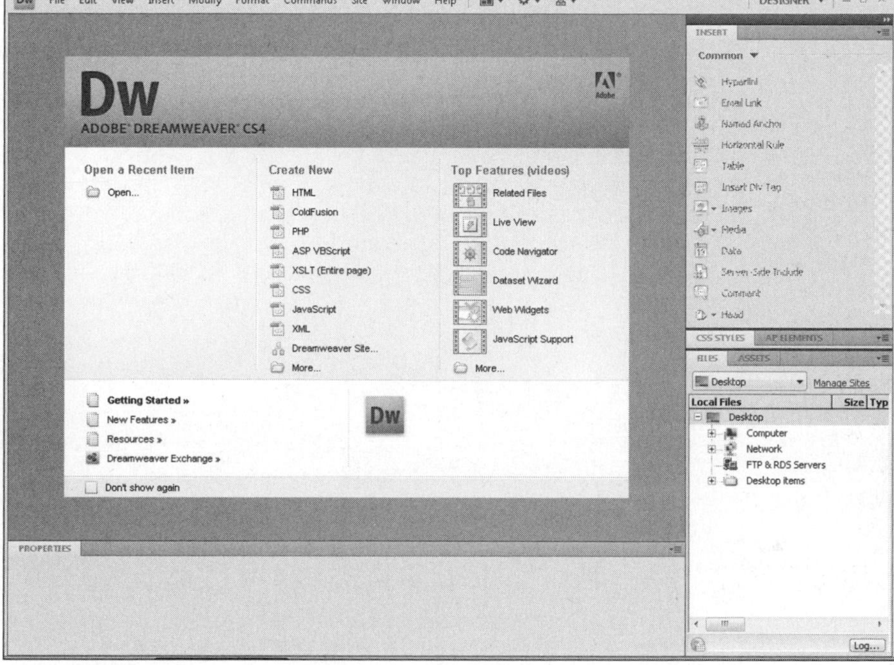

Figure 2-5: The Welcome screen provides a list of shortcuts for creating new files or opening existing pages in Dreamweaver.

Creating a page with the New Document window

You can also create a new page by using the New Document window available from the File menu, as you see in the following the steps:

1. **Choose File⇨New.**

   The New Document window opens.

2. **From the left side of the screen, select Blank Page.**
3. **From the Page Type list, select HTML and then choose Create.**
4. **From the Layout section, choose <none>.**
5. **Choose File⇨Save to save your page and give it a filename following the guidelines in the upcoming sections, "Naming new page files" and "Naming the first page index.html."**

You find many other options in the Dreamweaver New Document window, including a wide range of predesigned layouts and templates. For now, I start with a simple blank page. You find instructions for customizing CSS layouts in Chapter 6 and for working with templates in Chapter 9.

Get in the habit of saving new Web pages in your main root Web site folder as soon as you create them, even though they're still blank. As you create links or add images to your pages, Dreamweaver needs to be able to identify the location of your page. Although Dreamweaver sets temporary links until your page is saved, saving a page first is always best.

Naming new page files

Over the years, I've received many e-mail messages from panicked Web designers because of broken links caused by filename conflicts. Because these problems usually don't occur until after a Web site is published on a server, they can be especially confusing and difficult to understand. If you're publishing your Web site to a Web server that runs on Mac or Windows, the following may not apply to you; but if you're using a Web server that runs Unix or Linux (which is what many commercial Web hosting companies use), the following instructions are especially important. If you're not sure, follow these rules when you save Web pages, images, and other files on your site to be safe:

- **Include an extension at the end to identify the file type** (such as `.html` for HTML files or `.gif` for GIF images). Dreamweaver automatically adds the `.html` file extension to the end of HTML files (which works for most Web servers), but you can change the extensions in Dreamweaver's preference dialog box if necessary for your Web server. See the "Showing file extensions in Windows" sidebar on viewing file extensions in Windows.
- **Don't use spaces or special characters in the filename.** For example, don't name a Web page with an apostrophe, such as `cat's page.html`. If you want to separate words, you can use the underscore (_) or the hyphen (-). For example, `cat-page.html` is a fine filename. Numbers are okay in most cases, and capital letters don't generally matter.

The reason for all this fuss? Filenames are especially important in Web sites because they're included in the HTML code when you set links. Links with spaces and special characters work just fine when you test pages on a Mac or a PC computer, but the software programs used on many of the Web servers on the Internet don't understand spaces or special characters in links. Thus, links that don't follow these rules may get broken when you publish the site to a Web server. By following these rules, you ensure that the filename and the code in the link match.

Showing file extensions in Windows

Unless you change the settings, you won't see the file extension of your gifs, jpegs, or html pages on a Windows computer (although these extensions will be displayed in the Files panel in Dreamweaver).

To change these settings, open the Folder Options dialog box, as shown in the following figure, choose the View tab, and then deselect the Hide Extensions for Known File Types option. How you open the Folder Options dialog box depends on which version of Windows you're using; but if you search for Folder Options in the Help section, you can find it easily.

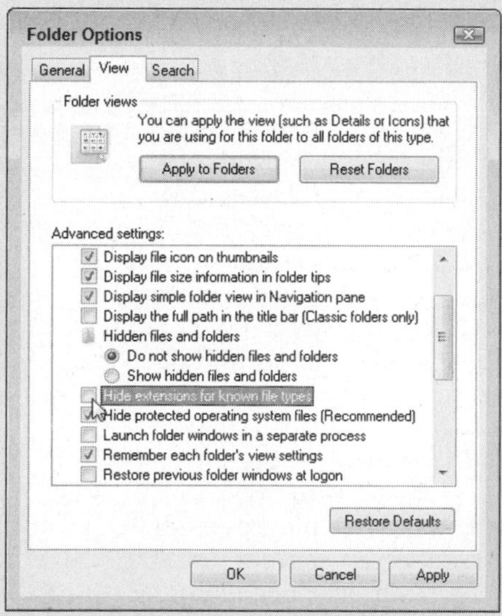

Naming the first page index.html

Another confusing rule, and one of the most important, is that the main page (or the *front page*) of your Web site must be called `index.html` (on some Windows-based servers, the first page should be named `default.html`). That's because most servers are set up to serve the `index.html` page first.

Essentially, when a Web browser comes to a domain name, such as DigitalFamily.com, the first page that opens is `index.html`. Similarly, when a Web browser is directed to a subfolder within a site, it also displays the index page first. As a result, if you create a `books` subfolder, for example, and inside that subfolder you include an index page as the main page, you can tell visitors to your site to simply enter **www.DigitalFamily.com/books** to arrive at the books page within your site. If you name the first page anything else, such as `books.html`, visitors have to type **www.DigitalFamily.com/books/books.html** to open the page.

The rest of the pages in your site can be named anything you like, as long as the names don't include any spaces or special characters (except the hyphen or underscore).

Bestowing a page title

When you create new pages, adding a page title right away is also good practice. You can add a page title by changing the text in the Title box at the top of the workspace. It's an easy detail to forget, but page titles are important because they play a role in the appearance of your site as well as behind the scenes:

- The title won't appear in the main part of your Web page, but it does appear at the top of a browser window, usually just to the right or left of the name of the browser. Pages on the Web look unfinished when the *untitled document* appears at the top of the browser window.
- The page title is also the text that appears in a user's Favorites or Bookmarks list.
- Many search engines give special priority to the words that appear in the title of a Web page.

Designing Your First Page

Many people are pleasantly surprised by how easily they can create a basic Web page in Dreamweaver.

If you're ready to plunge right in, create a page and click to insert your cursor at the top of the blank page. (See the previous section, "Creating New Pages," if you need to start from the beginning.) Type some text on the page, anything you like; you just need something to get started. In the example in Figure 2-6 (a little later in this chapter), I typed the text "I gotcha where I want ya." I'll use this as a headline in the simple page I'm creating to go with my lion photo.

In this chapter, I use a mix of CSS and HTML formatting options, although I mostly use HTML. In Chapter 5, you find more detailed instructions for creating CSS to control and manage formatting.

Formatting headlines with the heading tags

One of the best formatting options for headlines is the collection of heading tags. In HTML, there are many advantages to using heading tags (`<h1>`, `<h2>`, and so forth) to format text that serves as a title or headline. That's because heading tags are designed to be displayed in relative sizes, with `<h1>` the largest, `<h2>` smaller, `<h3>` smaller still, and so on through `<h6>`. That's valuable because no matter what the default text size is for a Web page (and text sizes can vary because of things like browser settings and computer platform), any text formatted with an `<h1>` tag is always larger than text formatted with `<h2>`.

Many search engines also give priority to keywords in text formatted with an `<h1>` tag because that tag is perceived to be the most important text on a page.

To format text with a heading tag, follow these steps:

1. **Highlight the text you want to format.**
2. **In the Property inspector, at the bottom of the workspace, make sure the HTML button on the left side of the inspector is selected.**
3. **Use the Format drop-down list to select a heading option (see Figure 2-6).**

   When heading tags are applied, the text automatically changes to display the heading's formatting options in design view.

In general, I find the Property inspector the easiest way to apply basic formatting, but you can also find these HTML formatting options under the Format drop-down list.

Adding paragraphs and line breaks

When you create page designs for the Web, you must work within many limitations that may seem confusing at first. Web design and print design are fundamentally different, and that can make even seemingly simple tasks more complicated than you might expect. How you create paragraph and line breaks is a good example.

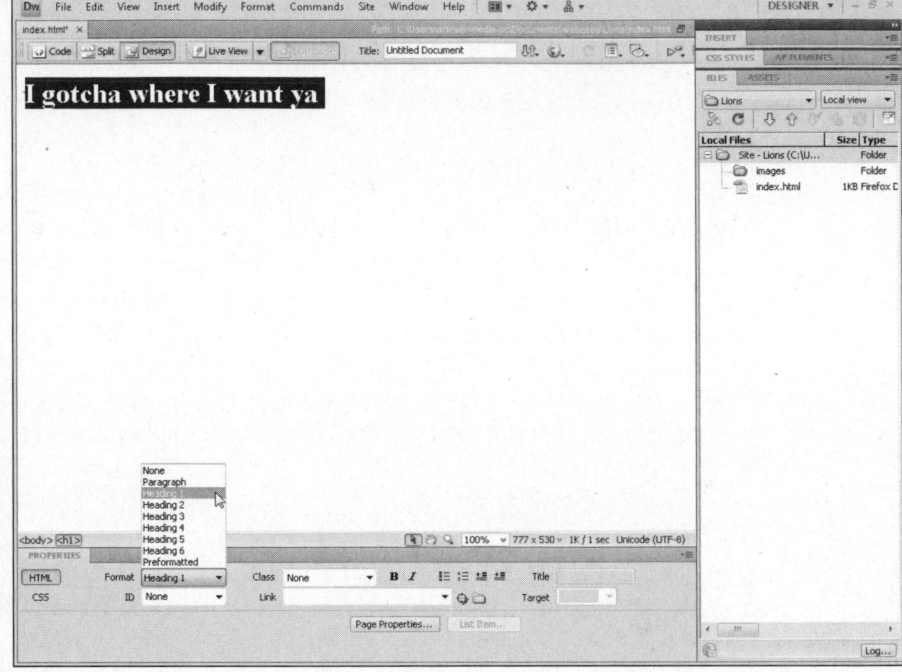

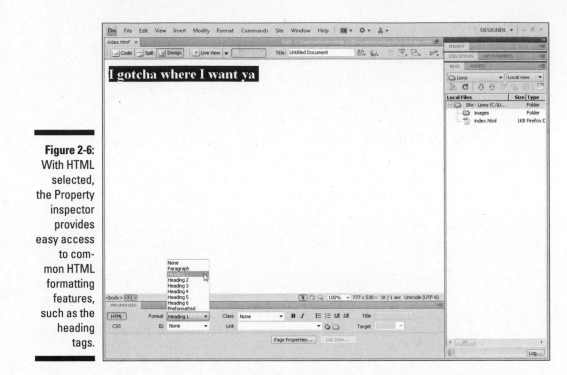

Figure 2-6: With HTML selected, the Property inspector provides easy access to common HTML formatting features, such as the heading tags.

If you're working in design view in Dreamweaver and press the Enter key (Windows) or the Return key (Mac), Dreamweaver inserts a paragraph tag, or `<p>`, in the code, which creates a line break followed by a blank line. If you want a line break without the extra blank line, hold down the Shift key while you press Enter (or Return) to get Dreamweaver to insert the `<br />` tag into the code, creating a single line break.

If you want to add a lot of space, you're best option is to use CSS to create a page layout with the spacing and alignment options you desire. (I cover CSS in Chapters 5 and 6.)

If you're working in code view and add space using the Enter or Return key, you add blank space within the code. Extra space in HTML code can be useful because extra space can make code easier to read, but it doesn't affect the way a page displays in design view or in a Web browser.

Inserting text from another program

Dreamweaver gives you many options to maintain formatting when you copy and paste text from another program. You can change the default for how Dreamweaver handles formatting when you choose Edit⇨Paste and alter the Preferences in the Copy/Paste category. And you can choose Edit⇨Paste Special to have all the options available each time you paste new content. Here are your four main options (and two ways to refine your choice):

- **Text Only:** Dreamweaver strips any formatting and inserts plain text.
- **Text with Structure:** Dreamweaver includes paragraphs, lists, tables, and other structural formatting options.
- **Text with Structure Plus Basic Formatting:** Dreamweaver includes structural formatting as well as basic formatting, such as bold and italic.
- **Text with Structure Plus Full Formatting:** In addition to the previous options, Dreamweaver includes formatting created by style sheets in programs, such as Microsoft Word.
- **Retain Line Breaks:** Line breaks are preserved, even if you don't keep other formatting options.
- **Clean Up Word Paragraph Spacing:** This option addresses a common problem with the way Microsoft Word's paragraph spacing is converted when content is pasted into an HTML file.

I cover formatting text in Chapter 5 because you need to understand some basics about CSS to best format text in a Web site. You find instructions for adding other content, such as images and links, to your page, in the upcoming sections.

Adding images

Now for the fun part. Adding an image to your Web page may seem almost magical at first because it's so simple with Dreamweaver. The challenge with Web graphics isn't adding them to your pages but creating good-looking images that load quickly in your viewer's browser. You need another program, such as Photoshop or Fireworks, to create, convert, and edit images. Dreamweaver just lets you place the images on your page.

For more information on finding and creating images, as well as keeping file sizes small, see Chapter 3. For now, I assume that you have a GIF or a JPEG image file ready and that you want to insert your image into your page. The two most common image formats you can use on your Web page are GIF and JPEG (which is often shortened to JPG), but the PNG file is increasingly used today because it's superior to the GIF format. ***Warning:*** PNG isn't fully supported in very old versions of some Web browsers. For the exercise that follows, you can use any image in GIF, JPEG, or PNG format.

If you don't have an image handy, you can download free images from my Web site at www.DigitalFamily.com/free. (You find instructions for downloading the free images on the site.)

Before inserting an image into a Web page, it's good practice to save the image inside your local root folder (the one you should have identified in the site definition process described in the "Defining a Web site in Dreamweaver" section, earlier in this chapter). Saving your image in your Web site's local root folder is important because you need to keep Web pages and images in the same location relative to each other in your Web site, or you risk broken image links when you publish your site to a server. Whether you save your images in an images folder or in any other place in the root folder is up to you, but it's common practice to save images in a folder called images.

If you insert an image into a page and the image isn't saved in the local root folder, Dreamweaver copies the image into the root folder of your site (directly into the images folder if you identified one during the site definition process). This happens automatically as Dreamweaver inserts the image into the page and the original image is left unchanged.

Many designers create an *images* folder so they can keep all their image files in one place. If you're working on a very large site, you may want to create multiple image folders to better organize your files.

To avoid breaking links or image references, always use the Files panel to move or rename files. When you do so, Dreamweaver automatically fixes the links. If you move or rename a file or folder outside Dreamweaver, the links break. You find more detailed instructions on testing and fixing links in Chapter 4.

Why can't I place images anywhere I want them?

You can't just place your cursor anywhere on a page and insert an image where you want it. This isn't a limitation of Dreamweaver; it's a restriction caused by how HTML is displayed on the Web.

By default, all images, text, and other elements are inserted starting at the top-left corner of the browser window. To create more complex layouts and position images precisely on a page, you're best option is to create a layout with CSS (which I cover in Chapter 6). You can also use an HTML table to position elements on a Web page (which I cover in Chapter 7).

Okay, assuming you've saved your page and the image you want to insert into your page is saved within your main root site folder (or you're ready to let Dreamweaver copy an image that is saved on your hard drive into your local root folder for you), you're ready for the easy part. Follow these steps to add an image on your Web page:

1. **Place your cursor on the page where you want to add the image.**

   I inserted my cursor under the headline at the beginning of the first paragraph.

2. **Double-click the Insert panel at the top right of the workspace to open it.**

   Note: The location of the Insert panel varies depending on the Workspace layout you've selected. These instructions assume you're using the designer layout option, which is the default when you first start Dreamweaver. Choose Window⇨Workspace Layout and then choose Designer to restore these default settings.

3. **Click the Images icon, located in the Common section of the Insert panel or click the small arrow to the right of the icon and then choose Image from the drop-down list.**

   The Select Image Source dialog box opens, displaying files and folders on your hard drive.

4. **Navigate to the folder that has the image you want to insert and double-click to select the image you want to insert into your page.**

5. **Enter alternate text in the Image Tag Accessibility Attributes dialog box.**

   If you have Accessibility options turned on in Preferences (the default), the Image Tag Accessibility Attributes dialog box appears. It's good practice to always add alternate text in this dialog box. To do so, simply enter text in the Alternate Text field. You can type any text in this field; it's meant to provide a description of the image. Alternate text won't appear on your Web page unless the image isn't visible, but it will appear in Internet Explorer when a user holds the cursor over the image. Alternate text is also important for Web surfers who use *screen readers,* or browsers that "read" Web pages to them, such as those with limited vision. For this reason, alternate text is required for accessibility compliance. A long description is considered optional under most accessibility guidelines. You can enter the address of a Web page with a longer description of the image in this field. You can also add or edit alternate text in the Property inspector after clicking to select the inserted image.

6. **Click OK.**

   The image automatically appears on the Web page.

7. **Click to select the image on your Web page.**

   Image options are displayed automatically in the Property inspector at the bottom of the page.

8. **Use the Property inspector to specify image attributes, such as alignment, spacing, and alternate text.**

   In the example shown in Figure 2-7, I set the alignment to Right, using the Align option at the very bottom right of the Property inspector. That's how I got the text to wrap to the left of the image. I've also added ten pixels of space with the H Space field to create a margin between the image and the text.

CSS makes it possible to create more precise formatting options. For example, H Space inserts space on both the left and right sides of an image. With CSS, you can create a style that applies margin space on any or all sides of an image.

With an image selected, the Property inspector enables you to specify many attributes for an image. Table 2-1 describes those attributes. If you don't see all the attributes listed in the table on your screen, click the triangle in the bottom-right corner of the Property inspector to expand the inspector and reveal all the image options.

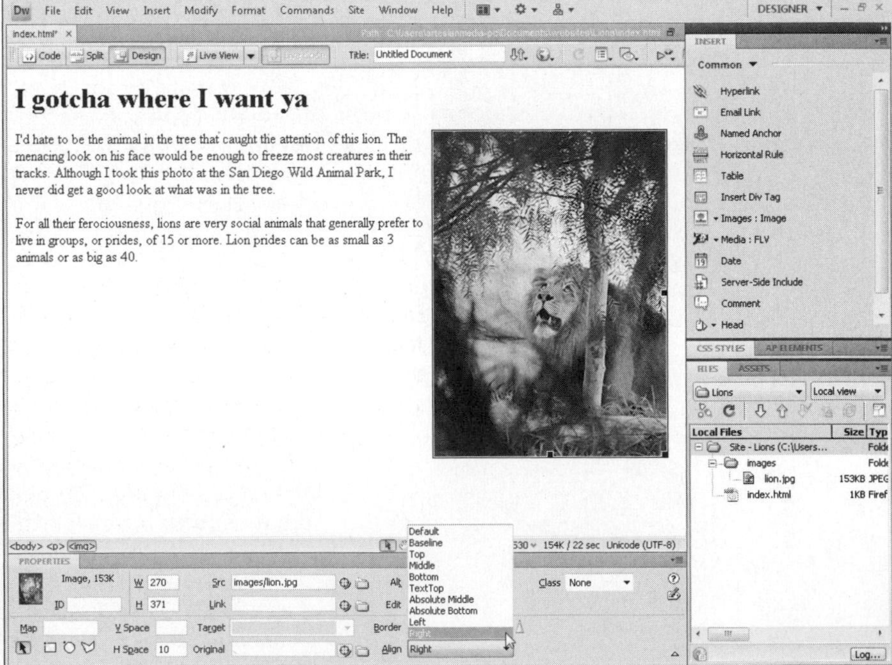

Figure 2-7: When an image is selected, the Property inspector provides easy access to common image attributes, such as alignment and spacing.

Table 2-1 Image Attributes in the Property Inspector

Abbreviation	*Attribute*	*Function*
Image	N/A	Specifies the file size.
ID	Name	Identifies image uniquely on the page — an important detail if you use behaviors or other scripts that target an image. Can be left blank.
Map	Map Name	Assigns a name to an image map. All image maps require a name.
Hotspot tools	Image Map Coordinates	Use the Rectangle, Oval, and Polygon icons to create image map hotspots for links. (See Chapter 3 to find out how to create an image map.)
W	Width	Dreamweaver automatically specifies the width of the image based on the actual size of the image dimensions.
H	Height	Dreamweaver automatically specifies the height of the image based on the actual size of the image dimensions.
Src	Source	Required. The *source* is the filename and path from the current document to the desired image. Dreamweaver automatically sets this when you insert the image.
Link	Hyperlink	This field displays the address or path if the image is used as a link. (For more about creating links, see "Setting Links" later in this chapter.)
Alt	Alternate Text	Use this field to add or edit alternate text.
Edit	Icons for Edit, Image Editing Settings, and Update from Original	Click the Edit icon to launch the image editor associated with Dreamweaver (you can change these settings in Dreamweaver's preferences dialog box). Use the Image Editing Settings icon to launch the Image Preview dialog box where you can make basic edits to an image. Choose the Update from Original icon to ensure that edits are made using the original image. ***Note:*** This setting works only if you've used an associated Adobe image editor to edit the image before inserting the image into the page.

(continued)

Table 2-1 *(continued)*

Abbreviation	***Attribute***	***Function***
V Space	Vertical Space	Measured in pixels, this setting inserts blank space above and below the image.
H Space	Horizontal Space	Measured in pixels, this setting inserts blank space to the left and right of the image.
Target	Link Target	Use this option when the image appears in a page where you want to control the target, such as when a page is part of an HTML frameset. If you want a link to open a new browser window, choose _blank. For instructions on targeting frames, see Chapter 8.
Border	Image Border	Measured in pixels, this attribute enables you to add a border around an image. I nearly always set the image border to 0 (zero) when using an image as a link to prevent an automatic border being added when an image is used as a link.
Icons for	Crop, Resample, Brightness and Contrast, and Sharpen	Use any of these icons to make minor alterations to an image in Dreamweaver. ***Note:*** Any changes made using these options permanently alter the image when the page is saved.
Class	CSS Setting	The Class field enables you to apply any class styles defined in Dreamweaver. To use this option, select any element in the workspace and then select any class style you want to apply from the drop-down list.

Although you can resize an image in Dreamweaver by clicking and dragging the edge of the image or by changing the Height and Width values in the Property inspector, I don't recommend you change an image size this way. Changing the height and width in the Property inspector doesn't actually change the size of the image, just the way it appears on the page. That's a problem for two reasons. First, using this option to make an image look larger or smaller can make the image look distorted. Second, using this option to make an image look smaller requires your visitor to download a larger file than necessary. If you do resize an image in Dreamweaver, a small circular icon appears to the right of the height and width fields. Click this icon, and Dreamweaver alters the HTML to return the image display to the actual size.

Setting Links

Dreamweaver is truly a dream when it comes to setting links. The most important thing to keep in mind is that a link is essentially an address (a URL) that tells a viewer's browser what page to go to when the viewer clicks the text or image containing the link.

To link to a page within your Web site, you can create a *relative link* that includes a path describing how to get from the current page to the linked page within your main root folder. A relative link doesn't need to include the domain name of the site, just instructions for a browser to get from one page within your site to another. Here's an example of what the code looks like for the relative link from the home page on my Web site at `www.DigitalFamily.com` to the Dreamweaver page in the books section, which is contained in a `books` folder:

```
<A HREF="books/dreamweaver.html">Dreamweaver Books</A>
```

Creating multiple pages to set links

Creating a new page to start a Web site may seem obvious but consider this: You may want to create a bunch of new pages before you get too far in your development, and you may even want to start organizing the new pages in subdirectories before you have anything on them. Doing so enables you to organize the structure of your site before you start setting links. After all, you can't link to a page that doesn't exist. If you plan to have five links on your front page to other pages in your site, go ahead and create those other pages, even if you don't put anything on them yet.

For example, say you're creating a site for your department at a big company. You're likely to want a few main pages, such as a page about your staff, another page about what you do, and a third page with general information and resources. At this initial stage, you could create four pages — one for the front page of the site and three others for each of the subsections. Name the front page `index.html` and name the other pages `staff.html`, `about.html`, and `general.html`. With these initial pages in place, you benefit from having an early plan for organizing the site, and you can start setting links more easily among the main pages of your site. See Chapter 4 for more tips on Web site planning and managing and testing links.

If you select the Root option instead of Relative in the Site Definition dialog box, this address would begin with a forward slash (as you see here) instructing the browser to begin at the root level:

```
<A HREF="/books/dreamweaver.html">Dreamweaver Books</A>
```

If you link to a page on a different Web site, create an absolute, or external, link. An *absolute link* includes the full Internet address of the other site. Here's an example of what the code would look like behind an absolute link if you created a link from your site to the Dreamweaver page in my books section:

```
<A HREF="http://www.digitalfamily.com/books/
            dreamweaver.html">Janine's Books</A>
```

If all that HREF code stuff looks like Greek to you, don't worry. The following section shows you how Dreamweaver sets links like this for you so you don't even have to look at this code if you don't want to. (I include these tips because I think it's helpful to have a little understanding of what's happening behind the scenes.)

Linking pages within your Web site

Linking from one page to another page in your Web site is easy. The most important thing to remember is to save your pages in your site's root folder (as described in the "Defining a Web site in Dreamweaver" section, previously in the chapter) before you start setting links. Here's how you create a link from one page in a Web site to another:

1. **In Dreamweaver, open the page where you want to create a link.**
2. **Select the text or image that you want to serve as the link (meaning the text or image that a user licks to trigger the link).**

   Click and drag to highlight text or click once to select an image. In this example, I selected the photo of the lion and I linked it to a page named `prey.html` located in the same folder.

3. **Click the Hyperlink icon in the Common Insert panel, at the top right of the workspace.**

   Alternatively, you can set a link by clicking the Browse button (the icon that looks like a file folder) just to the right of the Link field in the Property inspector.

And yet another alternative, you can click the Point to File icon (which looks like a circle with a dot in the middle) and then drag your cursor over the name of any file in the Files panel. When you click and drag, Dreamweaver extends a line from the link field to the file in the Files panel. Note, the file must be visible in the Files panel, thus you may need to open a subfolder to reveal the file before you can set a link this way.

4. **In the Hyperlink dialog box (see Figure 2-8), click the Browse icon to the right of the Link drop-down list.**

   The Select File dialog box opens.

Figure 2-8: The Hyperlink dialog box includes a number of link settings not available from the Property inspector, including Target options and accessibility settings.

5. **Click the filename to select the page that you want your image or text to link to, and then click OK (Windows) or Choose (Mac).**

   The link is set automatically, and the dialog box closes. Note that to test your links, you have to view your page in a browser, a process I cover in the "Previewing Your Page in a Browser" section, later in this chapter.

You can use the Target field in the Hyperlink dialog box, as shown in Figure 2-8, to "target" where your linked page opens. For example, the _blank option causes the linked page to open in a new browser window. The other options are most important when working with frames, which I cover in Chapter 8.

Setting links to named anchors within a page

Setting links to named anchors makes it possible to link to elements within the same page. A *named anchor link* is an HTML tag that can be inserted anywhere on a page to add a Name, which can serve as a target for a link. You can use a named anchor to link from an image or a text string on one page to another place on the same page, or to link from one page to a specific part of a different page. To create a named anchor link, sometimes called a *jump link,* first insert a named anchor in the place that you want to link to and then include that anchor in the link to direct the browser to that specific part of the page when a viewer follows the link.

Suppose that you want to set a link from the word *Tigers* at the top of a page to a section lower on the page that starts with the headline *Lions are Cooler than Tigers.* First insert a named anchor at the *Lions are Cooler than Tigers* headline and then link the word *Tigers* from the top of the page to that anchor.

To insert a named anchor and set a link to it, follow these steps:

1. **Open the page on which you want to insert the named anchor.**
2. **Place your cursor next to the word or image that you want to link to on the page.**

   You don't need to select the word or image; you just need a reference point that appears when the link is selected. For this example, I placed the cursor to the left of the headline *Lions are Cooler than Tigers.*
3. **Choose Insert⇨Named Anchor.**

   The Insert Named Anchor dialog box appears.
4. **Enter a name for the anchor.**

   You can name anchors anything you want (as long as you don't use spaces or special characters). Just make sure that you use a different name for each anchor on the same page. Then be sure that you remember what you called the anchor because you have to either type the anchor name to set the link or select it from the drop-down list in the Hyperlink dialog box, as you see in Step 8. In this example, I chose *tiger* as the anchor name because it's easy for me to remember.

5. **Click OK.**

   The dialog box closes, and a small anchor icon appears on the page where you inserted the anchor name. You can move an anchor name by clicking the anchor icon and dragging it to another location on the page.

   If you're curious about what this named anchor looks like in HTML, here's the code that appears before the headline in my example:

```
<A NAME="tiger" id="tiger"></A>
```

   Remember that Dreamweaver creates XHTML code, which is a strict version of HTML and requires that all code be in lowercase letters.

6. **To set a link to the named anchor location, select the text or image that you want to link from.**

   You can link to a named anchor from anywhere else on the same page or from another page. In my example, I linked from the word *Tiger* that appears at the top of the page to the anchor I made next to the headline.

7. **Click the Link icon in the Common Insert panel, at the top right of the workspace.**

8. **In the Hyperlink dialog box, use the small arrow to the right of the Link box to select the anchor.**

   Alternatively, you can set a jump link by using the Property inspector by typing a pound sign (#) followed by the anchor name.

   You can also select the text and drag a line from the Point to File icon (next to the Link text box) to the anchor icon. The anchor name automatically appears in the Link box, saving you from typing the name.

   In my example, I typed **#tiger** in the Link text box. The HTML code for this line looks like this:

```
<A HREF="#tiger">Tiger</A>
```

   If you want to link to an anchor named *tiger* on another page with the filename `coolcats.html`, type **coolcats.html#tiger** in the Link text box.

Linking to another Web site

Linking to a page on another Web site — called an *external link* — is even easier than linking to an internal link. All you need is the URL of the page to which you want to link, and you're most of the way there.

To create an external link, follow these steps:

1. **In Dreamweaver, open the page from which you want to link.**
2. **Select the text or image that you want to act as a link.**
3. **In the Link text box in the Property inspector, type the URL of the page you want your text or image to link to.**

   The link is set automatically. In the example in Figure 2-9, I created a link using the text San Diego Wild Animal Page to link to the park's Web site at `www.sandiegozoo.org`.

Although, you don't have to type the `http://` or even the `www.` at the beginning of a Web site address to get to a site in most browsers, you must always use the full URL, including the `http://`, when you create a link to another Web site in HTML. Otherwise, the browser can't find the correct external site address, and the visitor will probably end up on an error page.

Setting a link to an e-mail address

Another common link option goes to an e-mail address. Visitors can send you messages easily with e-mail links. I always recommend that you invite visitors to contact you because they can point out mistakes in your site and give you valuable feedback about how you can further develop your site.Setting a link to an e-mail address is just as easy as setting a link to another Web page. All you need to know is the e-mail address you want to link to and what text or image you want to use when you set the link.

To create an e-mail link, select the text you want to link and then click the E-mail Link icon in the Common Insert panel. In the E-mail Link dialog box, enter the e-mail address in the Link field and then click OK. If you want to use an image as an e-mail link, you must select the image in the main work area and then enter the e-mail link into the Link field of the Property inspector.

When you create an e-mail link with the Link field in the Property inspector, the e-mail links must begin with the code `mailto:` (no `//`). For example, if you typed a link to my e-mail address into the Property inspector, you'd need to type **mailto:janine@jcwarner.com**. Here's what the full line of code behind that e-mail link would look like:

```
<A HREF="mailto:janine@jcwarner.com">Send a message to
          Janine</A>
```

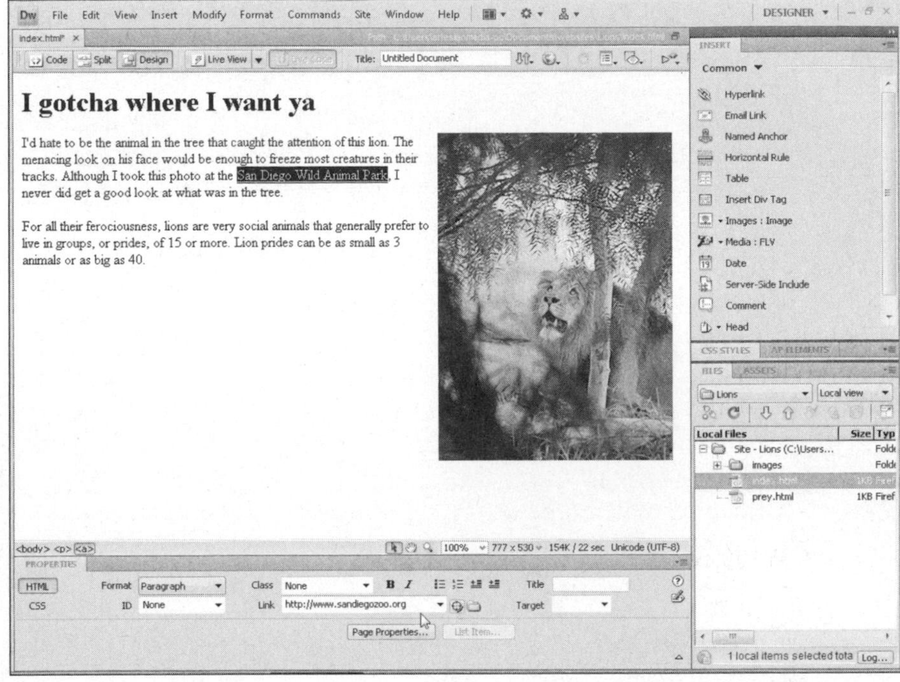

Figure 2-9: To set a link to another Web site, highlight the text or image you want to link and type the URL in the Link text box.

When visitors to your Web site click an e-mail link, their computer systems automatically launch their e-mail program and create a blank e-mail message to the specified e-mail address. This is a cool trick, but it can be disconcerting to your users if they don't expect it to happen, and it won't work if they don't have e-mail programs on their computers. That's why I always try to let users know when I use an e-mail link. For example, instead of just linking the words *Contact Janine,* I link the words *E-mail Janine.* Even better, I often link the actual e-mail address.

When you create an e-mail link on a Web page that will be displayed on the public Internet, you open yourself to spammers, some of whom use automated programs to "lift" e-mail addresses off Web pages.

Spam is the reason many sites don't include e-mail links, but instead use text, such as *Send e-mail to Janine at jcwarner.com.* Another alternative is to use the AddressMunger Web site to create e-mail links that include special code to hide them from spammers. Visit `www.AddressMunger.com` to read more. You can also use a form to get around this potential problem. By setting up a form with a script that delivers the form's contents to an e-mail address, you can shield your e-mail address from spammers while still making it easy for visitors to your site to send comments. You find instructions for creating forms in Chapter 12.

Changing Page Properties

You can change many individual elements on a page in the Property inspector, but if you want to make changes that affect the entire page, such as changing the background color of the entire page or changing the way links and text are formatted, use the Page Properties dialog box.

As shown in Figure 2-10, the Page Properties dialog box includes a list of categories on the left. Each of these reveals different options for specifying page settings. Some of these options are covered in other parts of the book, such as the Tracing Image feature (Chapter 9), and the Background Image feature (Chapter 3).

For now, to keep things simple, this section focuses only on changing the background and the text colors available from the Appearance categories, as shown in Figure 2-10, and the options in the Links (CSS) category. Note that the CSS options are recommended over HTML options. When you use the Appearance (CSS) options, Dreamweaver automatically creates corresponding styles for the Body tag.

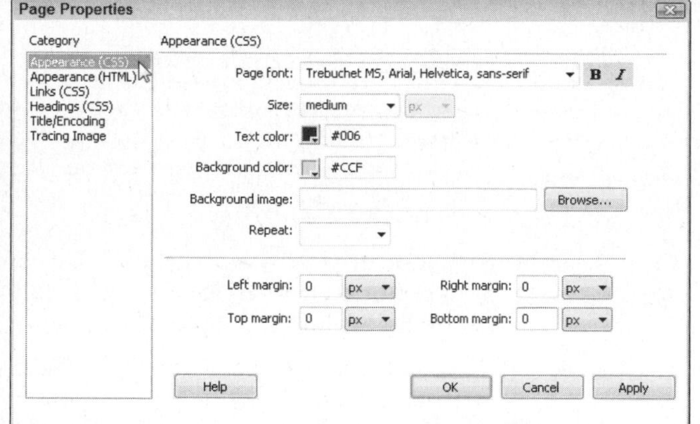

Figure 2-10: The Appearance (CSS) category in the Page Properties dialog box enables you to specify the text color, font face, font size, background, and margins.

Although you can apply global settings, such as text size and color, in the Page Properties dialog box, you can override those settings with other formatting options in specific instances. For example, you could set all your text to Helvetica in Page Properties and then change the font for an individual headline to Arial with the Font field in the Property inspector.

To change the font settings, the background and text colors, and the page margins for an entire page, follow these steps:

1. **Choose Modify➪Page Properties.**

   The Appearance (CSS) category of the Page Properties dialog box appears (see Figure 2-10).

2. **In the Page Font drop-down list, specify the fonts you want for the text on your page.**

   In this example, I set the font face to the collection that begins with the Georgia font. If you don't specify a font, your text appears in the font specified in your user's browser, which is usually Times.

3. **If you want all the text on your page to appear bold or italic, click the B or I, respectively, to the right of the Page Font drop-down list.**

   If you select one of these options, all your text appears bold or italic in the page.

4. **In the Size drop-down list, specify the font size you want for the text on your page.**

   Again, you can override these settings for any text on the page.

5. **Click the Text Color swatch box to reveal the color palette. Choose any color you like.**

   The color you select fills the color swatch box but won't change the text color on your page until you click the Apply or OK button.

6. **Click the Background Color swatch box to reveal the color palette. Choose any color you like.**

   The color you selected fills the color swatch box. The color doesn't fill the background until you click the Apply or OK button.

7. **If you want to insert a graphic or photograph into the background of your page, click the Browse button next to the Background Image box and select the image in the Select Image Source dialog box.**

   When you insert a background image, it automatically repeats or tiles across and down the page unless you choose the No-Repeat option from the Repeat drop-down list or use CSS to further define the display.

8. **Use the margin options at the bottom of the dialog box to change the left, right, top, or bottom margins of your page.**

   Entering **0** in all four of these fields removes the default margin settings that automatically add margin space at the top and left of a Web page, enabling you to create designs that begin flush with the edge of a browser.

9. **Click the Apply button to see how the colors look on your page.**

10. **Click OK to finish and close the Page Properties dialog box.**

When you change the background, text, or link colors, make sure the colors look good together and that your text is still readable. As a general rule, a light background color works best with dark text color and vice versa.

To change the link color and underline options, follow these steps:

1. **Choose Modify⇨Page Properties.**

   The Page Properties dialog box appears.

2. **In the Category list, select the Links (CSS) option.**

   The Links (CSS) category is displayed, as shown in Figure 2-11.

Figure 2-11: The Links (CSS) category enables you to change link colors, font face, and size, as well as to alter the display of the underlined or linked text.

3. **Specify the font face and size you want for the links on your page.**

   If you don't specify a font, your links appear in the same font and size specified for the text of your document.

4. **To the right of the Link Font drop-down list, click the B or I if you want all the links on your page to appear bold or italic, respectively.**

   If you select one of these options, all your links appear bold or italic unless you specify other formatting in the page.

5. **Specify a color for any or all link states.**

   The color you selected is applied to links on your page based on the link state. There are four link states, and all can be displayed in the same or different colors:

   - **Link Color:** This option controls the color in which a link appears when it is first displayed on a page.

- **Visited Links:** This option controls the color of links that a visitor has already clicked (or visited).
- **Rollover Links:** A link changes to this color when a user rolls a cursor over the link (also known as *hovering*).
- **Active Links:** A link changes to this color briefly while a user is actively clicking it.

6. **In the Underline Style drop-down list, specify whether you want your links underlined.**

   By default, all links on a Web page appear underlined in a browser, but many designers find the underline distracting and prefer to turn off underlining by selecting Never Underline. You can also choose Show Underline Only on Rollover to make the underline appear when a user moves a cursor over a link. Hide Underline on Rollover causes the underline to disappear when a user moves a cursor over a link.

7. **Click the Apply button to see your changes automatically applied to any linked text or other elements on your page.**
8. **Click OK to finish and close the Page Properties dialog box.**

When you change the link options and other settings in the Page Properties dialog box, Dreamweaver automatically creates styles corresponding to these settings and saves them in the CSS Styles panel, as shown in Figure 2-12. I cover Dreamweaver's CSS Styles panel in greater detail in Chapters 5 and 6.

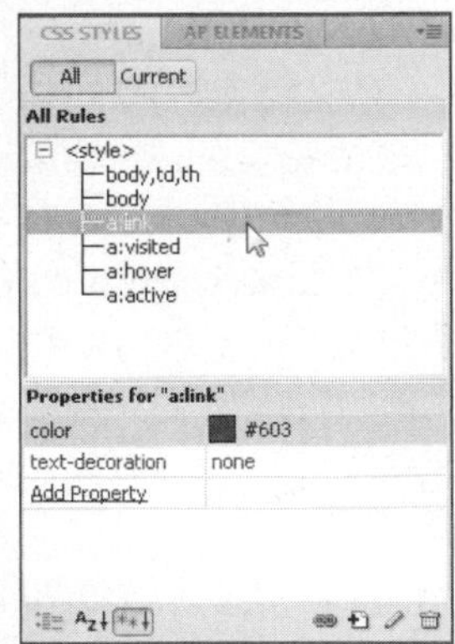

Figure 2-12: When you specify formatting options in the Page Properties dialog box, Dreamweaver automatically creates styles that appear in the CSS panel.

Adding Meta Tags for Search Engines

If you've heard of Meta tags, you probably associate them with search engines, and you'd be right. Meta tags are used for a variety of things, but one of the most common uses is to provide special text that doesn't appear on your page but is read by crawlers, bots, and other programs that scour the Web cataloging and ranking Web pages for Yahoo!, Google, and a long list of other search-related sites.

Some search engines read the Meta tags for keywords and descriptions. The first enables site designers to include a list of keywords they would like used to make their Web site a match when someone types the same keywords into a search engine. Unfortunately, Meta keywords have been so abused by Web designers attempting to mislead visitors about the true content of their Web pages that most search engines ignore the Meta keyword tag. Some search engines continue to recognize Meta keywords, however, and it won't hurt your ranking with any search engines if you use this Meta tag.

The Meta description tag is more widely used and is definitely worth using. This tag is designed to let you include a written description of your Web site and is often used by search engines as the brief description that appears in search results pages. If you don't include your own text in a Meta description tag, many search engines use the first several words that appear on your front page or some other collection of text from your page, usually based on formatting or placement on the page. Depending on your design, the first few words may not be the best description of your site, and you'll be better served by including your own Meta description.

Follow these steps to fill in the Meta description tag:

1. **Open the page where you want to add a Meta description.**

   You can use Meta descriptions on any or all pages on your Web site. (Many people using search engines to find your site may end up directly at internal pages if the content matches the search.)

2. **Choose Insert⇨HTML⇨Head Tags⇨Description, as shown in Figure 2-13.**

   The Description dialog box appears.

3. **In the Description text box, enter the text you want for your page description.**

   Don't add any HTML to the text in this box.

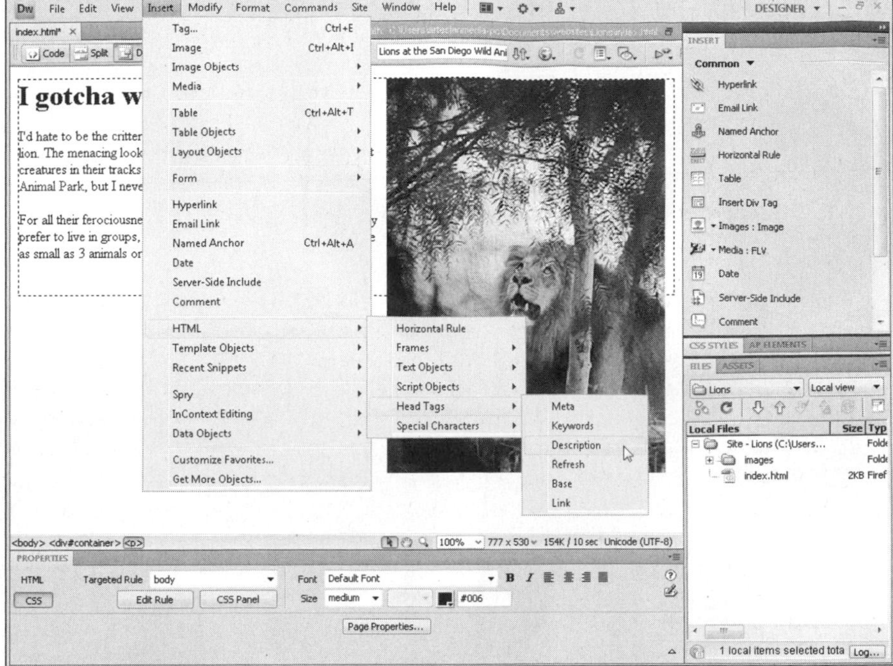

Figure 2-13: Many search engines use the text entered into the Meta description field as the description of your Web page in search results.

4. **Click OK.**

   The description text you entered is inserted into the Head area at the top of the page in the HTML code. Meta content doesn't appear in the body of the page.

If you want to add keywords, repeat Steps 1–4, choosing Insert➪HTML➪Head Tags➪Keywords in Step 2.

Previewing Your Page in a Browser

Although Dreamweaver displays Web pages much like a Web browser, not all interactive features work in Dreamweaver. To test links, for example, preview your work in a Web browser.

The simplest way to preview your work is to save the page you're working on and then click the Preview/Debug in Browser icon located at the top right of the workspace, as shown in Figure 2-14 (it looks like a small globe). You can also choose File➪Preview in a Browser.

When you install Dreamweaver, it automatically finds all the browsers installed on your computer and sets them up so that you can easily select them to preview your pages. It's always a good practice to test your pages in more than one Web browser because page display can vary. How many browsers you test your pages on depends on the audience you expect to visit your Web site, but most good Web designers test their pages on at least the latest two or three versions of Internet Explorer and Firefox. It's also good practice to preview your pages on both Macintosh and Windows computers because the page display might differ.

If you install more browsers on your computer, you can add them to the Browser Preview list by choosing Edit⇨Preferences (Dreamweaver⇨Preferences on a Mac) and then choosing Preview in Browser from the Category list. Click the plus sign at the top of the screen to add a browser and then navigate your hard drive to select the installed browser to add to the list. Alternatively, you can click the globe icon at the top of the workspace, as shown in Figure 2-14 and choose Edit Browser List.

Figure 2-14: Use the Preview/ Debug in Browser icon at the top of the workspace to open any page displayed in Dreamweaver in a Web browser.

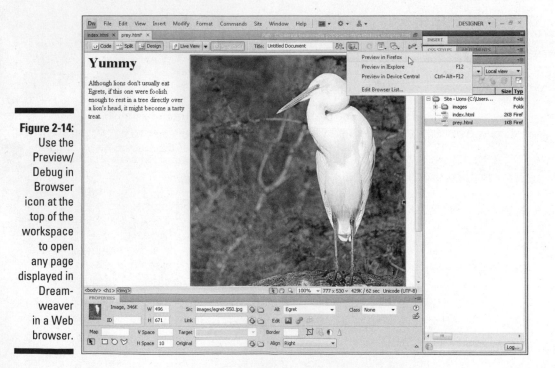

Chapter 3

Adding Graphics

In This Chapter

- Creating and optimizing images for the Web
- Inserting and aligning images
- Editing images
- Including a background image
- Using image maps

No matter how great the writing may be on your Web site, the graphics always get people's attention first. The key to making a good first impression is to use images that look great, download quickly, and are a good fit with the design of your Web site.

If you're familiar with using a graphics-editing program, such as Adobe Photoshop or Fireworks, to create graphics for the Web, you're a step ahead. If not, you find pointers throughout this chapter on how to convert images for the Web, what image formats to use, and how to optimize images for faster download times.

If your images are already in GIF, JPEG, or PNG format and ready for the Web, you can jump ahead to the "Inserting Images in Dreamweaver" section, where you find out how to place and align images, create image maps, and use an image as a background. You also discover some of Dreamweaver's built-in image-editing features, which enable you to crop images and even adjust contrast and brightness without ever launching an external image-editing program.

Comparing Adobe Web graphics programs

Most professional designers strongly prefer Adobe Photoshop, although I have to say I've been impressed with Photoshop Elements, which is a "light" version but offers many of the same features for a fraction of the cost. The following is a list of some of the most popular image-editing programs on the market today. All these image programs are available for both Mac and Windows:

- **Adobe Fireworks (`www.adobe.com/fireworks`):** Fireworks was one of the first image-editing programs designed to create and edit Web graphics. Originally created by Macromedia, the program is now part of the Adobe Web Suite and is fully integrated with Dreamweaver. Fireworks gives you everything you need to create, edit, and output Web graphics, all in one well-designed product. Although Fireworks lacks many of the advanced image-editing capabilities of Photoshop, it shines when creating Web graphics, and is especially popular among Web designers who rave about the ability to create a design in Fireworks that can easily be sliced and re-created in Dreamweaver.
- **Adobe Photoshop (`www.adobe.com/photoshop`):** By far the most popular image-editing program on the market, Photoshop is a widely used standard among graphics professionals. With Photoshop, you can create original artwork, edit and enhance photographs, and so much more. Photoshop has a wealth of powerful painting and selection tools in addition to special effects and filters that can be used to create images that go far beyond what you can capture on film or create with many other illustration programs. In previous versions, Photoshop came bundled with a program called *Image Ready,* a companion program designed for Web graphics. In CS3, those Web features were included in Photoshop; and in CS4, they've been enhanced, making it easier than ever to go back and forth between Photoshop and Dreamweaver.
- **Adobe Photoshop Elements (`www.adobe.com/elements`):** If you don't need all the bells and whistles offered in the full-blown version of Photoshop, Photoshop Elements is a remarkably powerful program — for about a sixth of the price. If you're a professional designer, you're best served by Photoshop CS4. But if you're a hobbyist or small business owner and want to create good-looking images without the high cost and learning curve of a professional graphics program, Elements is a great deal and well-suited to creating Web graphics.

If you have an Internet connection and want to do basic image editing for free, visit `www.photoshop.com/express` where you can use a free online version of Photoshop Elements.

Creating and Optimizing Web Graphics

The most important thing to keep in mind when creating images for the Web is that you want to *optimize* your images to make your file sizes as small as possible so that they download as quickly as possible.

How you optimize an image depends on how the image was created and whether you want to save it as a JPEG, PNG or GIF. You find instructions for optimizing images with Photoshop in the sections that follow, but the bottom line is this: No matter what program, format, or optimization technique you choose, your biggest challenge is finding the best balance between small file size and good image quality. Essentially, the more you optimize, the faster the image will download, but the compression and color reduction techniques used to optimize images can make them look terrible.

You can optimize images using compression techniques or color reduction and you can further reduce file size by reducing the physical size of an image. As a general rule, do any editing, such as adjusting contrast, retouching, or combining images before you reduce their size or optimize them because you want to work with the highest resolution possible when you're editing. Also, resize an image before you optimize it. You find instructions for resizing an image in the next exercise and instructions for optimizing in the sections that follow.

Resizing graphics and photos

Resizing images is important for two reasons: Your photos and graphics must be small enough to display well on a computer monitor. The smaller you make them, the more you reduce the file size and the faster your images will download to a user's computer.

Although you can change the display size of an image by altering the height and width settings in the Property inspector in Dreamweaver, you get much better results if you change the physical size of the image in an image editor instead. That's because when you alter the height and width in the HTML code, you simply instruct a Web browser to display the image in a different size. If you set the image larger, the image is likely to look fuzzy or distorted because not enough pixels are in the image for all the details to look good when the image is displayed larger than its actual size. If you set the code to display the image smaller than it is, you're requiring that your users download an image that's larger than necessary.

To enlarge or reduce the dimensions of an image, change the image size. Follow these steps:

1. **With an image open in Photoshop, choose Image⇨Resize.**

   If you don't want your original image to lose quality, make a copy of it and resize the *copy* for your Web site.

2. **In the Image Size dialog box, specify a height and width for the image.**

   As shown in Figure 3-1, I'm reducing the size of this image to 200 pixels wide.

The Image Size dialog box can be confusing at first because it has multiple options for changing image size and resolution. A simple strategy is to use the fields in the Pixel Dimensions area, at the top of the dialog box. With these options, you can alter the height and width of an image to a specified size in pixels or enlarge or reduce the image by any percentage, as shown in the drop-down list in Figure 3-1. (***Note:*** Make sure Scale Styles, Constrain Proportions, and Resample Image are all selected at the bottom of the dialog box.)

If you've checked the Constrain Proportions check box at the bottom of the dialog box in Elements, any changes you make to the height automatically affect the width (and vice versa) to ensure that the image proportions remain constant even if the height or width is altered.

3. **Click OK to resize the image.**

   If you want to return the image to its previous size, choose Edit➪Undo. Beware, after you save the image, the changes become permanent.

Most Web designers limit the resolution of an image to 72 pixels per inch (ppi) because that's all that displays on a computer monitor, and anything higher than that means the image is a larger size than necessary for the Web. If the image resolution is higher than 72 ppi, Photoshop automatically reduces the resolution when you use the Save for Web features, covered in the sections that follow.

Figure 3-1: When you resize an image in Photoshop in the Pixel Dimensions area, you can specify the new size in pixels or as a percentage of the original size.

Choosing the best image format

One of the most common questions about images for the Web concerns when to use GIF or PNG and when to use JPEG. Table 3-1 provides the simple answer.

Table 3-1 Image Formats for the Web

Format	*Best Use*
GIF	For line art (such as one- or two-color logos), simple drawings, animations, and basically any image that has no gradients or blends. GIF is also the best format for images that you want displayed with a transparent background.
PNG	PNG generally produces better-looking images with smaller file sizes than GIF for the same kinds of limited-color images. Just beware that really old browsers, such as IE 3, don't support the PNG format and that even newer browsers, such as IE 4, 5, and 6, have problems with full PNG alpha channel support.
JPEG	For colorful, complex images (such as photographs), images containing gradients or color blends, and any other images with millions of colors.

Saving images for the Web: The basics

If you're new to saving images for the Web, the following basics can help you get the best results from your files, your image-editing program, and ultimately, your Web pages. You can

- **Convert images from any format into the GIF, PNG, and JPEG formats.** For example, your TIF, BMP, and PSD image files can all be turned into a Web-friendly file format.
- **Optimize images that are already in GIF, PNG, or JPEG format.** This further reduces their file sizes for faster download over the Internet.
- **Use many programs to create Web graphics, but Photoshop is one of the best and easiest to use.** Under the File menu in Photoshop (and Photoshop Elements), you'll find the Save for Web option. (In Photoshop CS4, the option is Save for Web & Devices.) Fireworks provides a similar feature and although the dialog boxes are slightly different in each program, the basic options for compressing and reducing colors are the same.

When you use the Save for Web feature, Photoshop creates a new copy of your image with the settings you specified and leaves the original unchanged in the main Photoshop workspace.

See the upcoming sections "Optimizing JPEG images in Photoshop" and "Optimizing GIF and PNG images in Photoshop" for details about using the Save for Web feature.

- **Make image edits before you optimize.** It's always best to use the highest quality image possible when you're editing, so make sure to do all your editing, sharpening, and resizing before you use the Save for Web option. Similarly, if you want to make further changes to an image after you've optimized it, you'll achieve the best results if you go back a higher resolution version of the image rather than editing the version that's been optimized for the Web.

Optimizing JPEG images in Photoshop

The JPEG format is the best choice for optimizing continuous-tone images, such as photographs and images with many colors or gradients. When you optimize a JPEG, you specify how much compression should be applied, a process that makes the file size of the image smaller.

If you have a digital photograph or another image that you want to prepare for the Web, follow these steps to optimize and save it in Photoshop. If you're using Photoshop Elements or Fireworks, the process is similar although the specific steps may vary:

1. **With the image open in Photoshop, choose File⇨Save for Web & Devices (or File⇨Save for Web).**

   The Save for Web & Devices dialog box appears.

2. **In the top-left corner of the dialog box, choose either 2-Up or 4-Up to display multiple versions of the same image for easy side-by-side comparison.**

   In the example shown in Figure 3-2, I chose 2-Up, which makes it possible to view the original image on the left and a preview of the same image as it will appear with the specified settings on the right.

3. **On the right side of the dialog window, just under Preset, click the small arrow to open the Optimized File Format drop-down list and choose JPEG (this dialog window is open in Figure 3-2).**

4. **Set the compression quality.**

   Use the preset options Low, Medium, High, Very High, or Maximum from the drop-down list. Or use the slider just under the Quality field to make more precise adjustments. Lowering the quality reduces the file size and makes the image download more quickly, but if you lower this number too much, the image will look blurry and blotchy.

Photoshop uses a compression scale of 0 to 100 for JPEGs in this dialog window, with 0 the lowest possible quality (the highest amount of compression and the smallest file size) and 100 the highest possible quality (the least amount of compression and the biggest file size). Low, Medium, and High represent compression values of 10, 30, and 60, respectively.

5. **Specify other settings as desired (the compression quality and file format are the most important settings).**
6. **Click Save.**

   The Save Optimized As dialog box opens.
7. **Enter a name for the image and save it into the images folder in your Web site folder.**

   Photoshop saves the optimized image as a copy of the original and leaves the original open in the main Photoshop work area.

Repeat these steps for each image you want to optimize as a JPEG.

Figure 3-2: The JPEG format is best for photographs and other images with millions of colors.

Optimizing GIF and PNG images in Photoshop

If you're working with a graphic, such as a logo, cartoon character, or drawing that can be displayed in 256 colors or less, use the GIF or PNG formats and reduce the total number of colors used in the image as much as possible to reduce the file size. To help make up for the degradation in image quality that can happen when colors are removed, GIF and PNG use a dithering trick. *Dithering* involves alternating pixels in a checkerboard-like pattern to create subtle color variations, even with a limited color palette. The effect can smooth the edges in an image and make it appear that the image uses more colors than it does.

To convert an image to a GIF or PNG in Photoshop, follow these steps:

1. **With the image open in Photoshop, choose File⇨Save for Web & Devices (or File⇨Save for Web).**

   The Save for Web & Devices dialog box appears.

2. **In the top-left corner of the dialog box, choose either 2-Up or 4-Up to display multiple versions of the same image for easy side-by-side comparison.**

   In the example shown in Figure 3-3, I chose 4-Up, which makes it possible to view the original image, as well as three different previews of the same image as it would appear with the settings specified for each preview. In Figure 3-3, you see the same image with four different settings.

3. **On the right side of the dialog window, just under Preset, click the small arrow to open the Optimized File Format drop-down list and choose either GIF or PNG.**

4. **In the Colors box, select the number of colors, as shown in Figure 3-3.**

   The fewer colors you use, the smaller the file size and the faster the image will download. But be careful, if you reduce the colors too much (as I have in the bottom-right preview shown in Figure 3-3), you lose details. The ideal number of colors depends on your image; if you go too far, your image will look terrible.

5. **If you want to maintain a transparent area in your image, select the Transparency option.**

   Any area of the image that was transparent when you created the image in the editor appears transparent in the preview window. If you don't have a transparent area in your image, this setting has no effect.

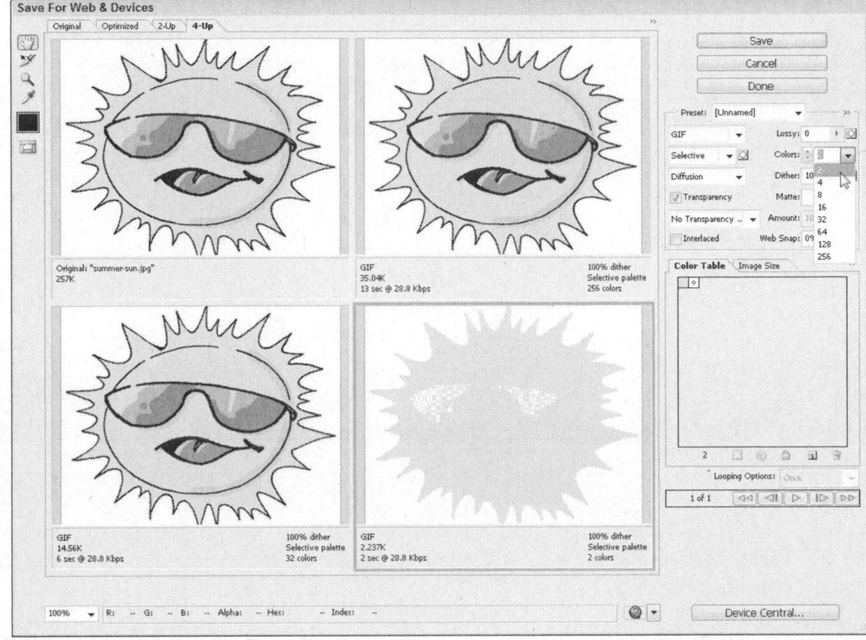

Figure 3-3: The GIF and PNG formats are best for images with limited colors, such as cartoons and line art.

Illustration by Tom McCain

Transparency is a good trick for making text or another part of an image appear to float on a Web page. That's because a transparent background doesn't appear on the Web page. You can select transparency as a background option in the New File dialog box when you create a new image.

6. **If you choose Transparency, also specify a Matte color.**

   Specify a matte color that matches the background your transparent image will be set against to ensure that the dithering along the transparent edge will blend in with the background. If you don't specify a matte color, the transparency is set for a white background, which can cause a *halo* effect if the image is displayed on a colored background.

7. **Specify other settings as desired.**

   The remainder of the settings in this dialog box can be left at their defaults in Photoshop.

8. **Click Save.**

   The Save Optimized As dialog box opens.

9. **Enter a name for the image and save it into the images folder (or any other folder) in your local root folder.**

Repeat these steps for each image you want to optimize as a GIF or PNG for your site.

Trial and error is a great technique in the Save for Web & Devices dialog box. In each of the three preview windows displaying optimized versions of the cool sun cartoon image in Figure 3-3, I used fewer and fewer colors, which reduced the file size. The version in the top left is the original, which has a file size of 257K. Reducing the image to 256 colors dramatically reduced the file size to 35K, but made little noticeable change to the image, as you see in the top right. In the bottom left, the image is reduced to 32 colors, which brought the size down to 14.5K, but still made little change to the image. In the bottom right, I reduced it to 2 colors, and although it's harder to tell in the black-and-white reproduction in this book, the image quality suffered dramatically and the mouth and sunglasses all but disappeared. In this last case, the small savings in file size are clearly not worth the loss of image quality.

How small is small enough?

After you know how to optimize GIFs and JPEGs and appreciate the goal of making them as small as possible, you may ask, "How small is small enough?" The answer is mostly subjective, but the following points are good to remember:

- **The larger your graphics files, the longer people have to wait for them to download before they can see them.** You may have the most beautiful picture of Mount Fuji on the front page of your Web site, but if it takes forever to download, most people aren't patient enough to wait to see it.
- **When you build pages with multiple graphics, you have to consider the cumulative download time of all the graphics on the page.** Even if each individual image is a small file size, they can add up. Unlike most things in life, smaller is definitely better on the Web.
- **Most Web pros consider anything from about 75K to 150K a good maximum *cumulative* size for all the elements on a given page.** With the increasing popularity of DSL and cable modems, many Web sites are starting to become a bit more graphics heavy and go beyond that size limit. However, anything over 150K is pushing the limit, especially if you expect people with dialup modems (56K and under) to stick around long enough to view your pages.

To make determining the total file size of the images on your page easy, Dreamweaver includes this information in the status bar of the current Document window, as shown in Figure 3-4. This number indicates the total file size of all the images and HTML on your page as well as the expected download time at a given connection speed. (You can set your own connection speed by choosing Edit⇨Preferences⇨Status Bar⇨Connection Speed. On a Mac, choose Dreamweaver⇨Preferences⇨Status Bar⇨Connection Speed.)

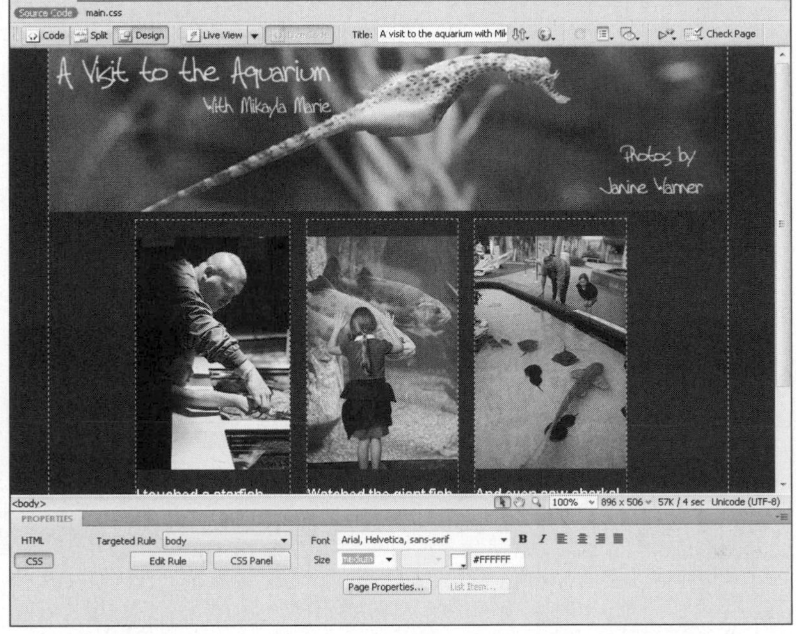

Figure 3-4: The Dreamweaver status bar indicates the total file size of all elements on a page and the estimated download time.

Inserting Images in Dreamweaver

Dreamweaver makes placing images on your Web pages easy and provides a variety of ways to do so, including choosing Insert⇨Image, clicking the Images icon in the Common Insert panel and selecting an image using the Insert image dialog box, or simply clicking an image name in the Files panel and dragging it onto the page.

To place an image on a Web page, follow these step-by-step instructions:

1. **Open an existing page or choose File⇨New to create a new page.**
2. **Make sure you save your page before inserting an image by choosing File⇨Save and saving it to your main site folder.**
3. **Place your cursor where you want to insert the image on the page.**
4.  **Click the Images icon on the Common Insert panel at the top of the work area (the icon looks like a small tree) or choose Insert⇨Image.**

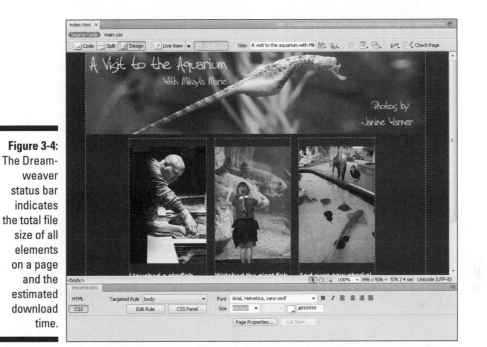

   The Select Image Source dialog box appears.

5. **Browse to locate the image you want to insert.**

   Depending on the computer system you use, there are different ways to preview images as you insert them. Here are three common options:

   - **On a PC with Windows XP,** choose Thumbnails from the View drop-down list (as shown in Figure 3-5) just to the right of the Look In field to display thumbnail versions of all the images in any open folder. You can also view a single preview of any selected image in the far right of the dialog box.
   - **On a PC with Windows Vista,** choose one of the icon options (small, medium, large, or extra large) from the View drop-down list just to the right of the Look In field to display thumbnail versions of all the images in any open folder. You can also view a single preview of any selected image in the far right of the dialog box.
   - **On a Mac,** choose the View as Columns option from the top left of the dialog, and you can view a single preview of any selected image in the far right of the dialog.

6. **To insert the image, double-click it or click once and then click OK.**

   The image automatically appears on the page.

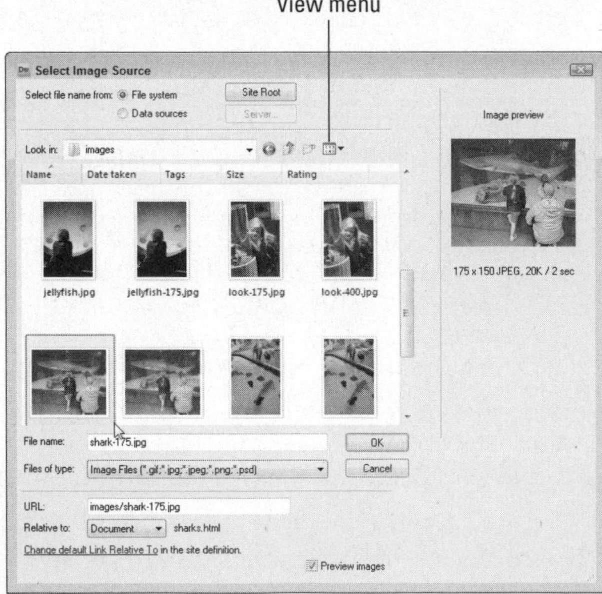

Figure 3-5: You can locate and preview the images in the Image Source dialog box.

When you insert an image file onto a page, you create a reference to the image from the page. The underlying code looks much like it does when you create a link from one page to another and then include the path from the image to the page. As a result, if your images and the pages they're linked to aren't in the same relative location on your hard drive as they are on your server, you break the reference to your images and they won't appear on your pages. (Instead, you get that ugly broken Images icon.) The best way to make sure that your images and files stay where they're supposed to in relation to one another is to save all your images in your images folder (or any other folder) in your local root folder and make sure they're located in the same folder or subfolder on your Web server. You find more information about creating and identifying a local root folder at the beginning of Chapter 2.

Aligning an Image with Text Wrapping

After you place an image on your Web page, you may want to align it so that text can wrap around it. In this section, you find the steps to do so with basic HTML. This option is useful if you want to use the simplest option for aligning an image in Dreamweaver and you're not familiar with using CSS. Before you get started, here are a few limitations of the HTML alignment option:

- The HTML alignment options enable you to align your images vertically or horizontally, but you can't do both at once to position images on either side of a page.
- The HTML alignment options don't really enable you to position images in relation to one another or in relation to text with much precision.

The best way to get around this limitation is to use Cascading Style Sheets (CSS) to create layout and alignment styles to control the positioning of all elements on a page. In Chapters 5 and 6, you find instructions for aligning and positioning images with CSS, which provides more precise, standards-based design options.

To align an image to the right of a page and wrap text around it on the left, follow these steps:

1. **Insert the image immediately to the left of the first line of the text.**

   The easiest way to do this is to place the cursor just before the first letter of text; then choose Insert⇨Image or click the Images icon in the Common Insert panel.

   If you want the text to wrap, don't put spaces or line breaks between the image and the text.

2. **Select the image.**

   The Property inspector changes to display the image attribute options.

3. **In the Property inspector, choose Right from the Align drop-down list.**

   The image aligns to the right, and the text automatically wraps around it, as shown in Figure 3-6.

To align the image to the left of the page with text wrapping around on the right, follow Steps 1 and 2, but choose Left from the Align drop-down list instead of Right in Step 3.

To prevent text from running against an image, click the image, find V and H spacing in the Property inspector, and enter the amount of space you want (the space is measured in pixels). Five to ten pixels is usually enough to prevent the text from bumping up against its edge. If you want to add space to only one side of an image, it's a bit more complicated, but you can more precisely control spacing with CSS using the instructions for aligning images and other elements, included in Chapter 5.

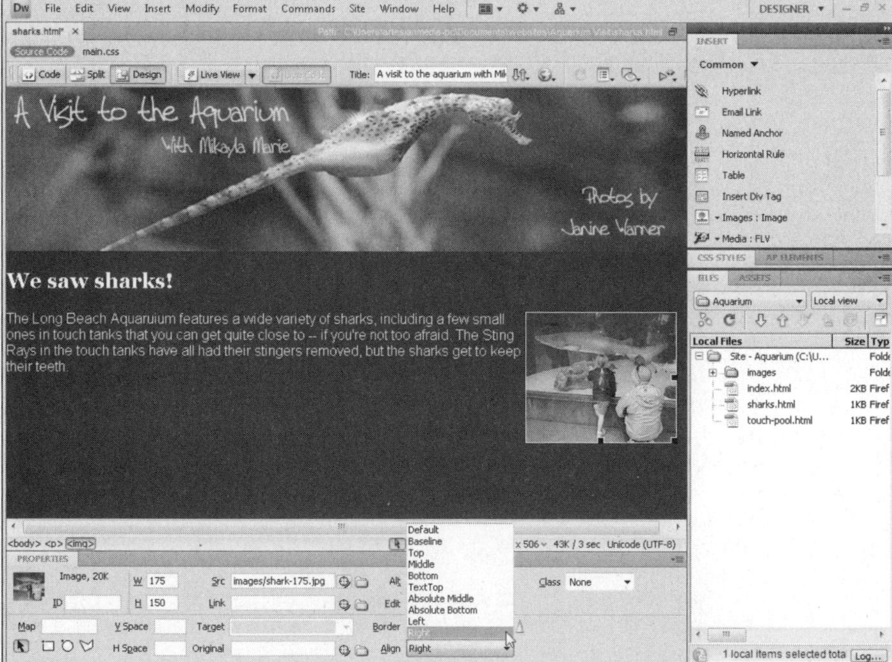

Figure 3-6: Use the Align drop-down list in the Property inspector to align an image to the right or left of a page.

Image Editing in Dreamweaver

The image-editing features in Dreamweaver enable you to make minor changes to images inside Dreamweaver without opening Fireworks, Photoshop, or any other graphics-editing program. These tools, as shown in Figure 3-7, are available from the Property inspector when an image is selected.

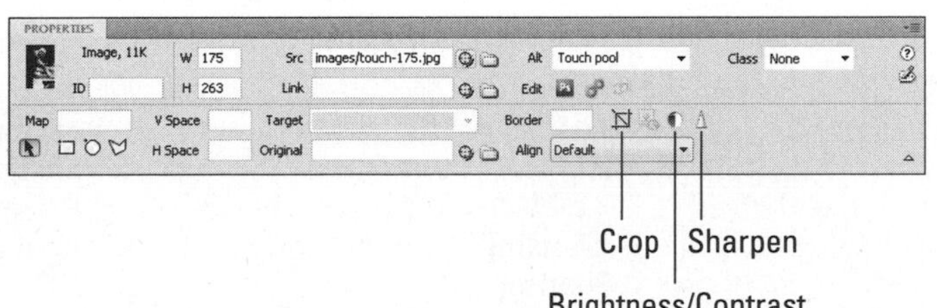

Figure 3-7: Use the image-editing tools to do basic image editing.

Before you get carried away editing your images, remember that Dreamweaver is primarily a Web page-creation application and isn't really designed to edit graphics. Although these tools can be useful, they shouldn't take the place of doing serious work on your graphics in a graphics application, such as Fireworks or Photoshop.

When you do use the tools for cropping, adjusting brightness and contrast, and sharpening an image, beware that you're changing the actual image (not just a copy of it). Make sure you're happy with these changes before you save the page you're working on. You can use the Undo feature in Dreamweaver to revert back several steps, but after you save the page, you can't undo changes to an image. To protect your original image, save a copy before editing it.

Cropping an image

Essentially, cropping an image is trimming it. To crop a graphic or photo, follow these steps:

1. **In the Document window, select the image you want to crop by clicking it.**

   The Property inspector changes to display the image's properties.

2. **Click the Crop icon (see Figure 3-8).**

   A dialog box appears, warning you that cropping changes the original image.

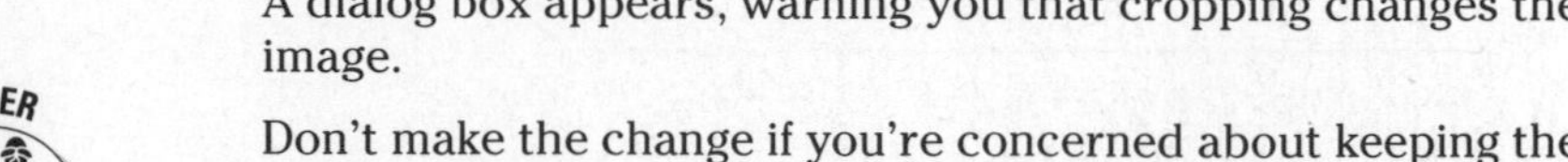

   Don't make the change if you're concerned about keeping the entire image available. If you're concerned, the best thing to do is to make a copy of the image and apply your cropping to the copy.

3. **Click OK.**

   A solid crop line with handles at the sides and corners appears over the image, as shown in Figure 3-8.

4. **Click and drag the handles to outline the area of the image you want to keep.**

   Any part of the image outside the crop line (and shaded) is deleted when the crop is completed.

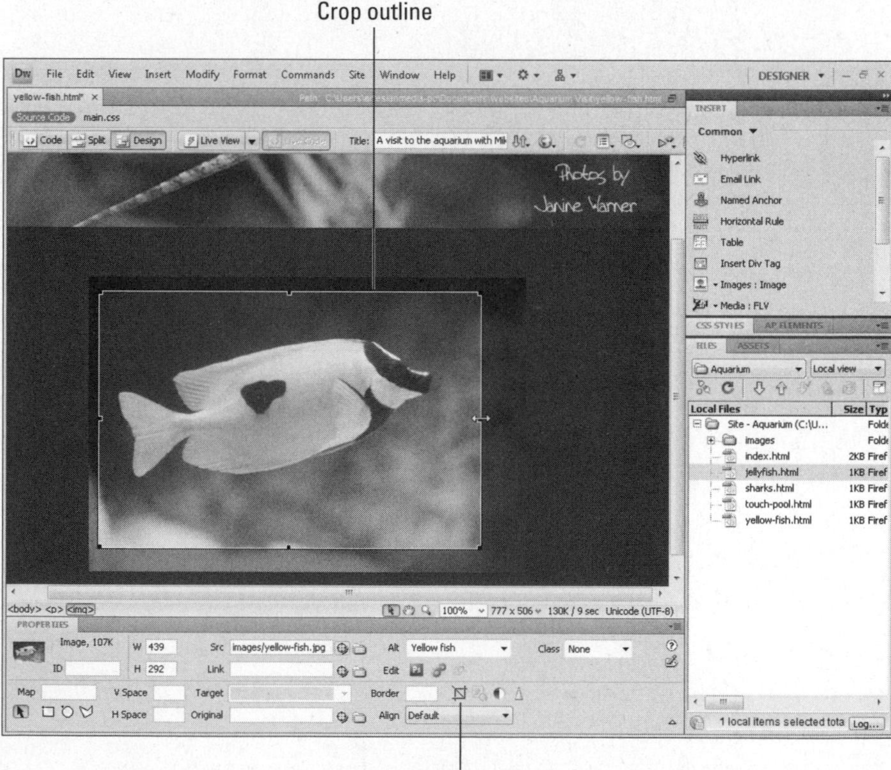

Figure 3-8: Define the area to crop by dragging the edges of the cropping tool outline.

5. **Double-click inside the box or press Enter (Return on a Mac).**

   The image is cropped.

You can undo cropping by choosing Edit⇨Undo. However, after you save the page, changes permanently apply to the image and can't be undone.

Adjusting brightness and contrast

Adjusting an image's *brightness* allows you to change the overall amount of light in an image. *Contrast* controls the difference between the light and dark areas of an image.

Using Dreamweaver's editing tools permanently alters the image when the page is saved. If you're concerned, the best thing to do is to make a copy of the image and make your adjustments to the copy.

To adjust brightness and contrast, follow these steps:

1. **In the Document window, select the image you want to alter.**

   The Property inspector shows the image properties.

2. **Click the Brightness and Contrast icon (labeled in Figure 3-7).**

   A dialog box appears, indicating that the changes you make are made to the original file.

3. **Click OK.**

   The Brightness/Contrast dialog box appears.

4. **Use the sliders to adjust the brightness and contrast settings of the image.**

   Make sure to select the Preview check box if you want to see how the changes affect the image as you move the sliders around.

5. **Click OK.**

   The settings take effect permanently when you save the page.

Sharpening an image

When you apply *sharpening* to an image, you increase the distinction between areas of color. The effect can be one of increased definition to the shapes and lines in an image.

Using Dreamweaver's editing tools permanently alters the image when the page is saved. If you're concerned, the best thing to do is to make a copy of the image and make your adjustments to the copy.

To sharpen an image, follow these steps:

1. **In the Document window, select the image you want to sharpen.**

   The Property inspector shows the image properties.

2. **Click the Sharpen icon (labeled in Figure 3-7).**

   A dialog box appears, indicating that your change is made to the original file.

3. **Click OK.**

   The Sharpen dialog box appears.

4. **Use the slider to adjust the sharpness of the image.**

   Make sure you select the Preview check box if you want to see how the changes affect the image as you move the slider.

5. **Click OK.**

   The image is sharpened, and changes are made permanently when you save changes to the page.

Optimizing images in Dreamweaver

Dreamweaver CS4 includes an Edit Image Settings icon that you can use to convert an image to the GIF, PNG, or JPEG format as well as optimize it by reducing the colors or increasing the compression, much as you can do in Photoshop or Fireworks. To use this feature, simply select any image in the Dreamweaver workspace and then click the Edit Image Settings icon in the Property inspector. (***Hint:*** It looks like a two small gears.)

Dreamweaver's editing tools permanently alter the image when the page is saved. If you're concerned, copy the image and make changes to the copy.

To optimize an image in Dreamweaver, follow these steps:

1. **In the Document window, select the image you want to optimize.**

   The Property inspector shows the image properties.

2. **Click the Edit Image Setting icon (see Figure 3-7).**

   A dialog box appears, indicating that your change is made to the original file.

3. **Click OK.**

   The Image Preview dialog box appears, as shown in Figure 3-9.

4. **In the Format drop-down list, select the image format you want.**

   You can select from GIF, JPEG, or PNG format.

5. **If you choose JPEG, use the slider that appears when you click the arrow next to Quality to select the level of compression. If you choose GIF or PNG, choose the number of colors desired.**

   The image is altered based on the settings you specify.

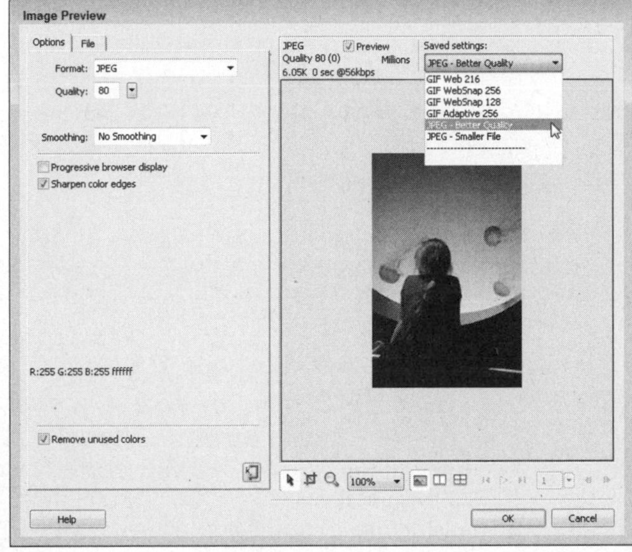

Figure 3-9: Define the area to crop by dragging the edges of the cropping tool outline.

You can also change other settings in the Image Preview dialog box, such as transparency settings for the GIF format, much as you would in Photoshop or Fireworks.

Opening an image in Photoshop or Fireworks from Dreamweaver

The Property inspector also includes an icon that makes it easy to open an image in Photoshop or Fireworks from within Dreamweaver. The Edit icon changes to the icon of the program specified in Dreamweaver's preferences.

To open an image in your preferred program, simply select the image in Dreamweaver, click the icon in the Property inspector, and watch your image appear as you've commanded.

Adobe has done some great work integrating the Photoshop and Fireworks programs into Dreamweaver. When you save changes to the image in Fireworks or Photoshop, they're automatically reflected in the version you've already inserted into a page in Dreamweaver.

To specify the image editor you want to associate with a file type in Dreamweaver's preferences, follow these instructions:

1. **Choose Edit⇨Preferences (Windows) or Dreamweaver⇨Preferences (on a Mac).**

   The Preferences dialog box opens.

2. **On the left, select the File Types / Editors Category, as shown in Figure 3-10.**

3. **In the left pane under Extensions, click to select .gif.**

   Dreamweaver lists a wide variety of file types here, and you can associate any or all of them with your favorite editors. To associate image editors with these graphic formats, select the GIF, PNG, and JPEG options one at a time and then continue with these steps.

4. **In the right pane, under Editors, click to select the editor you want associated with the .gif format.**

   In the example shown in Figure 3-10, Photoshop is listed already, so you can simply click Photoshop to select it. If you want to associate an editor that isn't on this list, such as Fireworks, click the plus (+) sign just above the Editors pane, browse to find the program on your hard drive, and select it to make it appear on the list.

5. **With the file type and program name selected, click the Make Primary button to associate the editor.**

   The editor specified as Primary is launched automatically when you select an image in Dreamweaver and click the Edit button in the Property inspector.

6. **Click to select .jpeg from the Extensions pane and repeat Steps 4 and 5.**

   You can continue with this process for any or all the other formats listed.

   To add additional file formats to Dreamweaver, click the plus (+) sign over the Extensions pane and type the extension beginning with a dot (.).

Figure 3-10: Use Dreamweaver's preferences settings to associate your favorite image editor.

Inserting a Background Image

Background images can add depth and richness to a page design by adding color and fullness. Used cleverly, a background image helps create the illusion that the entire page is one large image while still downloading quickly and efficiently. The trick is to use an image with a small file size that creates the impression of a large image. One way this works on the Web is to use the default settings for a background image, which cause the image to *tile* (repeat) across and down the page (see Figure 3-11).

Beware that certain backgrounds (such as the one shown in Figure 3-11) can make it difficult to read text placed on top. Choose your background images carefully and make sure your background and your text have plenty of contrast — reading on a computer screen is hard enough.

With CSS, you can have far greater control over the display of a background image. When you create a CSS background style, you can insert a background image that doesn't repeat or that repeats only across the Y axis or down the X axis of the page. When you insert an image using Dreamweaver's Page Properties feature, as shown in Figure 3-12, you can use the Repeat drop-down list to specify how the image repeats on the page, and Dreamweaver automatically creates a style for the page with these background settings. If you use the CSS Definition dialog box to further edit the background options in the body style, you can also specify where the background image is displayed on a page. (Find more on CSS background options in Chapter 5.)

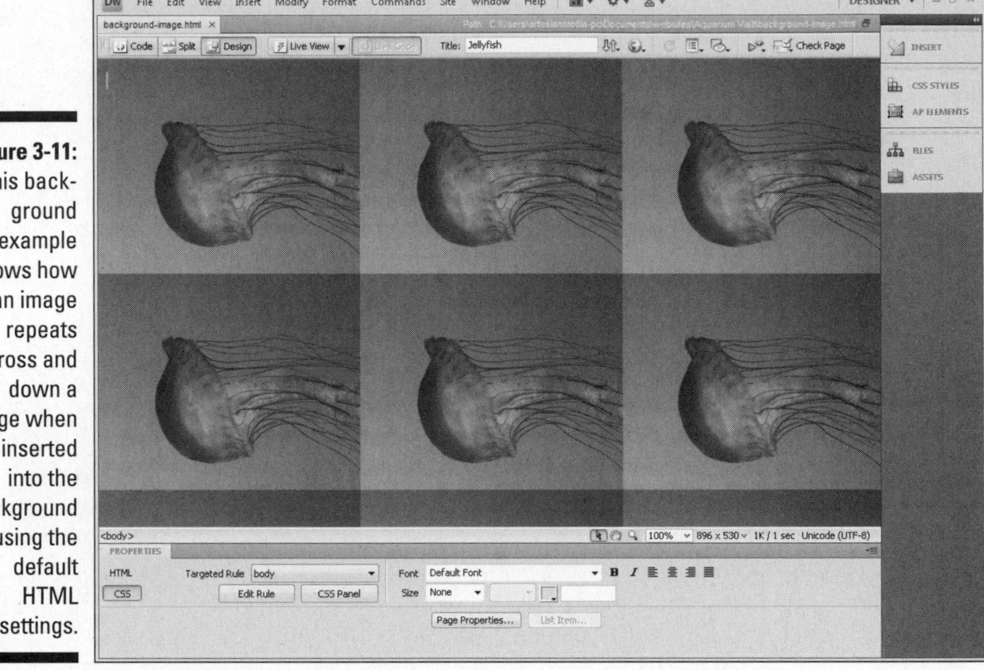

Figure 3-11: This background example shows how an image repeats across and down a page when inserted into the background using the default HTML settings.

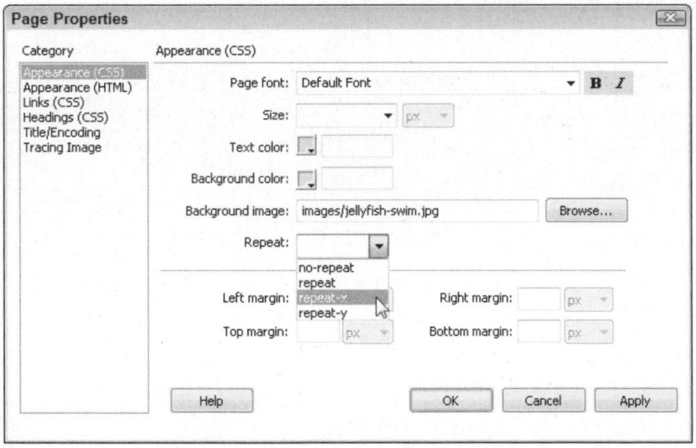

Figure 3-12: Settings control how a background image is repeated or not repeated on a page.

Creating Image Maps

Image maps enable you to create *hot spots* (clickable areas) in an image and link each area to a different Web page. A common use of an image map is with a geographic map, such as a map of the United States, that links to different locations, depending on the section of the map a visitor clicks. For example, if you have a national bank and want customers to find a local branch or ATM machine easily, you can create hot spots on an image map of the United States and then link each hot spot to a page listing banks in that geographic location.

Dreamweaver makes creating image maps easy by providing a set of simple drawing tools that enable you to create hot spots and set their corresponding links. To create an image map, follow these steps:

1. **Place the image you want to use as an image map on your page.**
2. **Select the image.**

   The image properties are displayed in the Property inspector.
3. **To draw your hot spot, choose a shape tool from the image map tools in the lower left of the Property inspector (labeled in Figure 3-13).**

   The shape tools (a rectangle, a circle, and an irregular polygon) allow you to draw regions on your images, called *hot spots,* each with a specific link. In the example shown in Figure 3-13, I'm creating hot spots on each creature in the aquarium touch pool so that I can link each one to a different page with additional information about the animal.
4. **With a shape tool selected, click and drag over an area of the image that you want to make *hot* (link to another page).**

   Here's how the different hot spot tools work:

   - **Rectangle:** When you click and drag, a light blue highlight appears around the region that you're making hot; this highlighted area indicates the active region. If you need to reposition the hot area, select the Pointer hotspot tool (labeled in Figure 3-13) and then select and move the region to the location you want. You can also resize the hot spot by clicking and dragging any of the corners.
   - **Circle:** The Circle tool works much like the Rectangle tool — just click and drag. To resize a circle hot spot, select the Pointer hotspot tool, and click and drag one of the small square boxes on its edges.
   - **Polygon:** The Polygon tool functions a little bit differently than the other two tools. To make a polygon selection, click the tool once for each point of the polygon shape you want to draw. The shape automatically connects the points while you click. When you're finished, switch to another map tool or click outside the image. You can change the size of the polygon or move any of its points by using the Pointer hotspot tool.

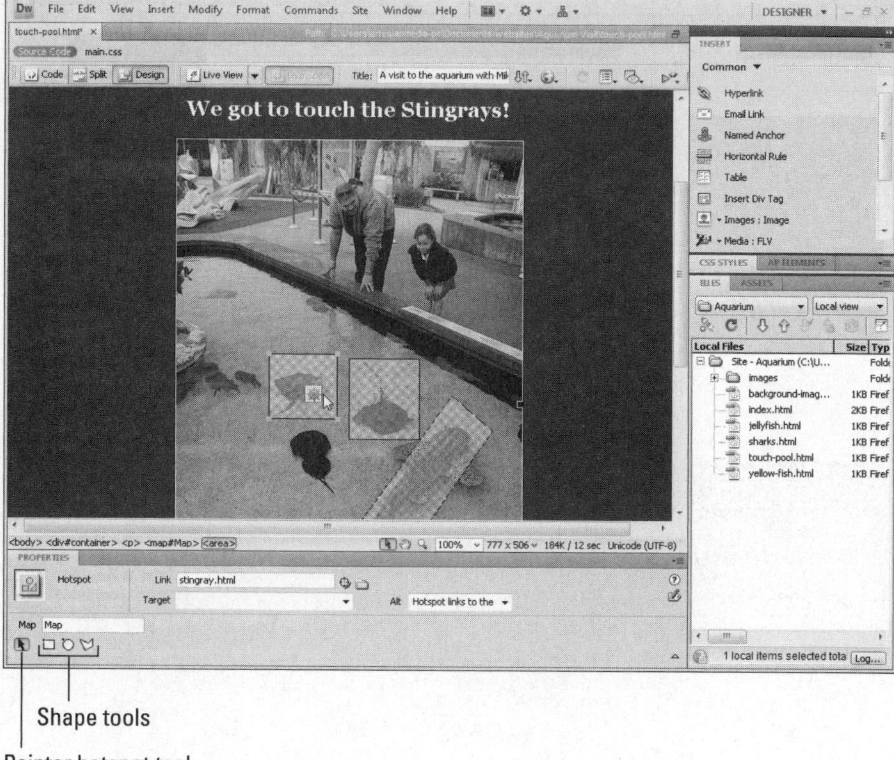

Figure 3-13: Use the image map tools in the Property inspector to create hot spots on an image that can be linked to different pages.

When prompted to describe the image map in the Alt field on the Property inspector, click OK to close the dialog box and then add a text description of the link in the Alt field in Hotspot properties of the Property inspector. The Alt field is for *alternative text* that doesn't appear on the page itself. This text is used by screen readers and other devices that *read* the code behind a page and need these descriptions of the hot spots in an image to better understand the image map.

5. **To link a selected hot area:**

   a. **Click the Browse icon, next to the Link text box (at the top of the Property inspector).**

   The Select File dialog box opens.

   b. **Browse to find the HTML file that you want to link to the hot spot on your image.**

   c. **Double-click the file to which you want to link.**

      The hot spot links to the selected page, and the Select File dialog box automatically closes.

   You can also type the path directly in the Link text box.

6. **To add more hot spots, choose an image and a shape tool, and repeat Steps 4 and 5.**

7. **To give your image map a name, type a name in the Map text field, just above the shape tools.**

   Giving your map (and all the hot spots it includes) a name helps to distinguish it in the event that you have multiple image maps on the same page. You can call the map anything you want, as long as you don't include spaces or special punctuation.

   When you finish, all your image map hot spots are indicated by a light blue highlight.

At any time, you can go back and edit the image map. Simply click and highlight the blue region on your image and drag the edges to resize the hot spot or enter a new URL to change the link.

Chapter 4

Managing, Testing, and Publishing a Site

In This Chapter

- Testing your site in different Web browsers
- Testing your site with the Dreamweaver Site Reporting feature
- Fixing broken links
- Managing your linked files
- Publishing your site on the Web
- Setting up FTP and other file transfer options
- Using Dreamweaver's site management features

If you're anxious to get your site online, jump ahead to midway through this chapter, where you find instructions for using Dreamweaver's publishing features in the "Publishing Your Site to a Web Server" section. But before you go live with your site, I recommend you spend a little time using Dreamweaver's testing features to make sure your pages are ready for the all the world to see. I cover these features at the beginning of this chapter.

At the end of this chapter, you find instructions for using Dreamweaver's site management features, which are designed to help teams of designers work better together. These include the Check In/Out feature, which prevents two people from working on the same page on a site simultaneously — an important feature if you want to make sure that one designer doesn't overwrite the work of another. And believe me, you want to do everything you can to prevent this situation.

If you want to work more on the design of your site before you move onto testing and publishing, feel free to skip ahead to the CSS chapters and other more advanced chapters that follow. You can always come back to this chapter when you're ready to put your work online.

If you're looking for information about Web hosting services and domain registration sites, find recommendations and tips for choosing the best hosting and domain services on my Web site at `www.DigitalFamily.com/dreamweaver`.

Testing Your Site in Different Browsers

One of the more confusing and frustrating aspects of Web design is that you can create a page that looks great in Dreamweaver and test it in a browser to confirm that it looks fine, only to discover later that it looks terrible in a different browser or on a different computer system. Web pages can look different from one system to another for many reasons, but the following issues are the most common culprits:

- **Browser differences:** Today, dozens of browsers are in use on the Web, not counting the different versions of each browser. For example, at the time of this writing, Internet Explorer (IE) 7 is the newest release from Microsoft, but a significant percentage of Web users haven't upgraded yet and are still using IE 6 or even earlier versions. Similarly, browser companies, such as Firefox and Safari, have now created a number of versions that are still in use on the Web. And each browser, as well as each browser version may display HTML and CSS code quite differently. This is because browsers have evolved over the years to support new technologies on the Web, but older browsers still in use may have trouble displaying everything you create on your Web pages. The other problem is that the companies that make Web browser don't all agree or follow the same standards (although most are getting better with their latest versions).
- **Hardware differences:** Another challenge comes from the differences between Macintosh and Windows computers. For example, the most fonts appear smaller on a Macintosh than on a PC (Times 12 on a PC looks like Times 10 on a Mac). Image colors can also vary from one computer to another.
- **Individual resolution settings:** The same Web page may look very different on a 21-inch monitor than it does on a 15-inch monitor. Even on the same monitor, different resolution settings can alter the way a page looks. On the PC, a common resolution is 1024 by 768 whereas on the Mac, the resolution is generally set much higher, making the design look much smaller, even if the monitor sizes are the same.

As a result of all these differences, the same Web page can look very different to the many people who visit a Web site. For example, Figure 4-1 shows a Web page in Internet Explorer on a PC, and Figure 4-2 shows the same page in Safari on a Macintosh. Notice that the text displays in a larger font size on the PC, changing the way the text wraps around the photo in the left column. This difference may seem subtle in this page design, but font size and other variations can lead to dramatic changes in the display of the same Web page.

Figure 4-1: A Web page displayed in Internet Explorer on a PC.

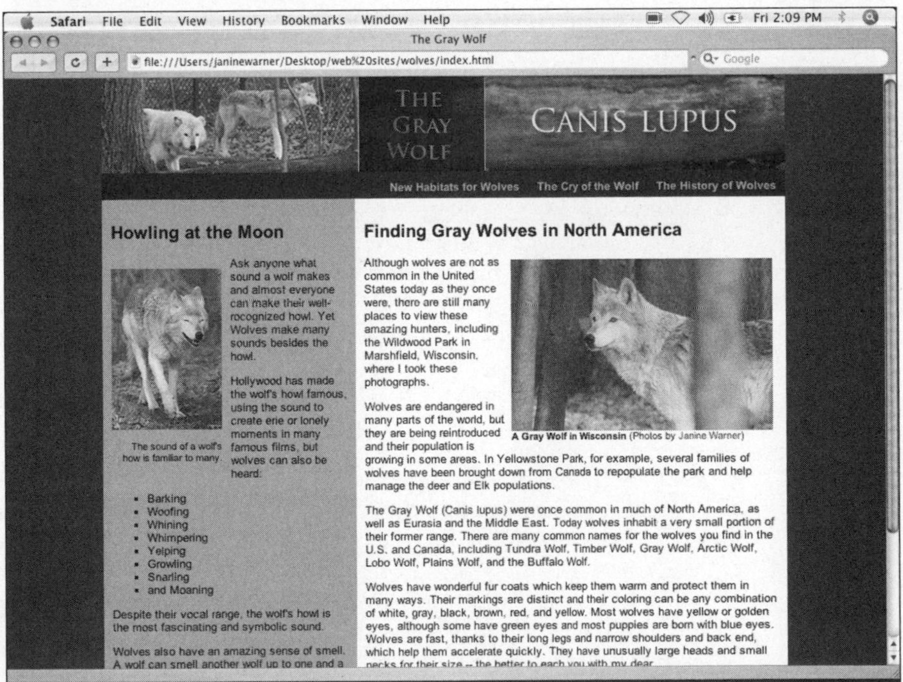

Figure 4-2: The same Web page displayed in Safari on a Mac.

This challenging aspect of the Web is at the root of many of the limitations and complications of creating good Web designs. With patience, testing, and an understanding of the tags and styles that are most problematic, you can create great Web sites that look good to most, if not all, of the people who visit your Web site.

Designing for browser differences

Getting your pages to look exactly the same across every browser in use on the Web is nearly impossible, unless you're willing to use only the simplest and most basic HTML formatting options. But such consistency is rarely worth losing the design benefits of CSS. Entire books and Web sites are dedicated to the best ways to design sites that look good on different browsers, especially when it comes to creating page designs with CSS.

Although I can't possibly cover all these strategies here, the following tips and options give you a good start:

- **Use Dreamweaver preview and testing features.** For instance, Dreamweaver enables you to preview pages in many different kinds of browsers, as I explain in Chapter 2. You can also test your pages with Dreamweaver's Browser Compatibility features, covered in the next section.
- **Use Dreamweaver's CSS layouts.** I also recommend that you start your CSS design work with one of the predesigned CSS layouts included in Dreamweaver because these are already designed to display well on many different systems. You find instructions for customizing those layouts in Chapter 6.
- **Create different versions of the same site or different style sheets.** This approach is extreme, but you can create different versions of the same site, each designed for the unique display settings of the different browsers and systems you expect your visitors will use. A script can then detect a user's system and deliver the best site version. This approach may be warranted for some special cases. For example, big sites, such as Google and Amazon, have created special versions of their sites for mobile devices. Even more common, now that CSS has become so popular, many designers create multiple external style sheets for the same page. For example, you can create one set of styles that are optimal for printing, another that are optimal for screen display, and yet another for mobile devices. You find instructions for creating and attaching external style sheets in Chapter 5.

- **Create a page that looks as good as possible on as many browsers as you consider important.** This is the solution many designers settle for. The page may not look *exactly* the same on every system, but mostly the same is often okay. Which browsers you design for depends on your audience. If you have good log files or visitor statistics, you can view a list of the browsers (and even the browser versions) used by visitors to your site. For example, you may be able to determine that 70 percent of your audience uses Internet Explorer 7, 20 percent uses Firefox 2, 6 percent uses Internet Explorer 6, and only 4 percent uses Safari. With that in mind, you may decide that you want to optimize your pages to display best in Internet Explorer, make sure they look almost if not equally good in Firefox, and not worry as much about all the details when the page is viewed in Safari, as long as the content is at least readable and the page doesn't look terrible.

If you want to create complex page designs with CSS and want your pages to look as good as possible on as many browsers as possible, a number of *hacks,* or workarounds, have been developed that can help ensure page designs look the same on a variety of browsers. Some of these tricks are relatively simple; others are extraordinarily complex, and unfortunately, every time a new version of a browser, such as IE or Firefox is released, those hacks will probably have to be adjusted. You find more information on designing CSS for different Web browsers in Chapter 7.

If you know that your visitors will be using only one browser — for example, if you're designing a corporate intranet and can require that all employees use Firefox 3 — your design work is simpler. Some public Web site designers resort to putting a note on the front page of a site advising anyone who visits that the pages display best in a particular browser. Although that may be warranted in some cases, I don't recommend it because you risk losing many potential visitors.

Using Dreamweaver's Browser Compatibility feature

In addition to being able to preview a Web page in any Web browser on your hard drive, Dreamweaver also includes a Browser Compatibility feature that can help you test for known issues among different browsers automatically.

To use this feature, open a page in Dreamweaver and choose File⇨Check Page⇨Browser Compatibility. You can also access this feature by clicking the Check Page drop-down arrow at the top right of the workspace and selecting Check Browser Compatibility from the drop-down list, as shown in Figure 4-3. Any recognized conflicts display in a report at the bottom of the workspace.

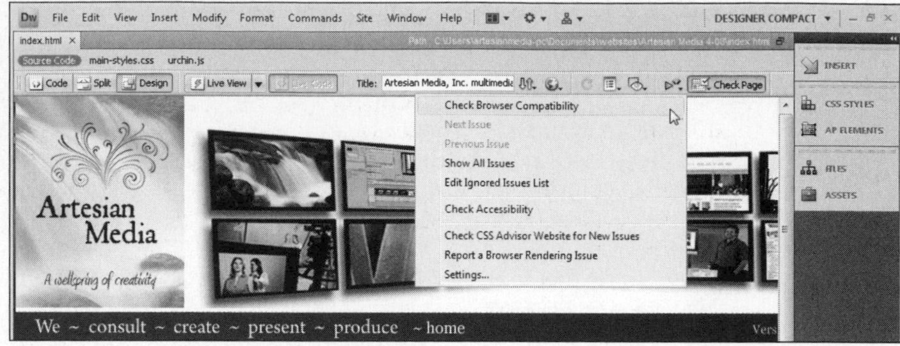

Figure 4-3: Access testing features, such as Check Browser Compatibility.

You can specify which browsers and browser versions you want to target by doing either of the following:

- Click the small menu icon at the top-left corner of the Browser Compatibility Check dialog box and choose Settings from the drop-down list to open the Target Browsers dialog box, as shown in Figure 4-4.
- From the Check Page drop-down list, choose Settings to open the Target Browsers dialog box, as shown in Figure 4-4.

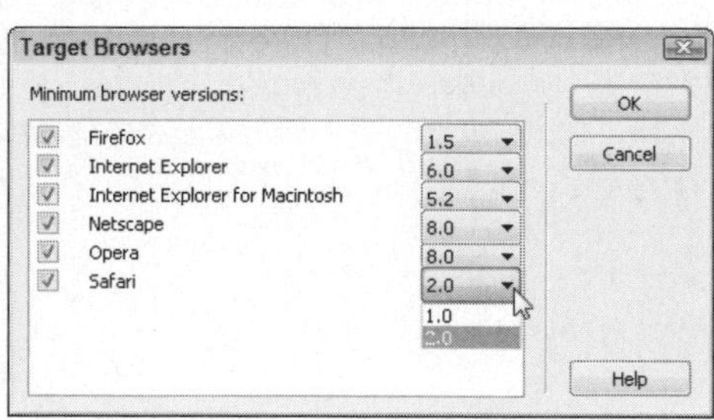

Figure 4-4: Specify the browsers and versions you want to target when you run a browser compatibility check.

Testing Your Work with the Site Reporting Features

Before you put your site online for the world to see, check your work using the Dreamweaver Site Reporting feature. You can create a variety of reports and even customize them to identify problems with external links, redundant and empty tags, untitled documents, and missing Alt text. You can easily miss things — especially when you work on a tight deadline — and what you miss can cause real problems for your viewers.

Before Dreamweaver added this great new feature, finding these kinds of mistakes was a tedious, time-consuming task. Now you can run a report that identifies these errors for you and use Dreamweaver to correct mistakes across your entire site automatically.

Follow these steps to produce a Site Report of your entire Web site:

1. **In the drop-down list at the top of the Files panel, select the site name. In the list that appears, select the site you want to work on.**

   Your site appears in the Files panel list only if you've completed the site setup process covered in Chapter 2.

2. **Make sure any open documents are saved by choosing File⇨Save All.**

3. **Choose Site⇨Reports.**

   The Reports dialog box appears (see Figure 4-5).

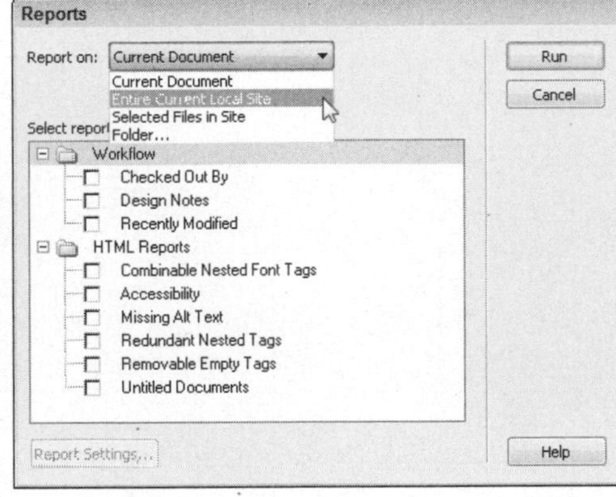

Figure 4-5: You can select any and all options, and you can run reports on a single page or the entire site.

4. **In the Report On drop-down list, choose Entire Current Local Site.**

   You can also choose to check only a single page by opening the page in Dreamweaver and then choosing Current Document in the Report On drop-down list. You can also run a report on selected files or on a particular folder. If you choose Selected Files in Site, you must have already selected the pages you want to check in the Files panel.

5. **In the Select Reports section, select the reports you want.**

   Table 4-1 describes the kind of report you get with each option. You can select as many reports as you want.

The Workflow options in the Select Reports section are functional only if you already enabled Check In/Out in the Remote Info section of the Site Definition dialog box and selected Maintain Design Notes in the Design Notes section of the Site Definition dialog box's Advanced tab. You can read more about the Site Definition dialog box in Chapter 2 and more about Design Notes and the Check In/Out in the "Making the Most of Dreamweaver's Site Management Features" section, later in this chapter.

6. **Click the Run button to create the report(s).**

   If you haven't already done so, you may be prompted to save your file, define your site, or select a folder. (See Chapter 2 for more information on defining a site in Dreamweaver.)

   The Results panel appears, as shown in Figure 4-6, displaying a list of problems found on the site. You can sort the list by different categories (filename, line number, or description) by clicking the corresponding column headings.

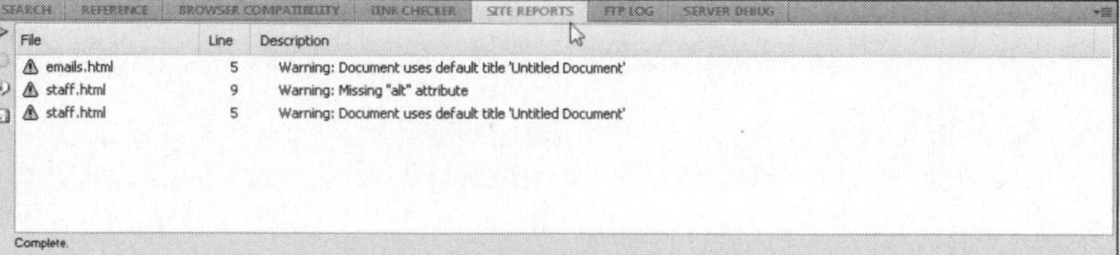

Figure 4-6: The Results panel displays a list of problems on your site.

7. **Double-click any item in the Results panel to open the corresponding file in the Document window.**

   You can also right-click (Windows) or Control+click (Mac) on any line of the report and choose More Info to find additional details about the specific error or condition.

8. **Use the Property inspector or another Dreamweaver feature to correct the identified problem and then save the file.**

Finding and Fixing Broken Links

If you're trying to rein in a chaotic Web site or if you just want to check a site for broken links, you'll be pleased to discover the Check Links feature. You can use Check Links to verify the links in a single file or an entire Web site, and you can use it to automatically fix all the referring links at once.

Here's an example of what Check Links can do. Assume that someone on your team (because you would never do such a thing yourself) changed the name of a file from `new.htm` to `old.htm` without using the Files panel or any of Dreamweaver's automatic link update features. Maybe this person changed the name using another program or simply renamed it in Explorer (Windows) or the Finder (Mac). Changing the filename was easy, but what this person may not have realized is that if he or she didn't change the links to the file when the file was renamed, the links are now broken.

If only one page links to the file that your clueless teammate changed, fixing the broken link isn't such a big deal. As long as you remember which file the page links from, you can simply open that page and use the Property inspector to reset the link the same way you created the link in the first place. (You can find out all the basics of link creation in Chapter 2.)

But many times, a single page in a Web site is linked to many other pages. When that's the case, fixing all the link references can be time-consuming, and forgetting some of them is all too easy. That's why the Check Links feature is so helpful. First, it serves as a diagnostic tool that identifies broken links throughout the site (so you don't have to second-guess where someone may have changed a filename or moved a file). Then it serves as a global fix-it tool. You can use the Check Links dialog box to identify the page a broken link should go to, and Dreamweaver automatically fixes all links referring to that page. The following section walks you through this cool process.

If you're working on a dynamic, database-driven site or if your site was altered with programming that was performed outside Dreamweaver, the Check Links feature may not work properly. This feature works best for sites with static HTML pages.

Checking for broken links

To check a site for broken links, follow these steps:

1. **In the drop-down list at the top of the Files panel, select the site name. In the list that appears, select the site you want to work on.**

   Link checking works only for sites listed in the Dreamweaver Site dialog box. For more information about the Site dialog box and how to set up a new site or import an existing one, see Chapter 2.

2. **Choose Site⇨Check Links Sitewide.**

   The Link Checker tab opens in the Results panel at the bottom of the page, just under the Property inspector, as shown in Figure 4-7. The tab displays a list of internal and external links. The tab also lists any pages, images, or other items not linked from any other page in the site — dubbed *orphans.* Unused images can waste space on your server, so this list is handy if you want to clean up old images or other elements you no longer use on the site.

Most service providers limit the amount of space on your server and charge extra if you exceed that limit. You can save valuable server space by deleting unused files, especially if they're image or multimedia files. But remember, just because you delete them from your hard drive doesn't mean they're deleted from the server. Make sure you remove them from the Remote Site window in the Files panel as well as the Local Site panel. (For more on using FTP and synchronization to update or delete files on your server, see the section, "Publishing Your Site to a Web Server," later in this chapter.)

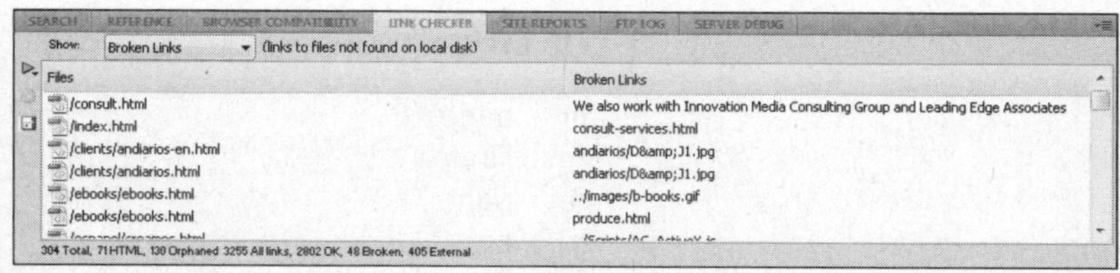

Figure 4-7: The report can be organized by broken links, external links, and unused files.

Fixing broken links

Broken links are one of the worst problems you can have on a Web site. After you identify a broken link in a site, fix it as soon as possible. Nothing turns off visitors faster than clicking a link and getting a `File Not Found` error page. Fortunately, Dreamweaver makes fixing broken links simple by providing quick access to files with broken links and automating the process of fixing multiple links to the same file.

After using the Link Checker tab described in the preceding section to identify broken links, follow these steps to use the Results panel to fix them:

1. **With the Results panel open at the bottom of the page, double-click a filename that Dreamweaver identifies as a broken link.**

   The page and its corresponding Property inspector open. The Results panel remains visible.

2. **Select the broken link or image on the open page.**

   For example, you can fix a broken image by selecting the broken image icon in the page and then reinserting it using the Property inspector to find the correct image name.

3. **In the Property inspector, click the folder icon to the right of the Src text box to identify the correct image file.**

(Alternatively, you can type the correct filename and path in the text box instead of using the browse option to find the correct image.) The Select Image Source dialog box appears. You fix links to pages just as you fix links to images, except you type the name of the correct file into the Link text box or click the folder icon next to it to find the file in your site folder.

4. **Click to select the filename of the correct image or file and then click OK.**

   The link automatically changes to reflect the new filename and location. If you replace an image, the image file reappears on the page.

Finding files by their addresses

If you're not sure where you saved a file or what you called it, but you can get to it with your browser, you can determine the filename and location by looking at the URL in the browser's address bar. Each folder in a Web site is included in the address to a page within that folder. Folder names are separated by the forward slash, /, and each filename can be distinguished because it includes an extension. For example, the URL in the browser's address bar of the page displayed in this figure tells me that the file is named `index.html` and is located in the `kiev` folder, which is a subfolder of the main folder for the Web site.

Similarly, you can identify the name and location of any image you're viewing on a Web page. If you're using Internet Explorer or Firefox, place your cursor over the image and right-click (Windows) or Control+click (Mac) and then choose Properties. The Element Properties dialog box includes the specific URL of the image, which has the name and folder (path). In the Element Properties dialog box shown in this example, you can see that the logo that appears in the top left of the page is `ArtesianMedia-logo.jpg` and is stored in an `images` folder. If you're using the Safari browser on a Mac, it works a little differently. Control+click an image and choose Open Image in New Window. In the new window, the image URL appears in the location bar.

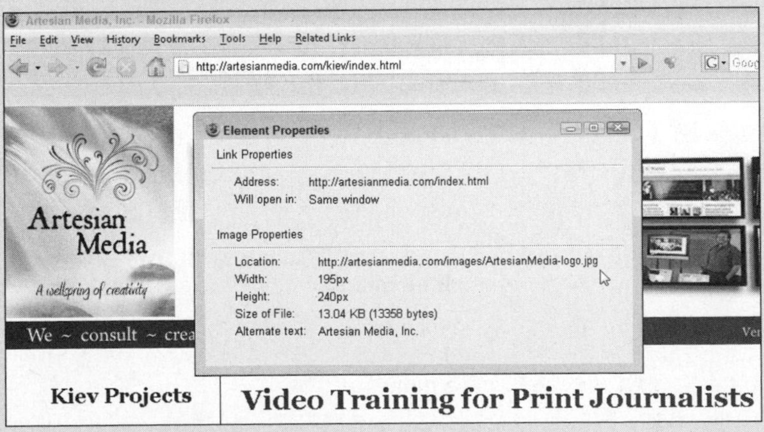

If the link that you correct appears in multiple pages and you fix the link using the broken link's Results panel, Dreamweaver prompts you with a dialog box asking whether you want to fix the remaining broken link references to the file. Click the Yes button to automatically correct all other references. Click the No button to leave the other files unchanged.

Managing Linked Files

Dreamweaver includes a variety of tools that help you manage the files and folders within a site without breaking links. You can use the Files panel to rename and rearrange files and folders, as well as create new folders, all with drag-and-drop ease.

You need to define your site for Dreamweaver's Files panel features to work. If you haven't already defined your site, turn to the instructions at the beginning of Chapter 2.

Moving and renaming files

To rearrange or rename files, follow these steps:

1. **Select the site you want to work on (if it's not already active) in the drop-down list at the top of the Files panel.**

   When you select a site by clicking the site name, the folders and files in that site appear in the Files panel.

2. **Click the plus (+) sign to open the main site root folder or any subfolder so that you can access the files.**

   Click the minus (–) sign to close a folder.

3. **In the Files panel, select the file or folder you want to move or rename or both.**

   To *move* a selected file or folder:

   a. **Drag the selected file or group of files into a folder.**

      Dreamweaver automatically changes all the related links. The Files panel works much like the Explorer window on a PC or the Finder on a Mac, except Dreamweaver tracks and fixes links when you move files through the Files panel. By contrast, if you move or rename site files or folders in the Finder or Explorer, you break any links set to or from those files.

When you move a linked file into a new folder in Dreamweaver, the Update Files dialog box appears with a list of links that needs to be updated, as shown in Figure 4-8.

b. **To adjust the links, choose Update.**

If you choose Don't Update, any links to or from that file are left unchanged.

To *rename* a selected file:

a. **Click twice on any filename or folder name.**

b. **When a box appears around the name, edit it just as you would a name in the Finder or Explorer and then press Enter (Return on a Mac).**

Again you're prompted with the Update Files dialog box to update any links affected by the filename change.

c. **Choose Update to adjust the links.**

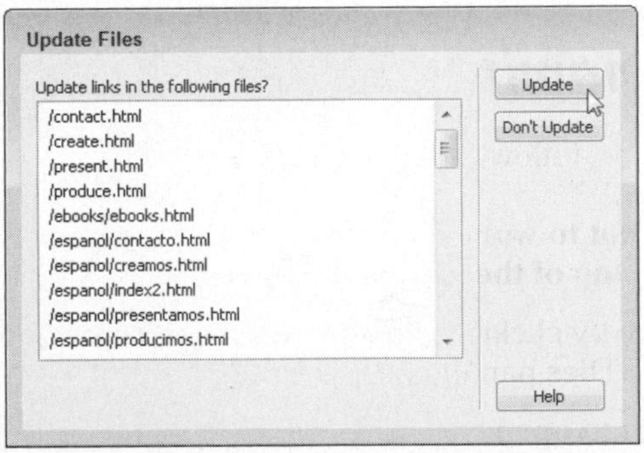

Figure 4-8: The Update Files dialog box lists all the files that will be changed during the update process.

Making global changes to links

If you want to globally change a link to point at a new URL or to some other page on your site, you can use the Change Link Sitewide option to enter the new URL and change every reference automatically. You can use this option to change any kind of link, including mailto, ftp, and script links. For example, if an e-mail address that you use throughout your site changes, you can use this feature to fix it automatically — a real timesaver. You can use this feature also when you want a string of text to link to a different file than it currently does. For example, you can change every instance of the words *Enter This Month's Contest* to link to `/contest/january.htm` instead of `/contest/december.htm` throughout your Web site.

To change a collection of links with the Change Link Sitewide feature, follow these steps:

1. **Make sure the site you want to work on is displayed in the Files panel.**

   See the preceding exercise for instructions on selecting a site.

2. **Choose Site➪Change Link Sitewide.**

   The Change Link Sitewide dialog box appears.

3. **Enter the old address and then enter the new address, or click the Browse button to identify files where you want to change the links.**

   You can use this feature to change any link, including e-mail links, links from one page to another within a site, or links to a different Web site.

4. **Click OK.**

   Dreamweaver updates any documents that include the specified links.

Any changes you make to links using Dreamweaver's automated link features occur only on the local version of your site on your hard drive. Make sure you upload all affected files to your Web server to ensure that all changes are included on your published site. To automatically reconcile changes on your local and remote sites, use Dreamweaver's Synchronize Files feature, which I describe later in this chapter.

Publishing Your Site to a Web Server

After you create your Web site, test it, and are ready to publish it on the Web, it's time to put Dreamweaver's publishing tools to work. Which features you use depends on the kind of Web server you use. If you're using a commercial service provider, you'll most likely need Dreamweaver's FTP features, which I cover in detail in the following section.

To access Dreamweaver's publishing tools:

1. **Choose Site➪Manage Sites.**

   The Manage Sites dialog box opens.

2. **In the list of defined sites, select the site you want to publish and then click the Edit button.**

   The Site Definition dialog box opens. If you haven't already defined your site, refer to the instructions for this important initial site setup process at the beginning of Chapter 2.

3. **Select the Advanced tab from the top of the Site Definition dialog box.**

   The Advanced options appear instead of the Site Definition Wizard available on the Basic tab.

4. **In the Category list, select the Remote Info category, as shown in Figure 4-9 (in the next exercise).**

5. **Click the Access drop-down arrow and select the publishing option that is best suited to your Web server and development environment. (In Figure 4-9, FTP is selected.)**

   Dreamweaver provides six Access options:

   • **None:** Select this option if you're not uploading your site to a server or if you're not yet ready to fill in these settings.

   • **FTP:** Select this option to use Dreamweaver's built-in File Transfer Protocol features, which I cover in detail in the following section. These are the settings you're most likely to need if you're using a commercial Web hosting service.

   • **Local/Network:** Select this option if you're using a Web server on a local network, such as your company or university server. For specific settings and requirements, check with your system administrator.

   • **WebDAV (Web-based Distributed Authoring and Versioning):** Select this option if you're using a server with the WebDAV protocol, such as Microsoft IIS.

   • **RDS (Rapid Development Services):** Select this option if you're using ColdFusion on a remote server.

   • **Microsoft Visual SourceSafe:** Select this option if you're using Microsoft Visual SourceSafe. Note this option is available only in Windows.

Setting up Web server access for FTP

To make your life simpler, Dreamweaver incorporates FTP capability so that you can easily upload your pages to a remote Web server. The FTP options include features that can help you keep track of changes you make to files on your hard drive and ensure that they match the files on your Web server.

To upload your site using FTP, you need the following information from your Web hosting service:

- FTP host name
- Path for the Web directory (this is optional but useful)
- FTP login
- FTP password

To access the FTP features in Dreamweaver:

1. **Follow the steps in the preceding section, choosing FTP in Step 5.**

   The dialog box in Figure 4-9 appears.

2. **In the FTP Host text box, type the hostname of your Web server.**

   The hostname should look something like `ftp.host.com`, `shell.host.com`, or `ftp.domain.com`, depending on your server. (In my example, I used `ftp.artesianmedia.com`.)

3. **In the Host Directory text box, type the directory on the remote site in which documents visible to the public are stored (also known as the *site root*).**

   The host directory looks something like `public_html/` or `www/htdocs/`. Again, this depends on your server.

4. **In the Login and Password text boxes, type the login name and password, respectively, required to gain access to your Web server.**

   If you check the Save box, Dreamweaver stores the information and automatically supplies it to the server when you connect to the remote site.

   This is your unique login and password information that provides you access to your server.

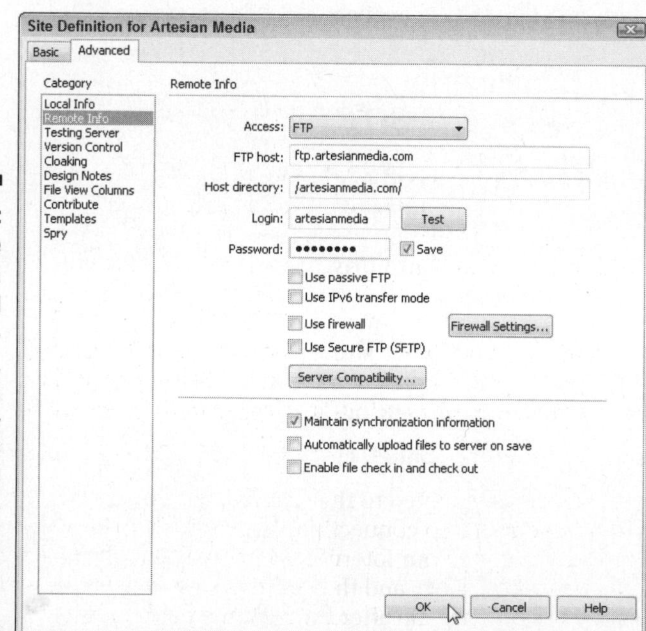

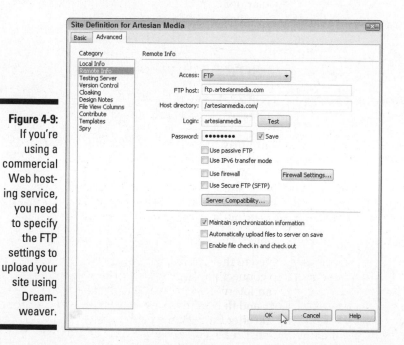

Figure 4-9: If you're using a commercial Web hosting service, you need to specify the FTP settings to upload your site using Dreamweaver.

Click the Test button to make sure you've entered everything correctly. If there are no problems, Dreamweaver responds with a box saying `Dreamweaver connected to your Web server successfully.` (*Note:* You must save the password to use the test feature, but you can deselect the Save Password box after you test if you prefer not to save the password in the program.)

5. **Select the Use Passive FTP or Use Firewall option only if your service provider or site administrator instructs you to do so.**

   If you aren't on a network but you do use a commercial service provider, you don't need to select either option.

6. **Click OK to save your Remote Info settings and close the Site Definition dialog box. Then click Done to close the Manage Sites dialog box.**

If you prefer to use a dedicated FTP program instead of Dreamweaver's built-in features, you can download FTP programs for the Mac and PC at the following Web addresses:

- `www.ipswitch.com`: A popular FTP program for the PC, WS_FTP, can be downloaded here.
- `www.cuteftp.com`: A popular Windows program, CuteFTP, can be downloaded from here.
- `www.fetchsoftworks.com` and `www.panic.com/transmit`: If you use a Macintosh computer, popular options are Fetch, available for download at the former, and Transmit, available for download at the latter.

Putting your Web site online

Now that your site is set up, upload pages on your server and retrieve them by using the built-in FTP capabilities of Dreamweaver.

To transfer files between your hard drive and a remote server, follow these steps:

1. **Make sure you've defined your site (as I describe in the beginning of Chapter 2), opened and displayed the site you want to upload in the Files panel, and used all the FTP settings described in the previous section.**

2. **In the top left of the Files panel, click the Connects to Remote Host icon.**

   If you're not already connected to the Internet, the Connects to Remote Host icon starts your dialup connection. If you have trouble connecting this way, try establishing your Internet connection as you usually do to check e-mail or surf the Web, and then return to Dreamweaver and click the Connects to Remote Host icon after establishing your Internet connection. When your computer is online, Dreamweaver should have no trouble automatically establishing an FTP connection with your host server.

If you still have trouble establishing a connection to your Web server, refer to the preceding section, "Setting up Web server access for FTP," and make sure that you specified the server information correctly. If you still have trouble, contact your service provider or site administrator to ensure that you have all the correct information for connecting to your server. Getting all this information set up correctly the first time can be tricky, and each service provider is different. (The good news is that after you get the connection working, you save it in Dreamweaver, which makes it super easy to reconnect in the future.)

After you establish the connection, you can move between views in this panel by choosing from the drop-down list at the top right, (visible in Figure 4-10). The main options are Local View, which displays files on your local hard drive, and Remote View, which displays files on the server.

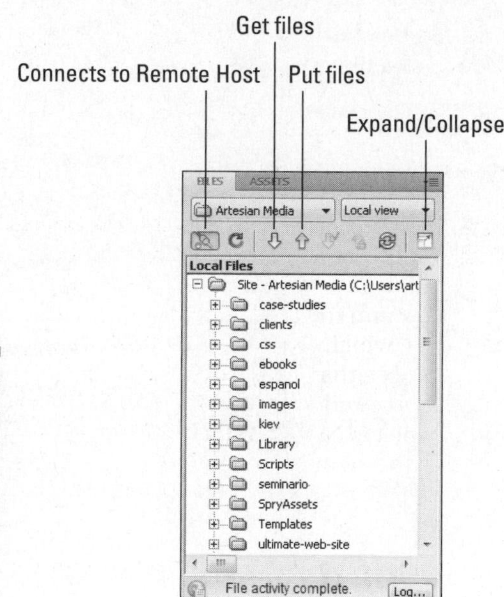

Figure 4-10: The row of icons across the top control FTP functions.

3. **To *upload* a file (transfer a file from your hard drive to your Web server), select the file from the Local View panel (which displays the files on your hard drive) and click the Put Files icon (the up arrow) in the Files panel.**

   The files are copied automatically to your server when you transfer them. You can select multiple files or folders to be transferred simultaneously.

After you upload files to you server, test your work by using a Web browser to view them online. Sometimes things that look and work fine on your computer (such as links) won't work on the server.

4. **To *download* files or folders (transfer files or folders from your Web server to your hard drive), select the files or folders from the Remote View panel (which displays the files on your server) and click the Get Files button (the down arrow) in the Files panel.**

   The files are copied automatically to your hard drive when you transfer them.

   Be aware that when you copy files to or from your server, the files you're transferring overwrite the files already at the destination. Dreamweaver notifies you about the overwriting if it notices you're replacing a newer file with an older one, but it can't always correctly assess the proper time differences. Take note of these warnings, but keep in mind that you can get warnings that aren't always accurate when they're based on the age of a file.

   When the transfer is complete, you can open the files on your hard drive.

You can see both the remote and local views simultaneously by clicking the Expand/Collapse icon on the far right side of the Files panel (labeled in Figure 4-10). To collapse this Site dialog box and return the Files panel to the side of the screen again, click the Expand/Collapse icon again.

The arrows with the check mark and the little lock at the top of the Files panel are for the Check In/Out feature, which enables you to keep track of who is working on a site and prevent more than one person making changes to the same page. These features are covered in the "Using Check In and Check Out" section, later in this chapter. The circle with the double arrows is for the Synchronize option covered in the section that follows.

Synchronizing local and remote sites

One of the most valuable features in Dreamweaver's FTP options is the capability to automatically synchronize the files on your hard drive with the files on your server. This is cool because it helps you keep track of which pages you've edited and ensures that they've been updated on the server. This may not matter much to you the first time you upload your site, or if you have only a few pages in your site. But if you have a large site and make frequent updates, this feature is a wonderful way to make sure all the changes you make get to your server. Dreamweaver also confirms which files are updated after you complete the synchronization.

Downloading an existing Web site

If you want to work on an existing Web site and you don't already have a copy of it on your local computer's hard drive, you can use Dreamweaver to download any or all the files in the site so that you can edit the existing pages, add new pages, or use any of Dreamweaver's other features to check links and manage the site's further development. The first step is to get a copy of the site onto your computer by downloading it from the server.

To download an existing Web site, follow these steps:

1. **Create a new folder on your computer to store the existing site.**
2. **Specify this folder as the local root folder for the site with Dreamweaver's site setup features.**

   Check out Chapter 2 for information on defining a site, if you're not sure how to do this.
3. **Set up the Remote Info dialog box.**

   I explain how to do this in the "Setting up Web server access for FTP" section.
4. **Connect to the remote site by clicking the Connects to Remote Host button, which looks like the ends of two cables, in the Files panel.**
5. **Click the Get Files button, which looks like a down arrow, to download the entire site to your local drive.**

   Sometimes your Web host has files on the remote server that you don't need to download. If you want to download only specific files or folders from the site, select those files or folders in the Remote Site pane of the Files panel and click the Get Files button. Dreamweaver automatically duplicates some or all of the remote site's structure, meaning the folders in the site but not all the files within them, and places the downloaded files in the correct part of the site hierarchy. Re-creating the folder structure on your local computer is important because Dreamweaver needs to know the location of the files as they relate to other parts of the site to set links properly. The safest option is to download the entire site; but if you're working on a large Web project, downloading a part and duplicating the structure enables you to work on a section of the site without downloading it all.

   If you're working on only one page or section of a site, generally choose to include *dependent files,* meaning any files linked from those pages, to ensure that links are set properly when you make changes.
6. **After you download the site or specific files or folders, you can edit them as you do any other file in Dreamweaver.**

Follow these steps to synchronize your Web site:

1. **Make sure the site you want to work on is selected and displayed in the Files panel.**
2.  **Click the Connects to Remote Host icon, in the top left of the Files panel, to log on to your remote site.**

3. **Click the Expand/Collapse icon (labeled in Figure 4-10) to expand the dialog box and view the remote and local sites simultaneously.**

   The Site dialog box displays both the remote and local views of the site. (To collapse this dialog box, click the Expand/Collapse icon again.)

4. **Choose Site⇨Synchronize.**

   The Synchronize Files dialog box appears.

5. **In the Synchronize drop-down list, choose whether to synchronize the Entire Site or Selected Files Only.**

6. **In the Direction drop-down list, choose which option you want to use to copy the files:**

   - **Put Newer Files to Remote:** This option copies the most recently modified files from your local site to the remote site. Click the Delete Remote Files Not on Local Drive box if you want those files removed from your Web site.
   - **Get Newer Files from Remote:** This option copies the most recently modified files from your remote site to the local site. Click the Delete Local Files Not on Remote Server box if you want to remove those files from your local copy.
   - **Get and Put Newer Files:** This option updates both the local and remote sites with the most recent versions of all the files.

   Make sure the Delete Remote Files Not on Local Drive box is not selected.

   Be careful of this feature when using Get or Put. As a general rule, I recommend you leave it deselected because you may have folders and files on the server, such as log files, that don't exist on your hard drive, and you don't want to delete them inadvertently.

7. **Click the Preview button.**

   The Site FTP dialog box displays the files that are about to be changed.

   Now you have the option to verify the files you want to delete, put, and get. If you don't want Dreamweaver to alter a file, deselect it from the Site FTP dialog box now or forever live with the consequences.

8. **Click OK.**

   All approved changes are automatically made, and Dreamweaver updates the Site FTP dialog box with the status.

9. **When the synchronization finishes, you can choose to save or not save the verification information to a local file.**

   I recommend that you save the verification information because it can be handy if you want to review your changes after synchronization is complete.

Setting Cloaking Options

The Dreamweaver Cloaking option enables you to exclude folders or files from all site operations, meaning they won't be uploaded to the live site when you're synchronizing or batching files back and forth. This feature is handy if you have sections of a site that you want to save but don't want visible to your viewers. For example, if you have a special holiday folder that you don't want visible during the rest of the year, you can use the Cloaking feature to save it locally, with the assurance that no one can accidentally publish the files with Dreamweaver until you uncloak them and publish them in December.

To use the Cloaking feature, follow these steps:

1. **Choose Site⇨Manage Sites.**
2. **Select the site you want to work on and then click Edit.**

   The Site Definition dialog box appears.
3. **If it's not already selected, click the Advanced tab at the top of the dialog box and choose the Cloaking category from the Category list on the left.**
4. **Select the Enable Cloaking box.**
5. **(Optional) To cloak files of a certain type, select the Cloak Files Ending With box and enter the extension(s) in the text field, as shown in Figure 4-11.**

   For example, if you want to cloak any original Photoshop files that may be saved in your local root folder so they don't upload and take up space on your server, enter the `.psd` extension. If you want to cloak more than one file type, separate each file extension with a space. Do not use a comma or other delimiter.
6. **Click OK to close the Site Definition dialog box and then click the Done button in the Define Sites dialog box to close it.**

   Files matching the extensions specified, if any, are now cloaked.
7. **(Optional) To manually cloak specific folders or files, select the folders or files in the Files tab of the Files panel.**
8. **Right-click (Windows) or Control+click (Mac) and choose Cloaking⇨Cloak.**

To uncloak files or folders, repeat Steps 7–8 and select Uncloak from the shortcut menu in Step 8. You can also use these steps to uncloak all the files in your current site, disable cloaking in the site, and change the cloaking settings.

If you disable cloaking for all files, any manual cloaking choices you've made are lost, even if you enable cloaking again later.

Editing Web pages online

If you're an experienced Web designer and just want to make quick changes to a site or use the FTP features to access files on a server without doing the site setup steps, Dreamweaver does enable you to use these features without completing site setup. To access FTP features and set them up quickly, choose Site⇨Manage Sites and then choose New⇨FTP & RDS Server from the Manage Sites dialog box. This shortcut enables you to work directly on your server using the FTP & RDS Server; however, Dreamweaver doesn't manage link checking, and none of the other site management features work.

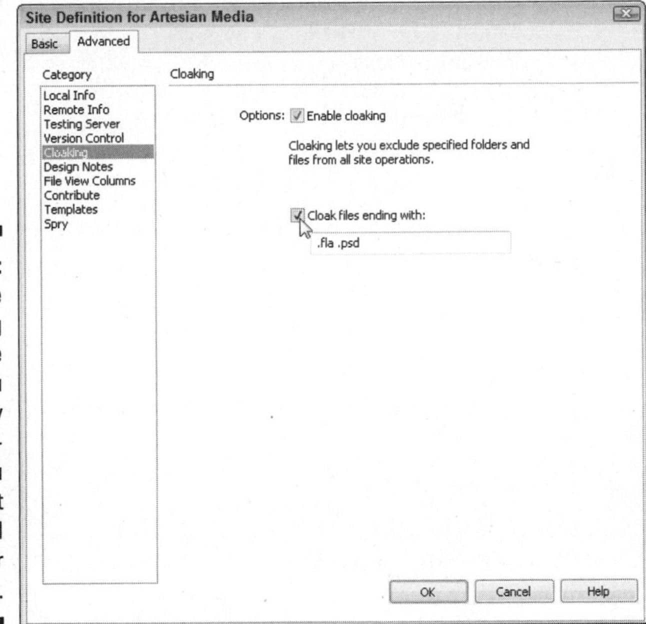

Figure 4-11: The Cloaking feature enables you to specify files or folders that you don't want transferred to your server.

Making the Most of Dreamweaver's Site Management Features

In the following sections, you find descriptions and instructions for using more of the options available from the Site Definition dialog box, including Design Notes, Check In/Out, and integrated e-mail. If you're the only person working on a Web site, you probably don't need the features described in this section because they're intended for use on sites developed by a team of people who need to communicate with each other and make sure they don't overwrite each other's work.

Using a testing server

The Testing Server option enables you to specify a development server, a necessary step if you're creating a Web site using the Dreamweaver dynamic page-creation features for developing sites using PHP, ASP, or ColdFusion. You find more information about using these options in Chapters 14 and 15.

Enabling Check In and Check Out

The Check In/Out feature is designed to keep people from overwriting each other's work when more than one person is working on the same Web site (a valuable feature if you want to keep peace among all the members of your Web design team). When a person working on the Web site checks out a file, other developers working on the site can't make changes to that file. When you check out a file, a green check mark appears next to the filename in the Files panel. If someone else checks out a file, you see a red check mark next to the filename.

To enable the Check In/Out feature, follow these steps:

These steps assume you've already set up the remote info for your site, using FTP or one of the other remote options. If you haven't yet done so, first complete the steps in the "Publishing Your Site to a Web Server," section earlier in this chapter.

1. **Choose Site⇨Manage Sites, select the site you want to work on, and click Edit.**
2. **In the Site Definition dialog box that appears, make sure the Advanced tab is selected and then select the Remote Info category on the left.**

   If you have not already selected a Remote Access option and filled in the fields, you will need to do so before you can set up Check In/Check Out.
3. **Select the Enable File Check In and Check Out option at the bottom of the Remote Info dialog box.**

   The dialog box expands to expose other options.

4. **(Optional) If you want files checked out whenever they're opened, select the Check Out Files When Opening option.**
5. **In the Check Out Name field, fill in the name you want associated with the files (presumably your name or nickname so other people working on the site know it's you).**
6. **In the Email Address field, fill in your e-mail address.**
7. **Click OK to save your changes and close the Site Definition dialog box.**

   With this Check Out feature, you can track which files a particular person is working on. The Email Address field is needed for Dreamweaver's integration with e-mail, which facilitates communication among developers on a site. See the next section for more information about integrated e-mail.

Using Design Notes

If you sometimes forget the details of your work or neglect to tell your colleagues important things about the Web site you're all working on, the Dreamweaver Design Notes feature may save you some grief.

Design Notes is ideal if you want to hide sensitive information from visitors, such as pricing structures or creative strategies, but make it available to members of your development team. Information saved as a Design Note in Dreamweaver can travel with any HTML file or image, even if the file transfers from one Web site to another or from Fireworks to Dreamweaver.

Essentially, Design Notes enable you to record information (such as a message to another designer on your team) and associate it with a file or a folder. Design Notes work a lot like the *comment tag* (HTML code that enables you to embed in a page text that won't appear in a browser) but with a bit more privacy. Unlike the comment tag, which is embedded directly in the HTML code of a page (and can be seen if someone views the source code behind a page on the Web), Design Notes are never visible to your visitors. The only way for a visitor to view Design Notes is to deliberately type the path to your notes subdirectory and view the notes files directly. You can even explicitly block this from being allowed, but only if you have administrative access to your server. To be even more secure, you can keep the notes on your hard drive and prevent them from ever being uploaded to your server — though, of course, your team members won't see your witty remarks.

When you create graphics in Adobe Fireworks, you can save a Design Note for each image file that's also available in Dreamweaver. To use this integrated feature, create a Design Note in Fireworks and associate it with the image. Then when you save the Fireworks image to your local Web site folder, the Design Note goes with it. When you open the file in Dreamweaver, the Design

Note appears when you right-click the image (Control-click on the Mac). This feature is a great way for graphic designers to communicate with other members of the Web development team.

Setting up Design Notes

To activate the Design Notes feature, follow these steps:

1. **Choose Site⇨Manage Sites.**

   The Manage Sites dialog box opens.

2. **Select the site you want to work on and then click the Edit button.**

   The Site Definition dialog box opens.

3. **Select the Advanced tab.**

4. **In the Category list at the left, choose Design Notes.**

   The Design Notes page appears.

5. **Select the Maintain Design Notes option.**

   With this option selected, whenever you copy, move, rename, or delete a file, the associated Design Notes file is also copied, moved, renamed, or deleted with it.

6. **(Optional) If you want your Design Notes to be sent with your files when they're uploaded to your server, select the Upload Design Notes for Sharing option.**

   If you're making notes only to yourself and don't want them to be associated with the page when you upload it to the server, deselect this option and the Design Notes will be maintained locally but not uploaded with your file.

7. **Click OK in the Site Definition dialog box and then click the Done button in the Manage Sites dialog box.**

   The Manage Sites dialog box closes.

The Clean Up button is useful after you've used Design Notes for a while. Click this button to delete any Design Notes that aren't associated with a file in the site. (This is useful for cleaning up Design Notes that correspond to pages, images, or other files that have been deleted from the site.)

Adding a note with Design Notes

To add Design Notes to a document, follow these steps:

1. **Open the file you want to add a Design Note to and then choose File⇨Design Notes.**

   The Design Notes dialog box opens (see Figure 4-12). You need to have a file checked out to add or modify a Design Note, but not to read a note.

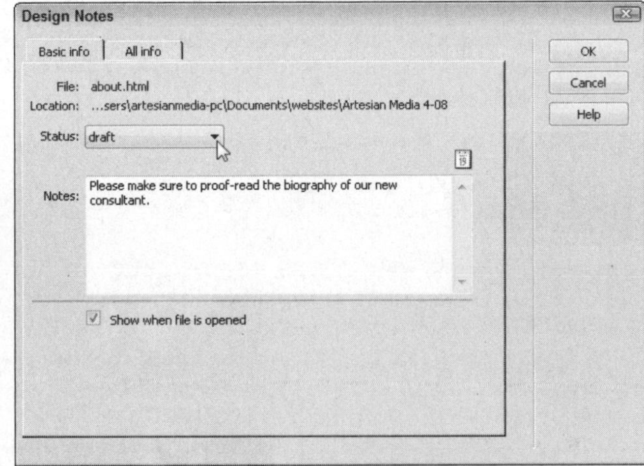

Figure 4-12: Design Notes make it easy to add messages to documents, images, and even entire folders.

2. **In the Status drop-down list, choose the status of the document.**

   Your options are Draft, Revision 1, Revision 2, Revision 3, Alpha, Beta, Final, and Needs Attention. You can choose any status, and you should set a policy with your design team about what each status means and how you use these options to manage your development.

3. **In the Notes text box, type your comments.**

4. **(Optional) To insert the current local date, click the Insert Date icon, which is just above the Notes text box.**

   The current date is inserted automatically.

   You can also select the Show When File Is Open check box. If this box is selected, the Design Notes appear whenever the file is opened so that they can't be missed.

5. **Click the All Info tab.**

   You can add other information that may be useful to developers of your site. For example, you can name a key designer (in the Name field) and define the value as the name of that person or the priority of the project (in the Value field). You may also define a field for a client or the type of file that you commonly use.

6. **Click the plus (+) button to add a new information item; click the minus (–) button to remove a selected item.**
7. **Click OK to save the notes.**

   The notes you entered are saved to a *notes* subfolder in the same location as the current file. The filename is the document's filename plus the extension `.mno`. For example, if the filename is `art.htm`, the associated Design Notes file is `art.htm.mno`. Design Notes are indicated in Site View by a small yellow icon that looks like a cartoon bubble.

Enabling Contribute features

Adobe Contribute is a program that was created so that people who don't know much about Web design can easily contribute to a Web site. Think of Contribute as sort of a Dreamweaver Light, except it doesn't work very well as a standalone program. Contribute was designed to work on sites designed in Dreamweaver, and a number of features have been carefully integrated to make that collaboration work smoothly. If you're working with other developers of a site who use Contribute, make sure you select the Enable Contribute Compatibility box in the Contribute category of the Site Definition dialog box.

Remembering Your History

You can keep track of what you're doing and even replay your steps with the History panel. The History panel also lets you undo one or more steps and create commands to automate repetitive tasks.

To open the History panel, as shown in Figure 4-13, choose Window⇨History. As soon as you open a file, the History panel starts automatically recording your actions as you work in Dreamweaver. You can't rearrange the order of steps in the History panel, but you can copy them, replay them, and undo them. Don't think of the History panel as an arbitrary collection of commands; think of it as a way to view the steps you've performed, in the order in which you performed them. This is a great way to let Dreamweaver do your work for you if you have to repeat the same steps over and over. It's also a lifesaver if you make a major mistake and want to go back one or more steps in your development work.

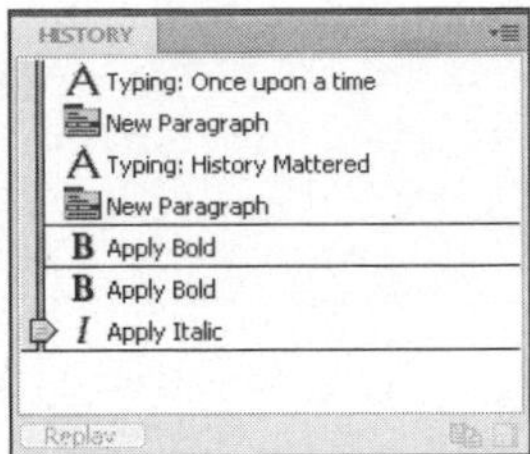

Figure 4-13: In the History panel, track what you do and undo or repeat steps easily.

Here's a rundown of how you can put the History panel to use:

- **To copy steps you already executed:** Use the Copy Steps option in the lower right as a quick way to automate steps you want to repeat. You can even select steps individually, in case you want to replay some (but not all) actions exactly as you did them.
- **To replay any or all steps displayed in the History panel:** Highlight the steps you want to replay and click the Replay button at the bottom of the History panel.
- **To undo the results of the replayed steps:** Choose Edit⇨Undo Replay Steps.
- **To apply steps to a specific element on a page:** Highlight that element in the Document window before selecting and replaying the steps. For example, if you want to apply bold and italic formatting to just a few words on a page, you can replay the steps that applied bold and italics to selected text.

Repeating your steps with Recorded Commands

You can automate repeat tasks using Dreamweaver's Recorded Commands feature, available from the Commands menu. Simply start the record option, execute any series of actions in Dreamweaver, stop, and save them. Then you just replay the recording to repeat the actions automatically. To use the Recorded Commands option, choose Commands⇨Start Recording and then carefully execute a series of steps that you want to be able to repeat. When you complete the steps you want to record, choose Commands⇨Stop Recording and name the command to save it. To play the actions back, choose Commands⇨Play Recorded Command and select your new command. Then kick back and watch the action; or better yet, take a break and get out of your office for a change.

You can also set the number of steps displayed in the History panel by choosing Edit➪Preferences (Windows) or Dreamweaver➪Preferences (Mac) and selecting General from the Category list on the left. The default is 50 steps, more than enough for most users. The higher the number, the more memory the History panel uses.

Using the Quick Tag Editor

If you're one of those developers who likes to work in the Dreamweaver Design area, sometimes referred to as the WYSIWYG (what you see is what you get) editing environment, but still wants to look at the HTML tags once in a while, you'll love the Quick Tag Editor.

The Quick Tag Editor, as the name implies, lets you quickly access HTML tags and enables you to modify, add, or remove an HTML tag without opening the HTML Source window. That means that while you're in the middle of working on a page in design view, you can view the HTML tag you're working on without switching over to code view. You can use the Quick Tag Editor to insert HTML, edit an existing tag, or wrap new tags around a selected text block or other element.

The Quick Tag Editor opens in one of three modes — Edit, Insert, or Wrap — depending on what you selected on the page before you launched the editor. Use the keyboard shortcut Ctrl+T (Windows) or ⌘+T (Mac) to change modes while the Quick Tag Editor is open.

You can enter or edit tags in the Quick Tag Editor just as you would in code view, without having to switch back and forth between code view and design view. To enter or edit tags in the Quick Tag Editor, follow these steps:

1. **With the document you want to edit open, select an image, text block, or other element.**

   If you want to add new code, simply click anywhere in the file without selecting text or an element.

2. **Choose Modify➪Quick Tag Editor.**

   You can also press Ctrl+T (Windows) or ⌘+T (Mac). Or, you can right-click the name of the element tag in the status bar at the bottom of the workspace.

The Quick Tag Editor opens in the mode that is most appropriate for your selection, as shown in Figure 4-14. For example, if you click an image or formatted text, it displays the current tag so that you can edit it. If you don't select anything or if you select unformatted text, the Quick Tag Editor opens with nothing in it, and you can enter the code you want to add. Press Ctrl+T (⌘+T) to switch to another mode.

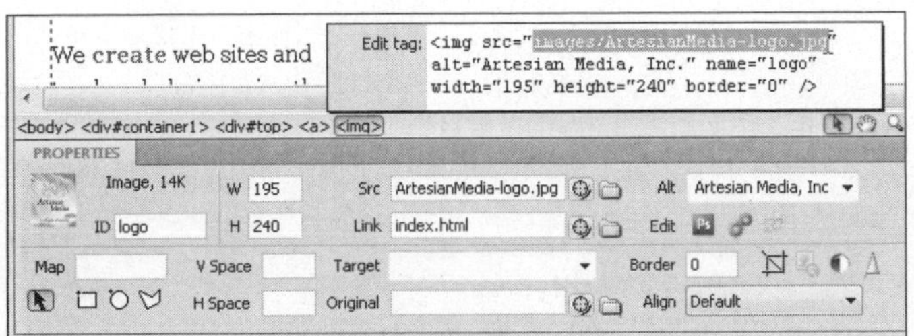

Figure 4-14: You can view and edit HTML tags in the Quick Tag Editor without switching to code view.

3. **To add a new tag or attribute, simply type the code into the Quick Tag Editor.**

   If you aren't sure about a tag or attribute, press the spacebar, and the Hints drop-down list appears automatically, offering you a list of all the tags or attributes available for the element you're editing. If this Hints drop-down list doesn't appear, choose Edit⇨Preferences⇨Code Hints (Windows) or Dreamweaver⇨Preferences⇨Code Hints (Mac) and make sure that the Enable Code Hints option is selected.

4. **To close the Quick Tag Editor and apply all your changes, press Enter (Windows) or Return (Mac).**

Part II

Appreciating Web Design Options

In this part . . .

The best way to create Web designs today is with Cascading Style Sheets (CSS). This part introduces you to the power and advantages of CSS, with two chapters on creating and using styles.

In Chapter 5, you find an introduction to CSS and a review of the CSS features in Dreamweaver. In Chapter 6, you move on to creating CSS layouts, using `<div>` tags and other block-level elements to create accessible, flexible designs.

In Chapter 7, you find out how to create tables, split and merge cells, and use table attributes. You also find tips about when to use tables and when CSS is the preferred option. In Chapter 8, you get an introduction to frames and discover how targeting makes it possible to open a link in a specific part of the page. In Chapter 9, you discover how the Dreamweaver templates can make creating Web pages faster, and best of all, how templates can save you time when you want to make changes to your page designs.

Chapter 5

Cascading Style Sheets

In This Chapter

- Introducing CSS
- Looking at CSS rule options
- Working in the CSS Styles panel
- Creating and editing CSS styles in the Property inspector
- Working with tag, class, and advanced style selectors
- Comparing internal and external style sheets

Want to add a little style to your pages? *Cascading Style Sheets (CSS)* are all the rave on the Web and with good reason. CSS is *the way* to create Web sites today if you want to follow the latest standards and develop sites that are accessible, flexible, and designed to work on a wide range of devices.

The concept of creating styles has been around since long before the Web. Desktop publishing programs, such as Adobe InDesign, and even word processing programs, such as Microsoft Word, have long used styles to manage the formatting and editing of text on printed pages. Using styles in a word processor, you can create and save styles for common features, such as headlines and captions. In print design, styles are great timesavers because they enable you to combine a collection of formatting options, such as Arial, bold, and italic, into one style and then apply all those options at once to any selected text in your document using a single style. You also have the advantage that if you change a style, you can automatically apply the change everywhere you've used that style in a document.

On the Web, you can do all that and more with CSS because you can use styles sheets for even more than just text formatting. For example, you can use CSS to create styles that align images to the left or right side of a page, add padding around text or images, and change background and link colors. You can even create more than one style sheet for the same page: one that makes your design look good on computers, another for cell phones, and a third a printed page.

For all these reasons (and more), CSS has quickly become the preferred method of designing Web pages among professional Web designers. If you haven't jumped on the CSS bandwagon yet, this chapter is designed to help you understand the basics of CSS, to introduce you to Dreamweaver's many CSS features, and to show you how to create and apply tag and class styles to text. Even if you've been working with CSS for a while, you may appreciate the review of CSS and Dreamweaver's style features before moving on to the more complex aspects of CSS covered in the next chapter. In Chapter 6, you find instructions for creating ID and Compounds styles, which enable you to use CSS to control the position of elements and to create styles that apply only to specific sections of a page. The lessons in Chapter 6 will help you design page layouts by combining HTML `<div>` tags and styles, and show you how to customize the predesigned CSS layouts included in Dreamweaver.

Introducing Cascading Style Sheets

One of the most powerful aspects of CSS is the way you can use it to make global style changes across an entire Web site. Suppose, for example, that you create a style for your headlines by redefining the `<h1>` tag to create large, blue, bold headlines. Then one fine day, you decide that all your headlines should be red instead of blue. If you aren't using CSS, changing all your headlines could be a huge undertaking — a matter of opening every Web page in your site to make changes to the font tags around your headlines. But if you're using CSS in an external style sheet, you can simply change the style that controls the headline in the style sheet, and *voilá!* Your headlines all turn red automatically. If you ever have to redesign your site (and believe me, every good site goes through periodic redesigns), you can save hours or even days of work if you've created your design with CSS.

CSS has many other advantages and a remarkably broad scope. The following partial list shows some of what you can do with CSS:

- Make global changes anywhere a style is applied simply by changing the original style in an external style sheet.
- Create styles for commonly used elements, such as headlines and captions, to create a more consistent design and speed the development process.
- Define styles that align and position elements, including images, tables, and `<div>` tags.
- Control padding and margin spacing with greater precision and add different amounts of space to each side of an element.
- Define font sizes in fixed or relative sizes with percentages, pixels, picas, points, inches, millimeters, ems, and exs (described in the sidebar, "Understanding CSS size options," later in this chapter).

- Add and remove borders around images, tables, <div> tags, and more. You can even add borders to only one side of an element to create dividing lines between elements and add visual interest to a page.
- Redefine existing HTML tags, such as the unordered list tag, which you can redefine to appear in a browser as a horizontal or vertical list with or without bullets. You can also replace standard HTML bullets with a variety of other bullet styles or an image.
- Control the display of a background image defining how and if it repeats on a page or within a container, such as a <div> tag or table.
- Change link colors, remove link underlining, and create rollover effects using text links.
- Create multiple styles for the same page. For example, you can create one style that uses a large text size for anyone who has trouble reading small print on the Web and another that's optimized for display on a small screen, such as a cell phone.

Understanding the basics of styles

Many people find CSS confusing at first because it's such a different approach to design than what you may be used to if you've worked in print. The following are three of the more confusing aspects of CSS for beginners:

- **Getting used to thinking about the styles on your site separate from your text, images, and other content.** For example, instead of simply applying formatting directly to a headline to make it bold, green, and 24 point, in CSS, you create a style for your headline that includes bold, green, and 24 point, save that style in a separate place in your document or in a separate file called an external style sheets, and then you apply the style to one or more headlines as a separate step. As a result, if you want to change the way your headline looks later, you don't go to the headline itself in your page to make the change. Instead, you edit the style in the style sheet, and it automatically changes any headlines formatted with that style.
- **Understanding all the different kinds of style selectors you can choose from, such as class, ID, and tag selectors.** No matter how you create your styles, each style definition, or *rule,* contains a selector and a declaration. The *selector* identifies the name and type of style; for example, the selector would be something like `#container` or `.caption`. The *declaration* defines the style and describes its properties, such as bold, blue, or 300 pixels wide. Dreamweaver's four selector types are described in detail in the section that follows.

- **Understanding when it's best to create external style sheets, internal style sheets, or inline styles, described in the section "Understanding rule definition options."**

And ultimately, you need to understand how CSS and HTML work together. So, for example, you can control the positioning and appearance of an HTML `<div>` tag by applying an ID style to the tag, or you can redefine a tag, such as the `<h1>` tag to change the way headlines look on a page.

If you're starting to feel baffled already (or at any point in this chapter), hang in there. After you read through the basic concepts and start creating and applying styles, all this should start making more sense. And remember, you can always come back and read through any or all these points again. After you've been using styles for a while, the details in the following sections are likely to have more meaning to you, but it's really hard to start using styles before you have a good overview of how they work.

Understanding style selectors

One of the first things you need to understand when you create new styles is which selector to use for which job. Each of the selector options has different naming restrictions and purposes. If you're completely new to working with styles, this may not make much sense yet, but I encourage you to read through all these descriptions of selectors so that you can appreciate your options before you move on.

Don't feel you have to memorize all this. Instead, consider folding down the corner on this page so you can refer to this list of selectors when you create your styles.

The following sections offer a description of each of the four selector option available from the New CSS Rule dialog box (as shown in Figure 5-1) in Dreamweaver CS4.

Figure 5-1: The four selector types.

Class selectors

The class selector is the most versatile selector option. Class styles can be used to format any element (from text to images to multimedia), and they can be used as many times as you like on any page in a Web site.

Class style names always begin with a period, and you can create class styles with any name as long as you don't use spaces or special characters (hyphens and underscores are okay). Thus you could create a style called caption for the text that appears before your pictures, and you could create a style called photo-credit to format the name of a photographer differently from the caption. In that case, your class styles would look like this:

```
.caption .photo-credit
```

Dreamweaver helps you with the period (or a dot). If you choose class as the selector type and forget to include a dot at the beginning of the name, Dreamweaver adds one for you. (***Note:*** Don't include any space between the dot and the style name.)

One other thing that can make styles confusing is that when you apply a class style to text or another element, the dot doesn't appear in the name when it's added to your HTML code. Thus, if you applied the `.caption` style to a paragraph tag to format the text under an image, it would look like this:

```
<p class="caption">This is a photo of an Egret in
          flight.</p>
```

Class styles must be applied to an element, such as the Paragraph tag shown in this example. Class tags can even be added to elements that are already defined by other styles.

When you create a class style in Dreamweaver, the style is displayed in the CSS Styles panel (as shown in Figure 5-3), and added to the CSS drop-down list in the Property inspector (as shown in Figure 5-2).

You can apply class styles using the CSS drop-down list, as shown in Figure 5-2. It's common to create styles to align images and other elements to the right or left of a page, and styles with the names `.float-right` and `.float-left` are included in most of the predesigned CSS layouts in Dreamweaver. These styles commonly include margin spacing to create a little white space between an image and text when text is wrapped around the aligned image, as shown in Figure 5-2.

For more details and step-by-step instructions for creating and applying styles with class selectors, see the section, "Using Class and Tag Styles in Dreamweaver," later in this chapter.

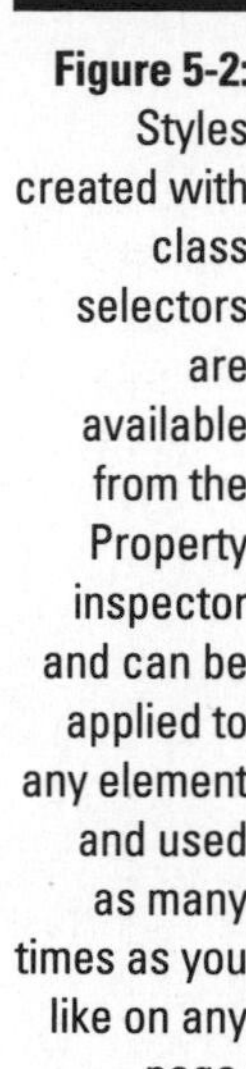
Figure 5-2: Styles created with class selectors are available from the Property inspector and can be applied to any element and used as many times as you like on any page.

ID selectors

Think of ID styles as the building blocks of most CSS layouts (you find out how to create layouts with these styles in Chapter 6). ID styles must begin with a pound (#) sign, and, similar to class styles, Dreamweaver adds a pound (#) sign to the beginning of the style name automatically if you forget to include it. (***Note:*** Don't include any space between the # and the style name.)

The ID selector option is a new addition to the CSS Rule dialog box in Dreamweaver CS4 (in CS3, you had to choose the Advanced option to create an ID style). Similar to class styles, you can name ID styles anything you like as long as you don't use spaces or special characters (again hyphens and underscores are okay). Thus an ID style used to identify the sidebar section of a page could look like this:

```
#sidebar
```

Similar to class styles, the # sign is not used in the HTML code when a style is applied to an element, such as a <div> tag like this:

```
<div id="sidebar">Between these tags with the sidebar ID
          style, you would include any headlines, text,
          or other elements in your sidebar.</div>
```

What's special about ID styles is that they should be used only once per page. This makes them ideally suited to formatting <div> tags and other block-level elements that are used to create distinct sections in a page. Thus, ID styles are great for creating page layouts where you want to define each section of a page only once.

In the predesigned CSS layouts included in Dreamweaver, all the designs are created by combining a series of <div> tags with ID styles using names like `#container`, `#header`, and `#footer` to identify the main sections of the design. In Figure 5-3, you can see how a collection of ID and Class styles are displayed in the CSS Styles panel after they're created. ID styles are also added to the ID drop-down list in the Property inspector, making them easy to apply to a selected element.

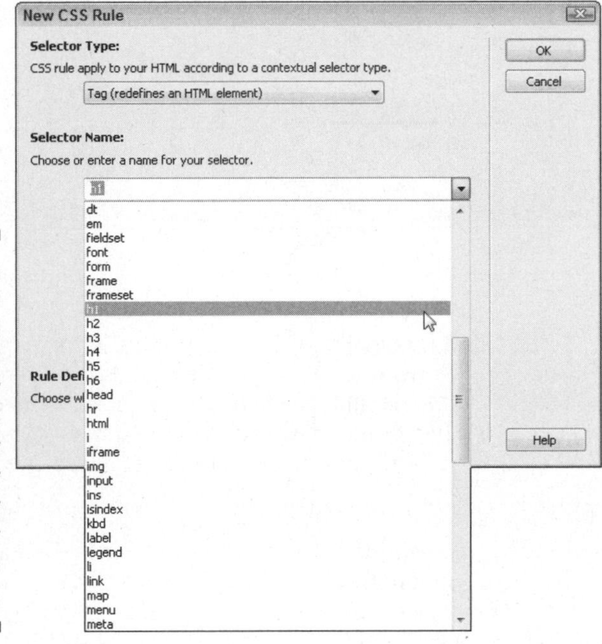

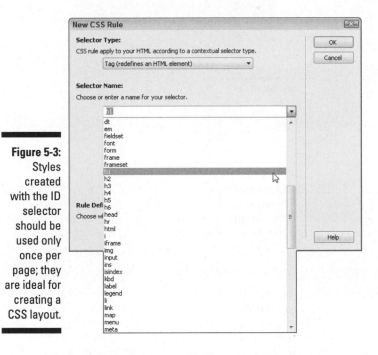

Figure 5-3: Styles created with the ID selector should be used only once per page; they are ideal for creating a CSS layout.

Tag selectors

The tag selector is used to redefine existing HTML tags. Select this option, shown in Figure 5-4, if you want to change the formatting options for an HTML tag, such as the <h1> (heading 1) tag or the <ul> (unordered list) tag.

In many cases, redefining existing HTML tags with CSS has advantages over creating new styles. For example, content formatted with the Heading 1 tag is well recognized on the Web as the most important text on a page. For that reason, many search engines give priority to text formatted with the Heading 1 tag. Similarly, the hierarchical structure of the <h1>–<h6> tags helps ensure that even if a visitor to your site changes the text size in his or her Web browser, text formatted with the Heading 1 tag is still larger relative to text formatted with an Heading 2 tag, which is larger than text formatted with the Heading 3 tag, and so on.

The ability to change the appearance of headings and other tags with CSS makes it possible to retain these advantages while still being able to use the font, size, color, spacing, and other formatting options that you prefer in your Web design. When you use the tag selector, the style definition is applied automatically to any text or other element that's been formatted with the corresponding tag. Thus, if you've formatted a headline with the `<h1>` tag and then create a new `<h1>` style, the formatting you used to define the style will apply automatically to the headline as soon as the style is created.

For details on working with tag selectors, see the section "Using Class and Tag Styles in Dreamweaver" later in this chapter.

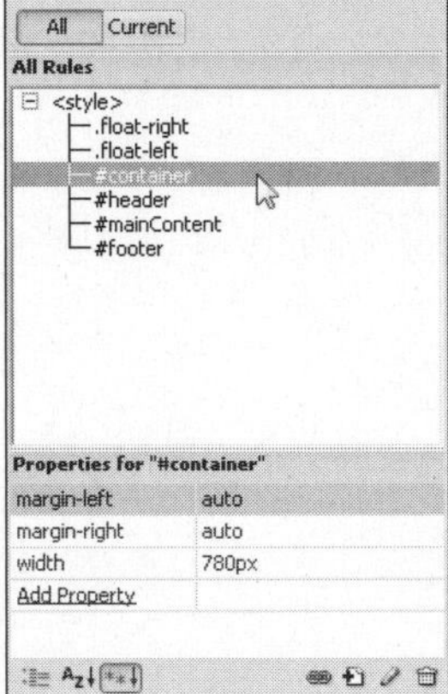

Figure 5-4: You can redefine the appearance of any HTML tag by creating a style with a tag selector.

Creating compound styles

The compound selector can be used to combine two or more style rules to create a style definition that displays only when one style is contained within another. Compound styles are useful when you want to do something like use the Heading 1 tag multiple times to format headlines in different ways on the same Web page. For example, you could create one style for headlines that appear in the main story area of a page and then create another style for headlines that appear in the sidebar on the page and still use the Heading 1 tag to format both.

Compound styles are created by combining ID, class, or tag styles and look like this:

```
#sidebar h1
```

(See Figure 5-5 for an example of how an `<h1>` style defined like this within a `#sidebar` ID style looks in the New CSS Rule dialog box.) Note that you must include a space between each name or tag in a compound style and that you don't include the brackets around tag in a style name. In this example, the style definition will apply only to `<h1>` tags that appear within another element, such as a `<div>` tag with an ID style `#sidebar`.

If a compound style combines more than one tag, it's written like this:

```
#sidebar h1 a:link
```

Again, you must include a space between each name or tag. In this example, you see a style that defines the appearance of the active link tag only when the link is located inside an element formatted with the `<h1>` tag that's also inside an element formatted with the `#sidebar` ID. A compound style like this makes it possible to create links that look different when they appear in a headline in the sidebar of a page than when they appear in another part of the sidebar.

After you figure out the differences among these style selector options and when they're best used, you're well on your way to mastering the art of creating Web pages with CSS in Dreamweaver. (Find more information about compound styles in Chapter 6.)

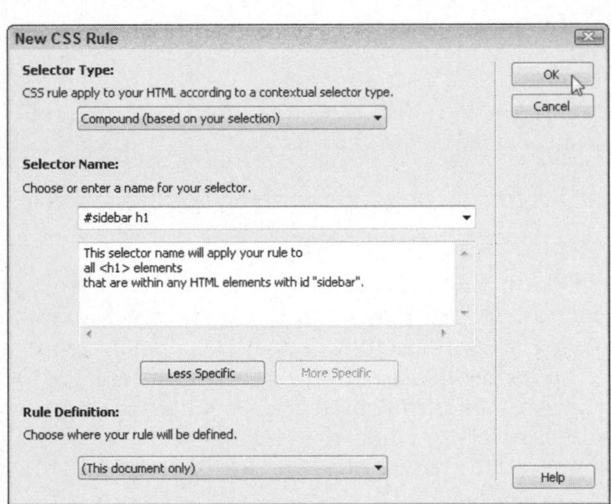

Figure 5-5: The compound style selector makes it possible to combine styles to create new style definitions that apply only to an area of a page already defined by an existing style.

Understanding rule definition options

You also have the option of creating internal, external, or inline styles. You can even use a combination of these options, or attach multiple external style sheets, to the same Web page.

- **Internal styles:** If you create internal styles, the CSS code is stored in the `<head>` area at the top of the HTML page you're working on, and the styles can be applied only to the page in which they were created.
- **External styles:** If you save your styles in an external style sheet, they're stored in a separate file with a `.css` extension. External style sheets can be attached to any or all the pages in a Web site in much the same way as you can insert the same image into multiple pages. You can also attach multiple external style sheets to the same page. For example, you can create one style sheet for styles that format text and another for layout styles. You can also create external style sheets for different purposes, such as one for print and one for screen display.
- **Inline styles:** Inline styles are created within a document at the place that a style is used and only apply to the element they're attached to in the document. These are generally considered the least useful of the three style sheet options because any changes to the defined style must be made to the code that contains the element, which means you lose many of the other benefits of styles, such as the ability to make global updates and create very clean, very fast-loading HTML code. For example, creating one style for all your headlines and saving it in an external style sheet is better than applying the style formatting options to each headline separately.

At the bottom of the New CSS Rule dialog box, shown in Figure 5-6, you find a Rule Definition drop-down list. Use this list to specify where and how you want to save each new style that you define. The options are:

- Choose **This Document Only** to create an internal style that can only be used in the open document.
- Choose **New Style Sheet File** to create the new style in an external style sheet and create a new external style sheet simultaneously.
- Choose any existing external style sheet that is attached to the page by selecting the name of the style sheet from the Rule Definition drop-down list. In Figure 5-6, I am selecting an existing style sheet with the name main.css.

If you are creating a style that you are likely to want to use on more than one page in your site, saving the style to a new or existing external style sheet is your best choice. If you save a style in an internal style sheet and later decide you want to add it to an external style sheet, you can move the style using the CSS Styles panel. You find instructions in the "Using External Style Sheets," section later in this chapter.

Why so many fonts?

Although you can specify any font you want for text on your Web pages, you don't have complete control over how that font appears on your visitor's computer. That's because the font you apply is displayed properly only if your visitors have the same font on their hard drives. To help ensure that your text appears as you intend, Dreamweaver includes collections of common fonts, grouped together in families, such as Arial, Helvetica, sans-serif, Georgia, Times New Roman, Times, and serif.

Here's how it works. When you apply a collection of fonts like these, the browser displays the formatted text in the first font available in the list. For example, if you choose the font collection that starts with Georgia and your visitors have Georgia on their hard drives, they'll see your text in Georgia. If they don't have Georgia, the text is displayed in the next font on the list that your visitors do have. In this case, Times New Roman; if they don't have that font, either, the text is displayed in Times; and if they don't even have Times (which would be very unusual), the browser looks for any serif font. (In case you're not familiar with font terms, *serif* describes fonts, such as Times, that have those little curly things on the edges of letters; *sans serif* means no curly things, which is what you get with a font like Arial.)

You can create your own font collections by selecting the Edit Font List option from the bottom of the Font-Family drop-down list in the Property inspector or the Type category of the CSS Rule definition dialog box. In the Edit Font List dialog box, shown here, use the plus and minus buttons at the top of the Edit Font List dialog box to add or remove a font collection. To add individual fonts to a collection, select the font name from the bottom right of the dialog box and use the double-left arrows to add it to a font list (use the double-right arrows to remove a font from a collection).

The only way to ensure that text appears in the font you want is to create the text in a graphic in a program, such as Photoshop or Fireworks, and then insert the graphic with the text into your page. That's not a bad option for special text, such as banners or logos, but it's usually not a good option for all your text because graphics take longer to download than text and are harder to update later.

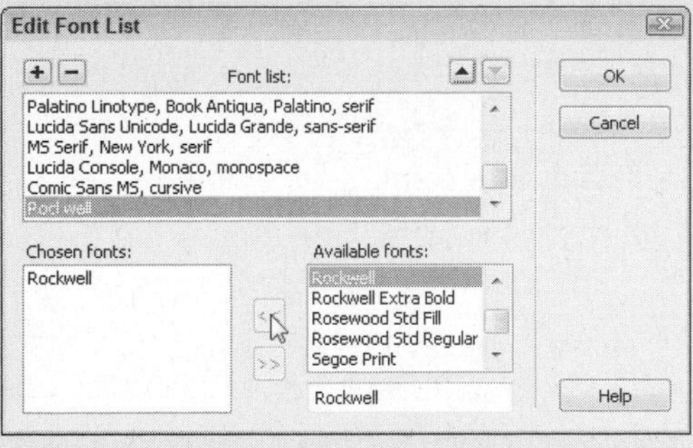

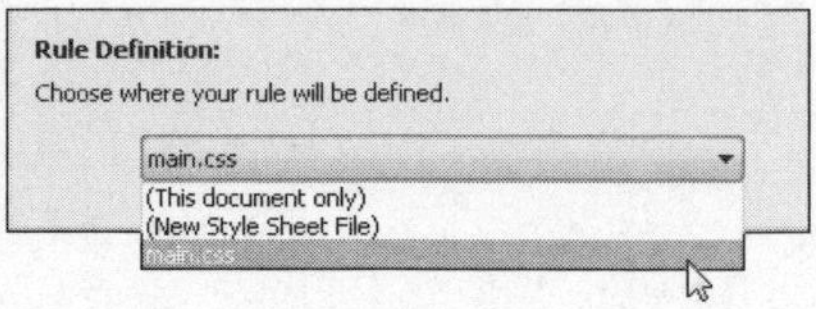

Figure 5-6: You can create an internal or external style sheet.

Looking at the code behind the scenes

If you *prefer* not to look the code behind your Web pages, it's helpful to at least have some familiarity with different kinds of tags, CSS, and other code that Dreamweaver creates for you when you design Web pages. The following examples show what the CSS code in an internal or external style sheet would look like in Dreamweaver for the following styles:

- An ID style created with the ID selector, that is named `#container`, and is defined as 780 pixels wide with the left and right margins set to auto (a cool trick for centering a CSS design, covered in detail in Chapter 6).
- A style created with a class selector, that is named `.caption`, and is defined as Verdana, Arial, Helvetica, sans-serif, small, italic, and bold.
- A style created with a tag selector to redefine the HTML tag `<h1>` — as Arial, Helvetica, sans-serif, large, and bold. (Note: because the Heading tags already include bold formatting, it is not necessary to include bold in the style definition.)

```
#container {
          width: 780px;
          margin-right: auto;
          margin-left: auto;
}
.caption {
          font-family:  Verdana, Arial, Helvetica, sans-
          serif;
          font-size: small;
          font-style: italic;
          font-weight: bold;
}
H1 {
          font-family: Arial, Helvetica, sans-serif;
          font-size: large;
}
```

Comparing CSS Rule Options

After you determine what selector type is best for your style and you decide whether you want to save it in an external or internal style, you're done with the New CSS Rules dialog box (described in the previous sections). You are ready to move on to the CSS Rule Definition dialog box and define the formatting and other options you want to include in your style. You find step-by-step instructions for creating new style rules later in this chapter. This section continues the overview to help you better understand your choices before you start creating a new style.

The CSS Rule Definition dialog box includes eight different categories, each with multiple options. All these choices can seem a bit daunting at first, which is why I've included this section with a general overview of the options in each category. Again, don't feel you need to memorize all these options; remember, you can always return to this section and use it as a reference when you're creating new styles.

In most cases, you'll only select a few options from one or two categories for each new style you create. Remember, you can always go back and edit styles to add or change options.

Not all the options in the CSS Rule Definition dialog box are supported by all the Web browsers in use on the Web today, so beware that the way styles are displayed on a Web page can vary depending on the browser. Similarly, some CSS options aren't included in Dreamweaver because they're not commonly supported. The following describes the options in each of the categories in the CSS Rule Definition dialog box, shown in Figures 5-7 through 5-14.

The Type category

The Type category features a collection of options that control the display of (you guessed it) the text in your pages. With the Type category selected (see Figure 5-7), you have the following formatting options:

- **Font-Family:** Specifies a font, a font family, or a series of families. You can add fonts to the list by choosing Edit Font List in the drop-down list. (For an explanation of why Dreamweaver includes font collections and how to create new ones, see the sidebar, "Why so many fonts?" earlier in this chapter.)
- **Font-Size:** Defines the size of the text. You can choose a specific numeric size or a relative size. Use the drop-down arrow to select from a list of options including pixels, picas, and percentages. For more on these options, see the sidebar "Understanding CSS size options."

Figure 5-7: The Type category in the CSS Rule Definition dialog box.

- **Font-Style:** Enables you to choose whether the text appears as normal, italic, or oblique. (Italic and oblique are rarely different in a Web browser, so stick with italic unless you have a specific reason not to.)
- **Line-Height:** Enables you to specify the height of a line on which the text is placed (graphic designers usually call this *leading*). You can specify line-height in a variety of ways including pixels, picas, and percentages. For more on these options, see the sidebar "Understanding CSS size options."
- **Font-Decoration:** Enables you to specify whether text is underlined, *overlined* (a line appears over the text), displayed with a strikethrough, or displayed with the *blink effect* (which makes text appear to flash on and off). You can also choose None, which removes all decorative effects.

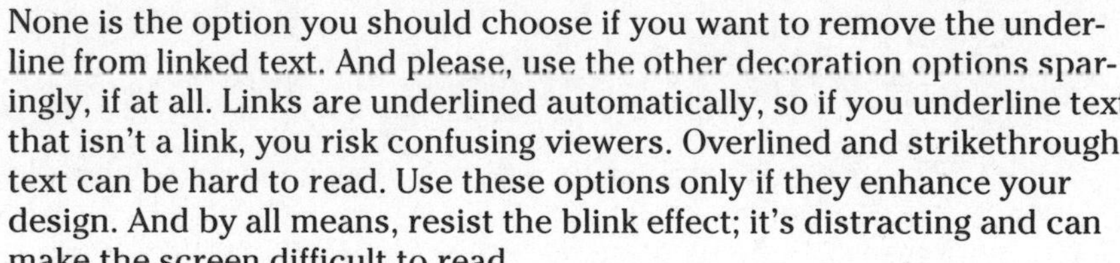

None is the option you should choose if you want to remove the underline from linked text. And please, use the other decoration options sparingly, if at all. Links are underlined automatically, so if you underline text that isn't a link, you risk confusing viewers. Overlined and strikethrough text can be hard to read. Use these options only if they enhance your design. And by all means, resist the blink effect; it's distracting and can make the screen difficult to read.

- **Font-Weight:** Enables you to control how bold the text appears by using a specific or relative boldness option.
- **Font-Variant:** Enables you to select small caps. Unfortunately, this attribute isn't supported by most browsers.
- **Font-Transform:** Enables you to globally change the case of selected words, making them all uppercase, all lowercase, with initial caps, or with no capitalization.
- **Color:** Defines the color of the text. You can use the color well (the square icon) to open a Web-safe color palette in which you can select predefined colors or create custom colors.

Understanding CSS size options

One of the more confusing aspects of CSS is that there are so many ways to specify sizes for fonts and other elements. If you're familiar with print, you'll probably recognize point sizes and pixel sizes, but these aren't necessarily the best options when you're designing for the Internet. On the Web, where display windows can vary from giant monitors to tiny cell phone screens, using relative sizes can help you create more flexible and adaptable deigns, something you can't do as well with fixed pixel or point sizes.

Many Web designers prefer to use relative sizes, such as the small, medium, and large. The advantage of this method is that the font size adjusts based on your visitor's settings while maintaining its relative relationship. Thus, text formatted as large displays larger than text formatted as small, no matter what the default font size. This enables you to maintain the hierarchy of text elements on a page, even if your user alters the default text size on a page (an option available to users in most Web browsers).

A variation on this approach is to specify a base, page-wide font size as medium (which is the default in most browsers), and then use percentages to make text larger or smaller, relative to that base size. For example, you could define the text in a caption style as 90 percent and your caption text would appear at 90 percent of the size of the rest of the text on the page. You could then make headlines 150 percent, for example, and subheads 125 percent.

Another size option is *em,* which is named after the letter *M.* When you use em as a measurement of size, the size is based on the font size of a capital letter *M* in the font face specified in a style. The *ex* option is similar, but it's based on the size of a lowercase *x* in the specified font face. Although these two options seem more complex (especially when you're new to Web design) these two sizes are popular for line spacing, as well as other settings, because the size is adjusted relative to the displayed text size. This can get confusing, but essentially, em and ex work similarly to percentages and are even better at adapting to different user settings and monitor sizes.

After you select the Type options for your style sheet, click Apply to apply them, and click OK to save the settings and close the CSS Rule Definition dialog box.

The Background category

The Background category in the CSS Rule Definition dialog box (see Figure 5-8) enables you to specify a background color or image for a style and to control how the background will be displayed on the page. You can use background style settings for any element of your Web page that can display a background, including `<div>` tags and Heading tags. For example, you could alter the `<body>` tag and include background settings that apply to the entire page, or you could create an ID style with a background setting that would add a background color only to an individual `<div>` tag. By including the background in the ID style of a `<div>` tag, you can limit the background to only display where the `<div>` tag is used.

In the example shown in Figure 5-8, I've defined the rule for an ID style named `#mainContent` to include a background image, which I'm further defining with the No-Repeat option. Another advantage of CSS is that it includes more precise control of background images than is possible with HTML, which by default, repeats a background image across and down a page.

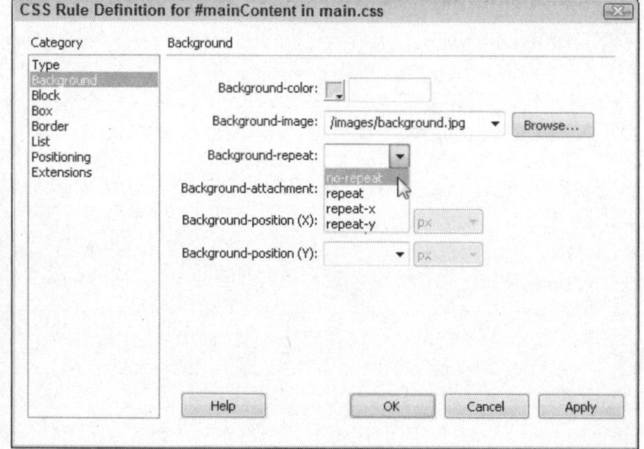

Figure 5-8: The Background category in the CSS Rule Definition dialog box.

You can choose from these Background options:

- **Background-Color:** Specifies the background color of a defined style. You can use the color well to open a Web-safe color palette in which you can select predefined colors or create custom colors.
- **Background-Image:** Enables you to select a background image as part of the style definition. Click the Browse button to select the image.
- **Background-Repeat:** Determines how and whether the background image tiles across and down the page. In all cases, the image is cropped if it doesn't fit behind the element to which the style is applied. The Repeat options are
  - **No-Repeat:** The background is displayed once at the top, left of the element.
  - **Repeat:** The background image repeats vertically and horizontally in the background of the element.
  - **Repeat-X:** The background repeats horizontally, but not vertically, in the background of the element.
  - **Repeat-Y:** The background repeats vertically, but not horizontally, in the background of the element.

- **Background-Attachment:** This property determines how the background behaves when the page is scrolled.
    - **Fixed:** The background remains glued to one place in the viewing area and doesn't scroll out of sight even when the Web page is scrolled.
    - **Scroll:** The background scrolls along with the Web page.
- **Background-Position (X):** Enables you to align the image left, center, or right, or to set a numeric value to determine the precise horizontal placement of the background. You can use horizontal positioning only with no-repeat or with repeat-y.
- **Background Position (Y):** Enables you to align the image top, center, or bottom, or to set a numeric value to determine the precise vertical placement of the background. You can use vertical positioning only with no-repeat or repeat-x.

The Block category

The Block category (see Figure 5-9) defines the spacing and alignment settings and is commonly used for styles that will define the display of text on a Web page.

You can choose from these Block category options:

- **Word-Spacing:** Defines the amount of white space inserted between words in points, millimeters (mm), centimeters (cm), picas, inches, pixels, ems, and exs.

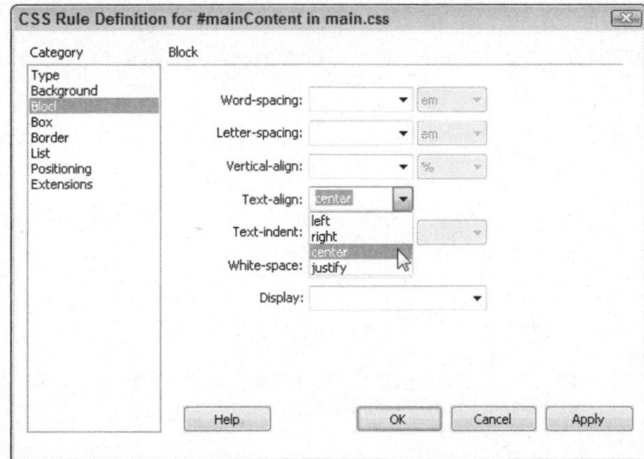

Figure 5-9: The Block category in the CSS Rule Definition dialog box.

- **Letter-Spacing:** Defines the amount of white space inserted between letters in points, millimeters (mm), centimeters (cm), picas, inches, pixels, ems, and exs.
- **Vertical-Align:** Aligns inline elements, such as text and images, in relation to the elements that surround them. Your options are Baseline, Sub, Super, Top, Text-Top, Middle, Bottom, and Text-Bottom, or you can set a numeric value. Note that not all Web browsers support all these options.
- **Text-Align:** Enables you to left, right, center, or justify your text. You can use this setting, for example, as part of the definition of an ID style when you want to align the contents of a <div> tag, such as centering the text in a footer.
- **Text-Indent:** Specifies how far the first line of text is indented. Negative numbers are allowed if you want the first line to begin off the page.
- **White-Space:** Tells the browser how to handle line breaks and spaces within a block of text. Your options are Normal, Pre (for preformatted), and Nowrap, which prevents elements from being separated if they must wrap to fit within a browser window or other container.
- **Display:** Indicates how to render an element in the browser. For example, you can hide an element by choosing None and change the positioning of an unordered list from horizontal to vertical, by choosing Inline.

The Box category

The Box category (see Figure 5-10) defines settings for positioning and spacing. As you can read in Chapter 6, these settings are ideal for creating page layouts with ID styles to position <div> tags.

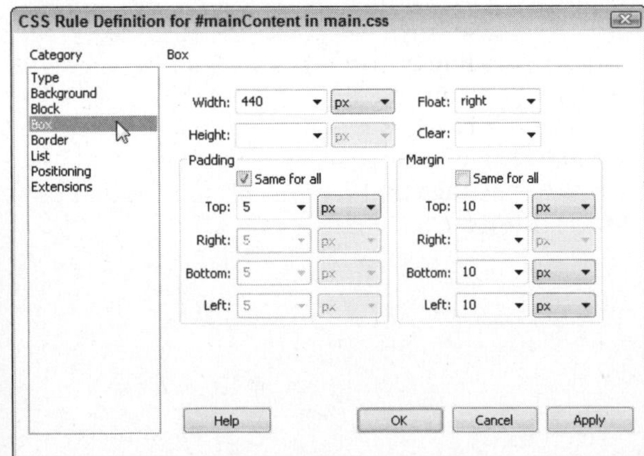

Figure 5-10: The Box category in the CSS Rule Definition dialog box.

You can use the Box category properties to set:

- **Width:** Enables you to specify a width for any element that can have its dimensions specified, such as a <div> tag. You can use pixels, points, inches, centimeters, millimeters, picas, ems, exs, or percentages for your measurements.
- **Height:** Enables you to specify a height for any element that can have its dimensions specified. ***Note:*** The height field is often left empty to enable elements, such as <div> tags, to expand to fit their contents.
- **Float:** Enables you to align elements, such as images and <div> tags, to the left or right of a page or other container causing text or other elements wrap around it.
- **Clear:** Prevents floating content from overlapping an area to the left or right, or to both sides of an element. This is a useful option for preventing overlapping of elements, especially when the Float option is used.
- **Padding:** Sets the amount of space within the borders of an element. For example, you can use padding to create space between the borders of a <div> tag and its contents. You can set padding separately for the top, right, bottom, and left. Padding is measured in pixels, points, inches, centimeters, millimeters, picas, ems, exs, and percentages.
- **Margin:** Sets the amount of space around the outside of an element. Margins can be used to create space between the edge of an element and other elements on the page, such as between an image and text or between two <div> tags. You can set the margin separately for the top, right, bottom, and left. Padding is measured in pixels, points, inches, centimeters, millimeters, picas, ems, exs, and percentages.

The Border category

The Border category defines settings — such as Width, Color, and Style — and are commonly used to define borders around images, tables, and <div> tags. As shown in Figure 5-11, you can specify border settings on all four sides of an element or create borders only on one, two, or three sides of an element. With this technique, you can use the border settings to create dividing lines between <div> tags that create columns or add separating lines above or below elements.

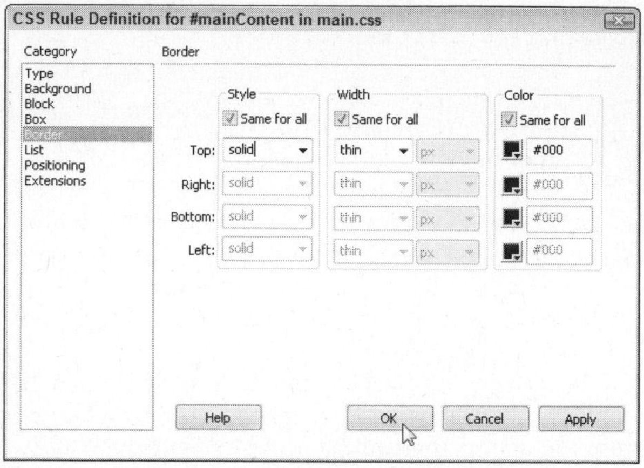

Figure 5-11: The Border category in the CSS Rule Definition dialog box.

The List category

The List category defines settings, such as the size and type of bullets for list tags. You can specify whether bullets are disc, circle, square, decimal, lower-roman, upper-roman, lower-alpha, upper-alpha, or none (see Figure 5-12). Choose None if you want to use the list tag with no bullet. If you want to use a custom bullet, you can use the Browse button to insert an image to be used as the bullet. You can also control the location of the list bullet in relation to the list item. In Chapter 6, you find instructions for redefining the unordered list tag to create rollover effects for links, a popular option for creating navigation rows and other collections, or lists, of links.

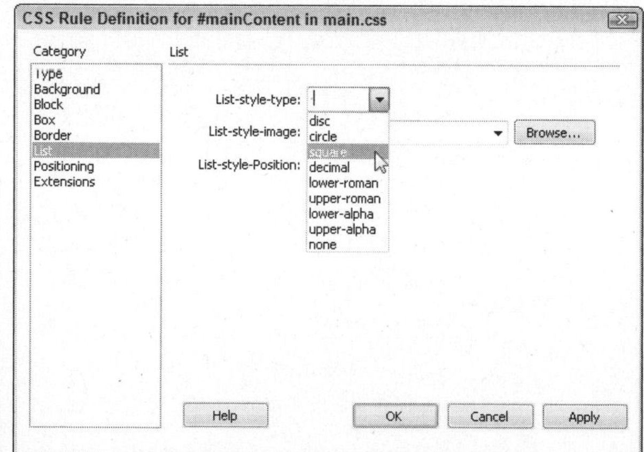

Figure 5-12: The List category in the CSS Rule Definition dialog box.

The Positioning category

The Positioning category (see Figure 5-13) enables you to alter the way elements are positioned on a page. As you can read in Chapter 6, positioning can dramatically change the way block-level elements appear in a browser. Block-level elements include table, list, header, paragraph, and `<div>` tags. For example, AP Divs in Dreamweaver are simply `<div>` tags that use absolute positioning to place elements in a specific part of a page.

To understand how positioning works, it's important to know that positioning is always determined relative to something else, such as another element on the page or the browser window. How you set up positioning depends on where your element is on the page and whether the element is inside another element, such as a `<div>` tag. Here are the Positioning options:

- **Position:** Enables you to specify the position of an element, such as a `<div>` tag. Options include
  - **Absolute:** Uses the top and left coordinates to control the position of an element relative to the upper-left corner of the browser window or the upper-left corner of an element that contains the element. (For example, the positioning of an AP Div contained within another AP Div is based on the position of the first AP Div.)
  - **Fixed:** Positions an element relative to the top-left corner of the browser. The content of an element using fixed positioning remains constant even if the user scrolls down or across the page.
  - **Relative:** Uses a position relative to the point where you insert the element into the page or relative to its container.
  - **Static:** By default, all HTML elements that can be positioned are static, which simply places the content at its location within the flow of the document.

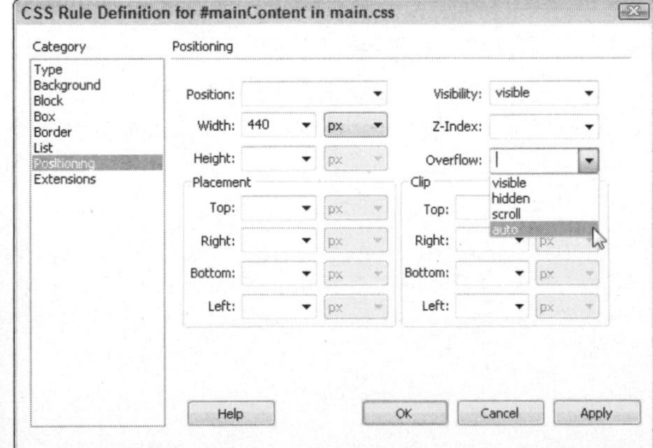

Figure 5-13: The Positioning category in the CSS Rule Definition dialog box.

- **Width, Height:** Enables you to specify a width and height that you can use in styles you apply to images, <div> tags, or any other element that can have its dimensions specified. These settings are the same as the Width and Height in the Box category and entering a value in either category caused the same value to appear in the other.
- **Placement:** Defines the size and location of an element within its containing element. For example, you can set the right edge of the element to line up with the right edge of the element that contains it. You can specify the Top, Right, Bottom, and Left options separately and you can use pixels, points, inches, centimeters, millimeters, picas, ems, exs, or percentages for your measurements.
- **Visibility:** Enables you to control whether the browser displays the element. You can use this feature, combined with a scripting language, such as JavaScript, to dynamically change the display of elements. For example, you can cause an element to appear on a page only when a user clicks a button and then make it disappear when the button is clicked again. The Visibility options are
  - **Inherit:** The element has the visibility of the element in which it's contained. This is the default.
  - **Visible:** The element is displayed.
  - **Hidden:** The element isn't displayed.
- **Z-Index:** Controls the position of an element, such as an AP Div, on the Z-coordinate, which controls the stacking order in relation to other elements on the page. Higher-numbered elements overlap lower-numbered elements.
- **Overflow:** Tells the browser how to display the contents of an element if the container, such as a <div> tag, can't fit the entire elements entire size.
  - **Visible:** Keeps content, such as an image or text, visible, even if it expands beyond the defined height or width of a container.
  - **Hidden:** Cuts off the contents if they exceed the size of the container. This option doesn't provide scroll bars.
  - **Scroll:** Adds scroll bars to the container regardless of whether the contents exceed the element's size.
  - **Auto:** Makes scroll bars appear only when a container's contents exceed its boundaries.
- **Clip:** When the content of an element overflows the space allotted and you set the Overflow property to Scroll or Auto, you can set the Clip settings to specify which part of the element is visible by controlling which part of the element is cropped if it doesn't fit in the display area.

The Extensions category

Extensions (see Figure 5-14) include filters and cursor options:

- **Page-Break:** Can be set for before or after an element to insert a point in a page where a printer sees a page break. This option enables you to better control the way a page is printed.
- **Cursor:** Defines the type of cursor that appears when a user moves the cursor over an element.
- **Filter:** Enables you to apply special effects, such as drop shadows and motion blurs. These are visible only in Microsoft Internet Explorer.

Now that you have the overview of all these options, here's another tip. You don't *have* to specify any of these settings when you create a new style in Dreamweaver. Any options you leave blank are controlled by the browser's default settings or other styles already applied to the page. For example, if you don't specify a text color in a class style named `.caption`, the text formatted with the style will remain black, the default color in most Web browsers, unless it has already been formatted by another style, such as a style that changes the color of all the text on a page. (You find instructions for changing the text color for an entire page in the "Using Page Properties to create styles for page-wide settings," later in this chapter.)

Figure 5-14: The Extensions category in the CSS Rule Definition dialog box.

Using the CSS Styles Panel

The CSS Styles panel, as shown in Figures 5-15 and 5-16, provides a great place to view, manage, organize, and edit CSS rules. To open the CSS styles panel, choose Window⇨CSS Styles or click the small double-arrow at the top of the panel group and then double-click CSS Styles.

You can also rename styles in the CSS Styles panel, but be careful. There are two ways to rename styles in the CSS Styles panel, and only one automatically changes the corresponding HTML code. If you don't change the name of a style in the style sheet and any place the style's used in your Web site code, the style no longer works. See the section, "Editing an existing style," later in this chapter, for details on this important difference and how to rename styles without breaking them. You find instructions for organizing style sheets in the section, "Moving, copying, and editing styles in an external style sheet," later in this chapter.

When you work with the CSS Styles panel, you can switch between two modes, accessible by clicking the All or Current tabs at the top-left of the panel. The following sections explain each mode in more detail.

Working with the big picture in All mode

The All tab, which is selected by default, displays a list of *all* the CSS rules defined in a document's internal style sheet and any attached external style sheets. When the CSS Styles panel is in All mode, you can do the following:

- **See the styles in a style sheet:** To view the styles in an internal or external style sheet in the CSS Styles panel, click the plus sign (the triangle on the Mac) to open the style sheet within the panel. You'll find the arrow (or triangle) next to the `<style>` tag if you're using an internal style sheet or next to the style sheet name if you're using an external style sheet attached to the page. Figure 5-15 shows a page with both internal and external style sheets.
- **View style properties:** Select a style in the CSS Styles panel, and its properties are displayed in the Properties pane at the bottom of the CSS Styles panel.
- **Edit styles:** Notice in Figure 5-15 that the h1 style is selected in the CSS Styles panel, and the definition of the style is displayed in the Properties pane at the bottom of the panel. You can edit existing styles by typing or using the drop-down lists in the Properties pane (these handy lists appear when you place your cursor in a field and are great for making quick changes). If you prefer to edit a style in the CSS Rule definition dialog box, described in detail in the previous section, double-click any style name and it opens automatically in the CSS Rule definition dialog box.

If you don't see any styles listed in the CSS Styles panel when the All tab is selected, you probably haven't defined any styles for the document or attached an external style sheet. Occasionally, however, the styles in an external style sheet won't display, even if the name appears in the Styles panel. (I've seen this happen sometimes when I open a file that was created in a previous version of Dreamweaver.) In this case, an easy solution is to simply reattach the style sheet by clicking the Attach Style Sheet icon (as shown in Figure 5-15), browsing to find the style sheet, and selecting it.

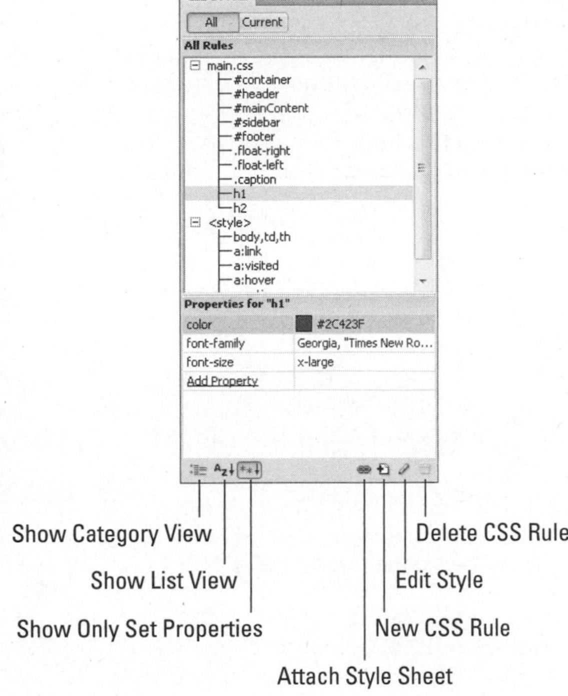

Figure 5-15: The CSS Styles panel, showing all the styles associated with the open document.

Looking closer at styles in Current mode

When you select the Current tab at the top left of the CSS Styles panel, you can view the styles *currently* applied to any selected element on a page, as shown in Figure 5-16.

Current mode is useful for identifying how styles are applied to a particular element and for troubleshooting when styles conflict.

The Current mode has three sections: the Summary for Selection pane, the About pane, and the Properties pane.

- **In the Summary for Selection pane,** you see the rules currently defined for the selected style. This pane is especially useful when you've created a complicated layout and are trying to understand how different styles may be affecting the same element.
- **In the About pane,** you see a text description of where a formatting option is defined for any rule selected in the Summary of Selection.
- **In the Properties pane,** you can edit, add, or delete style rules just as you can in All mode.

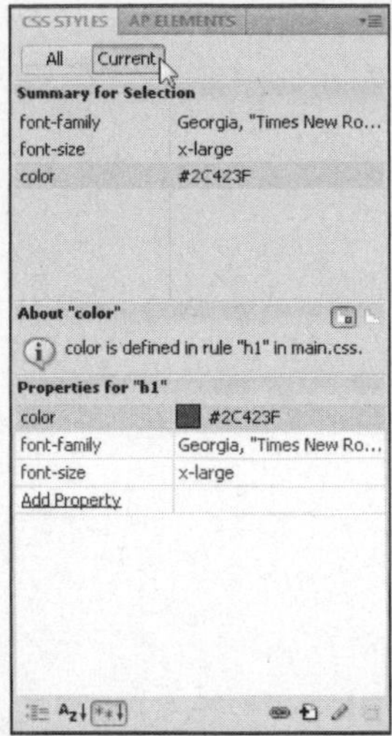

Figure 5-16: The Current mode of the CSS Styles panel, showing the styles applied to a headline selected in the open document.

Creating, attaching, and listing styles

In the bottom left of the CSS Styles panel, as shown in Figure 5-15, you see three small icons that make it easy to change among the Show Category, Show List, and Show Only Set Properties views. These options apply to the Properties pane in both Current and All modes. Here's how they work:

- **Show Category View:** Dreamweaver displays all the properties available for a selected rule organized by the category to which they belong. For example, all the font properties are grouped into a Font category.
- **Show List View:** Dreamweaver displays all the properties available to use for a rule organized alphabetically.
- **Show Only Set Properties:** In this view, Dreamweaver displays only the properties you've defined for a selected rule. This is the default setting, and the option shown in Figure 5-15. With this view option, get a quick look at the settings for the selected style.

The second set of icons, on the bottom right of the CSS Styles panel (also shown in Figure 5-15) aren't dependent on the view settings. From left to right, these icons represent

- **Attach Style Sheet:** Click this icon and browse to find any existing style sheet in a site to attach it to the open page.
- **New CSS Rule:** Click this icon to open the New CSS Rule dialog box and create a new style.

- **Edit Style:** Click this icon to open any style selected in the CSS Styles panel in the CSS Rule definition dialog box where you can edit it.
- **Delete CSS Rule:** Select any style name in the CSS Styles panel and click this trash icon to delete it.

Switching between CSS and HTML Mode in the Property Inspector

In CS4, Dreamweaver added new CSS controls to the Property inspector, a welcome addition designed to make it easier to create and edit styles as you format text and other elements on your pages.

In previous versions of Dreamweaver, the Property inspector displayed all the settings at once, but in CS4, the Property inspector was split into two sections. In Figure 5-17, you see the HTML mode of the Property inspector. In Figure 5-18, you see the CSS mode. Notice that there are buttons on the left side of the Property inspector to make switching between these two modes easy.

Figure 5-17: The HTML mode of the Property inspector.

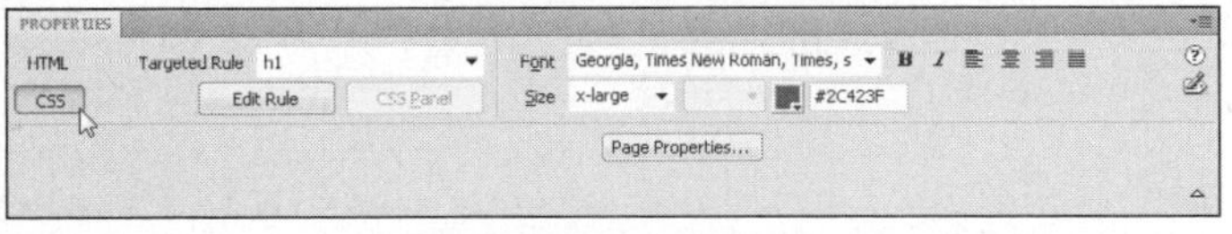

Figure 5-18: The CSS mode of the Property inspector.

If you're new to CSS and HTML, it can be a little confusing at first to understand the differences between these two modes. Essentially, if you use the formatting icons, such as bold and italic, in HTML mode, Dreamweaver adds HTML tags and attributes. If you use these same icons in CSS mode, Dreamweaver launches the New CSS Rule dialog box so that you can create a style that includes these formatting options.

In CSS mode, you can also choose to edit existing styles to add new formatting options to styles that are already applied to the page. This means that you can edit existing styles by simply selecting the style from the Targeted Rule drop-down list and then using the Font, Size, and other fields in the Property inspector to make any changes or additions.

Any time you edit an existing style that has already been applied to elements on a page, the changes you make to the style are automatically applied anywhere the style is used.

On the other hand, say you want to apply an existing style to an element on the page. For example, if you want to align an image with a class style or apply an ID style to a `<div>` tag, you want to be in HTML mode. To apply a style in this mode, select the element in the page where you want to apply the style and then use the Class or ID drop-down lists to select the style; Dreamweaver automatically applies it.

Similarly, if you want to apply an HTML tag, such as the Heading 1 tag, you want to be in HTML mode, but if you want to create or edit a CSS rule for the H1 tag, you want to do that from the CSS mode.

Using Class and Tag Styles in Dreamweaver

In the following sections, you find instructions for putting Dreamweaver's style features to use to create, apply, and edit styles with the class and tag selectors. In Chapter 6, you find instructions for working with styles created with the ID and compound selectors.

As you go through the steps to create a new style in Dreamweaver, you may be surprised by the number of options in the many panels and dialog boxes available for creating CSS. Remember, you can always refer to the descriptions of these many options, which are covered in detail in the earlier sections of this chapter.

Creating styles with the class selector

Using styles to format text in Dreamweaver is a relatively simple process. First, you define a style and then, as you see in the following steps, you apply it to an element on the page. In this section, you walk through the process of creating a class style that can be applied to any element on a page. In this example, you'll create a `.caption` class style and then, in the next section, you'll use `.caption` to format the text under a photo.

To define a new class style, create a new document or open an existing file, and then follow these steps:

1. **Choose Format⇨CSS Styles⇨New.**

   Alternatively, you can click the New CSS Rule icon at the bottom of the CSS Styles panel (refer to Figure 5-15).

   The New CSS Rule dialog box appears, as shown in Figure 5-19.

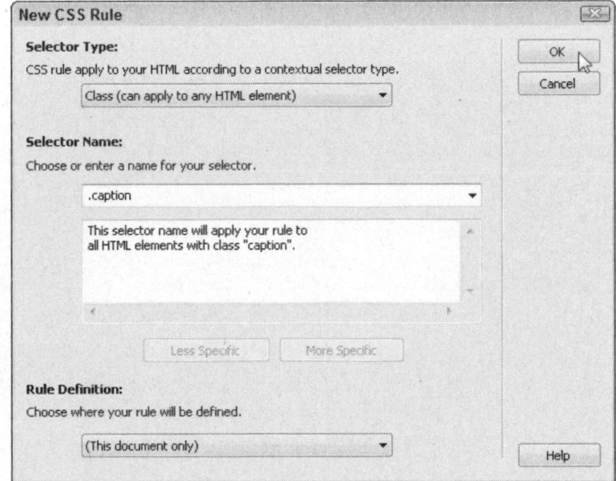

Figure 5-19: The New CSS Rule dialog box.

2. **Choose a selector type.**

   To create a class style, choose (you guessed it) Class from the Selector Type drop-down list.

3. **In the Selector Name field, type a new name for the style beginning with a dot (.).**

   For this example, type **.caption**.

   You can name a class style anything you like, as long as you don't use spaces or punctuation, but class style names must begin with a dot (.). If you choose the Class option and neglect to enter a dot at the beginning of the name, Dreamweaver adds one for you.

4. **From the Rule Definition drop-down list, choose This Document Only to create the new style in an internal style sheet.**

   An internal style sheet applies only to the current page. When you select this option, the style will be created and added to the top of the open HTML page in the `<head>` section.

   If you prefer, you can choose the New Style Sheet File option to create a new external style sheet as you create the style, or you can use the drop-down list to select any existing style sheet already attached to the page and add the new style to it.

5. **Click OK.**

   The CSS Rule Definition dialog box opens, as shown in Figure 5-20.

6. **Choose a category from the left of the CSS Rule Definition dialog box.**

   For this example, choose the Type category, as shown in Figure 5-20. (For a detailed description of each of the categories, refer to the "Comparing CSS Rule Options" section, earlier in this chapter.)

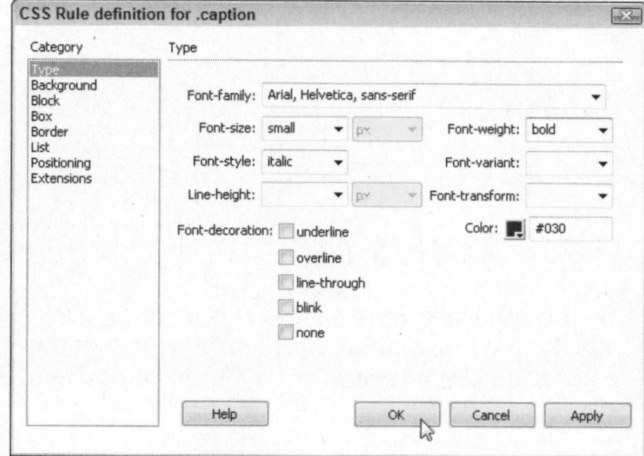

Figure 5-20: The Type category of the CSS Rule Definition dialog box.

7. **In the Font-Family field, choose a font list collection from the drop-down list or enter the name of a font.**

   For this example, I chose Arial, Helvetica, sans-serif. To use a font that isn't included, choose the Edit Font List option from the drop-down list and create a new font list using your own fonts. (For more on using fonts on the Web, see the sidebar, "Why so many fonts?" earlier in this chapter.)

8. **In the Font-Size drop-down list, choose the size you want for your caption style.**

   For this example, I chose Small. You can specify text sizes in pixels, picas, mm, and several other measurements. For an explanation of options, see the sidebar "Understanding CSS size options," earlier in this chapter.

9. **In the Font-Style drop-down list, choose a font style.**

   In this example, I chose Italic.

10. **In the Font-Weight drop-down list, choose a weight.**

    For this example, I chose Bold.

11. Click the color well and choose a color for the style.

Sticking to the default color swatches in the color well (the square icon) is certainly the quickest way to choose a color, but you can also create custom colors by clicking the icon that looks like a rainbow-colored globe in the upper-right corner of the color well and selecting a color from the System Color Picker. For this example, I chose a dark green color.

12. Click OK.

The new style name is added to the CSS panel, as shown in Figure 5-21, a little later in this chapter. If the new style isn't visible, click the plus sign (+) (or triangle on the Mac) next to the `<style>` tag to reveal the rules in the current style.

When you create a class style, such as the `.caption` style in this example, it's also added to the Class drop-down list in the Property inspector, as you see in the following section.

Applying class styles in Dreamweaver

Defining class styles in Dreamweaver is the time-consuming part. Applying them after you define them is the *time-saving* part. How you apply a style depends on the kind of style you've created. To apply a class style in Dreamweaver, follow these steps:

1. Open an existing document or create a new one and add some text, and then click and drag to select the text or other element to which you want to apply a style.

In this example, I've selected the text under the photograph in the page shown in Figure 5-21.

2. In the Property inspector (with the HTML features displayed), select the style from the Class drop-down list.

Notice that Dreamweaver provides a preview of the style by formatting the name in the drop-down list based on the specified options in the style definition (in this example, the `.caption` style is displayed as bold, italic, and green). When you choose a style, the selected text or other element automatically changes in the Document window to reflect the application of the style. In Figure 5-21, you see the caption style created in the previous exercise applied to the text below the photograph.

Another way to apply a style is to select an image, text, or other element and then choose the name of the style from the menu you see when you choose Format➪CSS Styles. You can also right-click (Control-click on the Mac), choose CSS Styles, and select a style name from the list of defined styles. I like to use the Property inspector because it's the only method that lets you preview how the style appears before applying it.

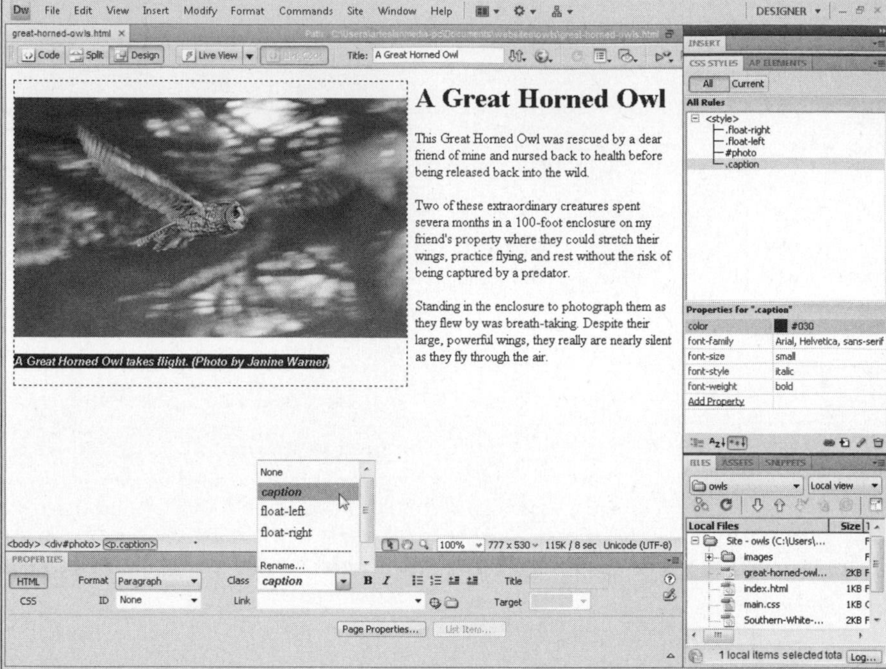

Figure 5-21: To apply a class style, select the text or other element in the main workspace, and then choose the style from the Class drop-down list in the Property inspector.

Removing class styles in Dreamweaver

To remove a class style from a selected text block or other element, make sure the Property inspector is in HTML mode, select the element where the style is applied in the Web page, and choose None from the Class drop-down list in the Property inspector (you can see this option in Figure 5-21).

You can also remove a style by right-clicking the tag the style is applied to in the tag selector at the very bottom of the workspace. The tag selector is a great feature for quick edits and for identifying elements on the page. As you see in Figure 5-22, when you right-click a tag name, a pop-up menu appears. If you don't see the tag that you want to edit in the tag selector, click to select the element in the Web page and the corresponding tag should appear in the tag selector. To remove or change a style using the tag selector, right-click the tag and then choose Class➪Set Class➪None to remove it, or select another class style from the menu to change the applied style.

Creating styles with the tag selector

In addition to creating new class styles, you can create styles that redefine existing HTML tags. When you create a style in the New CSS Rule dialog box using the tag selector option, you can alter the appearance, position, and other features of any an existing HTML tag.

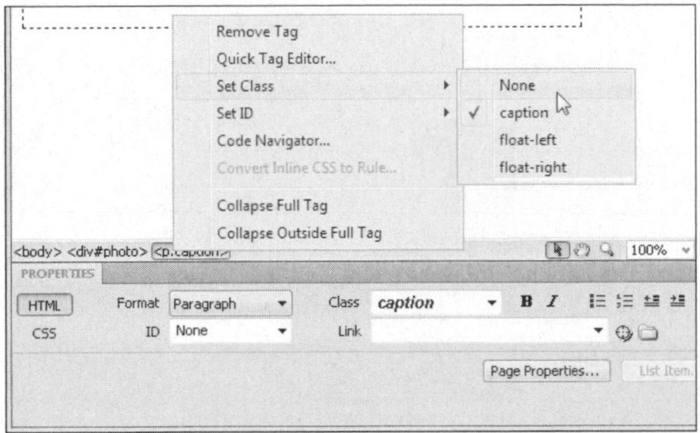

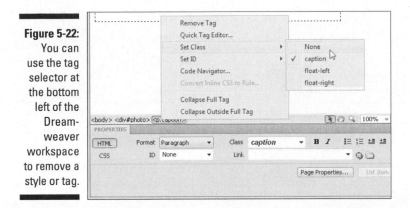

Figure 5-22: You can use the tag selector at the bottom left of the Dreamweaver workspace to remove a style or tag.

Because HTML tags already include formatting options, (for example, the Heading tags include formatting to style text in large and bold), when you create a style with a Tag selector, you have to consider the formatting options already associated with that tag. Any options you specify in the CSS Rule Definition dialog box will either be added to the existing formatting created by the tag, or the new rules will override the existing style. For example, in the exercise that follows, I redefine the `<h1>` tag by changing the headline font to Georgia, which will take the place of the default font Times, but I don't need to make bold part of the style definition because it's already included in the style for an `<h1>` tag.

When you redefine an existing HTML tag, you don't need to apply the style for the formatting to change. Wherever you've applied the HTML tag, the style definition settings are applied automatically.

You may ask "Why would I redefine the `<h1>` tag instead of just creating a new headline style as a class style?" or "What's the best scenario for using each of these options?" In "Creating styles with the class selector" earlier in this chapter, you find out how to create a new style class that you can *selectively* apply to any block of text on your page. But at times, using an existing HTML tag is better. Heading styles are especially important because they're well recognized on the Web as indicators of the most important text on a page.

To redefine an HTML tag, such as the `<h1>` tag, with the tag selector, create a new file or open an existing one and then follow these steps:

1. **Choose Format⇨CSS Styles⇨New.**

   Alternatively, you can right-click (Option-click on a Mac) anywhere in the CSS panel and choose New, or you can click the New CSS Rule icon at the bottom right of the CSS panel. The icon looks like a small plus (+) sign.

   The New CSS Rule dialog box opens, as shown in Figure 5-23.

2. **Choose Tag from the Selector Type drop-down list.**
3. **Choose the HTML tag you want to redefine from the Selector Name drop-down list.**

   You can also type to enter the name of a tag into the Selector Name field. In this example, I selected h1 to redefine the H1 heading tag.

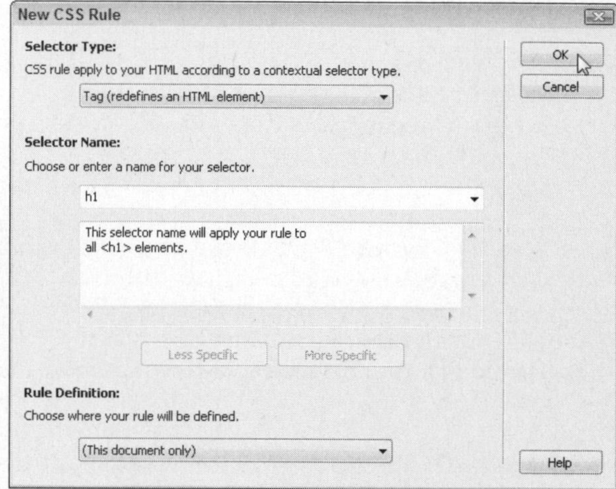

Figure 5-23: Use the tag selector to redefine an existing HTML tag, such as the <h1> tag.

4. **From the Rule Definition drop-down list, choose the This Document Only option to create the new style in an internal style sheet.**

   If you prefer, you can choose the New Style Sheet File option to create a new external style sheet as you create the style, or you can use the drop-down list to select any existing style sheet already attached to the page and add the new style to it.

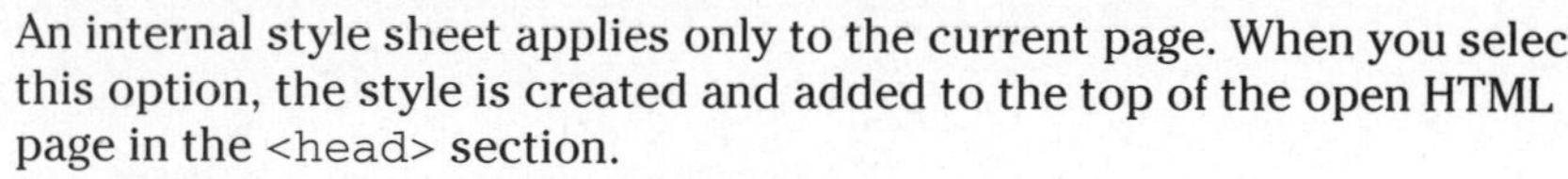

   An internal style sheet applies only to the current page. When you select this option, the style is created and added to the top of the open HTML page in the `<head>` section.

5. **Click OK.**

   The CSS Rule definition dialog box opens.

6. **Choose a category and specify the options you want to use to redefine the new tag style.**

   For this example, I redefined the `<h1>` tag to use the Georgia font instead of the default browser font, changed the size to extra large, and changed the text color to dark green.

7. **Click OK.**

   Any text or other element that you've already formatted with the HTML tag immediately changes to reflect the formatting in the new tag style definition.

If you want to be able to use the same HTML tag with different style definitions, you can create compound styles, as described in Chapter 6. See "Understanding style selectors" earlier in this chapter for an introduction to the different types.

Editing an existing style

You can change the attributes of any style after you create it by editing its style definitions. This is where some of the biggest advantages of Cascading Style Sheets come into play. You can make global changes to a page or even to an entire Web site by changing a style because when you edit the style, the changes are automatically applied to every element where you used the style. This is one of the reasons that external style sheets are so valuable because you can create styles that are used on any or all the pages in a site. Beware, however, that this can also lead to problems. If you decide that you want to edit a style when you use it on a new page, don't forget that you'll be changing the formatting everywhere else you've already used that style. In some cases, you may be better off creating new styles, rather than editing old styles.

You can create new styles by duplicating an existing style, giving it a new name, and then altering the style definitions. This is a time-saving trick when you want to create a new style that is similar to an existing one.

To edit an existing style, follow these steps:

1. **Open the CSS Styles panel by choosing Window⇨CSS Styles.**
2. **Select the name of an existing style in the CSS panel.**

   The corresponding definition settings are displayed in the Properties pane below it.
3. **Select any of the settings in the Properties pane and edit them.**

   Alternatively, you can double-click the name of any style in the CSS Styles panel to launch the CSS Rule Definition dialog box and edit the style there.

   - **If you edit a style definition in the Properties panel,** the changes are applied automatically as soon as you press the Return or Enter key or click outside the formatting field in the panel.
   - **If you edit a style in the CSS Rule Definition dialog box,** changes are applied automatically when you click the Apply button.
4. **Click OK to apply the changes and close the dialog box.**

Renaming existing styles

You can rename a CSS style in the CSS Styles panel in much the same way you'd rename a filename in the Files panel, by clicking to select the name and then typing a new name. Beware, however, that renaming a style in this way doesn't change its corresponding reference in the HTML code of your Web pages. If you change a name in the CSS Styles panel by simply typing a new name like this, you must also manually change the name in the corresponding page code, which can get complicated if you've used the style in many places.

For example, if you create an `.imagecaption` style and apply it to text in your Web page, and then later you decide to shorten the name of the style to `.caption`, make sure that every place you've used that style in your site is updated in the code where it's been applied, or the link to the style sheet will be broken.

If you want to rename a style and update the style references in the code at the same time, open any page where the style is used and follow these instructions:

1. **Open the CSS Styles panel by choosing Window⇨CSS Styles.**
2. **Right-click (Control-click) the name of an existing style in the CSS panel.**
3. **Choose Rename Class, as shown in Figure 5-24.**

   The Rename dialog box opens. (If you select a style created with another selector type, the options change. For example, if you select an ID style, the option will be Rename ID.)
4. **Type a new name in the New name field and click OK.**

   If you've already applied the style and the style is saved in an external style sheet, a dialog box opens offering to "Use Find and Replace to fix the documents that use this style?".

   If the style you want to rename is saved in an internal style sheet, the name will automatically be changed in the code anywhere the style has been applied. With internal style sheets, the Find and Replace dialog box does not open and you do not have all the options in this exercise. However, any changes that are made will be displayed in the Results panel, which automatically opens at the bottom of the workspace.
5. **Click Yes to automatically update references to the style in the code with the new style name.**

   The Find and Replace dialog box opens (see Figure 5-25) with the necessary search strings already filled in. Don't change these settings unless you know what you're doing with these advanced search strings and want to alter the way Dreamweaver renames the style.

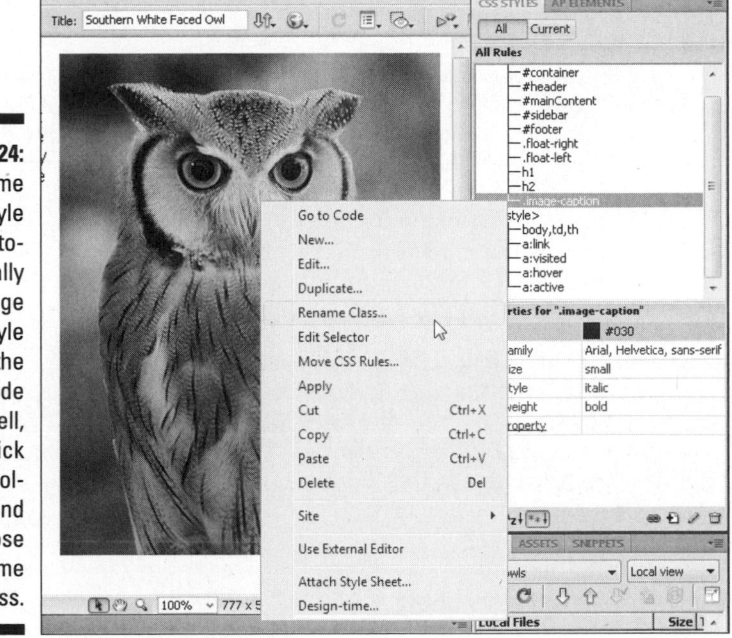

Figure 5-24: To rename a style and automatically change the style name in the page code as well, right-click (Control-click) and choose Rename Class.

6. **Click Replace All to automatically update all references to the style in the code.**

   Dreamweaver warns you that this operation can't be undone, but you can always rename the style again by repeating these steps if you change your mind.

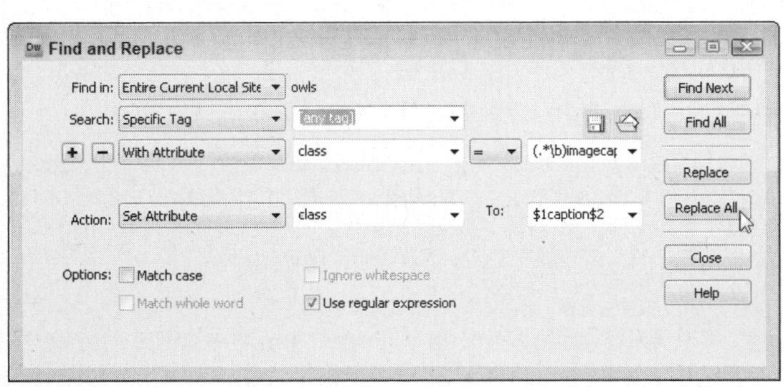

Figure 5-25: Dreamweaver automatically sets up the necessary search strings in the Find and Replace dialog box when you use the Rename style option.

Using Page Properties to Create Styles for Page-Wide Settings, such as Links

If you're like many designers, you probably don't like the underline that automatically appears under all the linked text in a Web page. In this section, you discover how easy it is to remove that underline and change the color, font face, and size for the links with Dreamweaver's Page Properties dialog box. You can also change other page-wide settings, such as the background color and page margins, from the Page Properties dialog box.

Although you can change link styles by redefining the anchor tag, as you'd create any style with a tag selector, the easiest way to alter all your link styles at once is to change them in the Page Properties dialog box. When you use this option, Dreamweaver automatically creates the corresponding tag selector styles and lists them in the CSS Styles panel. Other page-wide settings in this dialog box work similarly.

To change hyperlink and other styles with the Page Properties dialog box, open an existing page or create a new one and follow these steps:

1. **Choose Modify⇨Page Properties.**

   Alternatively, you can click the Page Properties button in the Property inspector. The Page Properties dialog box appears.

2. **In the Appearance (CSS) category, which is displayed when the Page Properties dialog box opens, you can specify page-wide font options, set a background color or image, and adjust the margins on a page.**

   When you alter these settings, Dreamweaver automatically creates a new style rule for the Body tag. If you want to edit these settings further in the future, you can do so by editing the Body tag or by returning to the Page Properties dialog box.

3. **Select the Links (CSS) category on the left of the Page Properties dialog box, as shown in Figure 5-26.**

4. **Specify a font face and size for your links.**

   If you want to use the same font size and face for your links as you use in the rest of the text on your page, it's best to leave these options blank; then if you change the text settings for the page, you won't have to remember to change them for your links as well.

5. **Specify colors for each hyperlink state by clicking in the corresponding color well and selecting a color from the Color dialog box.**

   You can change any or all the link color settings. If you don't specify a link color, the browser uses the default link color. Here's an explanation of each of the four link states:

- **Link Color:** The color in which your links appear when the page is first loaded and the linked page hasn't yet been visited by the browser. The corresponding HTML tag is <a:link>.
- **Visited Links:** The color your links change to after a browser has already viewed the linked page. The corresponding HTML tag is <a:visited>.
- **Rollover Links:** The color a link changes to as a user rolls a cursor over a link. The corresponding HTML tag is <a:hover>.
- **Active Links:** The color a link changes to as a user is actively clicking a link. The corresponding HTML tag is <a:active>.

6. **Select a style from the Underline Style drop-down list.**

   Many designers prefer to remove the underline that automatically appears under linked text by choosing Never Underline, as shown in Figure 5-26.

7. **Click OK.**

   The Page Properties dialog box closes, the style settings are automatically applied to any links on the page, and the corresponding styles are added to the CSS panel.

To fully test link styles, preview your page in a Web browser or click the Live View button at the top of the workspace. It's good practice to test link settings in a browser when you make changes like the ones in the preceding exercise. Take a look at how your links appear; for example, do the active and visited link colors look good against the background color of the page. Remember that any styles you create using the Page Properties dialog box affect *all* links on your page unless you specifically apply a different style to an individual link that overrides the redefined tag style. If you want to use different link styles in different parts of the same page, you can create compound styles, covered in Chapter 6.

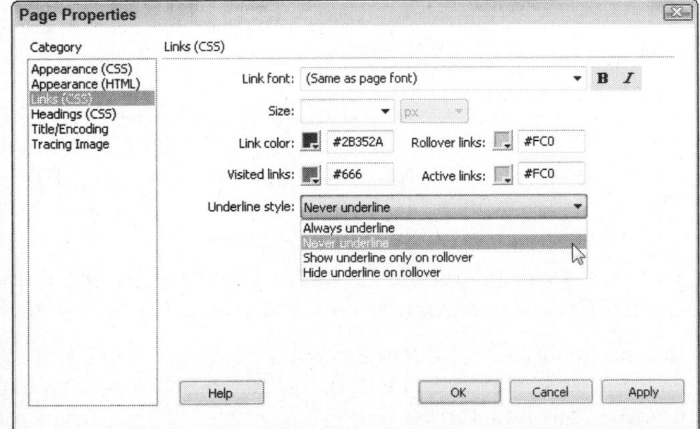

Figure 5-26: Use the Links (CSS) category in the Page Properties dialog box to change the style definitions for all four hyperlink states.

Using External Style Sheets

External style sheets (or *linked style sheets*) offer the greatest advantages with CSS. You can define styles for common formatting options used throughout an entire site, such as headlines, captions, and even images, which makes applying multiple formatting options to elements fast and easy. Using external style sheets also makes global changes easier because when you change a style in an external style sheet, you automatically change every element to which you applied the style throughout the site.

Internal style sheet information is stored in the Head section of the HTML code of the document you're working on, and styles in an internal style sheet can be applied only to the current document. If you want to create styles that you can share among multiple documents, use external style sheets. Don't worry if you've already created a bunch of styles in an internal style sheet and now wish they were in an external one — as you'll discover in this exercise, it's easy to move styles from one kind of style sheet to another.

Creating an external style sheet

You create external style sheets almost exactly the same way you create internal style sheets, except that external style sheets need to be saved as separate files. When you use Dreamweaver to create a new style, you have the option of creating that style in a new or existing external style sheet. If you choose to create a new style in a new external style sheet, Dreamweaver automatically creates the new file as you create the style and attaches the new style sheet to the page you're working on.

If you prefer, you can create a new CSS file just as you'd create any other new file in Dreamweaver by choosing File⇨New and then selecting CSS in the New Document dialog box. If you choose this option, attach the style sheet to the page you're working on as a separate step by choosing Format⇨CSS Styles⇨ Attach Style Sheet or by clicking the Attach Style Sheet icon at the bottom of the CSS Styles panel.

You must attach an external style sheet to every page where you want the styles to be used. When a style sheet is attached to a Web page, all the style definitions included in the style sheet become available for that page from the CSS Styles panel.

To create an external style sheet as you create a new style, follow these steps:

1. **Choose Text⇨CSS Styles⇨New.**

   The New CSS Rule dialog box appears.

2. **Choose a selector from the Selector Type drop-down list.**

   The four options — Class, ID, Tag, and Compound — are described in detail in the "Understanding style selectors" section, earlier in this chapter.

3. **Type a name into the Selector Name field or select an option from the Selector Name drop-down list.**

4. **Choose New Style Sheet File from the Rule Definition drop-down list.**

   This is the crucial step in creating a new external style sheet as you create the new style.

5. **Click OK.**

   The Save Style Sheet File As dialog box opens.

6. **Select a location in which to save the style sheet file.**

   Note that you should save the style sheet in the root folder of your Web site. You can save your CSS files in a subfolder, but remember that you must upload the CSS file to your Web server when you publish the site for the styles to work. (For more information on the root folder and how to define a site in Dreamweaver, see Chapter 2.)

7. **Enter a name for the style sheet in the File Name field.**

   You can name your style sheets anything you like; just don't use any spaces or special characters (hyphens and underscores are okay). Dreamweaver automatically adds the `.css`; just make sure you don't delete it.

8. **Click Save.**

   The CSS Rule Definition dialog box opens.

9. **Define the new style rule specifying all formatting options you want applied with the new style.**

   You find detailed descriptions of these options in the "Comparing CSS Rule Options" section earlier in this chapter.

10. **Click OK to save the new style, close the dialog box, and create the new external style sheet simultaneously.**

    Your new style is automatically saved in the new external style sheet and listed in the CSS Styles panel.

You must attach this external style sheet to every page where you want to use the styles that are saved in it. See the next section for step-by-step instructions.

Attaching an external style sheet to a Web page

After you create an external style sheet, you'll likely want to attach it to additional Web pages. Begin by opening the page to which you want to attach the style sheet and then follow these steps:

1. **Choose Window⇨CSS Styles.**

   The CSS panel appears.

2. **Click the Attach Style Sheet icon in the CSS panel (the first button in the lower-right area).**

   The Attach External Style Sheet dialog box appears (as shown in Figure 5-27).

3. **Click the Browse button and locate the CSS file in your site folder.**

   You can also enter a URL if you want to use a remote CSS file located on another Web site, but it's most common to use a style sheet contained within the Web site you're working on. Either way, Dreamweaver automatically sets the link to the style sheet for you, includes the style sheet link code at the top of the HTML file, and lists all the styles in the external style sheet in the CSS panel.

4. **Select the Link or Import option.**

   If you're attaching a style sheet to an HTML file, your best choice is almost always to choose Link, which is the default option. Choose Import if you want to create one master external style sheet that contains references to other style sheets, an advanced option that enables one style sheet to refer to another.

5. **In the Media drop-down list, choose an option.**

   With the Media drop-down list, you can specify the intended use for the style sheet. For example, if you've created a style sheet that formats your page for printing, choose the Print option. You can leave this option blank if you're attaching a style sheet to control the way the page will appear in a browser.

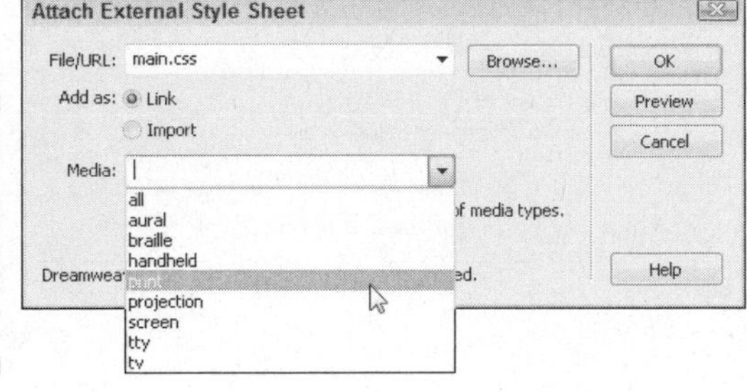

Figure 5-27: The Attach External Style Sheet dialog box.

6. **Click OK.**

   The dialog box closes, and the external CSS file is automatically linked to the page. Any styles you've defined in the external style sheet appear in the CSS Styles panel, listed under the name of the style sheet, and all the styles automatically become available for use on the page. In Figure 5-28, you can see that the main.css style sheet has been added to the CSS Styles panel. Internal style sheets are simply listed as `<style>`.

You can attach multiple style sheets to the same HTML page. For example, you can save all your text styles in one style sheet and all your layout styles in another and then attach both to the same document to make all the defined styles available to the page. Similarly, you create different style sheets for different purposes, such as one for printing the file and another for browser display.

Moving, copying, and editing styles in an external style sheet

After you attach an external style sheet to a document, you can move, copy, and edit styles as follows:

- **Moving styles:** Move any internal styles into the external style sheet by simply clicking the name of a style in an internal style sheet in the CSS Styles panel and dragging it onto the name of an external style sheet. In Figure 5-28, you can see that I'm moving a body style from the internal style sheet, which by default is `<style>`, into the external style sheet main.css. If you have attached more than one external style sheet to a document, you can also move styles from one external style sheet to another using click and drag.

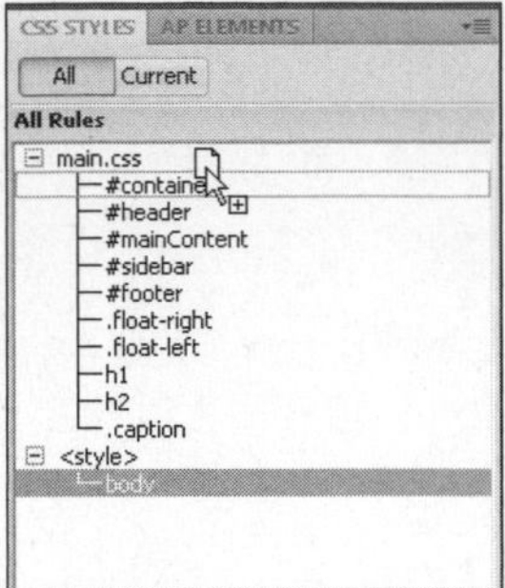

Figure 5-28: Click and drag to move styles from an internal to an external style sheet.

- **Copying styles:** You can copy styles from one document to another by right-clicking (Control-clicking on a Mac) a style name in the CSS Styles panel, choosing Copy, and then opening the document where you want to add the style, right-clicking (Control-clicking on a Mac) the name of an internal or external style sheet in the CSS Styles panel, and choosing Paste.
- **Editing styles:** You edit styles in an external style sheet the same way you edit styles in an internal style sheet: by clicking or double-clicking the style name in CSS Styles panel. (For more detailed instructions, see the section "Editing an existing style," earlier in this chapter.) Any changes you make to a style in an external style sheet are applied automatically to all the files to which the external style sheet is attached (remember, you must upload the style sheet to your Web server for the changes to take effect on the published version of the site).

If you want to edit a remote CSS file, download the file to your hard drive before you open it in Dreamweaver. In Dreamweaver, you open `.css` files by double-clicking them or choosing File➪Open, both of which open the style sheet in code view. Code view is the only view available for CSS files because they're text files and have no layout components. When you view an external style sheet this way, you can still use the CSS panel to edit any defined styles, even if the style sheet isn't linked to an HTML page. Be sure to save it when you finish editing it!

If you prefer, you can also edit the code by hand directly in code view. Figure 5-29 shows an example of a style sheet opened directly in Dreamweaver. Notice that the CSS Styles panel displays all relevant style information and gives you access to the CSS editing tools.

When you edit an external style sheet, you must upload it to your server before the style changes can be applied to pages on your live Web site.

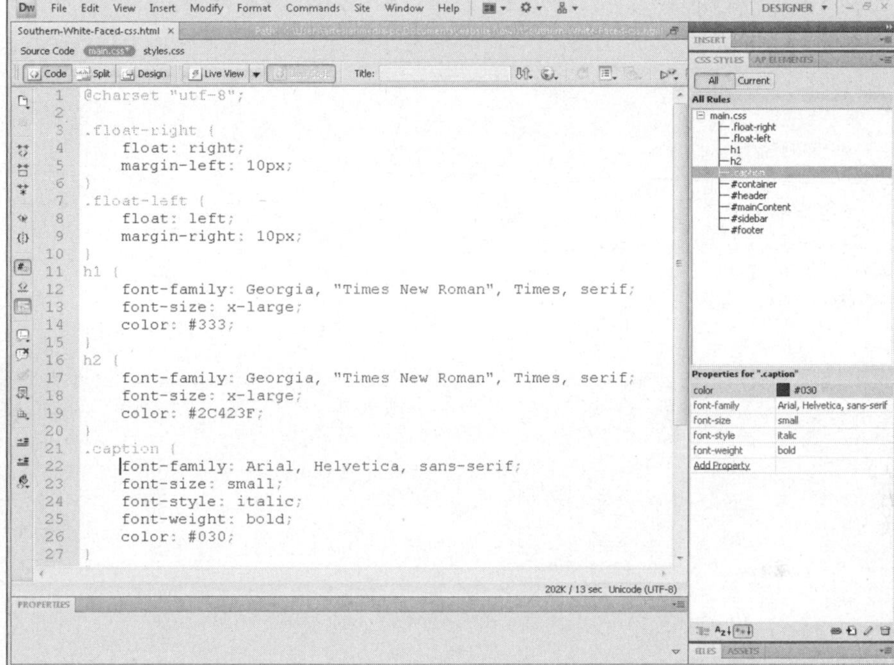

Figure 5-29: You can edit external style sheets (files with a .css extension) by opening them as you would any other document.

Using ready-made external style sheets

Adobe includes several sample style sheets for you to use in your Web sites. These come in the form of external style sheets that have been created with some popular styles to give you a jump-start in designing your pages. You can use these styles as-is or modify them to suit your needs.

To create a new external style sheet using one of the sample style sheets provided by Adobe, follow these steps:

1. **Choose File⇨New.**

   The New Document dialog box opens, as shown in Figure 5-30.

2. **Choose Page from Sample.**
3. **In the Sample Folder list, select CSS Style Sheet to display the list of CSS style collections**
4. **Select any of the sample styles listed under Sample Page.**

   A preview of styles is displayed in the far right of the New Document dialog box, as shown in Figure 5-30.

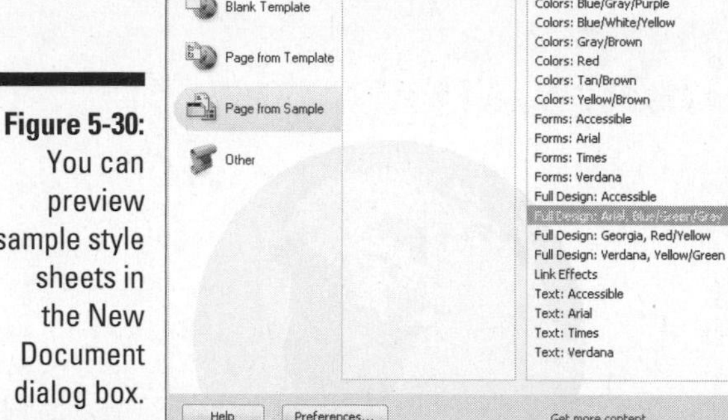

Figure 5-30: You can preview sample style sheets in the New Document dialog box.

5. **Select a style you like and click Create.**

   A new, untitled style sheet opens in code view.

6. **Choose File⇨Save (or Save As) and save the new style sheet in the root folder of the site where you plan to use it.**

To use the styles in a document, attach the new style sheet to an open file by following the instructions in the section “Attaching an external style sheet to a Web page,” earlier in this chapter.

When you do save a CSS file created from a sample style collection, Dreamweaver leaves the original style collection unchanged.

Chapter 6

Creating CSS Layouts

In This Chapter

- Creating page layouts with CSS
- Using Firefox to turn styles on and off
- Styling unordered lists for links
- Understanding the box model
- Comparing browser differences
- Using Dreamweaver's CSS layouts
- Creating custom CSS layouts
- Using Dreamweaver's AP Divs
- Working with conflicting styles
- Using the design time style sheet

Whether you're new to CSS or you've been struggling (I mean designing) with styles for years, Dreamweaver's many CSS features offer welcome assistance to even the most experienced designers.

One of the challenges with CSS is still a relatively new addition to the world of Web design, and browser support — which can make the difference between a beautiful Web page and a jumbled design that's unreadable — continues to change and evolve.

So Adobe dedicated the equivalent of decades of time (at least in Internet years) to designing a collection of CSS layouts that you can use to get a head start on many common page designs. Whether you're creating static HMTL pages or dynamic, database-driven sites with PHP, you can customize Dreamweaver's pre-styled layouts to create a broad range of Web site designs that are designed to display well in a wide-range of Web browsers. The first part of this chapter shows you how to work with these layouts and how to edit them to create your own designs.
If you prefer, you can create your own custom CSS layouts, and you find a few tips for doing so in the second part of this chapter. You also find instructions for creating a collection, or *list,* of links for a navigation bar using the `<ul>` tag, an increasingly recommended way to develop accessible navigation features.

Before you start this chapter, I recommend you at least skim through Chapter 5, where you find an introduction to CSS, a review of the many panels, dialog boxes, and inspectors you can use to create, apply, and edit styles in Dreamweaver, as well as instructions for creating CSS styles with class and tag selectors.

In this chapter, you move on to more advanced uses of CSS with instructions for creating styles with ID and compound selectors to position and align images, text, and other elements on a Web page.

Brace yourself. You're getting into some of the most complex Web design features that Dreamweaver has to offer, but I think you'll find the power and precision of these options well worth the effort. If you want to create Web designs that display well in a variety of browsers, screen sizes, and devices, and you want to ensure that your pages meet the latest Web standards, and are accessible to special Web browsers used by the disabled, CSS is clearly your best option. You start with customizing one of the predesigned layouts in Dreamweaver and then move on to creating custom CSS features from scratch.

Using CSS Layouts in Dreamweaver

Before you rush off to check out all the CSS layouts included in Dreamweaver, let me warn you: They're not much to look at when you first open them. They're intentionally designed with the most basic of formatting options and a dull gray color scheme — but fortunately color styles are some of the easiest to alter in CSS.

Comparing CSS layout options

Dreamweaver includes a variety of CSS layouts, designed with four distinct approaches to CSS. You'll find a longer description of each of these layout types in Dreamweaver's Help files, but essentially

- **Liquid layouts** are designed to expand and contract depending on the size of the browser window.
- **Fixed layouts** are centered within the browser and set to a width of 780 pixels.
- **Elastic layouts** use the ems measurement to adapt to different text sizes and other variations in display.
- **Hybrid layouts** use a mix of options.

In the examples shown in Figures 6-1 and 6-2, I've selected a design that creates a two-column, fixed layout, with a header and footer. In general, fixed layouts are an easier option to start with, but there are advantages to liquid designs because they're more flexible.

If you know the basics of editing styles, covered in the Chapter 5, you can adjust the width of columns, the formatting styles for text, and the alignment of any element on the page relatively easily. If you're new to CSS, altering one of these layouts may seem confusing at first, but trust me, it's certainly easier than creating a design from scratch.

Creating a new page with a CSS layout

No matter what you're experience level, the following tutorials are designed to help you appreciate how Dreamweaver's CSS layouts work, and to help you customize the layouts step-by-step to create your own page designs.

Figure 6-1 shows what a Dreamweaver CSS layout looks like when it's first created. Figure 6-2 shows the same layout after it's been customized. In the steps that follow, you find detailed instructions for editing this CSS layout. Although you find many different layout designs to choose from in Dreamweaver, the basic process for editing the CSS rules to customize one of these layouts is the same for them all.

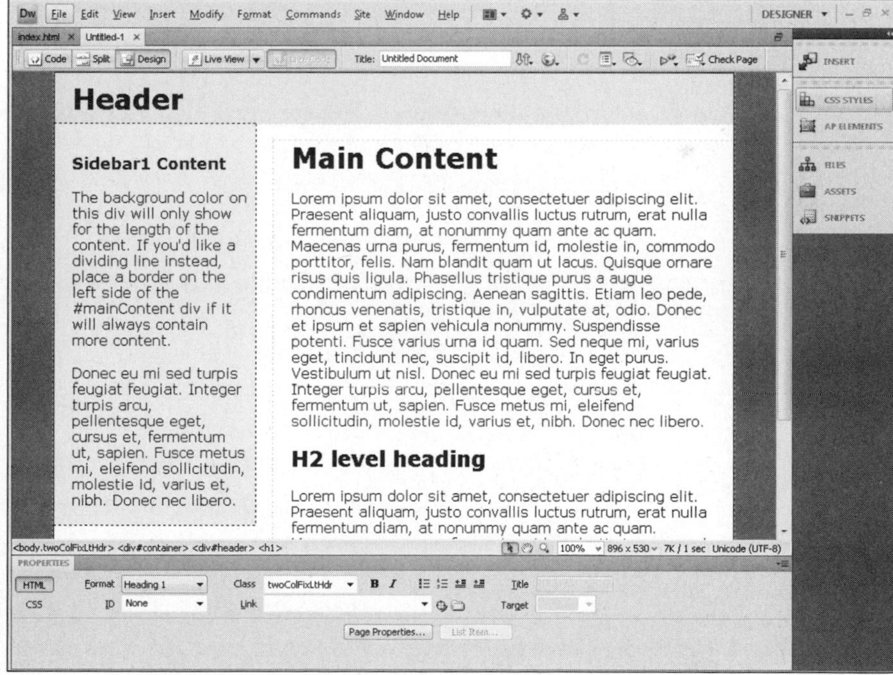

Figure 6-1: New pages created from Dreamweaver's CSS layouts are gray and dull.

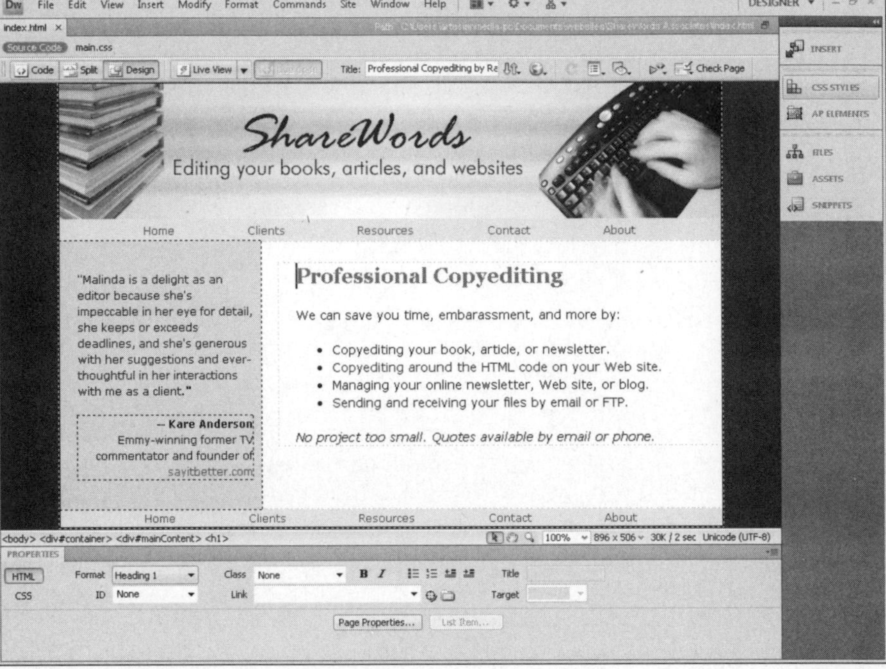

Figure 6-2: You can customize Dreamweaver's CSS layouts a little, or a lot, to create your own Web site designs.

To create a new page using one of Dreamweaver's CSS layouts, follow these instructions:

1. **Choose File⇨New.**

   The New Document dialog box appears (see Figure 6-3).

2. **Choose Blank Page from the left column and HTML from the Page Type column in the middle.**

   If you're working on a dynamic site, you can choose any of the options in the bottom part of the Page Type section, including ASP.NET, PHP, or ColdFusion and still use a CSS layout.

3. **Select any of the CSS layouts listed in the Layout section.**

   For this example, I chose 2 Column Fixed, Left Sidebar, Header and Footer.

   Notice in Figure 6-3, that when you select a CSS layout, a preview of the layout is displayed in the top right of the dialog box.

4. **From the Layout CSS drop-down list, choose the type of style sheet you want to create as you create the page.**

   Choose Add to Head to create an internal style sheet and include all the styles for the layout in the Head area of the new document.

Choose Create New File to create a new external style sheet with all the page styles as you create the new document with the design.

Choose Link to Existing File to add the style sheet information for the new document to an existing style sheet.

5. **Click Create.**

It's important to save all the pages of a Web site in the root folder. You find more about defining a Web site and specifying a root folder in Dreamweaver in Chapter 2.

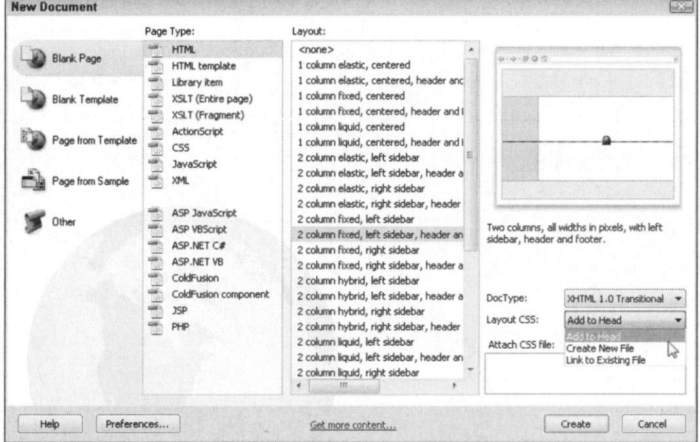

Figure 6-3: When you select the name of a CSS layout in the New Document dialog box, a preview is displayed in the top-right corner.

6. **Choose File⇨Save to save the page and styles.**

If you saved the styles in an external style sheet, you're prompted by a second dialog box to save the style sheet separately. If the styles are contained in an internal style sheet, they're saved automatically when you save the page.

Removing class styles from CSS layouts

All the CSS layouts in Dreamweaver are identified by a class style, such as `.twoColFixLtHdr` used in the layout shown in the style used in these two exercises. These class names are made up of abbreviations for the layout. In this case, `.twoColFixLtHdr` describes this layout as a two-column design with a fixed size, a left sidebar, and a header.

These class names are included at the beginning of each of the ID styles in this CSS layout, making all the ID styles compound styles, which can make identifying the IDs a bit more confusing. These styles work with this class style at the beginning because the class is attached to the `<body>` tag of the code in the page. Even though `.twoColFixLtHdr` isn't defined by

(continued)

(continued)

any rules, its presence in the <body> tag and at the beginning of the name of each of the ID styles enables the styles in this layout to work properly.

This class style can be handy for identifying the selected layout, but it also complicates the style names in a way that isn't necessary. If you want to simplify the style names in a design like this, you can remove the class style — just make sure you remove it from both the <body> tag and the style names of each ID style in the CSS Styles panel.

To remove a class style, follow these instructions:

1. **Click the Split view button at the top of the workspace to view the code in split view, as shown in this figure.**
2. **Find the <body> tag in the code (it appears just after any CSS styles and just before the content of the page begins).**
3. **Delete everything but the <body> tag and brackets.**

   In this example, you'd delete `class="twoColFixLtHdr"` (including the space) and leave <body>. When you do this, all the links to the ID styles break, and the page layout loses all the corresponding formatting, which changes the appearance dramatically. Don't worry. You can get it all back by following the next steps.
4. **Select just the class name at the beginning of an ID style in the CSS Styles panel and press the Delete or Backspace key.**

   For example, for `.twoColFixLtHdr #container`, select only `.twoColFixLtHdr` (including the space) and delete the entire class name and space, leaving only `#container`.
5. **Repeat Step 4 for each ID style that includes the class name.**

   When you delete the class name from the beginning of each of ID style in the CSS Styles panel, the page layout is restored in the workspace.

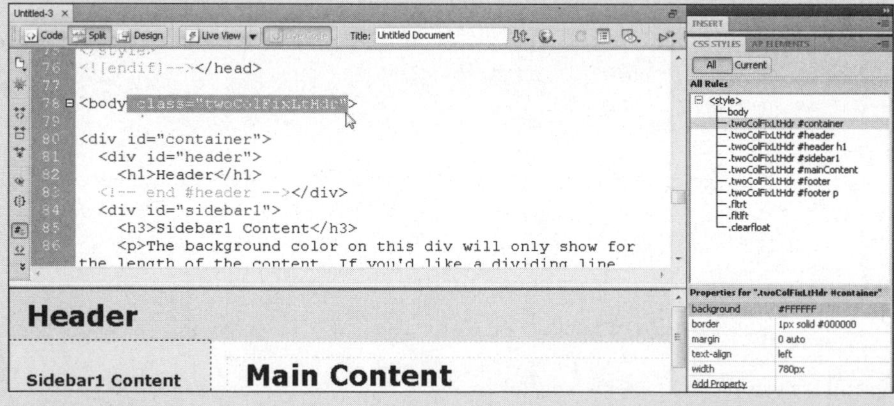

Editing the styles in a CSS layout

After you create a new page with a CSS layout, you have a seemingly infinite number of options for editing it, but first you have to determine which styles in the style sheet correspond to the elements you want to edit.

In this example, because I've chosen a fixed width layout, I know a style can be used to change the width of the layout area. Following a common practice of using `<div>` tags to contain elements on a page and using ID styles to describe how they should be displayed, Dreamweaver includes a `<div>` tag with an ID style named `#container`in every layout. To change the width of any of these designs, change the corresponding `#container`style, as shown in the following exercise.

The steps in the following sections explain how to edit the overall design of a page created with a Dreamweaver CSS layout. I've broken the process into several step lists to help you following along more easily. ***Note:*** The steps assume you're proceeding through the sections in order.

As you can probably imagine, there are many ways you can edit the styles in a CSS layout to create your own designs, and the process I explain in the following sections is just one them. I help you understand what you need to do to get started. After you set your basic page design, you can create as many additional styles as you desire. In the section "Styling an Unordered List for Links," for example, you find instructions for creating a series of styles to format a list of links with the `<ul>` and `<li>` tags to create a horizontal navigation bar with a simple rollover effect.

Getting started

To begin editing styles in a CSS layout, follow these steps:

1. **With the file open, choose Window⇨CSS Styles or click the CSS Styles button to expand the panel.**

   The CSS Styles panel opens or expands.

2. **Click the plus (+) sign (or a triangle on a Mac) next to the style sheet name to open the list of styles.**

   All the styles associated with the new page are listed.

   To change any element in the design of this page, edit the corresponding style.

3. **Select the name of any style listed in the CSS Styles panel.**

   The corresponding CSS rules defined for the style are displayed in the Properties pane at the bottom of the CSS Styles panel, as shown in

Figure 6-4. Clicking through the list of styles and reviewing their corresponding rules is a good way to get a quick overview of the design and to see where the various page formatting options are stored.

All the styles that include a # sign are ID styles, which correspond to `<div>` tags in the page code. These styles control the size and positioning of the main areas of the page and are named to correspond. For example, `.twoColFixLtHdr #header` controls the area at the top of the page design where you see the word *Header*. Similarly, `#sidebar1` controls the area with the headline *Sidebar1 Content*.

Figure 6-4: You can alter any of the styles in a CSS layout by editing its style definition in the CSS Styles panel.

Editing page-wide settings

To edit page-wide settings, such as the font face, size, and color of the text used throughout the page, follow these steps:

1. **Double-click the `body` style in the CSS Styles panel.**

   The CSS Rule Definition dialog box opens.

2. **Select the Type category and specify your desired Font settings.**
3. **Select the Background category and use the color well in the Background-Color field to specify a color for the entire background of the page.**

   Alternatively, you can enter any hexadecimal color code manually in the Background-Color field.

4. **Click the Apply button to preview your changes and then click OK to save the changes and close the dialog box.**

Customizing the Header area

To edit the Header area at the top of the page, follow these steps:

1. **Select the** `.twoColFixLtHdr #header` **style in the CSS Styles panel, as shown in Figure 6-4.**

   In the Properties pane, you can see that the `#header` style includes a definition for a background color, which is set to `#DDDDDD` (the hexadecimal code for the gray color displayed in the top of the page design where the word Header appears).

   All the CSS layouts in Dreamweaver are identified by a class style, such as `.twoColFixLtHdr` used in the layout shown in this example. Dreamweaver uses these class names to distinguish between the layouts, but they aren't necessary. If you prefer to simplify the ID styles names in your layout, you can remove the class name by following the instructions in the sidebar, "Removing class styles from CSS layouts."

2. **Click and drag to select the background color code and press the Delete key.**

   Removing the color code from the Background-Color field in the `.twoColFixLtHdr #header` style removes the background color from the Header area completely and returns that part of the page to the default color, which is white (unless it's been set to another color in another style).

3. **To change the background color, double-click the** `.twoColFixLtHdr #header` **style to open the CSS Rule Definition dialog box, select the Background category, and then use the color well in the Background-Color field to select another color.**

4. **Click and drag to select the word Header in the top part of the page in the workspace and press the Delete key.**

   The word Header disappears.

5. **To add your own text to the Header area, type the text as you would anywhere else on a Web page.**

6. **To add a graphic to the Header area, make sure your cursor is in the Header area, choose Insert⇨Image, and select the name of image you want to insert.**

   The image appears in the Header area.

7. **Remove any unwanted spacing.**

   The Header area of this (and nearly all the) CSS layouts in Dreamweaver includes extra space created by an `<h1>` tag and padding in the `#header` style. If you replace Header with text, you may want to maintain these spacing features, but if you add an image, as I have in this example, you probably want to get rid of this extra space. Here's how:

a. **Click to select the** `.twoColFixLtHdr #header` **style in the CSS Styles panel.**

b. **Click and drag to select the contents of the Padding field. In this example, select "0 10px 0 20px" in the Padding field in the Properties pane at the bottom of the CSS Styles panel and then press the Delete or Backspace key.**

   This completely removes all the padding from the Header area.

c. **Select the text or image you inserted into the Header area and then right-click the** `<h1>` **tag in the tag selector at the bottom of the workspace and choose Remove Tag from the pop-up menu, as shown in Figure 6-5.**

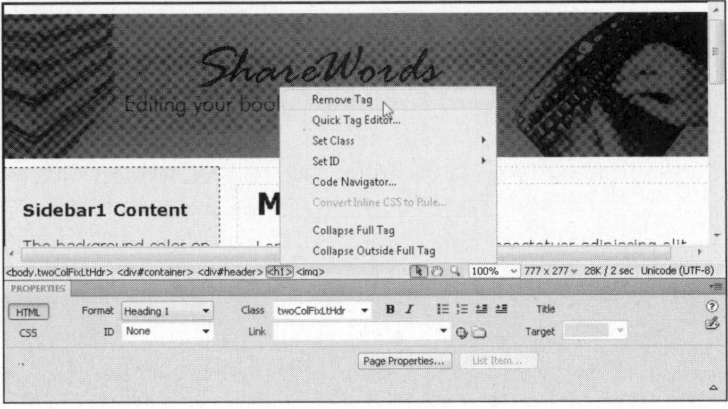

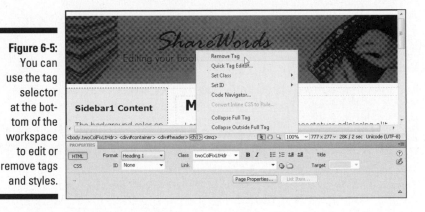

Figure 6-5: You can use the tag selector at the bottom of the workspace to edit or remove tags and styles.

Customizing the content areas

You may also want to adjust the width and padding of the content areas in your preset layout. When you're done, you're ready to add your own text to these areas. The following steps explain how:

1. **To change the width of the entire content area, select the** `.twoColFixLtHdr #container` **style in the CSS Styles panel.**

   The style definition appears in the Properties pane (refer to Figure 6-5).

2. **Select the size in the width field and type a new number with your desired page width.**

   In this example, I selected the width, which is set to 780, as shown in Figure 6-5, and I changed it to 760. When you alter the width of the `#content` style, as I did here, you change the width of the entire design because all the other `<div>` tags are contained within the `<div>` that's formatted with the `#content` style and they're all set to expand to fill the `#content <div>`.

3. **Replace the text in the sidebar and main content areas.**

   You can replace the text in any page created from a CSS layout just as you would in any other Web page. If you delete content, such as the headline in the sidebar, make sure you also delete any corresponding code, such as the `<h3>` tag, which formats the sidebar heading. You can most easily delete this code by using the tag selector, as shown in Figure 6-5.

4. **To change the width and background color of the sidebar, double-click the `.twoColFixLtHdr #sidebar1` style in the CSS Styles panel.**

   The CSS Rule Definition dialog box opens.

5. **Select the Background category and use the color well in the Background-Color field to specify a color.**

   Alternatively, you can enter any hexadecimal color code manually.

6. **Select the Box category and change the width, padding, and margin settings.**

   You can alter the width of the sidebar, the *padding* (the space inside the border of the sidebar), or the *margins* (the space outside the border of the sidebar).

7. **Click the Apply button to preview the changes and then click OK to save the changes and close the dialog box.**

   The changes are applied automatically to the design in the open page.

When you change the width of a sidebar in a Dreamweaver CSS layout, you must also change the corresponding margin setting in the `mainContent` style (as you see in the next step). The width in the sidebar style and the margin in the `mainContent` style are used in combination to control the positioning of the sidebar and `mainContent` `<div>`s in relation to each other.

8. **Double-click the `.twoColFixLtHdr #mainContent` style in the CSS Styles panel.**

   The CSS Rule Definition dialog box opens.

9. **Select the Box category and change the margin settings to correspond to the new width of the sidebar.**

   In this example, I changed the width of the sidebar from 200 to 300, so I need to change the corresponding margin setting in the `mainContent` style. You may not want to change the margin setting by the same amount as you changed the width of the sidebar because this can lead to a margin that may not look right in your page design. Instead, I recommend you experiment by changing the margin setting and then clicking the Apply button to see how the page looks.

10. **Choose File⇨Save to save the page and styles.**

    If you saved the styles in an external style sheet, you're prompted by a second dialog box to save the style sheet separately. If the styles are contained in an internal style sheet, they're saved automatically when you save the page.

After you edit a CSS layout to create the page design you want to use in your site, it's good practice to save the page as a template so that you can create additional pages with the same layout, without repeating all these steps to customize the styles. As you discover in Chapter 9, there are many advantages to using Dreamweaver's template features when you're designing a site with more than a few pages.

Here's a related tip: If you'll use the design as a template, make sure you save your styles in an external style sheet so that the style rules can be edited outside the template. Find instructions for creating external style sheets and for moving internal styles into an external style sheet in Chapter 5.

Turning Styles On and Off in Firefox

Even if you prefer another Web browser, I strongly encourage you to download and install the Firefox browser for testing your Web pages. Firefox is made for both Mac and PC computers and you can download it for free from `www.mozilla.com/firefox`.

Not only is it good practice to test your pages in more than one browser (at the very least, Internet Explorer and Firefox), the Firefox browser offers several special features and extensions that can help you better view your CSS and the CSS on other people's Web sites.

As shown in Figures 6-6 and 6-7, you can turn the styles that format a Web page on and off in Firefox. To turn off styles, choose View⇨Page Style⇨No Style. To turn on styles, choose View⇨Page Style⇨Basic Page Style. If the page includes additional style sheets, such as style sheets that increase the font size of a page to make it more accessible, you can select those styles instead.

The Web Developer Add On for Firefox adds many great features to the browser, including the ability to view an external style sheet on any Web site (that's right, you can look under the hood of other people's Web sites with this add-on). You can even view CSS style sheets by Media type so that you can see how a site, such as Disney.com, develops different style sheets for print, screen, and handheld devices. To find this valuable addition to Firefox, click the Add-Ons link at the top of the Firefox Web page and then search for Web Developer. The Add-Ons link, which is consistently rated with five out of five stars, is free, and takes only a few seconds to download and install.

Styling an Unordered List for Links

Here's a great CSS trick for turning a bulleted list into a navigation bar with a simple rollover effect. Using a bulleted list for navigation bars is a well-accepted convention for Web sites that meet current accessibility standards. A bulleted list is a logical choice for navigation elements because even if the style rules are removed, the links still stand out from the rest of the elements on the page and are clearly grouped together.

In Figures 6-6 and 6-7, you see the same Web page displayed in Firefox with the styles turned on and off. Notice that the navigation links are formatted in a simple, bulleted list when the styles are turned off but are displayed in a horizontal row with no bullets when styles are turned on.

Thanks to CSS, you can gain the benefits of styling a list of links with the unordered list tag and still format your links with any style you choose so that you don't have to keep those boring bullets and can align your links horizontally or vertically. Using CSS instead of images to create a rollover effect like the one featured in the following exercise not only makes your page more accessible, but it helps your page load faster, too.

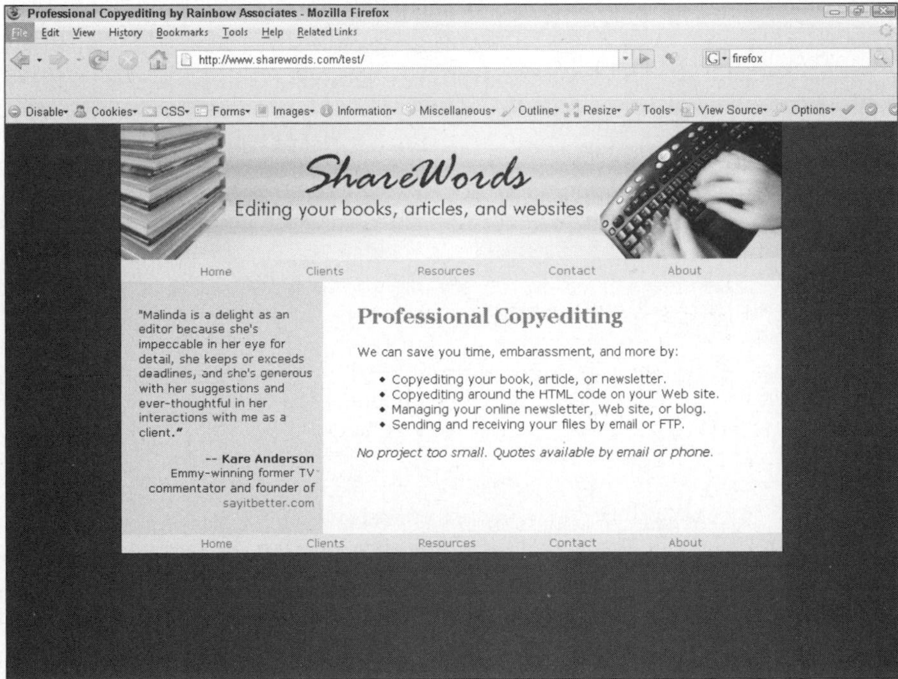

Figure 6-6: You can view the same Web page with styles turned on or off in the Firefox browser. In this image, the styles are turned on.

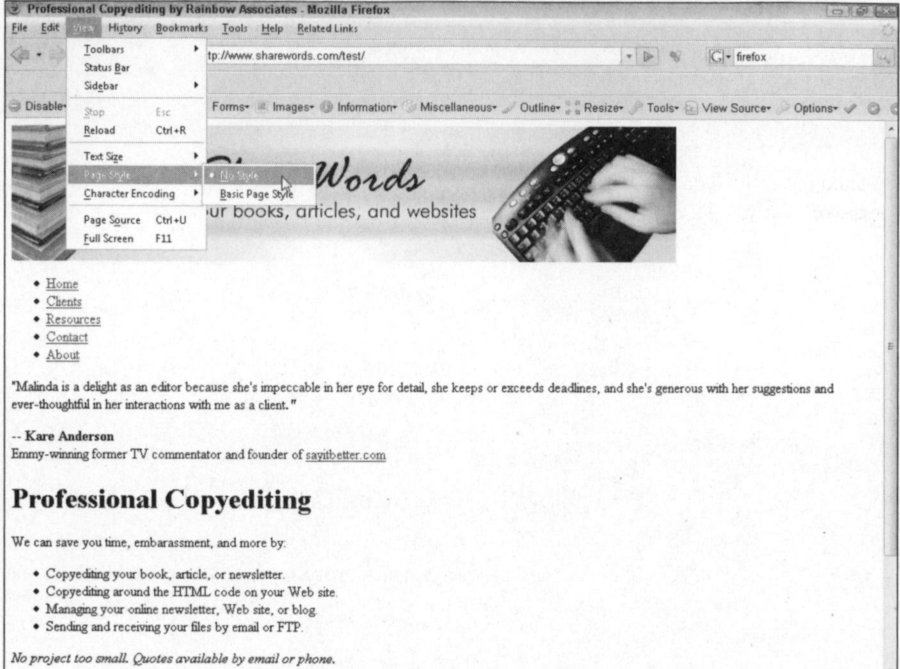

Figure 6-7: This is the same page shown in Figure 6-6, but the styles are turned off.

This exercise builds on the page design created in the earlier sections in this chapter, except that I've removed the class styles that were included at the beginning of each of the ID styles. This makes it simpler to create new styles within the `<div>` tags that are formatted by the ID styles. You find instructions for altering the styles in a CSS layout like this in the sidebar, "Removing class styles from CSS layouts" earlier in this chapter.

To create a navigation bar using CSS to redefine the unordered list and link tags, follow these steps:

1. **Place your cursor in the HTML page where you want your navigation bar to appear and then click the Div button in the Common Insert panel to insert a** `<div>` **tag.**

   The Insert Div Tag dialog box opens, as shown in Figure 6-8.

   When you're creating a list of links to serve as your navigation bar, it's best to store those links in a `<div>` tag at the top or side of the page where visitors to your site can easily find them.

2. **Specify an Insert option.**

   You can choose from a variety of options in the Insert drop-down list to more precisely control where the new `<div>` tag is added. If you're not sure, you can leave the Wrap around Selection option selected, even if you haven't selected anything.

Figure 6-8: The Insert Div Tag dialog box.

3. **Enter a name in the Class field or the ID field.**

   You can name the `<div>` tag anything you like as long as you don't use spaces or special characters (underscores and hyphens are okay). In this example, I chose to create an ID style, so I entered **navbar** in the ID field. (***Remember:*** ID styles are generally recommended for positioning `<div>` tags that make up part of the layout of a Web page.)

4. **Click the New CSS Rule button to create a new style for your Div ID as you insert the `<div>` tag.**

   The New CSS Rule dialog box opens.

5. **Select the Box category and specify the desired settings for the size, margins, and padding.**

   For the `navbar` shown in this example, I set the margins to 0, set the padding to 2 pixels, checked the All box to apply the same padding to all sides, and left the Height and Width fields blank, which means the `<div>` tag will expand to fit its contents and its container.

6. **Select the Background category and choose a background color or image.**

   If you don't specify a color or insert a background image, the color of the `navbar` `<div>` tag will be determined by the color of any `<div>` tag that contains it or by the specified page color. In this example, I've selected a lavender color to set the `navbar` apart from the rest of the design.

7. **Select the Type category and specify the font options.**

   If you don't specify any font settings, the text will be displayed in the font set for the page or the surrounding container.

   In this example, I've set the font to Verdana in the `<body>` tag, and because I don't want to change it, I left the Font-Family field blank. I do, however, want the text to display a little smaller in the `navbar` than it does in the rest of the page, so I've set the Font-Size to 90 percent, which will display the text in this `<div>` tag at 90 percent of the default text size for the page.

8. **Click OK to close the New CSS Rule dialog box and then click OK to close the Insert Div Tag dialog box.**

   The new `<div>` tag is added to the page and the `#navbar` ID style is created and listed in the CSS Styles panel. `Content for id "navbar" goes here` is inserted between the open `<div>` tag and the close `</div>` tag to make it easy to identify where you should add your own content within the `<div>` tag. Make sure to delete this text when you add your own content.

9. **Insert the text for each link into the** `navbar <div>` **area.**

   Make sure to separate each line of text with a Return (so that the text is formatted with a `<p>` tag in the code). If the lines aren't separated by paragraph tags, the unordered list won't be applied properly in the next step.

10. **To format the text as an unordered list, click and drag to select all the text in the** `navbar <div>` **and then click the Unordered List icon in the Property inspector.**

    If you haven't redefined the unordered list tag already, the text changes to the default settings of an unordered list, removing the space between each line and adding bullets.

11. **Set links from each text section just as you would link any other text block or image.**

    You find detailed instructions for setting links in Chapter 2, but the simplest way is to first select the text and then click the Link icon in the Common Insert panel. In the Hyperlink dialog box, enter the URL you want the text to link to or use the Browse button (which looks like a folder) to the right of the link field to locate the file you want to link to.

    If you haven't yet created the pages you'll link to, you can set a temporary link by entering a pound (#) sign in the Link field. This is important because in order for the styles that you create in the rest of this exercise to work, the text must be linked to something so that the link styles will apply.

12. **Create a new style to redefine the unordered list tag when it's displayed in the** `<div>` **tag with the** `#navbar` **ID by following these steps to create styles with the compound selector:**

    a. **Choose Format⇨CSS Styles⇨New.**

    b. **Under Selector Type, choose Compound.**

    c. **In the Selector Name field, enter** #navbar ul, **as shown in Figure 6-9, and then click OK.**

    d. **In the CSS Rule Definition dialog box, choose the Box category and set margins and padding to** 0.

    e. **Select the Same for All check box for both margins and padding to remove the margins and padding included in the** `<ul>` **HTML tag.**

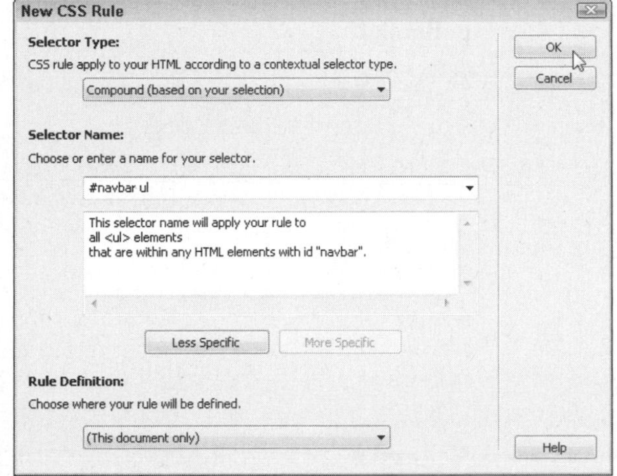

Figure 6-9: You can create a style to redefine any existing HTML tag.

f. **Click OK to save the style and close the dialog box.**

The spacing around the list of links formatted as an Unordered List disappears.

13. **Create a new compound style to redefine the list item tag by following these steps:**

a. **Choose Format➪CSS Styles➪New.**

b. **Under Selector Type, choose Compound.**

c. **In the Selector Name field, enter** #navbar ul li **(make sure to include spaces between each name) and then click OK.**

d. **In the CSS Rule Definition dialog box, select the Block category and set Display to Inline.**

This changes the style of the `<li>` tag from vertical to horizontal.

e. **Select the List category and set Type to None to remove the bullet.**

f. **Select the Box category and set margins left and right to 40 pixels.**

This separates the list items from one another in the horizontal list. You can change the setting to any measurement to create the amount of space between links that best fits your design.

g. **Click OK to save these settings and close the dialog box.**

14. **Create a new style to redefine the link tag by following these steps:**

a. **Choose Format➪CSS Styles➪New.**

b. **Under Selector Type, choose Compound.**

c. **In the Tag field, enter** #navbar a:link **and then click OK.**

d. **In the CSS Rule Definition dialog box, select the Type category and set Decoration to None by clicking the check box.**

   This removes the underline from linked text.

e. **Still in the Type category, change the text color to the color you want your links to appear when they're first loaded on a page.**

   I set the text color to a dark blue.

f. **Click OK to save these settings and close the dialog box.**

15. **Create a new style to redefine the hover link tag so that the link color will change when a user rolls a cursor over the link:**

    a. **Choose Format⇨CSS Styles⇨New.**

    b. **Under Selector Type, choose Compound.**

    c. **In the Tag field, enter** #navbar a:hover **and then click OK.**

    d. **In the CSS Rule Definition dialog box, select the Type category and set Decoration to None by clicking the check box.**

       This removes the underline from linked text. If you prefer to have the underline appear when a user rolls a cursor over a link, check Underline.

    e. **Still in the Type category, change the text color to the color you want your links to appear when users roll their cursors over the link.**

       I set the text color to a bright red color. The more dramatic the color difference between the `a:link` and `a:hover` colors, the more dramatic the rollover effect.

    f. **Click OK to save these settings and close the dialog box.**

16. **Create a new style to redefine the visited link tag so that the link color will change after a user clicks a link:**

    a. **Choose Format⇨CSS Styles⇨New.**

    b. **Under Selector Type, choose Compound.**

    c. **In the Tag field, enter** #navbar a:visited **and then click OK.**

    d. **In the CSS Rule Definition dialog box, choose the Type category and set Decoration to None by clicking the check box.**

    e. **Still in the Type category, change the text color to the color you want your links to appear after the link has been visited.**

       I set the text color to a light gray color. If you want the color to remain the same, set the `a:visited` link to the same color as the `a:link`.

    f. **Click OK to save these settings and close the dialog box.**

Creating compound styles

When you redefine tags, such as the unordered list and link tags, the new style applies to all uses of that tag within a page unless you define the tags as compound styles by including the name of their container as part of the style name.

For example, in the exercise in the "Styling an Unordered List for Links" section, instead of creating a new tag style with just the name of the `<ul>` tag, I created a new tag style called `#navbar ul` to redefine the `<ul>` tag only when it's contained within a `<div>` tag with an ID of `navbar`.

When you create advanced styles like this, use the name of the container followed by the tag name separated by a single space. In this example, I also created styles for the `<li>` and `<link>` tags in the same way, creating styles with names like `#navbar a:link`, `#navbar a:hover`, and `#navbar ul li`. You can create compound styles with multiple tags or styles to create more specific CSS rules, but you must include a space between each tag or style name.

17. **Click the Live View button at the top of the workspace or click the Preview button to view the page in a browser to see the effect of the link styles.**

Using CSS to Create Custom Page Layouts

This section is designed to help you better understand how Dreamweaver creates CSS layouts and introduces you to how to create your own custom CSS layouts. For starters, you explore the box model workflow, which forms the foundation of any CSS layout. You also discover some basics about margins versus padding and how CSS displays in different browsers.

Creating designs using the box model

The key to understanding the way CSS works when it comes to page layout is to think in terms of designing with a series of infinitely adjustable containers, or boxes. The entire process is often referred to as the *box model*. Think of the box model this way:

1. **Create `<div>` tags that span the full width of the page and stack one on top of another.**

Although you can use any HTML element for page layout, the `<div>` tag is used most often to create page layouts with CSS. `<div>` stands for *div*ision. Think of the `<div>` tag as simply a container to hold other content or to make a division on the page, separating one section of content from another. Unlike other HTML tags, the `<div>` tag has no inherent formatting features except to add a line break. Unless CSS is applied to a `<div>` tag, it can seem invisible on a page. And yet it has a powerful purpose because any content surrounded by an opening `<div>` tag and closing `<div>` tag becomes an object (or a box) that can be formatted with CSS.

2. **Add content, such as text and images, into each box.**

   Alternatively, you can create the CSS styles to position the boxes and then add content, but I find it easier to decide how to define the styles after I see at least some of the content in place.

3. **Tag content as needed, with the `<ul>` tag or `<p>` (paragraph) tag to contain your content.**

4. **With the content and boxes in place, create the styles that position each box to create the design you want for the page.**

   Most often, you assign each `<div>` tag an ID and then create an ID style to control how each container appears on the page. You give each ID style attributes to control the position, alignment, and other formatting options of each box and its contents. You can also specify such settings as margins, padding, and borders to add space and outlines around these containers.

Comparing block and inline elements

As a general rule, HTML tags can be divided into block elements and inline elements. *Block elements,* such as the `<div>` tag, interrupt the flow of the page, creating a box or block around which other page elements align. In HTML, block elements include the paragraph (`<p>`) tag, which creates a line break before and after it's used and doesn't allow anything to appear alongside it. Heading tags, such as `<h1>`, `<h2>`, and `<h3>`, and list tags, such as `<ul>` and `<ol>`, are also block elements.

In contrast, *inline elements* flow with text. For example, the `<strong>` and `<em>` tags are inline elements. You can place these elements one after another, and a new line break doesn't appear between each element. They simply flow with the text. For that reason, the `<span>` tag, which is an inline element, is a good choice for applying styles that you want to affect a small amount of text within a block, such as when you want to add a little color to text contained within `<p>` tags.

ID style names always begin with a # sign and must match the corresponding ID assigned to the block element, in this case <div> tags in the HTML code. For a quick reference to style selectors and their corresponding HTML code, see the sidebar, "CSS options at a glance." For a more detailed explanation of CSS selectors, see Chapter 5.

Comparing margins and padding

When it comes to design, one of the more confusing aspects of the box model is the way margins and padding work:

- **Padding** adds space inside an element. Think of padding as a way to add a cushion around the inside of a box so that your content doesn't bump into the sides of your box.
- **Margins** add space outside an element. Think of margins as a way to add space between boxes and other elements on a page, such as text and images, so that they don't bump into each other.

In Figure 6-10, you see a <div> tag with a corresponding ID style that creates the thin black border around the <div> tag, which defines it as follows:

500 pixels wide
25 pixels of padding inside the <div> tag border
50 pixels of margin spacing outside the <div> tag border

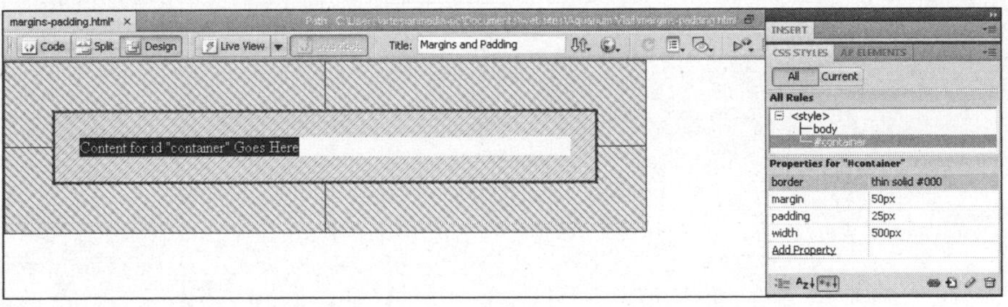

Figure 6-10: Padding is added to the inside of an element, and margins are added to the outside.

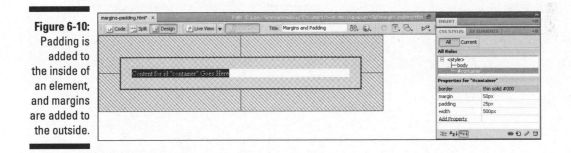

Here's the confusing part:

- **Padding adds to the specified width.** If you specify a width for a <div> tag (or any other box element), as I have in Figure 6-10, the total width is increased by the padding. In my example, the <div> tag will fill 550 pixels of space on the page: 500 pixels for the width plus 25 pixels on each side of padding.

- **Margins add to the total space taken up by an element in a page.** The margins of the <div> tag style are set to 50 pixels, so the <div> tag is positioned 50 pixels from the top and left of the page and no other element will display closer than 50 pixels on the right or bottom. This prevents the display of any other element in that space and it means that the <div> tag effectively takes up all of that space on the page.
- **Borders add to the specified width, too.** The ID style for the <div> tag also includes border settings, which cause the dark border to surround the <div> tag. The thin border adds another 2 pixels to each side of the <div> tag (4 pixels total).

Thus, the total space on the page that will be filled by the <div> tag is 654 pixels:

500 pixel width
50 pixels total of padding
4 pixels of border
100 pixels for the 50 pixel margin on each side

As you see in the exercise that follows, understanding how styles affect the width of elements is especially important when you want to place two or more containers side by side, such as the three photos contained within <div> tags in the page design shown in Figure 6-11.

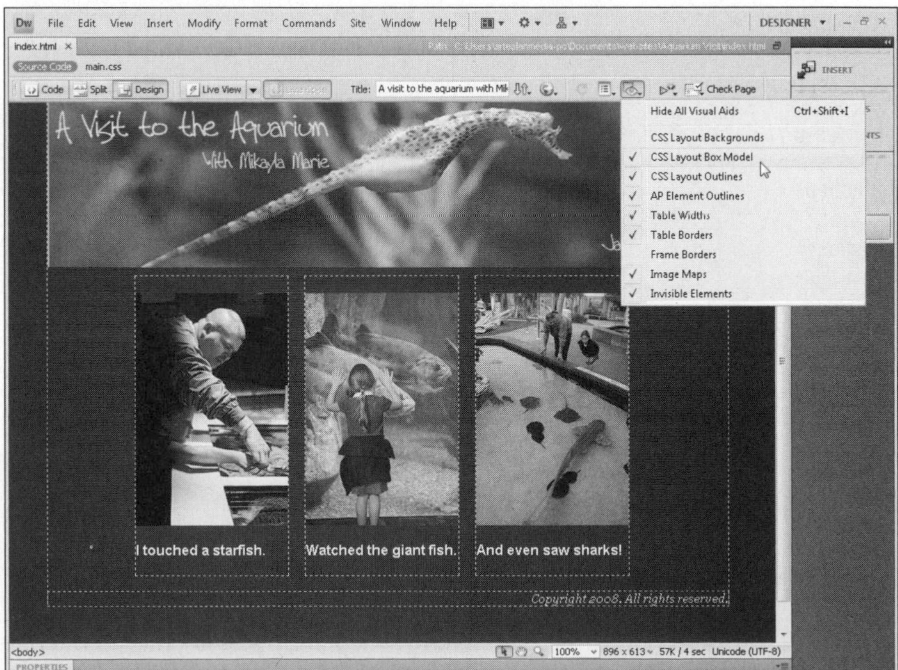

Figure 6-11: This page design was created using the CSS box model.

Note that in the example shown in Figure 6-11, I've set the margins for the entire page to 0. This is an easy setting to make in the Page Properties dialog box, available by clicking the Page Properties button in the Property inspector or by choosing Modify⇨Page Properties.

When you alter the margin settings in the Page Properties dialog box, Dreamweaver automatically creates a new tag style by redefining the `<body>` tag. Setting page margins to 0 means that any content on the page will be aligned from the very top and left edges of the browser window when the page is displayed in a Web browser. If you don't change the page margins, most Web browsers will display the contents of a Web page 10 pixels from the top and left edges of the browser window.

Displaying CSS in different browsers

Neither Dreamweaver nor I can show you exactly how your Web pages will look to everyone who may ever view them on the Web because different browsers display Web pages differently, especially older browser versions that don't include standards-compliant support for CSS (and many other advanced Web design features, for that matter).

If you want your Web pages to look exactly the same in every browser that might ever visit your pages, you have to create very simple designs that don't use any of the latest Web design features. If you want to create more advanced page designs and want your pages to look exactly the same in all the most recent browser versions (including Internet Explorer versions 5 and up), you'll have to move on to more advanced CSS training when you're finished with this book and explore the "hacks" that have been developed to get around browser differences. You'll find many books, Web sites, and training videos dedicated to advanced CSS training.

For a list of more advanced CSS training resources online and off, visit `www.DigitalFamily.com/dreamweaver` and look for the article on "Where to learn advanced CSS tips and tricks."

For the purposes of this book, I've designed pages that are consistent in their display on IE 6 and later, Firefox 1.5 and later, and Safari and Firefox on the Mac. I can't cover all the CSS hacks needed to design CSS layouts for every browser in use on the Web today, but the browsers that I targeted with these designs represent the majority of Web browsers your visitors are likely to use.

One of the advantages of using the predesigned CSS layouts in Dreamweaver is that they're designed with browser differences in mind and, unless you edit them heavily, should display well in the vast majority of Web browsers. When you create custom CSS designs, like the one covered in the next section, "Creating a Custom CSS Layout," keep in mind that you run the risk of creating designs that can look quite different from one browser to another.

Splitting the view

If you're creating a series of <div> tags to position content on a Web page, you may find it easier to keep track of the <div> tags if you use Dreamweaver's split view, which enables you to see the code view and design view simultaneously. To split the workspace area, choose View⇨Code and Design or click the Split view button, located just under the Insert panel at the top of the workspace.

If you select an image, text, or another element on a page in design view, it's automatically highlighted in code view, a great feature that makes it easier to find your place in the code when you're trying to troubleshoot what's happening behind the scenes.

I like to use split view to keep an eye on the code as I create page designs, especially when I'm inserting <div> tags, because it can be hard to keep track of how <div> tags are arranged and nested when you're using only design view.

I leave it to you to decide whether to worry about visitors with older browsers and whether to explore more advanced CSS training when you're finished here. At the very least, this is why I always recommend that you test your page designs in a variety of Web browsers, and on both Macs and PCs, whenever possible. With a little trial and error, you can often find ways to create even complex designs that look good across many different systems.

Creating a Custom CSS Layout

There are many approaches to creating layouts with CSS. You can create fluid layouts that expand and contract to fill the browser window no matter how wide or narrow, and you can create fixed layouts that remain a specified width no matter how wide the browser window. When you create fixed-width designs, such as the example in this section, it's good practice to center the design on the Web page so that it appears to float in the middle of the page no matter what the size of the browser window.

The following exercise walks you through the creation of the design shown in Figure 6-11 using a series of <div> tags created within a <div> tag with an ID named #container. The corresponding container style defines the container with a fixed width of 760 pixels. As you see in Step 4 in the later section "Styling the container <div> tag," the trick to centering a <div> tag with a style is to set the left and right margins to Auto. This makes the browser display an equal amount of margin space on each side of the container and effectively centers the <div> tag and all its content in the page. This is an important trick because <div> tags and other block-level elements have no center option.

Work through the following sections in order to create a fixed-width, three-column layout with a header and footer area using CSS and <div> tags. I've broken the key tasks into individual sections.

Setting up the page and the boxes

1. **Choose File⇨New and then choose Blank Page from the left column, HTML from the Page Type options in the middle, and <none> from the Layout section.**

   Alternatively, you can use one of the predesigned CSS layouts listed under the Layout section covered in "Using CSS Layouts in Dreamweaver" earlier in this chapter.

2. **Save the page in the root folder of the Web site.**

   It's important to save all the pages of a Web site in the root folder. You find more about defining a Web site and specifying a root folder in Dreamweaver in Chapter 2.

3. **Choose Modify⇨Page Properties and specify the page-wide options.**

   The Page Properties dialog opens.

   For this example, I set the page margins to 0 and the Background color to a dark blue color.

   Note that when you use the Page Properties dialog box, Dreamweaver creates the corresponding CSS styles for the <body> tag, saves them in an internal style sheet at the top of the HTML document, and displays the new styles in the CSS Styles panel. (You find instructions for moving internal styles into an external style sheet in Chapter 5.)

4. **Click the Insert Div Tag button in the Common Insert panel, as shown in Figure 6-12.**

   The Insert Div Tag dialog box opens.

   This is the first of a series of <div> tags you'll add to the page, and these steps can get a bit tricky, but the goal is simple — to insert a <div> tag for each section of content that you want to appear on the page. For this design (shown completed in Figure 6-11) I need five <div> tags; one to serve as the container for the entire design, which can also contain the banner image at the top; one for each of the three photos I want to line up in the three columns; and one for the footer, where I'll add my copyright information at the bottom of the page.

5. **In the Insert Div Tag dialog box, enter the container name in the ID field and then click OK.**

   A <div> tag is inserted into the page with the words: `Content for id "container" Goes Here.`

Although you can create styles for your <div> tags as you create them by clicking the New CSS Rule button, I often find it simpler to first create the <div> tags and name then, add the content to the <div> tags, and then go back and create the styles after the content's in place.

6. **Make sure your cursor is inside the `<div>` tag you just created, press Enter (Return) to add a paragraph break, and then click the Insert Div Tag button in the Common Insert panel to add another `<div>` tag inside the first one.**

   The Insert Div Tag dialog box opens.

7. **In the Insert Div Tag dialog box, enter** photo1 **in the ID field and then click OK.**

   A `<div>` tag is inserted into the page with the words: `Content for id "photo1" Goes Here.`

8. **Make sure your cursor is inside the first `<div>` tag named `container`, and just below the second `<div>` tag named `photo1`, and click the Insert Div Tag button in the Common Insert panel to add another `<div>` tag.**

9. **In the Insert Div Tag dialog box, enter** photo2 **in the ID field and then click OK.**

   A `<div>` tag is inserted into the page with the words: `Content for id "photo2" Goes Here.`

10. **Make sure your cursor is inside the first `<div>` tag named `container`, and just below the third `<div>` tag named `photo2`, and click the Insert Div Tag button in the Common Insert panel to add another `<div>` tag.**

11. **In the Insert Div Tag dialog box, enter the name** photo3 **in the ID field and then click OK.**

    A `<div>` tag is inserted into the page with the words: `Content for id "photo3" Goes Here.`

12. **Make sure your cursor is inside the first `<div>` tag named `container`, and just below the fourth `<div>` tag named `photo3`, and click the Insert Div Tag button in the Common Insert panel to add another `<div>` tag.**

13. **In the Insert Div Tag dialog box, enter the name of the footer in the ID field and then click OK.**

    A `<div>` tag is inserted into the page with the words: `Content for id "footer" Goes Here.`

If you've entered all the <div> tags correctly, your page should look like Figure 6-12. If you have accidentally created one <div> tag inside another when you don't mean to, choose Edit⇨Undo, move your cursor, and try again. You can also use split view: Position your cursor in the HTML code to get it where you want it and use the Insert Div Tag button in the Common Insert panel. See the sidebar "Splitting the view" for tips on how to use this approach.

14. **Add content to each <div> tag.**

    You can add content to each of your <div> tags as you would add content anywhere else on a page. For this example, I used the Insert Image icon in the Common Insert panel to add the images and then I typed in the text for the captions and copyright information.

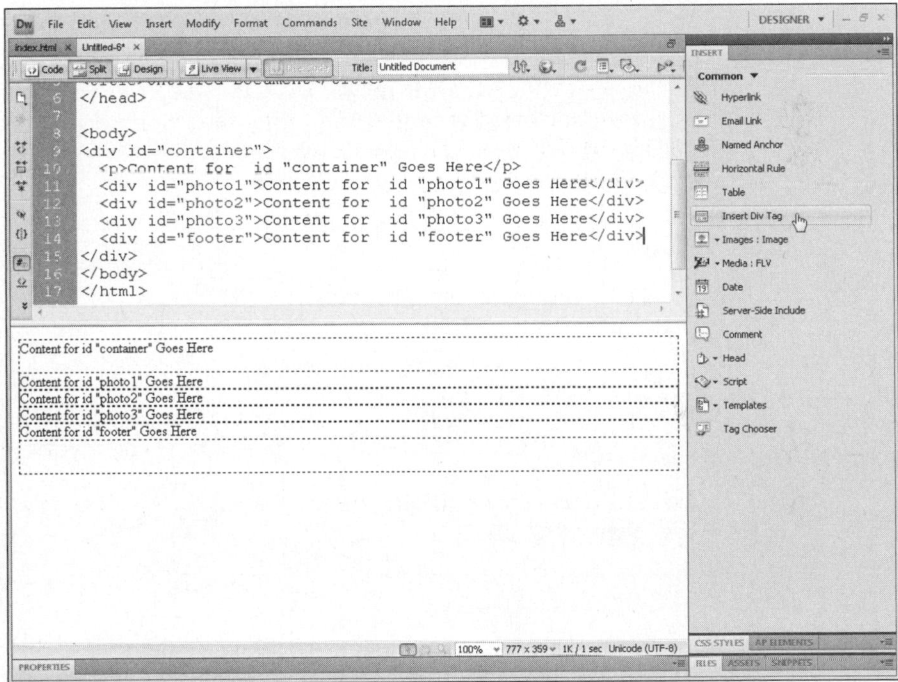

Figure 6-12: You can create a CSS layout like the one shown in Figure 6-11 by first creating a series of <div> tags like you see here.

Styling the container <div> tag

Think of the container <div> tag as the <div> tag that *contains* all the others. The styles you set for it create the overall width of the design you create with all the other <div> tags and other elements you insert inside the container <div> tag. To set the styles for the example in this section, follow these steps:

1. **Place your cursor at the beginning of** `Content the id "container" Goes Here`.

2. **Click the New CSS Rule icon (hint: it looks like a small piece of paper with a plus sign (+) over it) at the bottom of the CSS Styles panel.**

   The New CSS Rules dialog box opens. Because your cursor was inside the container `<div>`, `#container` should already be entered into the Selector Name field. If it's not, type it in exactly as you entered the name when you created the container `<div>`. If anything else is included in the Selector Name field, such as the `<p>` tag, delete it so that only `#container` remains.

3. **Leave the Rule Definition drop-down list set to This Document Only and click OK.**

   The CSS Rule definition for `#container` opens.

4. **In the CSS Rule Definition dialog box, specify the formatting settings.**

   As shown in Figure 6-13, for the container `<div>` tag in this example, I set the width to 780 pixels. Here's the trick to centering a `<div>` tag like this: Set the left and right margins to Auto. That way a browser automatically adds an equal amount of margin space to each side of the `<div>` tag, effectively centering it on the page.

5. **Click the Apply button to preview the style and then click OK to close the CSS Rule Definition dialog box and save the style.**

   When you create an ID style that matches the name of an ID assigned to a `<div>` tag, the style is applied immediately when you click the Apply button. (Make sure the ID and the style name are an exact match. If you add an extra space or mistype a character, this won't work.)

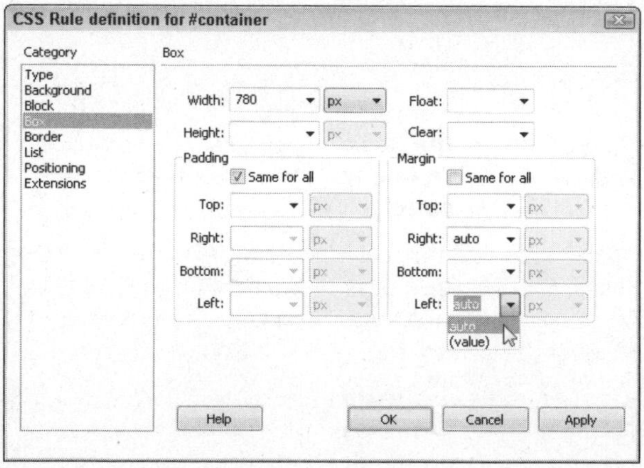

Figure 6-13: Set the left and right margins to Auto in the Box settings to center a <div> tag on a page.

Creating columns in the design

To ensure that your layout will work with three columns (at least that's the number of columns in the example for this section), calculate how wide to define the styles for each of your photo <div>s. Yes, that means you have to do a little math, and yes, you're certainly welcome to get out a calculator or make a sketch on scrap paper (or, as I prefer, do both). With this prep work out of the way, you're ready to create styles for the columns. The following steps walk you through the process:

1. **Calculate the width and positioning of the <div> tags that create the three columns in the design.**

   Let me walk you through the way I'd calculate this design. First, I know I set the width for the `#container` to 780 pixels so I know that's all the space I have to work with. Next, I know that each of the photos is 175 pixels wide, so I know that I have to subtract 175 times 3 (which is 525 pixels) from 780. That leaves me with 235 pixels to create margins between my three photos and the left and right side of my container. If I want to space them evenly, I'd then need to divide 235 by 3, but I've decided that I'd rather group the three photos in the middle of the design and leave more space on the right and left.

   So, I decide arbitrarily that I want 20 pixels of margin space between each of the images in the center area of the page and then I split up the remaining space on each side of the group of three photos. That means I need to subtract 40 pixels from 235, which leaves me with 195 pixels to split between the two sides. Because you can't use fractions of pixels, I put 98 pixels on the left and leave 97 pixels on the right.

   With the calculations complete, you're ready to define the styles for the three columns by creating ID styles for each of the photo <div>s. In addition to setting the width, padding, and margins for each style, I also used the Float option to align the <div>s to the left so that they align next to each other.

2. **Place your cursor inside the `<div>` you named `photo1` and then click the New CSS Rule icon (the one with the plus sign [+] over it) at the bottom of the CSS Styles panel.**

   The New CSS Rules dialog box opens. Because your cursor was inside the `photo1 <div>` tag, `#photo1` should already be entered into the Selector Name field. If it's not, type it exactly as you entered the name when you created the <div> tag.

   If one <div> tag is contained within another, as you see in this case where the `#photo1 <div>` tag is inside the `#container <div>` tag, then both names appear automatically in the Selector Name field. In this case, you have the option of deleting the name of the first div to create a simple ID style, or keeping both names to create a compound style which will only work if the styles are used together.

3. **Leave the Rule Definition drop-down list set to This Document Only and click OK**

   The CSS Rule definition for `#photo1` opens.

4. **Click to select the Box category and specify Width, Float, and Margin settings, as shown in Figure 6-14.**

   For the `photo1` `<div>` tag in this example, I set the width to 175 pixels, exactly the size of the photo. Next, choose Left from the Float drop-down list to align the `<div>` tag to the left side of the page. Now here's the tricky part, I want this `<div>` tag to be 98 pixels from the left side of my container, so I want to set the Left margin to 98 pixels. Finally, I set the Top, Right, and Bottom margins to 10. (I'll set the inside margins of the other two photos to 10 pixels to achieve a 20-pixel wide margin between them.)

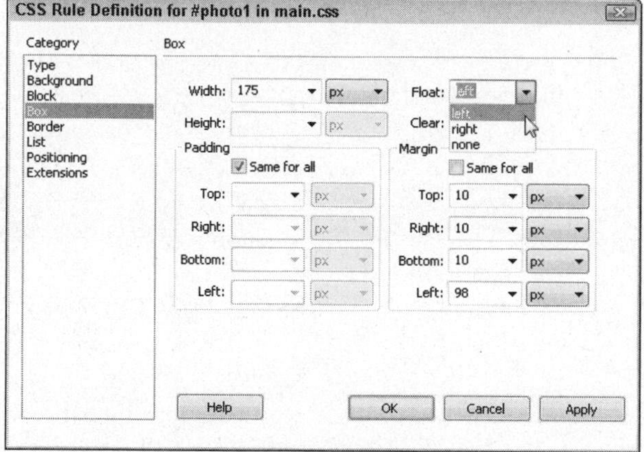

Figure 6-14: Use the Box settings to define the Width, Margin, and other settings.

5. **Click the Apply button to preview the style click OK to close the CSS Rule Definition dialog box and save the style.**

   The style is applied automatically, and the first photo aligns to the left, 98 pixels from the left side of the page.

6. **Place your cursor inside the `<div>` tag you named `photo2` and then click the New CSS Rule icon (the one with the plus sign [+] over it) at the bottom of the CSS Styles panel.**

   The New CSS Rules dialog box opens. Because your cursor was inside the `photo2` `<div>` tag, `#photo2` should already be entered into the Selector Name field. If it's not, type it exactly as you entered the name when you created the `<div>` tag.

7. **Leave the Rule Definition drop-down list set to This Document Only and click OK**

   The CSS Rule definition for #photo2 opens.

8. **Click to select the Box category and specify Width, Float, and Margin settings.**

   For the photo2 <div> tag in this example, I set the width to 175 pixels, exactly the size of the photo. Next, choose Left from the Float drop-down list to align the <div> tag to the left side of the page so it will float up next to the first photo. And finally, select the Same for All box under Margin and enter 10 in the Top field. A 10 automatically appears in all four margin fields because Same for All is selected.

9. **Click the Apply button to preview the style and then click OK to close the CSS Rule Definition dialog box and save the style.**

   The style is applied automatically, and the second photo aligns to the left, 20 pixels from the first photo.

10. **Place your cursor inside the <div> tag you named photo3 and then click the New CSS Rule icon (the one with the plus sign [+] over it) at the bottom of the CSS Styles panel.**

    The New CSS Rules dialog box opens. Because your cursor was inside the photo3 <div> tag, #photo3 should already be entered into the Selector Name field. If it's not, type it exactly as you entered the name when you created the <div> tag.

11. **Leave the Rule Definition drop-down list set to This Document Only and click OK**

    The CSS Rule definition for #photo3 opens.

12. **Click to select the Box category and specify Width, Float, and Margin settings.**

    For the photo3 <div> tag in this example, I set the width to 175 pixels, exactly the size of the photo. Next, choose Left from the Float drop-down list to align the <div> tag to the left side of the page so it will float up next to the second photo. And finally, enter 10 pixels in the Top, Bottom, and Left Margin fields.

    Leave the Right Margin field blank for photo3. Because it's aligned to the left, you don't need to specify the margin space on the right, and leaving this blank allows for greater flexibility if the page is viewed in an older browser version (some older browsers display margins differently; leaving this blank can prevent the third photo from wrapping down below the first two in older browsers).

13. **Click the Apply button to preview the style and then click OK to close the CSS Rule Definition dialog box and save the style.**

    The style is applied automatically, and the third photo aligns to the left, floating up to position 20 pixels from the second photo.

Wrapping up the custom layout

The last phase in creating the custom CSS layout example in this section is to style the footer and then make any additional changes you want to the design.

To create a style for the footer, in this example, use the Clear option to keep the footer positioned at the bottom of the page layout. If you're creating a multi-column design like the one in this example, and you use the Float option to align the columns to the left or right, you run the risk that the footer `<div>` tag at the bottom of the design will be displayed on top of or beside the columns instead of below them.

The reasons for this get complicated, but it has to do with how box elements change when you use the Float setting and take them out of the flow of the page. Because column heights can vary due to text size, differences in different browsers, and computer platforms, it's almost impossible to create columns of text on a Web page that will always be displayed with the same height. As a result, it's good practice to use the Clear option to ensure that the footer remains at the bottom of the design no matter what. Using the Clear option also ensures that the container will surround all the content on the page when it's displayed in a browser.

Follow these steps to create a style for the footer `<div>` tag:

1. **Place your cursor inside the footer `<div>` tag and then click the New CSS Rule icon (the one with the plus sign [+] over it) at the bottom of the CSS Styles panel.**

   The New CSS Rules dialog box opens. Because your cursor was inside the footer `<div>`, `#footer` should already be entered into the Selector Name field. If it's not, type it exactly as you entered the name when you created the `<div>` tag.

2. **Leave the Rule Definition drop-down list set to This Document Only. and click OK.**

   The CSS Rule definition for `#footer` opens.

3. **Click to select the Box category and specify the Padding and Clear settings.**

First, set the Padding to 10 with the Same for All button selected to add a little space around the copyright text in the footer.

Next, choose Both from the Clear drop-down list. This forces the footer to *clear* all the columns above it and ensures that the footer appears at the very bottom below all the content of the page.

After you style the footer, you can still add any other styles you want to format the text, images, and other elements in the design. To achieve the final design you see in Figure 6-11, I created styles to alter the text formatting of the captions as well as the copyright text in the footer. Using styles created with a class selector works well for this kind of formatting, which you can find more about in Chapter 5.

Positioning Elements with AP Divs

AP Divs, or *layers* in Dreamweaver 8, permit precise positioning of elements on an HTML page. Think of an AP Div as a container for other elements, such as images, text, tables, and even other layers. You can put this container anywhere on an HTML page and even stack these containers on top of each other.

With AP Divs, you can position text blocks and images exactly where you want them on a page by specifying the distance of the AP Div from the top and left sides of a page or from any other container, such as another `<div>` tag. With AP Divs, you can also layer, or stack, elements on top of each other by changing the Z Index setting.

Because an AP Div is a container, you can manipulate everything in it as a unit. For example, you can move one AP Div so that it overlaps another. You can even make AP Divs invisible and use JavaScript or another scripting language to change visibility dynamically.

Creating AP Divs

To create an AP Div, follow these steps:

1. **Choose Insert➪Layout Objects➪AP Div.**

   A box representing an empty AP Div appears at the top of the page, outlined in blue. Alternatively, you can click the Draw AP Div button in the Layout Insert panel and then click and drag to create a new AP Div anywhere in the work area.

2. **To reposition an AP Div on the page, click anywhere along the outline of the AP Div to select it and then drag it to the desired location.**

   When you hold the mouse over the outline of the AP Div, the cursor turns to a four-pointed arrow (or a hand on the Macintosh). You also see eight tiny, square handles around the perimeter of the box.

3. **Click and drag any handle to resize the AP Div.**
4. **To add content to an AP Div, insert your cursor inside the AP Div.**

   A blinking cursor appears inside the AP Div box.

5. **Choose Insert⇨Image.**

   The Select Image Source dialog box appears.

6. **Click the filename of the image you want to insert and then click OK.**

   The Image Tag Accessibility Attributes dialog box opens.

7. **Fill in the Alternate Text and Long description fields and then click OK.**

   The image is inserted into the AP Div.

8. **Enter any text you want in the AP Div by typing or using copy and paste as you would to add text anywhere else on a Web page.**

   AP Divs can be problematic when you're working with text because text size can change in Web pages when displayed on different computer platforms, and users can change the text size in their browsers. If you've created AP Divs that are sized to fit tightly around the text in the size it appears on your computer, the layout can change dramatically when the page is displayed on another computer. For example, if the text size is larger, the text can get cut off or overlap other elements on the page. The best way to avoid this problem is to leave the height unspecified. This enables the AP Div to adjust to fit the content so that nothing is positioned under the AP Div in the layout and thus nothing is likely to get hidden if the text overlaps the AP Div.

9. **To change AP Div settings in the Property inspector, click the little tab (which appears in the upper-left area of the AP Div when it's selected).**

   The Property inspector displays the AP Div settings, including its coordinates in relation to the left and top of a browser window when the AP Div is selected: L (for left), T (for top).

   As shown in Figure 6-15, the AP Div in this example is exactly 300 pixels from the left side of the browser window and 175 pixels from the top. In addition to using the click-and-drag method to move a layer, you can change a layer's position by entering numbers in the position boxes: L (number of pixels from the left edge of the page) and T (number of pixels from the top of the page). You can also change the height and width of an AP Div by entering a size in the width (W) and in the height (H) fields in the Property inspector.

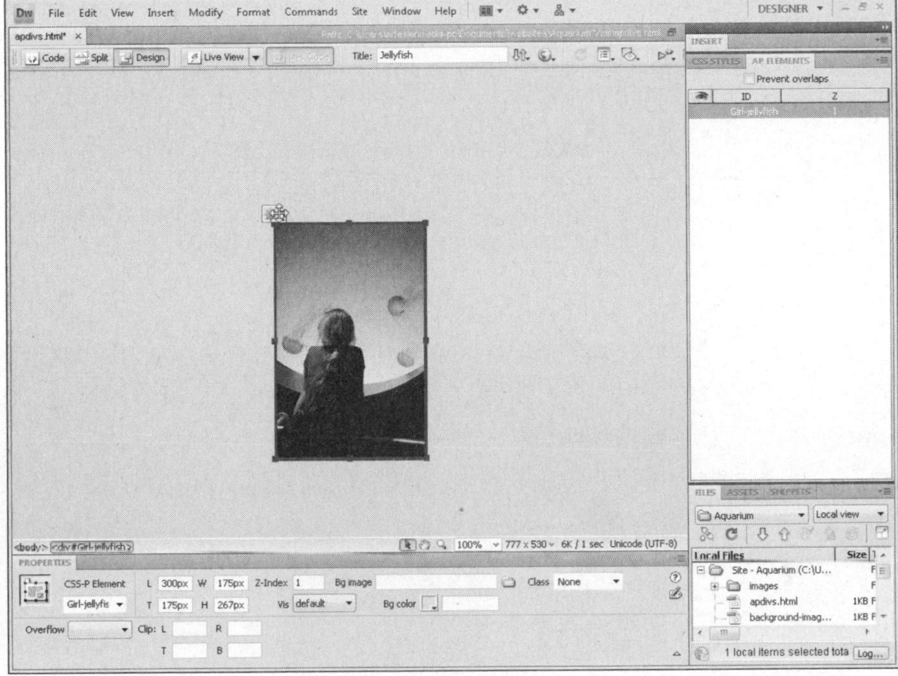

Figure 6-15: Change the height and width of an AP Div in the Property inspector.

10. **Name your AP Div by typing a name in the AP Div ID text box in the upper-left corner of the Property inspector.**

    When you create a new AP Div, Dreamweaver automatically names your AP Div for you, starting with `apDiv1`, `apDiv2`, and so on. I find it easier to keep track of AP Divs when I change the name to something more descriptive, especially if I'm working with lots of AP Divs on a page.

You must select the AP Div in the main work area first for its properties to appear in the Property inspector, where you can rename the AP Div and change the height, width, left, top, and other settings.

Stacking and changing visibility of AP Divs

A powerful feature of AP Divs is their maneuverability: You can stack them on top of each other and make them visible or invisible. To stack AP Divs, simply drag one AP Div on top of another. Unlike other elements in a Web page, AP Divs give you complete layout control by including the capability to overlap one another. You can use AP Divs to position and layer any element on a page. For example, to overlap images, simply place each image in a separate AP Div and then move one AP Div so that it overlaps the other. To let you control which AP Div is on top, Dreamweaver provides two ways to change the stacking order with the Z Index. You can change the Z Index from the Property inspector or the AP Elements panel (see Figure 6-16). To open the AP Elements panel shown in Figure 6-16, choose Window➪AP Elements.

To change the stacking order and visibility of AP Divs, follow these steps:

1. **Open a page that has two or more layers on it, such as the page with the jellyfish photos, as shown in Figure 6-17.**

Figure 6-16: The AP Elements panel can be used to change the visibility and stacking order of AP Divs.

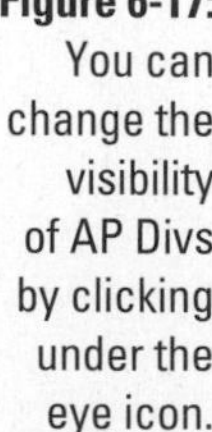

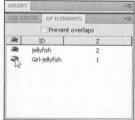

Figure 6-17: You can change the visibility of AP Divs by clicking under the eye icon.

2. **Select an AP Div by clicking anywhere on the border outline of the AP Div.**
3. **Choose Window➪AP Elements to open the AP Elements panel.**

   The AP Elements panel lists any AP Divs that have been inserted into a Web page.

   If you're familiar with layers in Adobe Photoshop or Macromedia Fireworks, you may find some similarities here, such as the eye icon to control visibility and the capability to drag AP Divs around in the panel to change their order.

4. **Reorder the stacking of the AP Divs by changing their corresponding Z Index numbers in the Property inspector or in the AP Elements panel.**

   The lowest number is the bottommost layer. The highest number is the topmost layer. To change the stacking order, simply select the number under the Z Index field and enter a higher or lower number.

5. **Click the eye icon to the left of any AP Div in the AP Elements panel to turn the layer visibility on or off.**

   If no eye appears, the visibility is set to the default, which usually means *on,* except in the case of nested AP Divs. (You find out about nested AP Divs in the next section.) If the eye is open, the AP Div is visible on the screen and in the browser. If the eye is closed, the layer is invisible.

   If you want to prevent any of your AP Divs from overlapping, select the Prevent Overlaps check box in the AP Elements panel.

Managing Conflicting Styles

Be careful when you apply more than one style to the same element (something that's easier to do than you may realize). The styles may conflict, and because browsers aren't always consistent in how they display styles, the results can be inconsistent and undesirable.

For the most part, the latest versions of Firefox and Internet Explorer display all attributes applied to any element, even if they're from different style rules, as long as the styles don't conflict. If they do conflict, browsers prioritize styles depending on how the styles have been defined and the order in which they appear. The method for determining this priority is what cascading is all about.

Cascading refers to the way in which multiple styles can apply to — or cascade over — the same element on a page. Because multiple styles can affect the same element, CSS has many rules to help prevent conflicts. These rules determine the priority each style should receive as a browser interprets styles. Style priorities are organized in a hierarchical order and work in a kind of a top-down fashion, similar to the way water cascades over rocks as it flows down a stream.

To help you better understand how styles cascade, consider this example. You can create a style for an entire page by redefining the `<body>` tag, the HTML tag that surrounds all the content displayed in the main window of a browser. So, for example, you could redefine the `<body>` tag with a rule that makes the default font for all text on your page Arial. Then you could redefine the `<h1>` tag with a rule that makes your headlines Garamond. And then the browser would have to determine how to display your headline based on this conflicting information. Should the headline be Arial because the page font is set to Arial in the `<body>` tag or should it be Garamond because that's the font in the `<h1>` tag?

To resolve this kind of conflict, CSS follows a hierarchy that can get rather complicated, but one of the simplest things to remember is that the closer a style is to an element (more specifically, a style defines an element), the higher that style's priority. So, as you might imagine, the headline style overrides the page style because it more specifically defines the style of the headline than the body style, which applies to the entire page.

CSS selectors also follow a hierarchy. Styles created with ID selectors are given priority over styles created with class, and both are given higher priority than styles that use the tag selector to redefine existing HTML tags. When styles have the same priority, deciding which is highest comes down to which style most specifically applies to an element.

Another basic guideline is that CSS rules get the highest priority, followed by HTML presentation attributes (for example, `align`, `color`, `face`, and `bgcolor`), followed by the browser default settings (font type and font size, for example). CSS rules always get the highest priority in any scenario. But within CSS, internal style sheets have priority over external style sheets, and *inline styles,* which are styles defined within the line of HTML code where the tag appears, get the highest priority.

Using Design Time Style Sheets

After you become savvy about using style sheets, you'll find that working with external style sheets affords the most power because you can link to them from multiple pages in your site rather than having to create a new internal style sheet for each page in your site. You have the added advantage in that you can easily alter your styles in just one place if you need to make changes after styles are applied. Even better, you can create multiple external style sheets as part of the design process and use a Dreamweaver feature — *design time style sheets* — to switch between them as you work on your document.

One benefit of the design time style sheets feature is that you can view how different external style sheets affect your page without linking to them. This feature is a great way to quickly switch between style sheets in a document and explore various what-if scenarios with the style sheets you create before you apply them. You may begin to like this feature because you can play around with and explore the full power of CSS. After you decide that you like a particular style sheet, you can apply it to your page as you do any other style sheet.

Design time style sheets affect only the appearance of styles in Dreamweaver. Because they're not real links, they show up only at runtime when a Dreamweaver document is open. Design time style sheet info is also stored in a design note file. If you want to preserve your design time style sheet info, be sure that you don't delete the corresponding design note file.

To set up design time style sheets, follow these steps:

1. **Choose Format⇨CSS Styles⇨Design-Time.**

   The Design Time Style Sheets dialog box appears.

2. **To work with a specific style sheet, click the Add Item button (+) above the Show Only at Design Time field.**

   The Select File dialog box appears, and you can select a CSS file. Remember that CSS files usually end with a `.css` extension. You can also add multiple CSS files by clicking the Add button again.

3. **To hide a specific style sheet, click the Add Item button (+) above the Hide at Design Time field and select from the Select File dialog box the style you want to hide.**

4. **To delete a listed style sheet from either category, select the style sheet and click the Remove Item button (–) to delete it.**

Chapter 7

Coming to the HTML Table

In This Chapter

- Introducing HTML tables
- Creating your tables in Standard mode
- Sorting your table data
- Importing data from other programs
- Working with tables for spacing and alignment
- Nesting your tables

In the early days of Web design, HTML tables offered one of the only options for creating complex page layouts. By splitting and merging table cells and using them as containers for text and images, Web developers could create intricate page designs despite the limits of HTML. Most were frustrated by this solution.

Using tables to create designs was far from ideal, and we often had to resort to special tricks, such as using a clear GIF to control spacing (see the sidebar, "The transparent, or clear, GIF trick," later in this chapter). But at least with tables you could position text, images, and other elements, anywhere you wanted on a page (well, almost anywhere). For example, you could use a table to align two columns of text side by side with a headline across the top like the format you might see in a newspaper or magazine. Because you could make the borders of a table invisible, you could use tables to create these kinds of designs without the table itself being visible on the page.

Today CSS has completely changed the way Web pages are created. Tables are still an ideal way to present tabular data on the Internet: For example, just about any content you could display in a spreadsheet can be formatted easily and effectively with a table. But tables are no longer the recommended solution for creating any other page layouts. Today, most professional designers use CSS to create page designs because these pages download faster, are easier to update, and are more flexible and accessible than tables ever were. Chapters 5 and 6 are dedicated to CSS and the latest developments in Web design.

This chapter is designed to help you appreciate how to create and edit tables in Dreamweaver. Even though tables are no longer *recommended* for most Web page layouts, you still find them used on many Web sites; so I've included a few tips for working with tables for page layouts, as well as formatting and sorting tabular data with tables in Dreamweaver.

Creating HTML Tables

Tables are made up of three basic elements: rows, columns, and cells. If you've ever worked with a spreadsheet program, you're probably familiar with tables. Tables in HTML are quite similar when it comes to working with tabular data. In most cases, you'll want to create a row of headings along the side or top of a table and then columns and rows that can be populated with text, images, and other data.

The code behind an HTML table is a complex series of `<tr>`, `<th>`, and `<td>` tags that indicate table rows, table header, and table data cells, respectively. Figuring out how to type those tags so that they create a series of little boxes on a Web page was never an intuitive process. If you wanted to merge or split cells to create rows or columns with varying numbers of cells, you faced a truly complex challenge.

Thank the cybergods that you have Dreamweaver to make this process easy. With Dreamweaver, you can easily

- Create tables and modify both the appearance and the structure of a table by simply clicking and dragging its edges.
- Add any type of content to a cell, such as images, text, and multimedia files — even nested tables.
- Use the Property inspector to merge and split cells, add color to the background or borders, and change the vertical and horizontal alignment of elements within a cell.

You can create tables in Standard or Expanded mode in Dreamweaver:

- **Expanded mode,** as shown in Figure 7-1, makes it easier to select inside and around tables by adding space around table borders. However, the display of a table changes in Expanded mode — it literally expands table cells. The added space makes editing content within tables easier, but the added space also changes the display.
- **Standard mode,** as shown in Figure 7-2, is more consistent with how tables will appear in a browser, so generally do most of your table editing, especially resizing and moving tables, in this mode.

You can switch between these two modes by clicking the Standard and Expanded mode buttons in the Layout menu bar at the top of the work area, as shown in Figures 7-1 and 7-2.

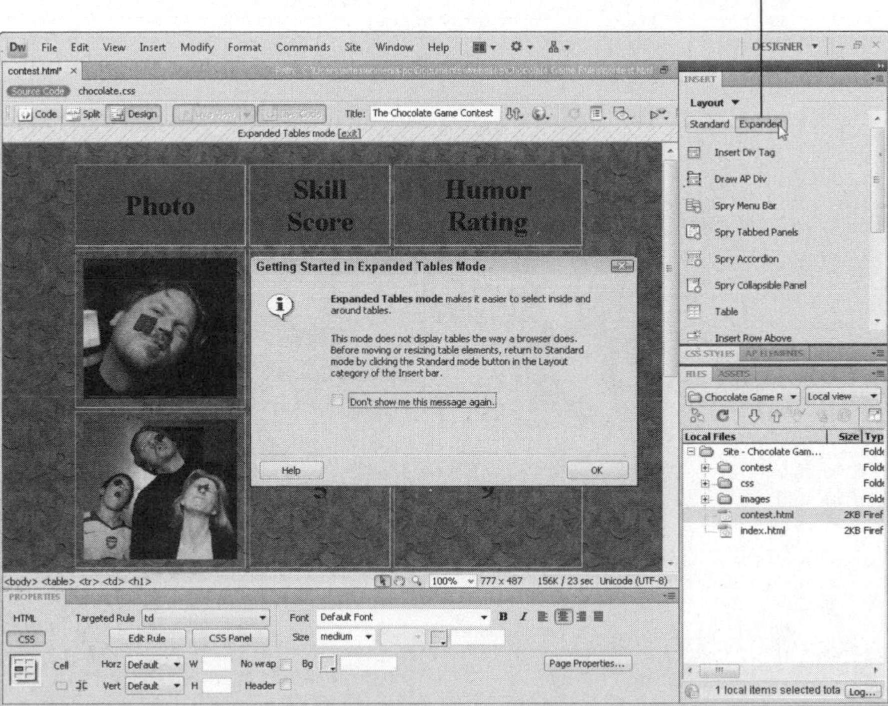

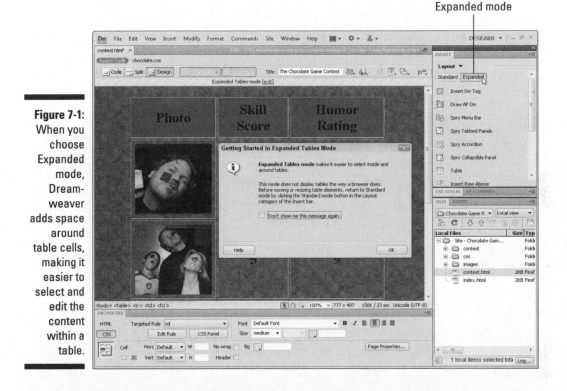

Figure 7-1: When you choose Expanded mode, Dreamweaver adds space around table cells, making it easier to select and edit the content within a table.

How wide should you make a table?

Designers often wonder how wide to make a table when they're using tables to control page layout. My advice is that if you're designing your pages for an 800 x 600 screen resolution (still a popular resolution among Internet users), a safe bet is to make your table no more than 780 pixels wide and center it in the middle of the page. That leaves a little room on each side to prevent the appearance of sideways scrollbars and causes the table to "float" in the middle of the page if users have a larger monitor. You also have the option of specifying a percentage width. For example, you can set the width of a table to 80 percent, and the table will fill 80 percent of the browser window no matter how wide the screen or the resolution of the monitor.

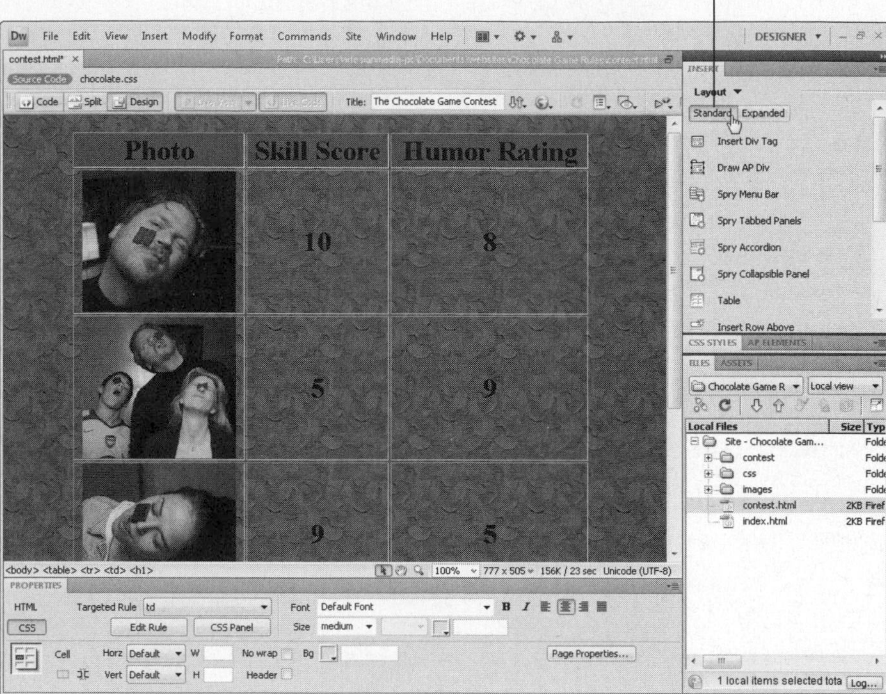

Figure 7-2: In Standard mode, Dreamweaver's table display is more consistent with how the layout will look in a Web browser, such as Firefox or Internet Explorer.

Creating Tables in Standard Mode

Although Expanded mode is useful for selecting and editing the contents of a table, Standard mode is best for creating tables. The following tips can help you create a table, and the sections that follow explain how to further refine it:

- **You can insert a table by choosing Insert⇨Table or by clicking the Table icon in the Common or Layout Insert panel.**
- **When you insert a new table, the Table dialog box, as shown in Figure 7-3, makes it easy to specify many table settings at once.** Don't worry about getting them all perfect; you can always change these options later.
- **You can edit all the table options, except the Accessibility options, in the Property inspector.** When you select a table or cell, the attributes appear in the Property inspector at the bottom of the work area. Click the border of any table to select the entire table, and the Property inspector displays the table options, as shown in Figure 7-4. To view all the options, click the expander arrow in the lower-right corner of the Property inspector. (All these options are described in the next section.)

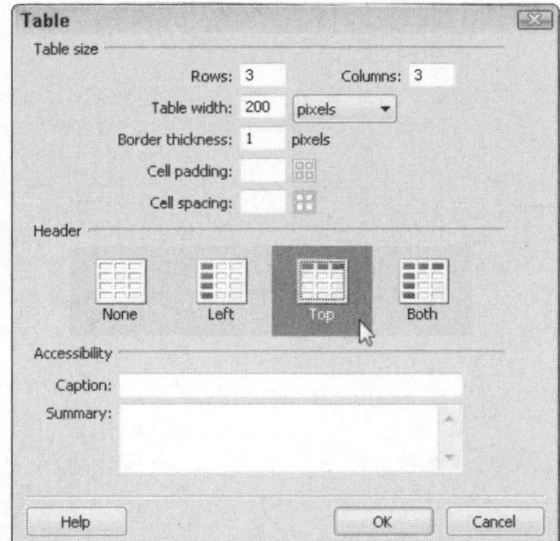

Figure 7-3: When you insert a table into a Web page, you can specify many table settings in this dialog box.

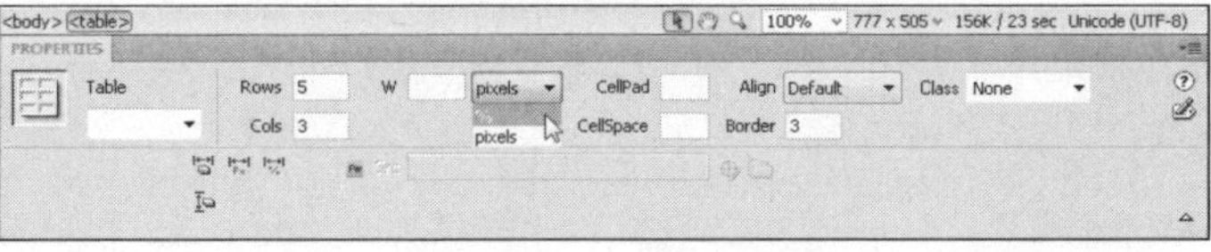

Figure 7-4: The Property inspector when a table is selected.

- **Select a table with the Select Table command.** If you're having trouble selecting the table (sometimes selecting the entire table and not just an individual cell is tricky), simply place your cursor anywhere inside the table and choose Modify➪Table➪Select Table.

Choosing your table's appearance

When you select a table in Dreamweaver, the Property inspector gives you access to the following table options for customizing the appearance of your table:

- **Table:** Provides a text area where you can enter a name for a table. This name, or ID, is useful for targeting the table in scripts.
- **Rows:** Displays the number of rows in the table. You can alter the size of the table by changing the number. Be careful, though: If you enter a smaller number, Dreamweaver deletes the bottom rows — contents and all.

- **Cols:** Displays the number of columns in the table. You can alter the size of the table by changing the number. Again, if you enter a smaller number, Dreamweaver deletes the columns on the right side of the table — contents and all.
- **W (width):** Displays the width of the table. You can alter the width by changing the number. You can specify the width as a percentage or a value in pixels. Values expressed as a percentage increase or decrease the table's size relative to the size of the user's browser window or any enclosing container, such as another table or a <div> tag.

  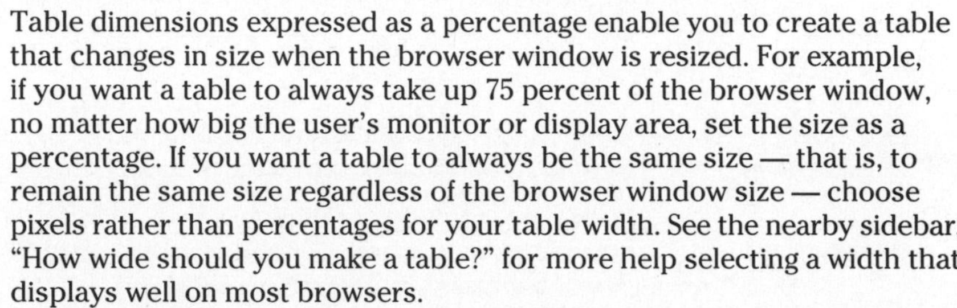

  Table dimensions expressed as a percentage enable you to create a table that changes in size when the browser window is resized. For example, if you want a table to always take up 75 percent of the browser window, no matter how big the user's monitor or display area, set the size as a percentage. If you want a table to always be the same size — that is, to remain the same size regardless of the browser window size — choose pixels rather than percentages for your table width. See the nearby sidebar, "How wide should you make a table?" for more help selecting a width that displays well on most browsers.

  If a table is inserted inside another container, such as a <div> tag or a table with a fixed width, it doesn't change size based on the browser window but is sized based on the container.

  Note: In Dreamweaver CS4, you no longer find an H (height) field. As a best practice, most designers don't specify a height for a table because the contents of a table, such as the font size text is displayed in) may change from one visitor to another (depending on user's system and settings).
- **CellPad:** Specifies the space between the contents of a cell and its border.
- **CellSpace:** Specifies the space between table cells.

Make sure the table fits the contents

Be aware that table cells automatically adjust to accommodate whatever you insert into them. For example, if you create a cell that's 100 pixels wide and then insert a 300-pixel-wide image, the table cell expands to fit the image. This can cause problems if the overall size of the table isn't set wide enough to accommodate all the objects within the table cells. When you build your tables, be aware of the size of the images and multimedia files you're inserting into cells or you may have unpredictable results. For example, if you set a table to a total width of 400 pixels and then insert 600 pixels worth of images, the table is forced to adjust in a way that contradicts the settings, when it does, some content may get cut off or expand beyond the desired width of the page layout. Worse yet, the table may not appear the same in all browsers as different browser try to accommodate these errors in different ways.

- **Align:** Controls the alignment of the table. The options are Default, Left, Center, and Right. As a general rule, the Default setting aligns the table from the left side of the browser window or other container.
- **Border:** Controls the size of the border around the table. The larger the number, the thicker the border. If you want the border to be invisible, set it to 0.
- **Class:** Provides easy access to style sheet options. (See Chapters 5 and 6 for more on CSS.)
- **Clear and Convert:** The icons in the lower-left area of the Property inspector (click the expander arrow in the lower-right corner to view them) provide these formatting options:
    - **Clear Row Heights** and **Clear Column Widths** enable you to remove all height and width values at one time.
    - **Convert Table Widths to Pixels** and **Convert Table Widths to Percents** enable you to automatically change Width settings from percentages to pixels. Pixels specify a fixed width; a percent setting means the browser automatically adjusts the specified percentage of the browser display area.

You can also apply formatting options and change the attributes of any element, such as text, an image, or a multimedia file, that you've placed within a table cell. To do so, click to select the element and then use the options in the CSS or HTML Property inspector to make any desired changes, just as you would if the element wasn't in a table cell.

Making tables more accessible

When you develop tables, you can do a few simple things to make your Web pages and your content, more accessible. One of the most important is to use the Table Header (`<th>`) tag for table headings. The `<th>` or Table Header tag works much like the `<td>`, Table Data tag, to create table cells, except that the `<th>` tag adds bold formatting and centering to content. You can alter the formatting of the `<th>` tag by creating a tag style (see Chapter 5 for how to do that), but make sure you use the `<th>` no matter what, as any content that's contained in that tag will be recognized by screen readers and other programs as the header content of the table.

When you create a new table, don't skip the Accessibility options at the bottom of the Table dialog box (refer to Figure 7-3). They're important for anyone who uses a browser that *reads* Web pages, such as those used by people with limited vision. If you enter a table caption, it's displayed within the table. (You can specify with the Align Caption option where the caption appears.) The Table Summary doesn't appear in a Web browser and is used only to describe the table for visitors who can't *see* the table of contents.

Specifying cell options

In addition to changing overall table settings, you can specify options for individual cells within a table. When you select a cell, which you can do by clicking to place the cursor anywhere inside the cell area, the Property inspector changes to display the individual properties for that cell (see Figure 7-5), such as the formatting and alignment of the contents of a particular cell.

In Dreamweaver CS4, the Property inspector features both HTML and CSS settings. CSS settings are generally preferred and work the same for the contents of a table cell as they do for content anywhere else on a Web page. (See Chapters 5 and 6 for more on using CSS.)

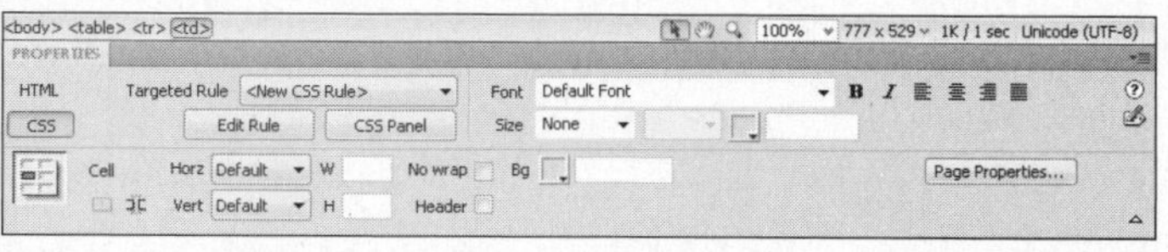

Figure 7-5: The Property inspector displays cell properties when <td> or <th> tags are selected.

You can also change multiple cells at the same time. For example, suppose that you want to have some (but not all) cells in your table take on a certain color background and style of text. You can apply the same properties to multiple cells by selecting more than one cell at a time before choosing the settings in the Property inspector. To select adjacent cells, press the Shift key while clicking to select cells. To select multiple cells that aren't adjacent, press the Ctrl key (the ⌘ key on the Mac) and click each cell you want to select. Any properties you change in the Property inspector apply to all selected cells.

If you're having trouble selecting an individual cell because it contains an image, click the image and then use either the ← or → key on your keyboard to move the cursor and deselect the image, which activates the Property inspector and displays the options for that cell.

When one or more cells are selected (they have to be adjacent for this to work), the top half of the Property inspector controls the formatting of text and URLs within the table cells. The lower half of the Property inspector provides these table cell attribute options (refer to Figure 7-5):

- **Merge Cells icon:** Merges two or more cells. To merge cells, you must first select two or more cells by clicking and dragging or by pressing either the Shift or Ctrl key while selecting multiple cells.
- **Split Cell icon:** Splits one cell into two. When you select this option, a dialog box lets you specify whether you want to split the row (you split the cell horizontally) or the column (you split the cell vertically). You can then specify the number of columns or rows, which controls how many times the cell divides. Note that you can apply the Split Cell option to only one cell at a time.
- **Horz:** Controls the horizontal alignment of the cell contents.
- **Vert:** Controls the vertical alignment of the cell contents.
- **W:** Controls the width of the cell.
- **H:** Controls the height of the cell.
- **No Wrap:** Prevents word wrapping within the cell. The cell widens to accommodate all text while you type or paste it into a cell. (Normally, the excess text just moves down to the next line and increases the height of the cell.)
- **Header:** Formats a cell's contents by using a header tag, which displays the text in bold and centered by default in most Web browsers.
- **Bg (color):** Click in the color well to select a background color from the color palette or enter a hexadecimal color code into the text field. If you use the color palette, the hexadecimal code is entered automatically into the Bg color field.

Formatting multiple columns in a table

When you're working with lots of cells in a table, you may want to format multiple cells in the same way. Dreamweaver makes that task easy, whether you want to align numbers, make the headings bold, or change the color scheme. Before you start planning how to line up all your numbers perfectly, be aware that you don't have as much control in HTML as you have in a program, such as Excel, where you can align numbers to the decimal point. You can, however, align the content of columns to the left, right, or center. Thus, if you use the same number of digits after the decimal point in all your numbers, you can get them to line up. For example, if one price is $12.99 and another is $14, express the latter as $14.00; then, when you right align, the numbers line up properly. (If your columns still aren't lining up the way you want them to, consider using a monospace font, such as Courier, which lines up better.)

The steps in this section explain how to create a table in Standard mode and align all the data cells to the right so that the numbers or other content align consistently. You can use these exercises also to align the contents of table cells to the left or center and to apply other formatting options, such as bold or italic. In these steps, I insert the data into the table after I create the table in Dreamweaver.

If you want to import data from a table you've created in a program, such as Word or Excel, see the section, "Importing Table Data from Other Programs," later in this chapter. If you're working with a table that already has data in it and just want to format or align the cells, go directly to Step 7.

If you're starting from scratch, create a new, blank HTML page and follow these steps from the beginning:

1. **Make sure that you're in Standard mode. (Choose View⇨Table Mode⇨Standard Mode.)**

2. **Click to place the cursor where you want to create a table.**

   In both Standard and Expanded modes, tables are created automatically in the top-left area of the page, unless you insert them after other content.

3. **Click the Table icon on the Common or Layout Insert panel.**

   Alternatively, you can choose Insert⇨Table. The Insert Table dialog box appears.

4. **In the appropriate boxes, type the number of columns and rows you want to include in your table.**

   Remember you can always add or remove cells later with the Property inspector.

5. **Specify the width, border, cell padding, and cell spacing.**

6. **Choose the header option that best corresponds to the layout you want for your table to create a row of header cells across the top, side, or both.**

7. **Add a caption and summary in the Accessibility section and click OK.**

   The table automatically appears on the page.

8. **Click to place the cursor in a cell and then type the data you want in that cell. Repeat for each cell.**

   Alternatively, you can use Edit⇨Paste Special to insert columnar data from another program, such as Excel.

9. **Select the column or row for which you want to change the alignment.**

   Place the cursor in the first cell in the column or row you want to align; then, click and drag your mouse to highlight the other columns or rows that you want to change.

10. **Choose an alignment option from the Horz (horizontal) or Vert (vertical) drop-down lists in the Property inspector, as shown in Figure 7-6.**

    The content of the cell adjusts to match the selected alignment option.

Alternatively, you can access many formatting options, including alignment options, by selecting a table and then right-clicking (Windows) or Control-clicking (Mac).

You can also apply other formatting options, such as bold or italic, to selected cells and their contents by choosing the option from the from the Property inspector.

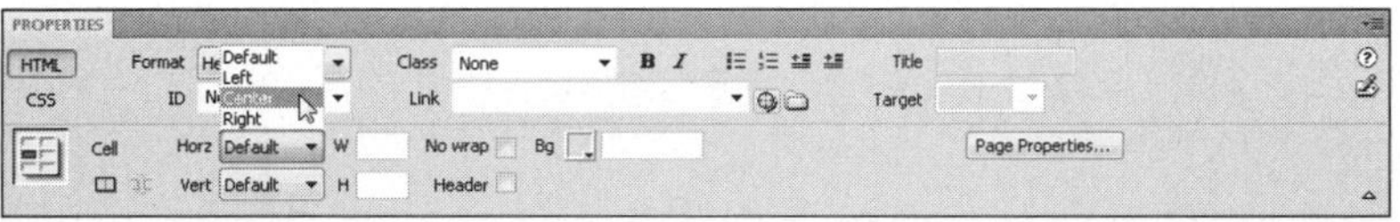

Figure 7-6: The Property inspector displaying the Table options.

If you want to format one cell in a column or row differently from the others, click to place the cursor in just that cell and then click one of the formatting options in the Property inspector. You can also choose to align multiple cells that aren't *contiguous* (they don't touch each other) by pressing and holding the Ctrl key (⌘ on the Mac) in Windows while you click the cells you want to select. Any options you change on the pop-up menu or in the Table Property inspector apply to all selected cells.

You can also use CSS to format the cells within a table. To do so, select the cell or cells, click the CSS button in the Property inspector, and use the CSS options to create and apply styles while you format the table. You find instructions for creating styles, which can be applied to tables as well as any other elements in a Web page, in Chapters 5 and 6.

Vertical alignment solves common problem

If you're having trouble getting the contents of adjacent cells to line up with each other, setting vertical alignment to Top may solve your problem. A common frustration when you're building tables is that you have two or more rows side by side with text in one and images in the other, and you want the top of the image and the top of the text to line up. Often they don't line up because they're different lengths, and the table is trying to adjust the contents to best use the space within their respective cells. The solution is simple: Select all the cells you want to align, and in the Property inspector, change vertical alignment to Top. Seemingly like magic, all the content jumps right to the top of the cells and lines up perfectly. This is such a common problem that I routinely set the vertical alignment of table cells to Top.

Merging and splitting table cells

Sometimes, the easiest way to modify the number of cells in a table is to *merge* cells (combine two or more cells into one) or *split* cells (split one cell into two or more rows or columns). With this technique, you can vary the space in table sections and customize their structures. For example, you may want a long cell space across the top of your table for a banner and then multiple cells below it so that you can control the spacing between columns of text or images. The following two sets of steps show you how to merge and split cells in a table.

To merge cells, create a new HTML page or open an existing HTML file and follow these steps (see Chapter 2 for more information on creating files):

1. **Choose Insert⇨Table and create a table with 4 rows and 4 columns, a 75 percent width, and a border of 1.**
2. **Choose the header option that best corresponds to the layout you want for your table to create a row of header cells across the top, side, or both.**
3. **Add a caption and summary in Accessibility section.**
4. **Click OK.**

   The table appears on the page.
5. **Highlight two or more adjacent cells by clicking and dragging the mouse from the first cell to the last.**

   You can merge only cells that are adjacent to one another and in the same row or column.
6. **Click the Merge Selected Cells icon, in the lower-left region of the Property inspector (as shown in Figure 7-7), to merge the selected cells into a single cell.**

   The cells are merged into a single cell by using the Colspan or Rowspan attributes. These HTML attributes make a single cell merge with adjacent cells by spanning extra rows or columns in the table.

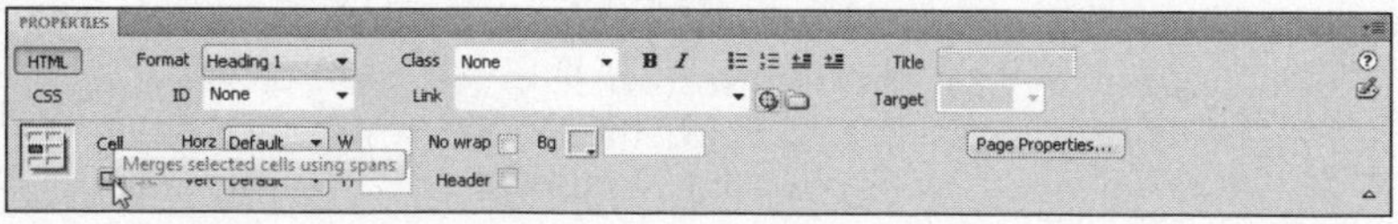

Figure 7-7: The Property inspector includes small icons that merge and split cells.

To split a cell, create a new table or open a page with an existing table and follow these steps:

1. **Click to place the cursor inside any cell you want to split.**
2. **Click the Split Selected Cell icon, in the lower-left region of the Property inspector.**

   The Split Cell dialog box appears.
3. **Select Rows or Columns in the dialog box, depending on how you want to divide the cell.**

   You can split a cell into however many new rows or columns you want.
4. **Type the number of rows or columns you want to create.**

   The selected cell is split into the number of rows or columns you entered.

Sorting Table Data

When you're working with lots of columnar data, you want to be able to sort that data just as you do in a spreadsheet program, such as Excel. In Dreamweaver, you can sort data even after it's formatted in HTML (something you couldn't easily do before). You still don't have as many options as you do in Excel. For example, you can sort an entire table based on a specified row, but you can't sort different rows individually.

To use the Sort Table Data feature, create a new, blank HTML page, add a table with several rows and columns, and add some content. (I explain how in the preceding section.) You may also open an existing page with a table of columnar data. Then, follow these steps:

1. **Select the table you want to sort.**

   Place the cursor in any cell of the table you want to sort.
2. **Choose View⇨Table Mode⇨Standard Mode.**
3. **Choose Commands⇨Sort Table.**

   The Sort Table dialog box appears, as shown in Figure 7-8.
4. **Specify which column you want to sort by and then choose Alphabetically or Numerically; and Ascending or Descending.**

   You can set up one or two sorts to happen simultaneously and opt whether to include the first row and whether to keep the `<tr>` (Table Row) attributes with a sorted row by selecting Keep All Row Colors the Same.

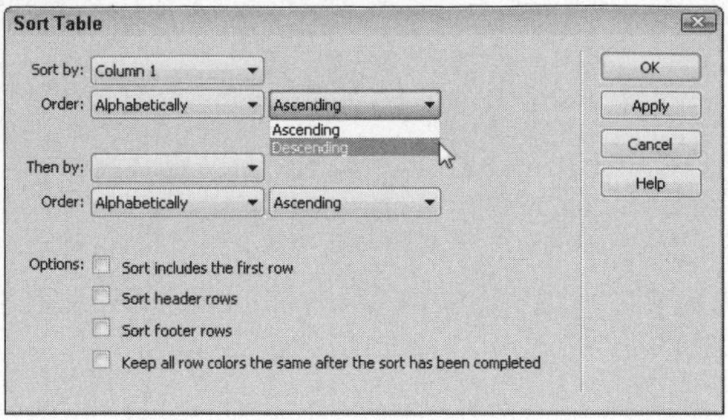

Figure 7-8: You can sort cell contents alphabetically or numerically, even after they're formatted in HTML.

5. **Click OK.**

   The selected cells are sorted, just as they are in a program, such as Excel. (Pretty cool, huh?)

Importing Table Data from Other Programs

Manually converting financial data or other spreadsheet information can be tedious. Fortunately, Dreamweaver includes a special feature that enables you to insert table data created in other applications, such as Word or Excel. To use this feature, the table data must be saved from the other program in a *delimited* format — the columns of data are separated by tabs, commas, colons, semicolons, or another type of delimiter. Most spreadsheet and database applications, as well as Microsoft Word, enable you to save data in a delimited format; files with a CSV (Comma Separated Values) file extension are one example. Consult the documentation for the application you're using to find out how. After the data is saved in a delimited format, you can import it into Dreamweaver.

To import table data into Dreamweaver after it's been saved in a delimited format (such as CSV) or in its native application (such as Access or Excel), create a new, blank HTML page or open an existing file and follow these steps to import the data:

1. **Choose File⇨Import⇨Tabular Data or choose Insert⇨Table Objects⇨Import Tabular Data.**

   The Import Tabular Data dialog box appears (see Figure 7-9).

2. **In the Data File text box, type the name of the file you want to import or use the Browse button to locate the file.**

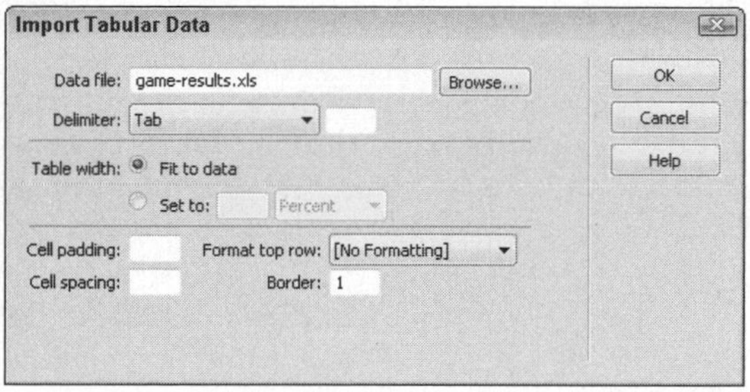

Figure 7-9: You can import tabular data into Dreamweaver from other programs, such as Excel.

3. **In the Delimiter drop-down list, select the delimiter format you used when you saved your file in the native application.**

   The delimiter options are Tab, Comma, Semicolon, Colon, and Other. You should have made this choice when you exported the data from the original program in which you created it, such as Excel or Access. If you don't remember what you chose, you can always go to the original program and export the data again. You must select the correct option for your data to import correctly.

4. **Select the table width.**

   If you choose Fit to Data, Dreamweaver automatically creates the table to fit the data being imported. If you choose Set, you must specify a percent or pixel size.

5. **(Optional) Specify the cell padding and cell spacing only if you want extra space around the data in the table to be created.**

6. **(Optional) Choose an option from the Format Top Row drop-down list only if you want to format the data in the top row of the table.**

   Your options are Bold, Italic, or Bold Italic.

7. **Specify the border size.**

   The default is 1, which puts a small border around the table. Choose 0 if you don't want the border to be visible. Choose a larger number if you want a thicker border.

8. **Click OK to automatically create a table with the imported data.**

Dreamweaver also enables you to export data from a table into a delimited format. This capability is useful if you want to export data from a Web page so that you can import it into another program, such as Word or Excel, or into a database program, such as FileMaker or Access. To export data from Dreamweaver, place the cursor anywhere in the table and choose File➪Export➪Table. In the Export Table dialog box, choose from the options on the Delimiter drop-down list (you can choose Tab, Space, Comma, Semicolon, or Colon). From the Line Breaks drop-down list, specify the operating system (you can choose Windows, Mac, or UNIX).

Using Tables for Spacing and Alignment

Tables have long been used on the Web to create page layouts that require more than basic alignment of elements on a page. In the early days of Web design, using tables was one of the only ways you could get around many of the limitations of basic HTML and accomplish some otherwise impossible design feats, such as evenly spacing bullets, creating columns side-by-side on a page, and spanning headlines or images across multiple columns.

Today, CSS offers a much better option for these kinds of designs, but many people are still using tables and you may have Web sites that you created in this way (or you may inherit a design that uses them). If you're working on a site that's designed with tables to create a page layout for any content that isn't tabular, such as the Chocolate Game Rules page, as shown in Figure 7-10, consider redesigning the page layout with `<div>` tags and CSS, which are covered in detail in Chapter 6.

Figure 7-10: Many two-column page layouts, such as the one shown here, were created with HTML tables.

Nesting Tables within Tables

Placing tables within tables, or *nested tables,* can help you create extremely complex designs. For example, with a table that contains all the scores of all the baseball games in a season, you could add a smaller table inside one cell to include detailed stats of an exceptional game. You create nested tables by inserting a table within a cell of another table.

The best Web designs communicate the information to your audience in the most elegant and understandable way and are easy to download. To make sure that your designs don't get too messy, remember these guidelines:

- A table within a table within a table is nested three levels deep. Anything more than that gets hairy.
- Pages that use nested tables take longer to download because browsers have to interpret each table individually before rendering the page. For some designs, the slightly longer download time is worth it, but in most cases, you're better off adding or merging cells in one table, as I explain in the section "Merging and splitting table cells," earlier in this chapter. One situation that makes a nested table worth the added download time is when you want to place a table of financial or other data in the midst of a complex page design.

To place a table inside another table, follow these steps:

1. **Click to place the cursor where you want to create the first table.**
2. **Choose Insert⇨Table.**

   The Insert Table dialog box appears.
3. **Type the number of columns and rows you need for your design.**
4. **Set the Width option to whatever is appropriate for your design and then click OK.**

   The table is sized automatically to the width you set.
5. **Click to place the cursor in the cell in which you want to place the second table.**
6. **Repeat Steps 2–4, specifying the number of columns and rows you want and the width of the table.**

   The new table appears inside the cell of the first table.
7. **Type the information that you want in the nested table cells as you would enter content in any other table.**

Chapter 8

Framing Your Pages

In This Chapter

- Introducing HTML frames
- Creating frame pages
- Knowing when *not* to use frames
- Setting targets and links
- Changing the properties of frames

Using HTML frames to create a Web site is a little like putting pink plastic flamingos on your front lawn — some people love them, some people hate them.

Thus making the most of frames requires appreciating not only the best way to create frames but also the best ways to use them and why so many Web designers have vowed never to use them. Many experienced Web designers say you should never use frames because they can confuse visitors as they navigate around a site and because frames hide the actual URL of each page (only the main address of the main frame page is displayed in a browser, even when a visitor clicks a link that opens another page in the frameset).

These are valid reasons to avoid using frames, but I still think it's important to include instructions for creating frames in this book. Afterall, even if all you want to do is redesign a site that was created with frames, you still need at least a basic understanding of how frames work just to deconstruct the existing site before you re-create it in a new layout option, such as the much-preferred CSS approach covered in Chapter 6.

Overall, I try to take a non-judgmental approach to frames — I don't *recommend* frames, but I can think of a few instances when frames come in handy, such as when you want to bring in content from another Web site and still maintain your own navigation and logo. Of course, you should do this only with permission from the other site (see the sidebar later in this chapter, "Resist using frames when linking to other Web sites").

Frames are used, for example, by a number of universities and other large institutions to rein in the many different designs created by different departments while still providing some consistent navigation and branding.

Frames aren't the only way to solve the problem of many Web designers working on one site, but they are a common approach to this common problem.

For all these reasons, this chapter covers how to build HTML framesets in Dreamweaver and also discusses when frames are most useful and when you may be better off avoiding them. Frames add a wide range of design possibilities, but they can also be frustrating to viewers. As you go through this chapter, consider not only how to create frames but also whether they are really the best solution for your Web site project.

Introducing the Basics of HTML Frames

Frames enable you to display multiple HTML pages in one browser window and control the content of each framed area individually. Web pages that use frames are split into separate sections — or individual *frames.* All the frames together make up a *frameset.* Behind the scenes, each frame of the frameset is a separate HTML file, which makes a page with frames a little complicated to create, even with Dreamweaver.

If you choose to create your frame files in a text editor, you have to juggle multiple pages, working on one frame at a time, and you can see what you create only when you preview your work in a browser. The visual editor in Dreamweaver makes creating frames a lot easier because you can view all the HTML files that make up the frameset at the same time and can edit them while they appear in the way in which they will appear in a browser.

Web developers commonly use frames to create a design with two or more sections within one browser window. Each section consists of a different HTML page, and you can place links in one section that, when selected, display information in another page in a different section of the frameset within the same browser window.

As a navigational feature, frames enable you to keep some information constant while changing other information in the same browser window. For example, you can keep a list of links visible in one frame and display the information each link brings up in another frame, as the site shown in Figure 8-1 does.

You can create as many frames as you want within a browser window. Unfortunately, some people overuse them and create designs that are so complex and broken up that they're neither aesthetically appealing nor easily navigable. Putting too many frames on one page can also make a site hard to read because the individual windows are too small. This has led many Web surfers to passionately hate frames. And some sites that rushed to implement frames when they were first introduced have since either abandoned frames or minimized their use.

Figure 8-1: With frames, you can display multiple pages in one browser window.

Here's a list of guidelines when using frames:

- **Don't use frames just for the sake of using frames.** If you have a compelling reason to use frames, create an elegant and easy-to-follow frameset. But don't do it just because Dreamweaver makes creating them relatively easy.
- **Limit the use of frames and keep files small.** Remember that each frame you create represents another HTML file. Thus, a frameset with three frames requires a browser to fetch and display four Web pages (each page file plus a fourth that holds them all together). Displaying them all in one browser may dramatically increase download time.
- **Turn off frame borders.** Browsers that support frames also support the capability to turn off the border that divides frames in a frameset. If you turn off the borders, your pages look cleaner. Frame borders, as shown in Figure 8-1, are thick and an ugly gray, and they can break up a nice design. You can change the color in the Property inspector, but I still recommend that you use them only when you feel that they're absolutely necessary. I show you how to turn off frame borders in the "Changing Frame Properties" section toward the end of this chapter.
- **Don't use frames when you can use CSS instead.** By far the preferred way to create a page layout today is to use CSS, covered in Chapters 5 and 6. If your goal is to create a layout for photos, like the one featured in this chapter, consider also using the Swap Image behavior covered in Chapter 10.

- **Don't place frames within frames.** The windows get too darned small to be useful for much of anything, and the screen looks horribly complicated. You can also run into problems when your framed site links to another site displayed in your frameset. The "Resist using frames when linking to other Web sites" sidebar provides many more reasons to limit using frames inside of frames.
- **Put in alternate** `<noframes>` **content.** The number of users surfing the Web with browsers that don't support frames becomes smaller every day. Still, showing them *something* other than a blank page is a good idea. I usually put in a line that says, "This site uses frames and requires a frames-capable browser to view." `<noframes>` content can also be read by search engines, which may otherwise fail to catalog the content within framed pages.

Understanding How Frames Work

Frames are a bit complicated, but Dreamweaver helps make the whole process of creating them somewhat easier. When you create a Web page with frames in Dreamweaver, remember that each frame area is a separate HTML file, and Dreamweaver saves each frame area as a separate page. You also want to keep track of which file displays in which of the frames so that you can aim links properly.

Figure 8-2 shows a simple frameset example with three frames, each containing a different HTML page and different text (*Page 1, Page 2,* and *Page 3*) so that I can clearly refer to them in the following numbered steps.

In addition to the files that appear in each frame, create a separate HTML file to generate the frameset. This page doesn't have a `<body>` tag, but it describes the frames and tells the browser how and where to display them. This gets a little complicated but don't worry: Dreamweaver creates the frameset HTML file for you. I just want to give you a general understanding of all the files that you're creating so that the following steps make more sense.

To help you understand how this works, look at the example in Figure 8-2. In this document, you see three frames, each displaying a different HTML page. The fourth HTML file that makes up the frame page *contains* the other frames but doesn't show up in the browser. This file is the frameset file, and it describes where and how each frame is displayed. For example, whether they're on the left, right, top, or bottom of the page and how large they are. The frameset file also contains other information, such as the name of each frame, which is used to specify which frame a link opens into, or *targets.* You find out more about linking frames in the "Setting Targets and Links in Frames" section, later in this chapter.

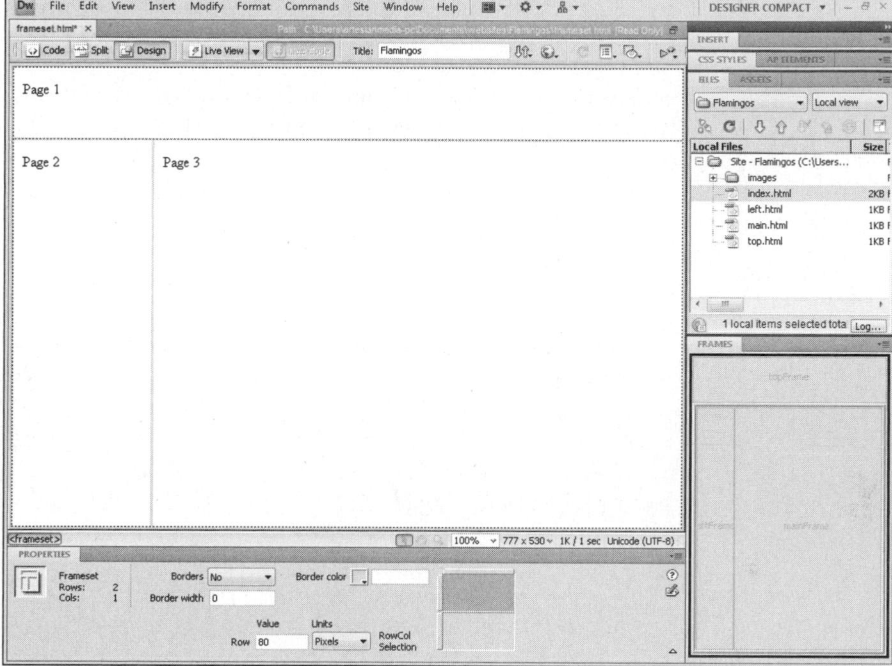

Figure 8-2: This three-frame frameset is comprised of four different HTML files: index.html, left.html, main.html, and top.html.

Creating a frameset in Dreamweaver

When you create a frameset page in Dreamweaver, you create multiple pages — the frameset file and each of the files that will be displayed initially within the frameset. When you edit the *content* of any of the frames in a frameset, you're editing not the frameset file but the files that populate the framed regions within the frameset.

If you're not using a program like Dreamweaver, you have to edit each of the files in a frameset separately, but Dreamweaver makes designing with frames easier by letting you edit the content of each frame in the *context* of the frameset as it will be displayed in a browser. If you can grasp this concept, you've come a long way toward understanding how frames work and how to use Dreamweaver to create and edit them. If it hasn't sunk in yet, read on. After you start creating and editing framesets, all these concepts should make a lot more sense.

You can create frames in three ways in Dreamweaver:

- The simplest method is to use a predesigned frameset from Dreamweaver's Samples collection. See the next section, "Creating a frameset from a sample."

- The second method is to create a page and then choose a predefined frameset from the Layout Insert panel, covered in the upcoming section "Creating a frameset using the Layout Insert panel."
- The third method, which can also be used to alter a frameset created by either of the first two methods, is to split a single HTML file into two or more sections, which then become separate pages within a frameset. To split a page into two frames, choose Modify➪Frameset and then choose any of the four options: Split Frame Left, Split Frame Right, Split Frame Up, or Split Frame Down to divide the page accordingly.

When you split a page that isn't yet part of a frameset, Dreamweaver automatically generates an untitled page with the `<frameset>` tag and then additional untitled pages appear in each of the frames within the frameset. When that happens, you're suddenly managing more than just one page. This concept is important to understand because you have to save and name each of these pages as a separate file, even though Dreamweaver makes it appear as though you're working on only one page that's broken into sections.

In general, I recommend that you save new HTML files before inserting anything into them. However, the opposite is true when you work with frame files in Dreamweaver. Wait until after you create all the frames in your frameset and *then* save them one at a time; otherwise, tracking your files can get even more complicated and confusing. I explain more in the "Saving files in a frameset" section, later in this chapter.

Creating a frameset from a sample

To create a simple frameset in Dreamweaver, such as the one shown in Figure 8-2, follow these steps:

1. **Choose File➪New.**

   The New Document dialog box opens, as shown in Figure 8-3.

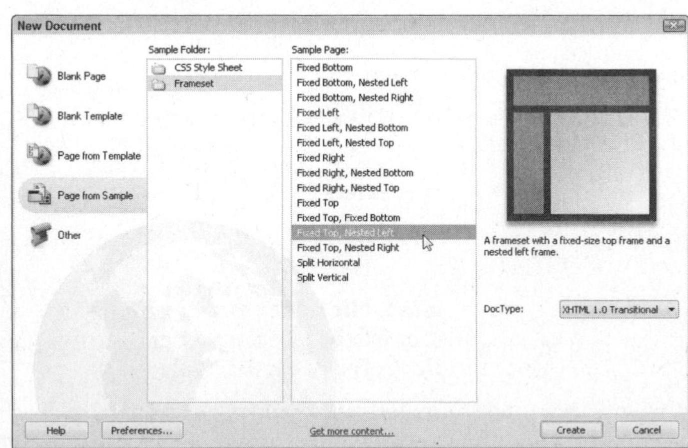

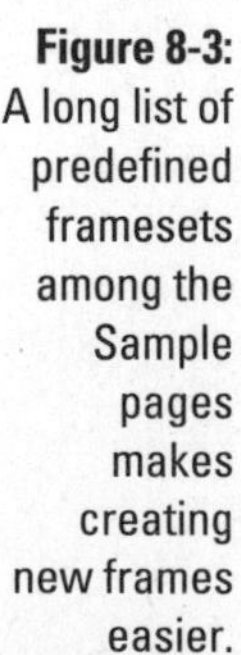

Figure 8-3: A long list of predefined framesets among the Sample pages makes creating new frames easier.

2. **From the icons on the left, select Page from Sample.**

3. **In the Sample Folder list, select Frameset.**

   The predefined framesets are displayed in a list under the Sample Page category.

4. **In the Sample Page list, select a Frameset design.**

   When you click to select the name of a predefined frameset, a preview is displayed in the far right of the dialog box, as shown in Figure 8-3.

5. **Click the Create button.**

   The frameset is created automatically and opens in Dreamweaver's workspace. If you have Accessibility alerts turned on in Dreamweaver's Preferences, you're prompted with an alert and an Accessibility dialog box, where you can enter Accessibility attributes for the frameset.

6. **Click and drag any of the bars dividing the frames to adjust the size of the frame area.**

7. **To edit each section of the frameset, click inside the frame that you want to work on and edit it as you would any other HTML page.**

   You can type text, insert images, create tables, and add any other features just as you do for any other page.

   For instructions on saving all the files in a frameset, continue with the instructions in the section "Saving files in a frameset," later in this chapter.

Creating a frameset using the Layout Insert panel

Another way to create frames is to select a predefined frameset from the Frames drop-down list, as shown in Figure 8-4. You find the Frames icon in the Layout Insert panel (available by clicking the Layout tab from the Insert panel at the top-right of the work area in the Designer workspace layout).

To create a framed page with the Frames icon on the Layout Insert panel, follow these steps:

1. **Choose File⇨New⇨Blank Page.**

2. **In the Page Type list, select HTML and then in the Layout list, select <none>.**

3. **Click the Create button to create a new blank page.**

   A blank HTML page is created and opens in the main Dreamweaver workspace.

4. **From the Layout Insert panel, click the Frames icon; in the drop-down list, select the design that most closely approximates the type of frameset you want to build (refer to Figure 8-4).**

   The selected frameset is created automatically and opens in the Dreamweaver workspace, replacing the blank HTML page created in Step 3.

Viewing frame borders

If you don't see the borders of your frames displayed in Dreamweaver's workspace, as you see in Figures 8-1, 8-2, and 8-4, you may need to change the View settings in Dreamweaver. To make frame borders visible, click to place your cursor in one of the frames within your frameset and choose View➪Visual Aids➪Frame Borders. Your frame borders appear automatically in the workspace. To hide frame borders in Dreamweaver's workspace, choose View➪Visual Aids➪Frame Borders again. Note that this doesn't turn off the display of frame borders in a browser. If you don't want your borders to be seen by visitors to your site, turn off frame borders, as described in the "Changing frame borders" section later in this chapter.

Don't worry if it isn't exactly the design you want; you can alter it later.

5. **Modify the frameset as needed.**

   You can resize the frames by clicking and dragging the borders.

   You can also split frames by choosing Modify➪Frameset and then choosing to split the frame left, right, up, or down.

To save your files, continue with the instructions in the next section, "Saving files in a frameset."

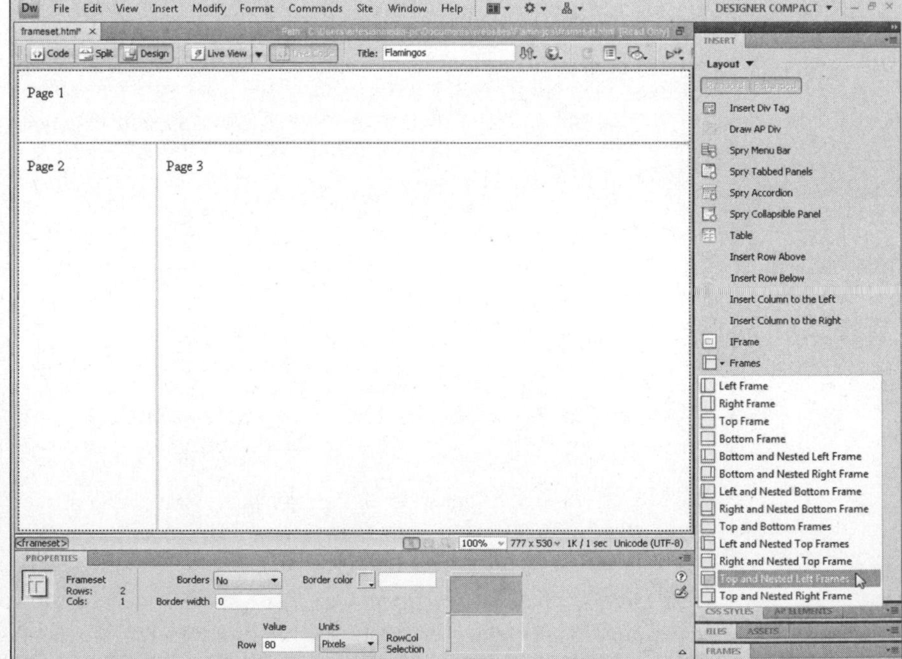

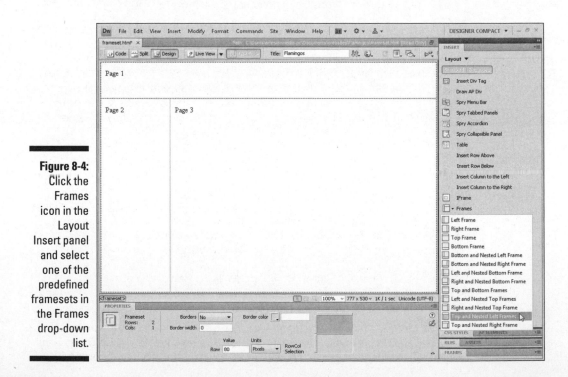

Figure 8-4: Click the Frames icon in the Layout Insert panel and select one of the predefined framesets in the Frames drop-down list.

Saving files in a frameset

No matter what approach you take to create a frameset, you can choose from any of these three options to save any or all your frame documents. No matter which option you choose to save your pages, make sure you save them within the main root folder of your Web site. (See Chapter 2 for more on using Dreamweaver's site definition features to establish a main root folder for your site.)

Similarly, after you save and name your documents the first time, you have the following options for saving a frame or the whole frameset again after you edit them:

- **Save the whole shebang:** If you haven't yet saved the frameset, choosing File➪Save All saves all files in your frameset prompting you separately for a name for each frame. If you've already saved and named the files, the Save All command is useful when you make changes to several of the frames and want to save all the changes at once. I prefer this option, which is covered in detail in the following exercise, especially the first time you save a frameset.
- **Save just one frame:** To save an individual frame displayed in a frameset without saving all the other frames, place your cursor in the frame you want to save and choose File➪Save Frame and save or name it just as you save any other individual page. Dreamweaver saves only the file for the frame in which your cursor is located.
- **Save only the page that defines the frameset:** First, make sure the entire frameset is selected (you can do this by clicking in the upper-left corner of the workspace) and then choose File➪Save Frameset. If you haven't selected the entire frameset, the Save Frameset option doesn't appear on the File menu. ***Remember:*** This page doesn't appear in any of the frames; it simply defines the entire display area, specifying which of the other pages appears in each frame as well as the position and size of the frames.

When you create a frameset, no matter which approach you take to create the frameset, it's good practice to wait to save your pages until *after* you've created all your frames. Saving all your frames at once can make it easier to name them in a way that will help you keep track of them later. Remember, a frameset consists of at least two HTML files, even though it appears as if you're working on only one file in the Dreamweaver workspace. (That said, I still recommend you save the files before you start adding content to your pages, to make sure you don't lose your work if your system or the program crashes.)

To save all the files in a frameset at once, follow these steps:

1. **Choose File➪Save All.**

   The Save As dialog box appears, asking you to name the file and designate a folder to save it in. This is the first of several Save As dialog boxes you see (how many depends on how many pages your frameset contains).

2. **Enter a name for the first file in the frameset.**

   Dreamweaver suggests a name, but you can choose your own.

The first file you're prompted to save when you use the Save All option, is the *frameset* file (the file that holds all the other frames in place). You can tell this by looking at the Dreamweaver Document window behind the Save As dialog box: The entire document has a thick dotted highlight around it, representing the frameset.

3. **Browse your hard drive to locate the desired folder for the HTML files and then click the Save button.**

   The first frameset file is saved, and a new Save As dialog box appears for the next one. After you save all the frames, the Save As dialog box disappears.

Carefully naming the files as you save them helps identify which area they represent. Notice that when you're prompted to save each file, Dreamweaver indicates the frame area by highlighting it with a dark, on-screen border behind the dialog box. I like names like `frame1.html` and `frame2.html`, or `leftframe.html`, `rightframe.html` because such names can help you distinguish between the files later.

Setting Targets and Links in Frames

One of the best features of frames is that you can change the contents of each frame separately within the Web browser. This feature opens a wide range of design possibilities that improves navigation for your site. One common way to use a frameset is to create a frame that displays a list of links to various pages of your site and then opens those links into another frame on the same page. This technique makes it possible to keep a list of links constantly visible and makes navigation a lot simpler and more intuitive.

Setting links from a file in one frame so that the pages they link to open in another frame is like linking from one page to another, and that's essentially what you're doing. What makes linking within a frameset distinctive is that, in addition to indicating which page you want to open with the link, you have to specify which frame section it *targets* (opens into).

But before you can set those links, you need to do a few things: First, you need to create some other pages that you can link to (if you haven't done so already). Create new pages as you would create any other pages in Dreamweaver, using any of the templates or sample page options, and then save each of the pages individually. If your pages already exist, you're more than halfway there; it's just a matter of linking to those pages.

The other thing you have to do before you can set links is to name each frame so that you can specify where the linked file loads. If you don't, the page just replaces the frameset altogether when someone clicks the link, and this defeats the purpose of using frames in the first place.

Naming frames

Naming a *frame* is different from naming the *file* that the frame represents. You find out how to name the files in the previous section, "Saving files in a frameset." The *frame name* is like a nickname that allows you to distinguish your frames from one another on a page and refer to them individually — this becomes important when you set links and want to target a link to open in a particular area of the frameset. The filename is the name of the HTML file for the frame. The frame name is the nickname you refer to when you want to set links.

You can see the names of your frames in the Frames panel, as shown on the right in Figure 8-5. If you've used one of Dreamweaver's predefined framesets, the frames are named something like `topFrame` and `mainframe`. If you're happy with the names that Dreamweaver automatically assigned to your frames, you can skip the following steps. If you created frames by splitting a document, the frames don't have a name and you must complete the following steps before you can target your frames.

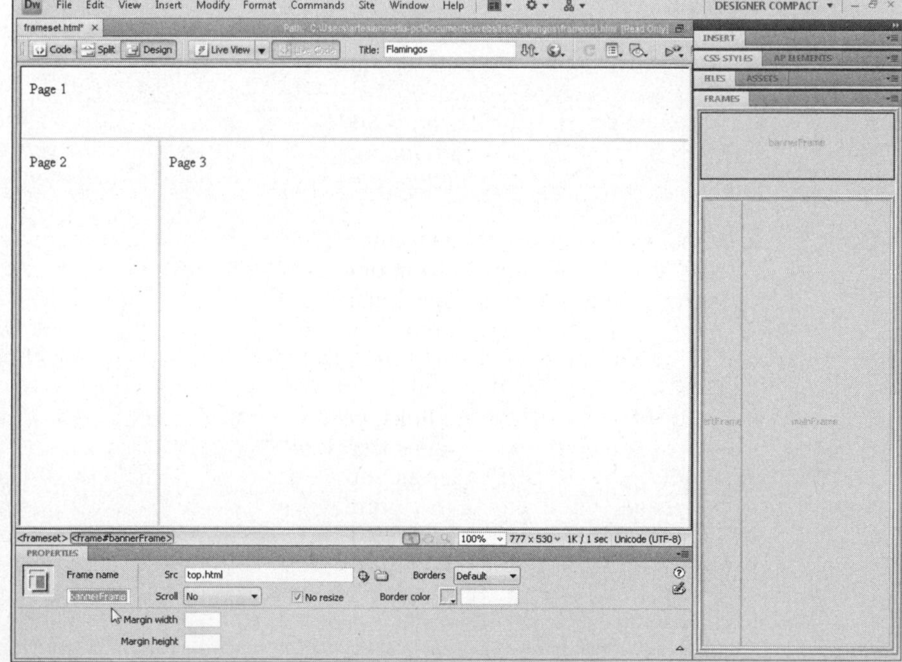

Figure 8-5: The Frames panel provides access to frame properties, such as frame names.

Resist using frames when linking to other Web sites

I understand that most people don't want to lose viewers to another site when they create a link, but that's the nature of the Web. If your site is designed well, you shouldn't have to worry about losing people. Instead, you should show them around your informative site and then politely guide them to other resources that they may find of interest — and let them go. If you link to another site and target that link within your frames, you keep users captive and usually leave them annoyed with you for taking up valuable browser space and making it harder to navigate to the site they've followed your link to visit. By displaying content from other sites within one or more of the frames in your site, you risk doing yourself far more harm than good.

If you insist on using frames when you link to another site, do so discreetly by placing a small, narrow frame across the bottom of the screen or the left side — not a wide band across the top, and certainly not more than one frame that still contains information from your site. Not only is this rude and ugly, but some people have been sued by sites that charged that using frames when the sites linked misled visitors into thinking the content belonged to the visitors when the content didn't.

Another reason not to use frames when you link to someone else's site is that other sites use frames, too. If you link a site that uses frames into a site that uses frames, you quickly create a mess of frames within frames that makes navigation confusing at best. Not everyone knows you can get out of frames by right-clicking a link in Windows, or clicking and holding a link on a Mac, and choosing Open Frame in Separate Window. Now that you know this trick, at least you can get out of a framed situation if you ever find yourself trapped in one.

To name a frame in a frameset or change the name of a frame, follow these steps:

1. **Open an existing frameset or create a new one.**

   See the "Creating a frameset in Dreamweaver" section, earlier in this chapter, if you don't know how to create a frameset.

2. **Choose Window➪Frames.**

   The Frames panel opens to the right of the work area (see Figure 8-5). The Frames panel is a miniature representation of the frames on your page that enables you to select different frames by clicking the corresponding frame area within the panel.

3. **Click to place your cursor in the area of the Frames panel that corresponds to the frame you want to name.**

   In Figure 8-5, I selected the top frame. You can click to select any of the frames in the panel. The Property inspector displays the properties for that particular frame. You can make any changes to the frame's properties by altering the properties in the Property inspector after selecting the frame.

You can also select the entire frameset by clicking the border around all the frames in the Frames panel. The Frames panel allows you to select only one frame or frameset at a time.

4. **In the Frame Name text box on the left side of the Property inspector, type a name for the frame.**

   Dreamweaver assigns names automatically when you save the files in a frameset. In the example shown in Figure 8-5, Dreamweaver assigned the names `topFrame`, `mainFrame`, and `leftFrame`. You can leave these names as is or change them to anything else in the Property inspector (just don't use spaces or special characters in the names).

   In the example, I changed `topFrame` to `bannerFrame`. Name your frames in a way that makes sense to you and helps you remember what they are so you can better target them.

5. **Choose File⇨Save Frameset to save the frameset page.**

   The frameset is the file you don't see in the display area that describes the other frames and contains information, such as frame names.

   Remember, you can save any individual frame by placing your cursor in the frame and choosing File⇨Save, or you can save all the files in your frameset (including the frameset page) by choosing File⇨Save All. Refer to the "Saving files in a frameset" section, earlier in this chapter, for more information on saving frames.

Now that you identified or changed the names of your frames, you're ready to start setting links that target frames. Don't close these files yet — you want to use them to follow the steps in the next section to set links.

I like to save my work on a regular basis so that I never lose more than a few minutes of work if my system crashes or the power goes out. Be aware, however, that when you work with frames, you need to save all your pages to save your work.

Setting links to a target frame

Setting links in a frameset requires some preliminary work. If you jumped to this section without creating a frameset or naming your frames, you may want to refer to the sections earlier in this chapter. If you already have a frameset, have named the frames, and just want to find out how to set links, this section is where you want to be.

Setting links in a frameset is like setting any other links between pages, except you need to specify the *target frame* — the frame where the linked page will appear when a user clicks the link. For example, if you want a link in the left frame to control what's in the main frame, specify the main frame as the target in the link. If you don't specify a target, the link opens in the same frame the link is in. Because the most common reason to use frames is to keep navigation links in one frame and open their corresponding pages in another, you probably want to target a frame when you set a link.

If this seems confusing, don't fret. After you try the following steps, it should become clear how targets work in framesets:

1. **Open an existing frameset or create a new frameset.**

   In Figure 8-6, you see that I'm using the Pink Flamingo Web site, which I created to use as an example in this chapter.

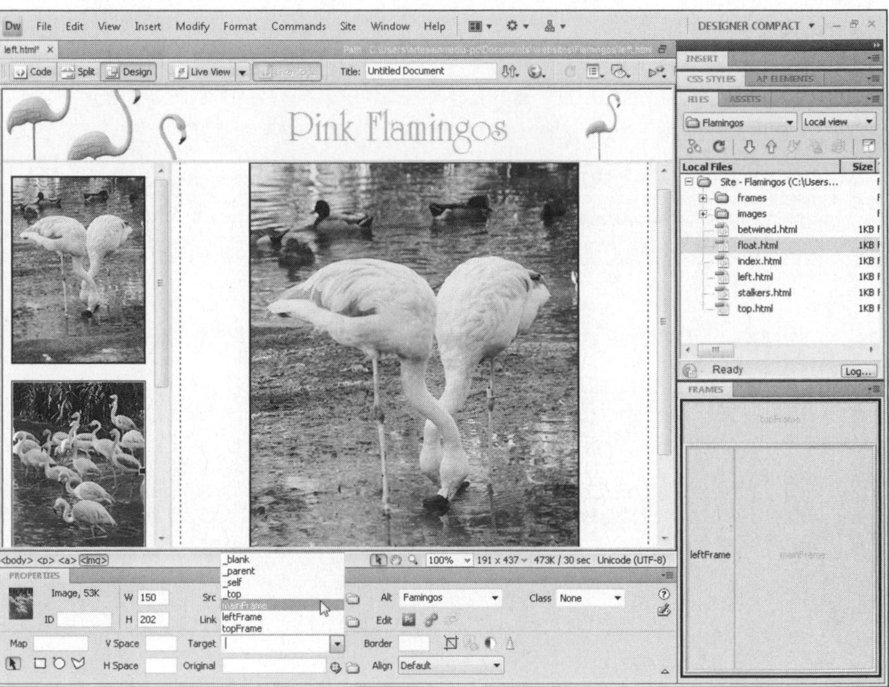

Figure 8-6: Use the Target field in the Property inspector to specify where a linked page will appear within a frameset.

2. **Highlight the text or click to select the image you want to serve as the link.**

   In my example, I selected the second thumbnail image in the left column. Note that the process of targeting a link works the same whether you're creating a link with text or an image.

3. **In the Property inspector, enter any URL in the Link text box or use the Browse button to select the page you want to link to.**

   In my example, I used the Browse button to set a link to the file `stalkers.html` (this page includes a larger version of the thumbnail picture that I've selected).

4. **In the Target drop-down list in the Property inspector, choose the name of the frame that you want the link to open into.**

   In my example, I selected the frame *mainframe* as the target. Choose the name that corresponds to the frame where you want your linked page to open. Notice that Dreamweaver conveniently lists all the frames you named in your document in the Target drop-down list, which I have open in Figure 8-6.

   The result is shown in Figure 8-7. When the frameset appears in a browser and a user clicks the second thumbnail of the photo that features more than a dozen flamingos in the left frame, the `stalkers.html` page with a larger version of that photo appears in the main frame area.

Figure 8-7: The selected link opens the page and targets the main frame area.

You can't test your links until you preview your work in a browser, and you have to save all your framed pages to ensure that your preview will work properly. To save all the pages in a frameset, choose File➪Save All.

Comparing target options

You have many options when you target links in a frameset. As shown in the preceding section, "Setting links to a target frame," you can specify that a linked page opens in another frame within your frameset. In addition, you can set linked pages to open in the same frame as the page with the link, to open a completely new page with no frames, and even to open a second browser window and display the page without affecting the original framed design. Table 8-1 provides a list of target options and what they mean. You can find all these options in the Target drop-down list in the Property inspector.

The Target drop-down list in the Property inspector is activated only when you select a linked image or section of text — a link must be in the Link field of the Property inspector before you can set a target.

Table 8-1 Understanding Target Options

Target Name	*What It Does*
_blank	Opens the linked document into a new browser window or tab.
_parent	Opens the linked document into the parent file of the page that has the link. (The *parent* is the file, frame, or frameset that contains the frame with the link.)
_self	Opens the linked document in the same frame as the original link, replacing the current content of the frame. This is the default option and usually doesn't need to be specified.
_top	Opens the linked document into the outermost frameset, replacing the entire contents of the browser window.

Changing Frame Properties

When you get more sophisticated with frames, you may want to further refine your frames by changing properties, which enables you to turn off frame borders, change the frame or border colors, limit scrolling, and so on. To access these options in Dreamweaver, choose Window⇨Frames, click inside the Frames panel in the area that corresponds to the frame that you want to change, and then use the Property inspector to access the options I describe in the following four sections. Figure 8-8 shows the Property inspector as it appears when you select a frameset in the Frames panel.

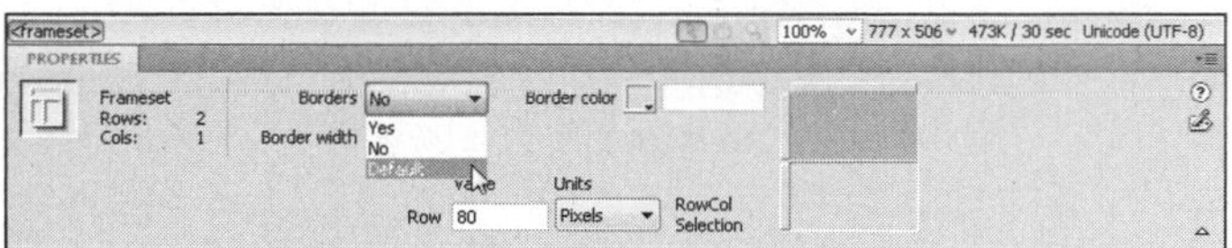

Figure 8-8: The selected frames or framesets and their properties are visible in the Property inspector.

Changing frame borders

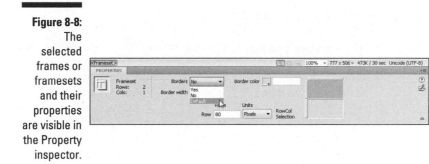

The best thing you can do with a frame border is to turn it off. You can turn off the borders for your site by choosing No from the Borders drop-down list in the Property inspector for either the frameset or for any of the individual frames in the frameset. Your other options include Yes, which forces the borders to be visible, and Default, which usually means Yes. In the case of individual frames, however, the Default option inherits the settings from the parent frameset.

You can make global border settings by using the Property inspector and applying the settings to the frameset. To select the frameset so that its properties are visible in the inspector (refer to Figure 8-8), click the border that encloses the frameset in the Frames panel.

If you choose to keep your borders visible, you may want to customize the color by clicking the Border Color square in the Property inspector and then choosing a color from the color palette.

If you select a specific border, the Property inspector also enables you to specify the border width. Simply enter a value in pixels in the Border Width text field to change the width of the selected border.

Frame border colors aren't well-supported by all browsers and may not display as you intend. Most designers simply turn off frame borders, but if you do keep them, make sure your design still looks okay if the borders are thick and grey, which is the default. Many browsers, including recent ones, don't display a different border color.

Changing frame sizes

The easiest way to change the size of a frame is to select the border and drag it until the frame is the size you want. When you select the border, the Property inspector displays the size of the frame, enabling you to change the size in pixels or as a percentage of the display area by entering a number in the Row or Column text boxes. If you specify 0 width for your frame borders, you may not see them on the page in order to drag and resize them. If this is the case, you can view the borders by choosing View➪Visual Aids➪Frame Borders, and Dreamweaver indicates the borders with a thin gray line that you can easily select.

Changing scrolling and resizing options

Scrolling options control whether a viewer can scroll up and down or left and right in a frame area. As shown in Figure 8-9, the scrolling options for frames are Yes, No, Auto, and Default. As a general rule, I recommend leaving the Scroll option set to Auto because a visitor's browser can then turn on scrolling if necessary. That is, if the viewer's display area is too small to see all the content of the frame, the frame becomes scrollable. If the content fits within the visible boundaries, the scroll arrows don't appear.

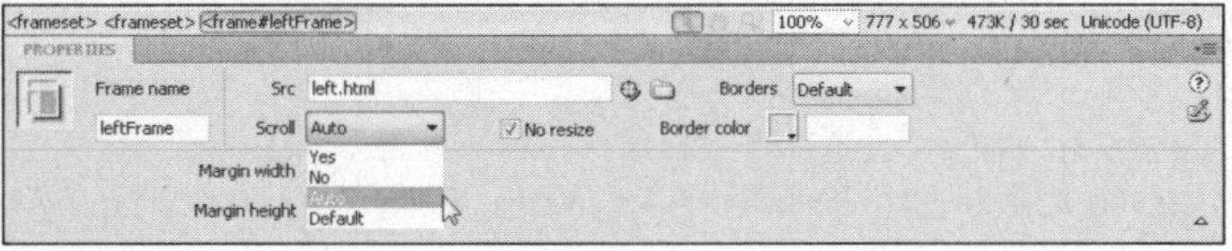

Figure 8-9: The Scroll options list in the Property inspector.

If you set this option to Yes, the scroll arrows are visible whether they're needed or not. If you set it to No, they won't be visible, even if that means your viewer can't see all the content of the frame — a sometimes dangerous proposition because then there's no easy way to scroll. Default leaves it up to the browser. In most browsers, the Default option results in the same display as the Auto option, but Default yields unpredictable results. As a general rule, using Auto is best.

Also note the No Resize option in Figure 8-9. If you select this option, a visitor to your site can't change the size of the frames. If you leave this option deselected, your user can select the border and drag it to make the frame area smaller or larger, just as you can when you develop your frames in Dreamweaver. Generally, I like to give viewers control, but I sometimes select the No Resize option if I want to ensure that my viewers can't alter the design in their browser.

Setting margin height and width

The Margin Width and Margin Height options enable you to specify the amount of margin space around a frame. Normally in a browser window, a small margin is visible between the edge of the window and any content, such as images or text. That's why you can't normally place an image on your page flush against the edge of the browser. With frames, though, you can actually control the size of the margin or even eliminate the margin.

I generally recommend that you set the margin to at least two pixels and make the margin larger if you want to create more space around your content. If you want to get rid of the margin, set it to 0 and any images or text in the frame appears flush against the edge of the frame or the browser window if the frame touches the edge of the browser. If the frame touches another frame, you can use this technique to create the impression of seamless images across frames.

Chapter 9

Coordinating Your Design Work

In This Chapter

- Creating many pages quickly with a template
- Making changes to multiple pages with templates
- Using Dreamweaver's Library for frequently used elements
- Designing a Web page with the Dreamweaver Tracing Image feature

Strive for consistency in all your designs — except when you're trying to be unpredictable. A little surprise here and there can keep your Web site lively. But, most Web sites work best and are easiest to navigate when they follow a consistent design theme. Case in point: Most readers take for granted that books don't change their designs from page to page, and newspapers don't change headline fonts and logos every day. Books and newspapers want to make life easier for their readers, and consistency is one of the primary tools for making sure readers find publications familiar. That doesn't mean you should limit modern Web design to what's possible in print, but it does mean we can all learn a thing or two from hundreds of years of print design.

Dreamweaver offers several features to help you develop and maintain a consistent look and feel across your site. In this chapter, you discover three of my favorite Dreamweaver features — templates, Library items, and the Tracing Image feature. Find out how they combine to make your design work faster and easier to manage, and you'll be well on your way to simplifying your work even before you start. The most important feature covered in this chapter is the ability to create templates. Templates in Dreamweaver not only make it easy to create pages with consistent design elements, they make it easy to update those pages later when things change — and things always change.

Templating Your Type

You can choose from many different kinds of templates to create Web sites; and you can find many places on the Web where you can buy them or even download them for free. At its simplest, a *template* is a ready-made page design, usually created in a way that makes it easy to add your own text and images. Some templates are customizable so that you can change design elements, such as colors, images, or fonts.

Dreamweaver takes this concept a few leaps further. Not only can you create templates that can be used to create new pages quickly and easily, you can also use Dreamweaver's templates to make global changes to all the pages created from a template.

Templates are best used in the following scenarios:

- **Templates are definitely the way to go when you're creating a number of pages that share the same characteristics, such as the same background color, navigation elements, or logo.** I recommend that you use a template any time you create a site with more than a few pages. For example, you might create a template that includes your logo, a row of links at the top and bottom of each page, and styles for the text colors and fonts. After you create a template with all these features, you can use it as the basis for all the other pages in your site. This approach makes it faster and easier to create a series of pages that share the same navigation, logo, and so on. If you ever decide to change one of these elements, such as your logo, you can change it once in the template and automatically update all the pages created from the template in your site.
- **If you want to use different design elements in different sections, you can even create more than one template for a site.** For example, if you're creating a Web site for a bed-and-breakfast inn, you might create one template for all the pages where you want to show off the rooms in the inn and another for a collection of pages that features great places to hike in the area.

  When creating multiple templates for a Web site, you may benefit from a *nested* template, a template whose design and editable regions are based on another template.

  For example, you can create a main template for elements that appear on every page across an entire site, such as a navigation bar. Then for secondary templates, start with the main template and add nested templates that have design variations for a section (or sections) of a site.

- **Templates are valuable when you're working with a team of people with varying skill levels.** For example, say you're building a site for a real-estate company and want to let the employees update the sales listings without messing up the page design. The fact that templates have locked regions can protect the most important elements of a page, making it easy for sales staff to add new information without accidentally breaking navigation elements or other consistent features.

The most powerful aspect of Dreamweaver's template feature is the capability to make global changes to every page created from a template. Even if you're working alone on a site, this aspect of templates can save hours (or even days) of time as the site grows and changes over time.

Creating Templates

Creating a template is as easy as creating any other file in Dreamweaver. You can start by creating an HTML Template page much as you would any other page. You can also choose File⇨Save As to turn any existing page into a template. The main difference is that the extension for a template file is `.dwt` (Dynamic Web Template), and template files are stored in a special Templates folder. When you create your first template in a Web site, Dreamweaver automatically creates a Templates folder in the root folder of your Web site and stores all your `.dwt` template files in this folder. Templates must be kept in this common Templates folder for the automated features in Dreamweaver to work properly.

The template features work only if you define your Web site in Dreamweaver. If you haven't gone through the setup process to define your root site folder yet, see Chapter 2 and complete those set up steps first.

Creating editable and uneditable regions

Perhaps the most difficult concept to grasp when it comes to templates is how editable and uneditable regions work and why they're important. Here's the short answer (I get into the details later in this chapter).

When you create a template design, every aspect of the design is locked automatically, or uneditable, until you designate it as an *editable region* — areas of a template that can be changed in any page created from the template. The steps for making a region editable are relatively simple (you find detailed instructions in the exercises that follow). When you create a new page from a template, *only* the areas you've designated as editable regions can be altered. If you want to make global changes with a template, only the areas that you've left uneditable can be used to make changes across multiple pages.

For example, suppose you create a design for an online magazine with the logo and navigation bar at the top of the page and the copyright and navigation links at the bottom, and you leave all these areas uneditable. Then you create a design area in the middle of the page where a story and photo can be added to each page created from the template and you designate that area as an editable region. When you create new pages from the template, you can replace the photo and story on each page because they're in editable regions, but you can't change the logo, navigation links, or copyright because they're in uneditable regions.

Now imagine that you've used this template to create many pages that are exactly the same, except that each features a different story and photo in the middle area designated as the editable region. Then one day you decide to change the logo for your company, so you need to change that section of the page on all the pages you've created. If the logo is in an uneditable region of the template, no problem. You simply open the template file and edit the logo on that one page. When you save the template, the new logo is applied automatically to all the pages created from that template. That saves a ton of time because you don't have to replace the logo on each page. You could make the same kinds of global changes to the navigation links at the top and bottom of the page because they're also in uneditable regions.

In contrast, if you make changes to the editable region in the template, those changes aren't applied to the pages created from the template. This is important because you wouldn't want to make a global change that overwrites all the individual stories and photos you've inserted into each page. It comes down to this: *Locked* areas of a template (areas you don't designate as editable) can be changed only in the template itself, and those changes can then be applied automatically to all the pages created from that template. Areas of a template designated as editable can be changed in any page created from the template, but those areas can't be updated automatically by changing the template.

If you're still a little confused after all this theory, don't worry, you'll get to see all this in action in the sections that follow.

Creating a new template

To create a template that you can use to create new pages, follow these steps:

1. **Choose File➪New.**

   The New Document window opens.

2. **In the list on the left, click the Blank Template option, as shown in Figure 9-1.**

3. **In the Template Type list, choose HTML Template.**

   You can also choose from a variety of other template options, including templates for ASP (Active Server Pages), ColdFusion, JSP (Java Server Pages), and PHP (a recursive acronym for Hypertext Preprocessor). These file types are used when creating dynamic Web sites. Find an introduction to creating dynamic Web sites in Chapters 14 and 15. In this example, I'm creating a new HTML page template.

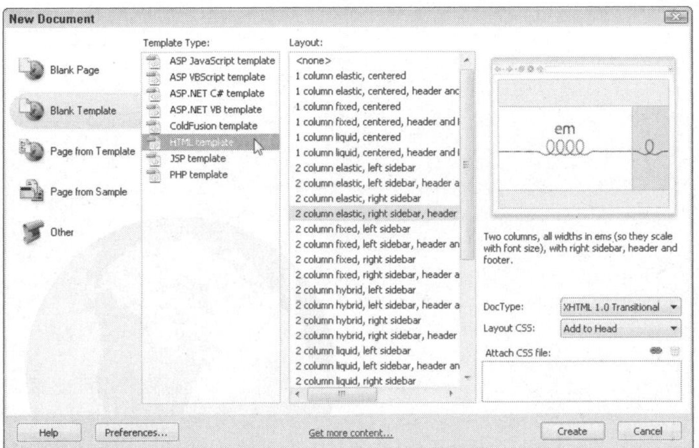

Figure 9-1: The Templates panel displays a list of all available templates in the selected site and provides access to template editing functions.

Why the head section is editable by default

In a new template, all elements are locked by default except for the document head section, which is indicated by the <head>, </head> tags. These tags enable you to change the title in any page created from a template or to insert JavaScript if you use behaviors on the page (covered in Chapter 10). For the template to be of much use for building new pages, you must make areas in the body of the page editable as well. Remember that you can always go back to the template later to alter the design, make more areas editable, or lock areas so they can't be changed.

In previous versions of Dreamweaver, if you created a template from an existing HTML page using the File⇨Save As feature to save the file as a `.dwt` template file, the head section wasn't turned into an editable region automatically. If you're working with Dreamweaver CS4, you shouldn't have this problem unless you are creating a template by saving a page that was created in previous version of Dreamweaver. If there are no template tags around the head section of a page, you can't edit the Title of the page and you can't add features that use JavaScript, such as those created with Dreamweaver's Spry AJAX widgets or Behaviors. To solve this problem you can recreate the template from a new file in Dreamweaver CS4 or you can manually add the template code to the head region of the existing file. Find instructions for adding the code manually on my Web site at `www.DigitalFamily.com/dreamweaver`.

4. **In the Layout area, choose** <none> **to create a blank page or select any of the predesigned CSS layouts.**

   Dreamweaver's many CSS layout options provide a great headstart to creating a new page design. Instructions for how to customize Dreamweaver's CSS layouts are included in Chapter 6.

5. **Click the Create button.**

   A new blank template is created and opens in the main work area, and the New Document dialog box closes.

6. **Choose File⇨Save.**

   If you haven't disabled the dialog box, a warning appears stating that the template doesn't have any editable regions and asking whether you really want to save it. Click Yes to continue.

7. **Click OK to save the page as is for now.**

   The Save as Template window appears, as shown in Figure 9-2.

8. **Give the template a name and a description, as shown in Figure 9-2.**

   The description field is optional but can be useful if you have many templates and want to keep notes about them. Note that the Save as Template dialog box includes a list of any templates that already exist in the site. The dialog box also includes a Site field at the top with a drop-down list that includes all the sites you've defined in Dreamweaver. This makes it possible to save a template into any site you've defined when you created it.

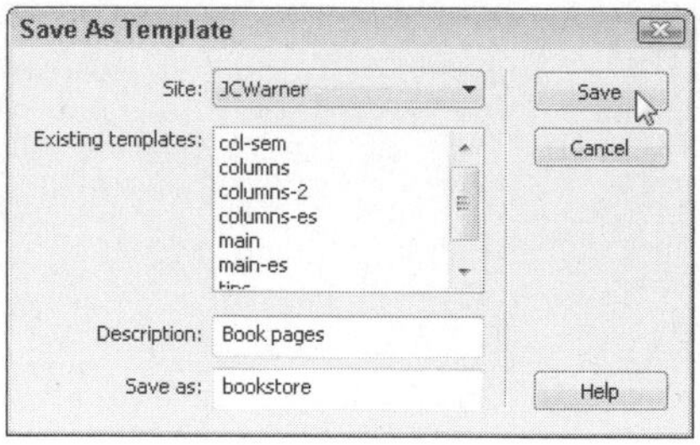

Figure 9-2: The Save as Template window displays existing templates.

9. **Click Save and the template is saved automatically with a** `.dwt` **extension.**

   The `.dwt` extension designates the file as a Dreamweaver template. You can now edit this page as you edit any other HTML page, inserting images, text, and so on.

10. **Choose Modify➪Page Properties and specify the page-wide settings.**

    Use the Page Properties dialog box to specify background, text, and link colors, as well as other options that apply to the entire page. (Page properties options are covered in Chapter 2.)

    When you set page properties, Dreamweaver creates the corresponding CSS styles in the template file and displays them in the CSS panel. You find more information about CSS editing options in Chapters 5 and 6.

11. **Create a design for the page by adding images, text, and other elements as you would in any other Dreamweaver file.**

    You find instructions for adding all these features to your pages throughout this book. Again, remember, you create a page design in a template just like you would in any other Web page.

12. **To create an editable region:**

    a. **Select any image, text block, or content area, such as a `<div>` tag.**

       If you choose to start with a blank page, type to enter some text and select it so that you can follow along with this exercise.

       Tip: If you've designed your pages with `<div>` tags and CSS, as covered in Chapter 6, a good option is to select the div for an entire section. A handy way to do that is to use the tag selector at the bottom of the workspace to select the div, as shown in Figure 9-3.

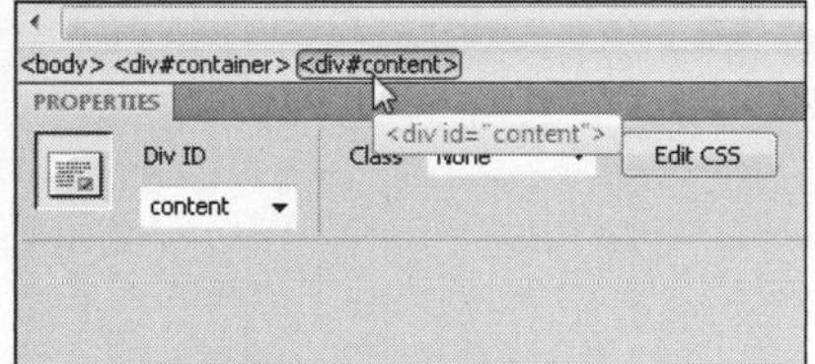

Figure 9-3: To select an entire section of a page, select the corresponding tag, such as a <div> tag, by using the tag selector at the bottom of the page.

b. **Choose Insert➪New Template Object➪New Editable Region (as shown in Figure 9-4).**

The New Editable Region dialog box opens.

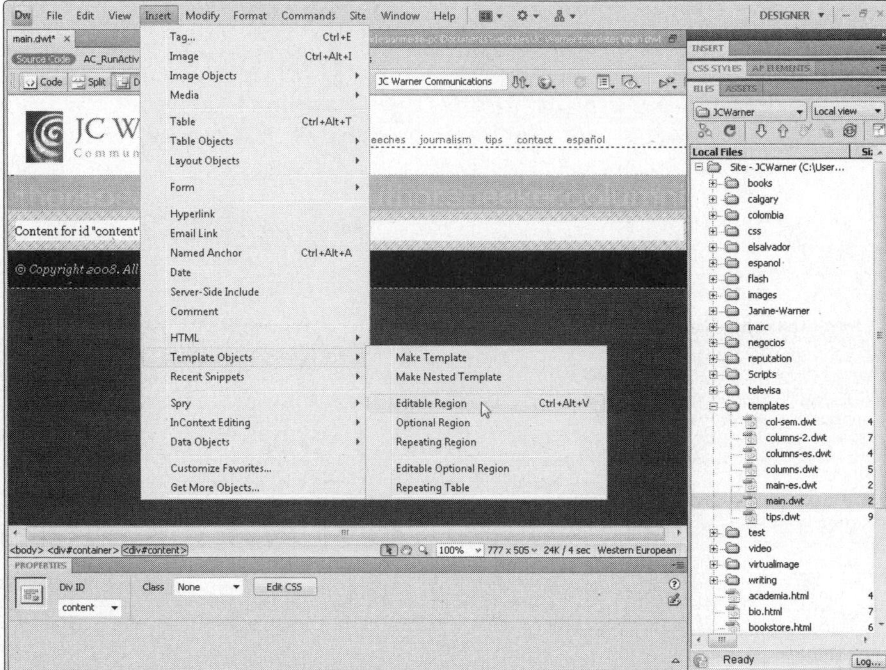

Figure 9-4: You can select any element in a template page, such as an image, or any area, such as a <div> tag shown here, and make it an editable region.

13. **When you finish designing the page, choose File➪Save to save your template.**

    When you save a new template page or you save an existing page as a template, Dreamweaver automatically adds the `.dwt` extension and saves the file into a Templates folder. If you don't already have a Templates folder in your local root folder, Dreamweaver creates one for you. (If Dreamweaver doesn't automatically create a Template folder, make sure you create a new Templates folder and save all your template files inside it.) For templates to be listed in the New Document window, they must be saved in a Templates folder.

If you save a template in Dreamweaver before you specify any editable regions, you're prompted with a warning because templates aren't useful without editable regions. You don't have to create editable regions before you save a template, but you can't make any changes in any pages created from a template until you create one or more editable regions. You can always go back and add editable regions later, so it's not a problem if you want to save your work before you create editable regions.

Saving any page as a template

Sometimes you get partway through creating a page before you realize that you're likely to want more pages just like it and you should create a template so you don't have to re-create the same page design over and over. Similarly, you may be working on a page that someone else created that you want to turn into a template. No matter where the original page comes from, creating a template from an existing page is almost as easy as creating a new template from scratch.

To save a page as a template, follow these steps:

1. **Open the page that you want to turn into a template.**

   Choose File➪Open and browse to find your file. Or open the site in the Files panel and double-click the file to open it.

2. **Choose File➪Save as Template, as shown in Figure 9-5.**

   The Save as Template dialog box appears (refer to Figure 9-2).

Figure 9-5: You can save any HTML page as a template.

3. **In the Site drop-down list, choose a site.**

   The menu lists all the sites you've defined in Dreamweaver. By default, the site you've defined and opened in the Files panel is selected when the dialog box opens. If you're working on a new site or haven't yet defined your site, read Chapter 2 for information on defining the site.

   You can use the Save as Template option to save a page as a template into any defined site, which makes it easy to save a page design from one site as a template for another site.

4. **In the Save As text box, type a name for the template.**
5. **Click the Save button.**

   If you haven't disabled the dialog box, a warning appears stating that the template doesn't have any editable regions and asking whether you really want to save it. Click Yes to continue.

   Notice that the file now has the `.dwt` extension, indicating that it's a template. You can now make changes to this template the same way you edit any other template.

6. **Update links in the template.**

   When you save a new template page or you save an existing page as a template, Dreamweaver automatically adds the `.dwt` extension and saves the file into a Templates folder. (If Dreamweaver doesn't automatically do this, make sure you create a new Templates folder and save all your template files inside the Templates folder in your root site folder.) Because your original file probably wasn't saved in the Templates folder, any links to other pages or images must be updated when the file is saved. Click OK and Dreamweaver corrects any links in the file as it saves the file in the Templates folder.

7. **Make any changes that you want and then choose File⇨Save.**

   You edit a template just as you edit any other page in Dreamweaver.

8. **To create an editable region:**

   a. **Select any content area, image, or text.**

   b. **Choose Insert⇨Template Object⇨New Editable Region (as shown in Figure 9-4).**

      The New Editable Region dialog box opens.

   c. **Give the new region a name.**

      The region you define as editable becomes an area that can be changed in any page created from the template. You can create multiple editable regions in any template.

d. **Click OK.**

The editable region is enclosed in a highlighted area with a tab at the top left, identified by the name you gave the region.

9. **When you finish designing the page, choose File➪Save to save your completed template.**

Making attributes editable

In addition to making any element in a page editable, you can also make the attributes of any element editable. This step is only necessary if you want to make an attribute editable when the tag itself is not editable. For example, when you want to make it possible to change the color attribute of an H1 heading without making it possible to change the heading tag itself. To create editable attributes in a template, follow these steps:

1. **In any Dreamweaver template, select an item that you want to make an editable attribute.**

In the example shown in Figure 9-6, I selected an image and am in the process of making one of the image attributes editable.

Figure 9-6: Select any heading, image, or other tag and use the Modify menu to make the attributes of that tag editable.

2. **Choose Modify➪Templates➪Make Attribute Editable.**

   The Editable Tag Attributes dialog box appears, as shown in Figure 9-7.

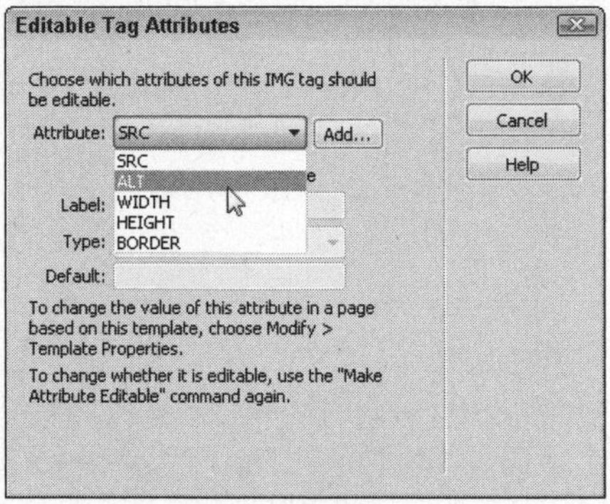

Figure 9-7: Identify which attributes you want to be editable.

3. **From the Attribute drop-down list, choose the attribute you want to make editable.**

   The attribute options vary depending on whether you select an image, text, or other element on the page.

   If the attribute isn't listed, click the Add button. In this example, I selected the `ALT` attribute of the image tag.

4. **Click OK to make the attribute editable and close the dialog box.**

Creating a new page from a template

After you create a template, put it to use. You can use one template to create or modify all the pages in your Web site or create different templates for different sections. For example, in a site, such as my profile site at `www.JCWarner.com` shown in these examples, you might create one template for each of the sections or use one template for all the pages in the site. After you create a template or a collection of templates, using a template to create a new page is similar to creating any other HTML page.

To use a template to create a page, follow these steps:

1. **Choose File➪New.**

   The New Document window opens.

2. **In the list on the left, click the Page from Template option, as shown in Figure 9-8.**

3. **In the Site list in the middle of the page, choose the name of the site that contains a template you want to use.**

   The templates in the selected site appear in the Template for Site section just to the right of the Site list in the New Document window (see Figure 9-8).

4. **In the Template for Site list, select the template you want to use.**

   Notice that when you click the name of a template, a preview of the selected template appears on the far right of the New Document window. In the example shown in Figure 9-8, I selected the main template from the JCWarner site.

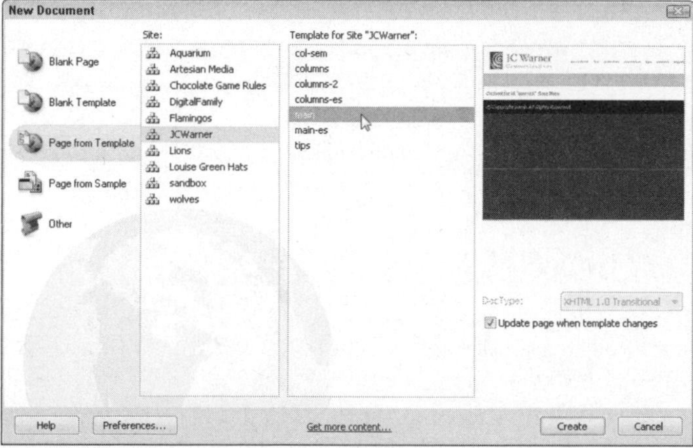

Figure 9-8: From the New Document window, you can preview and select any template saved in any defined Web site to create a new page.

5. **Click the Create button.**

   A new page is created from the template and appears in the main work area.

6. **Edit any of the regions of the page that are editable with Dreamweaver's regular editing features and save the file as you would save any other HTML page.**

When you create new pages from a template, you can change only the editable regions in each file created from the template. When you edit a template, only the regions that aren't defined as editable can be used to make global changes to all the pages created from the template.

Making Global Changes with Templates

One of the greatest advantages of using templates is that you can automatically apply changes to all the pages created with a template by altering the original template. For example, if I created a series of pages with the main template shown in the preceding example, I could make changes to those pages by editing any of the uneditable regions in the template.

To update files in a site that were created from a template, follow these steps:

1. **Open the template file.**

   Note that template files are distinguishable by the `.dwt` extension and are saved in the Template folder.

2. **Use Dreamweaver's editing features to make any changes you want to the template.**

   Remember that only changes to uneditable regions are updated automatically. In this example, the logo and navigation elements are locked regions and can be edited to make global changes.

3. **Choose File⇨Save.**

   The Update Template Files dialog box appears, as shown in Figure 9-9.

4. **Click the Update button to modify all pages listed in the Update Template Files dialog box. Click the Don't Update button to leave these pages unchanged.**

   If you click Update, Dreamweaver automatically changes all the pages listed in the Update Template Files dialog box to reflect any changes made to uneditable regions of the template.

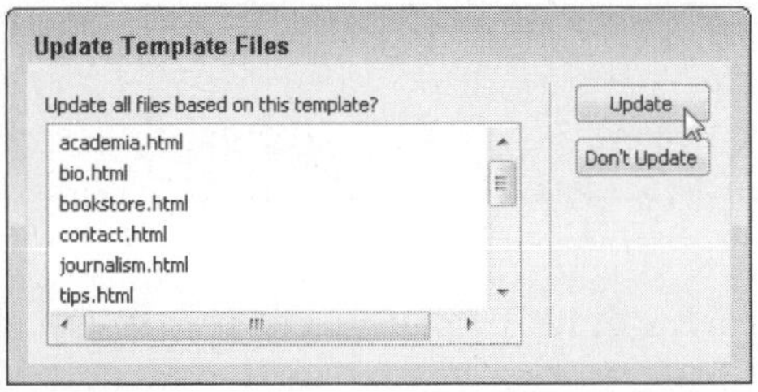

Figure 9-9: You can update all files created from a template.

Identifying a template

If you're not sure which template was used to create a page, you can open the template while you have the page open, make changes to the template, and update all the pages created with it by following these steps:

1. **Open a document that uses the template that you want to change.**
2. **Choose Modify⇨Templates⇨Open Attached Template, as shown in Figure 9-10.**

   The template opens.

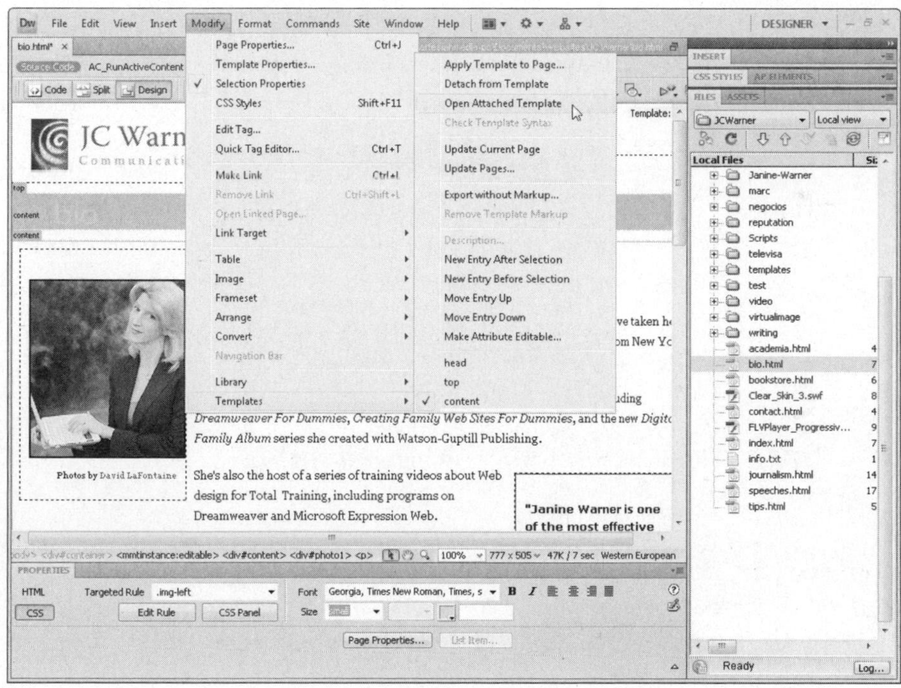

Figure 9-10: You can open an attached template from within any page created from a template.

3. **Use Dreamweaver's regular editing functions to modify the template as you would edit any page or template.**
4. **Choose File⇨Save.**

   The Update Template Files dialog box appears (refer to Figure 9-9).

5. **Click the Update button to modify all the pages listed in the Update Template Files dialog box. Click the Don't Update button to leave these pages unchanged.**

   If you choose Update, Dreamweaver automatically changes all the pages listed in the Update Template Files dialog box.

If you have a page open that was created from the template, the changes will automatically be applied, but you'll need to save the page before closing it to save the changes.

You can also apply changes to all the pages created from a template with the Update Pages option. To do so, open the template, and then make and save your changes without applying those changes to pages created with the template. Anytime later, you can choose Modify➪Templates➪Update Pages to apply the update.

Attaching and detaching templates

You can apply a template to an existing page by attaching it, and you can remove a template from a page by detaching it. When you apply a template to an existing document, the content in the template is added to the content already in the document. If a template is already applied to the page, Dreamweaver automatically matches any editable regions that have the same name in both templates and opens a dialog box with a list of regions, including any that don't match.

You can remove or detach a template from a page if you no longer want changes to the original template to affect the page created with the template. Detaching a template also unlocks all regions of a page, making it completely editable. You can detach a template by choosing Modify➪Templates➪Detach from Template. This action makes the file fully editable again, but any future changes you make to the template aren't reflected on the detached page.

You can apply a template to an existing page by using any one of the following techniques:

- Choose Modify➪Templates➪Apply Template to Page and then double-click the name of a template to apply it to the page.
- Drag the template from the Template Assets panel into the Document window. To open the Template Assets panel, click the Assets tab behind the Files panel tab and then click the Templates icon. You can also choose Window➪Assets.

If the editable regions don't match, Dreamweaver asks you to match inconsistent region names in a dialog box. After the region conflicts are resolved, click OK.

Reusing Elements with the Library Feature

The Library feature isn't a common feature in other Web design programs, so the concept may be new to you even if you've been developing Web sites for a while. The Library feature is handy when you have a single element you want to reuse on many pages, such as a copyright statement you want to appear at the bottom of each page or even something as complex as a row of navigation links.

A *Library item* is a snippet of code that can contain almost anything, including image references and links. After you save a section of code in the Library, you can insert it into any page with drag-and-drop ease. If you ever need to change a Library item (by adding or changing a link, for example), simply edit the stored Library item and Dreamweaver automatically updates the contents of the Library item on any or all pages where it appears throughout the site.

Like templates, Library items are a great way to share the work of your best designers with less experienced ones. For example, one designer can create a logo and another can create the navigation elements, and then these can be placed in the Library and made available to the entire team. You have more flexibility with Library items than templates because they're elements you can place anywhere on any page, even multiple times. Libraries aren't shared among sites the way templates are, but you can copy and paste the same Library item from one site into another.

Library items can't contain their own style sheets because the code for styles can appear only as part of the head area of an HTML file. You can, however, attach an external style sheet to a Library item to see how the styles affect the display of the Library item, but the same styles must be available on each page where the Library item is used for the styles to be applied. (For more on style sheets, see Chapters 5 and 6.)

Creating and Using Library Items

The following sections show you the steps for creating a Library item, adding one to a page, and editing and updating a Library item across multiple pages. For these steps to work properly, you must do them in sequential order. Before creating or using Library items, you must first define a site and open it in the Files panel. (See Chapter 2 for instructions on defining a site in Dreamweaver.)

Creating a Library item within an existing page works well because you can see how the item looks before you add it to the Library. You can edit an item after it's in the Library, but it may not look just as it will on a Web page. For example, Library items don't include <body> tags when they're saved in the Library, so link colors are displayed as default blue when viewed in the Library, even if the link colors have been changed to, say, purple in the <body> tag of the page.

Creating a Library item

To create a Library item that you can use on multiple pages on your site, follow these steps:

1. **Open any existing file that has images, text, or other elements on the page that you want to save as a Library item.**
2. **From this page, select an element or collection of elements that you want to save as a Library item, such as the copyright information that appears at the bottom of this page.**
3. **Choose Modify⇨Library⇨Add Object to Library.**

   The Library Assets panel opens and displays any existing Library items. Your new Library item appears as *Untitled.*
4. **Click to select Untitled and replace it by typing a new name as you would name any file in Explorer on a PC or the Finder on a Mac.**

   In the example shown in Figure 9-11, I've named the Library item copyright.

   When you create a Library item, Dreamweaver automatically saves it to the Library. Naming Library items makes them easier to identify when you want to use them. You can then easily apply Library items to any new or existing page in your site by following the steps in the next exercise.

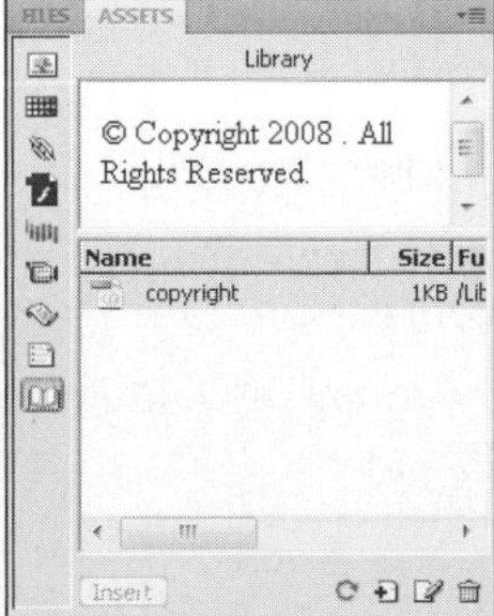

Figure 9-11: The Assets Library panel.

Adding a Library item to a page

You can easily add elements from the Library to your pages by simply dragging them from the Assets panel to the page. When you add a Library item to a page, the content is inserted into the document and a relationship is established between the content on the page and the item in the Library. This is important because it enables you to edit the Library item later and apply the changes to all pages where the item appears, but it also means that you can't edit the item on the page where it's inserted. You must edit Library items from within the Library, as you see in the following section.

To add a Library item to a page, follow these steps:

1. **Create a new document in Dreamweaver or open any existing file.**
2. **From the Files panel, click the Assets tab, and then click the Library icon.**

   The Library opens in the Assets panel (refer to Figure 9-11).
3. **Drag an item from the Library to the Document window.**

   Alternatively, you can select an item in the Library and click the Insert button. The item automatically appears on the page. After you insert a Library item on a page, you can use any of Dreamweaver's formatting features to position it on the page.

Highlighting Library items

Library items are highlighted to distinguish them from other elements on a page. You can both customize the highlight color for Library items and show or hide the highlight color in the Preferences dialog box. To change or hide Library highlighting, follow these steps:

1. **Choose Edit⇨Preferences (Windows) or Dreamweaver⇨Preferences (Mac).**

   The Preferences dialog box appears.
2. **In the Category section on the left, select Highlighting.**
3. **Click the color box to select a color for Library items and then select the Show box to display the Library highlight color on your pages.**

   Leave the box blank if you don't want to display the highlight color.
4. **Click OK to close the Preferences dialog box.**

Making global changes with Library items

One of the biggest timesaving advantages of the Dreamweaver Library feature is that you can make changes to Library items and automatically apply those changes to any or all pages where the Library item appears. To edit a Library item, follow these steps:

1. **From the Files panel, click the Assets tab and then click the Library icon.**

   The Library opens in the Assets panel (refer to Figure 9-11).

2. **Double-click any item listed in the Library to open it.**

   Dreamweaver opens a new window where you can edit the Library item.

   Because the Library item is just a snippet of code, it won't have a `<body>` tag in which to specify background, link, or text colors. Don't worry about this — the Library item acquires the right settings from the tags on the page where you insert it.

3. **Change the Library item as you would edit any element in Dreamweaver.**

   For example, you can change a link, edit the wording of text, change the font or size, and even add images, text, and other elements. In this example, I changed the date for the copyright from 2008 to 2009.

4. **Choose File➪Save to save changes to the original item.**

   The Update Library Items dialog box opens, displaying a list of all the pages where the Library item appears.

5. **To apply the changes you made to the Library item on all the listed pages, click the Update button. If you don't want to apply the changes to all the pages where the Library item appears, click the Don't Update button.**

   If you clicked the Update button, the Update Pages dialog box appears and shows the progress of the updating. You can stop the update from this dialog box, if necessary.

If you want to create a new Library item based on an existing one without altering the original, follow Steps 1–3, and in place of Step 4, choose File➪Save As and give the item a new name.

Editing one instance of a Library item

If you want to alter a Library item on a specific page where you've inserted it, or if you want to make changes to just a few pages, you can override the automated Library feature by detaching it, or breaking the link between the original item in the Library and the item inserted into the page.

After you break a connection, you can no longer update that page's Library item automatically.

To make a Library item editable, follow these steps:

1. **Open any file that contains a Library item and select the Library item.**

   The Property inspector displays the Library item options, as shown in Figure 9-12.

Figure 9-12: You can detach a Library item in the Property inspector.

2. **Click the Detach from Original button.**

   A warning message appears, letting you know that if you proceed with detaching the Library item from the original, you can no longer update this occurrence of it when the original is edited.

3. **Click OK to detach the Library item.**

Using a Tracing Image to Guide Your Layout

The Tracing Image feature is especially popular among designers. The concept dates back to the earliest days of design. The Tracing Image feature enables you to use graphics as guides for your page designs, much as you might copy a cartoon through thin transparent paper.

The Tracing Image feature is ideal for people who like to first create a design in a program, such as Photoshop or Fireworks, and then model their Web page after it. By using the Tracing Image feature, you can insert any Web-ready image into the background of any Dreamweaver page. Then you can position `<div>` tags or insert tables or other elements on top of the tracing image, making it easier to re-create your design in Dreamweaver. You can use JPG, GIF, or PNG images as tracing images and you can create them in any graphics application that supports these formats.

Although the tracing image appears in the background of a page, it doesn't take the place of a background image and won't appear in a browser.

To add a tracing image to your page, follow these steps:

1. **Create a new page or open an existing page in Dreamweaver.**
2. **Choose Modify➪Page Properties.**

   The Page Properties dialog box opens.
3. **In the Category list, select Tracing Image.**

   The Tracing Image options appear on the right, as shown in Figure 9-13.

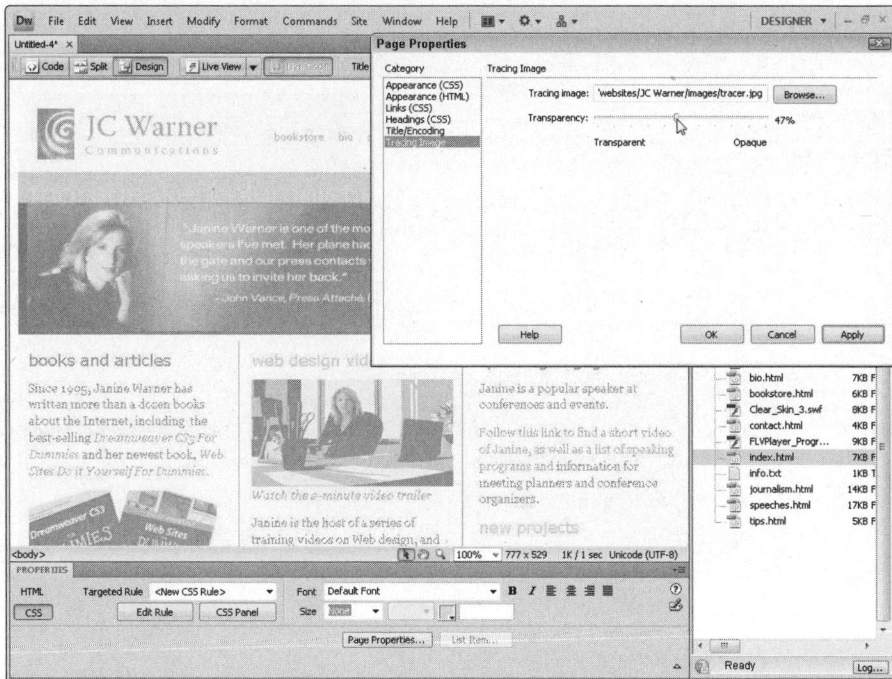

Figure 9-13: The Page Properties dialog box lets you set a tracing image to use when laying out your HTML page.

4. **Click the Browse button to locate the image you want to use as a tracing image.**

   The Select Image Source dialog box appears.
5. **Click the image you want to trace from and then click Apply to preview how the image looks behind the page.**

6. **Set the opacity for the tracing image with the Transparency slider.**

   Lowering the transparency level causes the tracing image to appear faded, which makes distinguishing between the tracing image and content on the page easy. You can set the transparency level to suit your preferences, but somewhere around 50 percent works well with most images.

7. **Click OK.**

   The tracing image appears in the Document window and the dialog box closes.

You have a few other options with the Tracing Image feature. Choose View➪Tracing Image to reveal the following options:

- **Show:** Hides the tracing image if you want to check your work without it being visible but don't want to remove it.
- **Align with Selection:** Enables you to automatically line up the tracing image with a selected element on a page.
- **Adjust Position:** Enables you to use the arrow keys or enter X, Y coordinates to control the position of the tracing image behind the page.
- **Reset Position:** Resets the tracing image to 0, 0 on the X, Y coordinates.
- **Load**: Enables you to add or replace a tracing image.

After you have the tracing image in place, you can use it as a guide while you design your page. Because the tracing image is behind the page, it won't interfere with your design work, and you can add any elements over the tracing image that you could add to any other Web page. Use the tracing image as a reference as you insert and position `<div>` tags, images, and other elements.

Part III

Making It Cool with Multimedia and JavaScript

"Evidently he died of natural causes following a marathon session animating everything on his personal Web site. And no, Morganstern – the irony isn't lost on me."

In this part . . .

Dreamweaver's behaviors make it possible to use JavaScript to create interactive features, such as rollover images and pop-up windows. The multimedia options help your Web pages sing, dance, and delight. In Chapter 10, you find an introduction to the Behaviors panel and step-by-step instructions for creating rollovers, image swaps, and more. You also find instructions for using the Dreamweaver Spry menu to create advanced AJAX features, such as drop-down menus and collapsible panels. In Chapter 11, you find out how to add multimedia files, such as sound, video, and Flash animations, to your Web pages. In Chapter 12, you discover that Dreamweaver has all the tools you need to create forms for your Web site. In Chapter 13, you discover the Spry features.

Chapter 10

Adding Interactivity with Behaviors

In This Chapter

- Adding behaviors to your Web page
- Creating image rollovers
- Using the Swap Image behavior
- Launching a new browser window
- Editing your behaviors
- Enhancing Dreamweaver with extensions

Want to add cool effects like rollovers and pop-up windows? Dreamweaver's behaviors make it easier than ever to create these kinds of interactive features with a JavaScript scripting language.

Behaviors are ready-to-use scripts that can be customized to create a variety of features. You can apply behaviors to almost any element on an HTML page and even to the entire page itself. For example, you can use the Swap Image feature to create an interactive slide show or the Open Browser Window option to play a video in a small, separate browser window.

In this chapter, I introduce you to the Behaviors panel and show you how to use some of Dreamweaver's most popular options.

Brushing Up on Behavior Basics

When you start working with behaviors in Dreamweaver, you can get up and running more easily if you start with this basic introduction to how they work and the terminology they use. When you set up a behavior, you can choose from a number of *triggers,* or *events,* such as `OnMouseOver` or `OnClick`. Consider this slightly corny example: If you tickle someone and make the person laugh, you used an event to trigger an action. Dreamweaver would call the tickling the *event* and the laughter the *action.* The combination is a Dreamweaver *behavior.*

You may already be familiar with the *rollover* behavior, when one image is switched for another. In a rollover, putting your mouse over an image is the *event.* The *action* is the switching of the original image for another image, as shown in Figure 10-1. Rollovers are common in navigation. You can create rollovers with simple effects that use two images, as long as the images are exactly the same size. Alternatively, you can use the Swap Image behavior to create much more complex effects, such as causing any or all the images on a page to change when any other element is triggered.

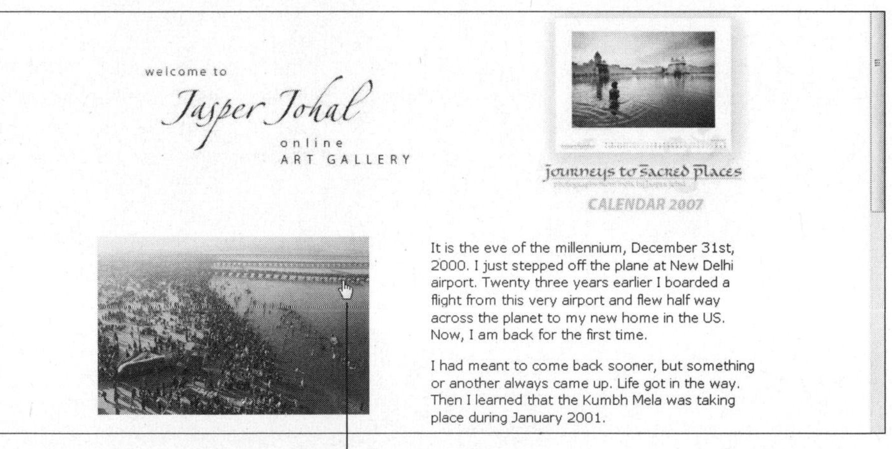

Figure 10-1: When a cursor rolls over one of the images on this page, a second image is displayed in its place.

Dreamweaver includes about 20 behaviors, and you can download and install more. (You find instructions in the "Installing New Extensions for Behaviors" section, at the end of this chapter.)

Specifying the target browser for behaviors

In addition to the behaviors loaded on your computer, the number of behaviors available in the Behaviors panel is controlled by the Show Events For setting, which enables you to see only those behaviors that will work in the target browser for your site. To access these options, follow these steps:

1. **Choose Window➪Behaviors to open the Behaviors panel.**
2. **Click the small arrow just under the plus sign and select Show Events For (second from the last at the bottom of the drop-down list).**
3. **Select the HTML level or browser versions you want to target.**

   In the example shown in the figure, I chose IE 6. The higher the browser version you select, the more behaviors are available. When you specify a target browser, you limit the behaviors to only those that will work in the selected browser and later versions. Behaviors that aren't supported by that browser version are dimmed and unavailable. ***Note:*** Behaviors may also be dimmed if they aren't available for a selected element.

Check out Chapter 1 for more on browser differences and selecting a target browser.

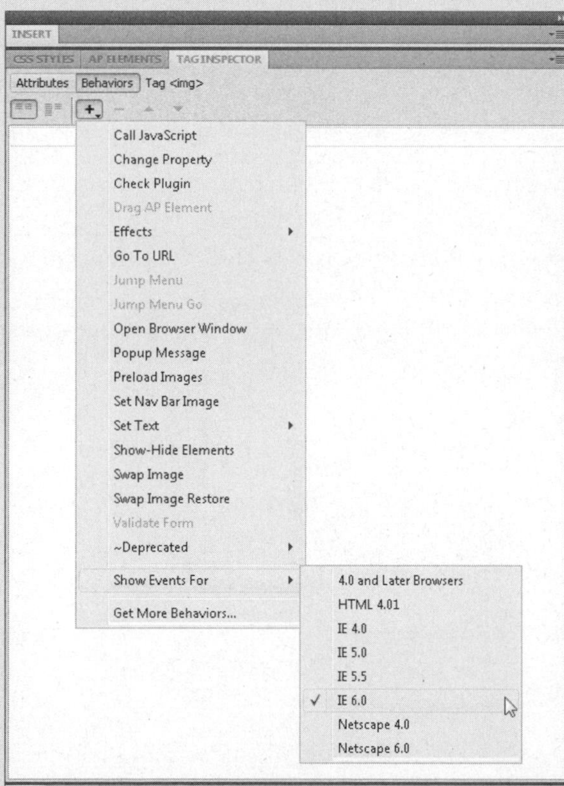

Creating a Rollover Image

Rollover images, as the name implies, are designed to react when someone rolls a cursor over an image. The effect can be as dramatic as a picture of a dog being replaced by a picture of a lion, or as subtle as the color of a word changing as one image replaces another. Either way, this is one of the most common JavaScripts in use on the Web and it's such a popular feature that Dreamweaver includes a special dialog box just for rollovers.

In the section that follows, you find instructions for using the Behaviors panel, where Dreamweaver stores most of the Behaviors included in the program. In this section, you find instructions for using the Insert Rollover Image dialog box, which makes creating a simple rollover effect one of the easiest behaviors to apply.

You can create more complex rollover image effects, with the Swap Image option from the Behaviors panel, which makes it possible to change multiple images at the same time, as you see in the following section.

To create a simple rollover effect with Dreamweaver's Insert Image Rollover dialog box, follow these steps:

1. **Place your cursor on the page where you want the rollover to appear.**

   Rollover effects require at least two images: one for the initial state and one for the rollover state. You can use two different images or two similar ones, but both should have the same dimensions. Otherwise, you get some strange scaling effects because both images must be displayed in exactly the same space on the page.

2. **Choose Insert⇨Image Objects⇨Rollover Image.**

   Alternatively, you can use the drop-down list available from the images icon in the Insert panel and select Rollover Image.

   The Insert Rollover Image dialog box appears, as shown in Figure 10-2.

3. **In the Image Name box, name your image.**

Insert Rollover Image

Image name: photos

Original image: images/boat_birds_310.jpg Browse...

Rollover image: images/crowds_85_310.jpg Browse...

Preload rollover image

Alternate text: East India Photos

When clicked, Go to URL: Gallery_One/index.html Browse...

OK

Cancel

Help

Figure 10-2: Select the original and rollover images.

Before you can apply a behavior to an element, such as an image, the element must have a name so that the behavior script can reference it. You can name elements anything you like as long as you don't use spaces or special characters.

4. **In the Original Image box, specify the first image you want visible. Use the Browse button to locate and select the image.**

   If the images aren't already in your site's root folder, Dreamweaver copies them into your site when you create the rollover. (If you haven't already defined your site in Dreamweaver, see Chapter 2 for more on this important preliminary step.)

5. **In the Rollover Image box, enter the image you want to become visible when visitors move their cursors over the first image.**

   Again, you can use the Browse button to locate and select the image.

6. **Select the Preload Rollover Image check box to load all rollover images into the browser's cache when the page first loads.**

   If you don't choose to do this step, your visitors may experience a delay because the second image won't be downloaded until a mouse is rolled over the original image.

7. **In the When Clicked, Go to URL box, enter any Web address or browse to locate another page in your site that you want to link to.**

   If you don't specify a URL, Dreamweaver automatically inserts the # sign as a placeholder in the code.

   The # sign is a common technique for creating links that don't link anywhere. Because there are many great uses for rollover images that don't link to another page, this is a useful technique. Just remember that if you do want your rollover to link, you need to replace the # sign with a link to another page.

8. **Click OK.**

   The images are set up automatically as a rollover.

9. **Click the globe icon at the top of the workspace to preview your work in a browser where you can test how the rollover works.**

Adding Behaviors to a Web Page

Dreamweaver offers a number of behaviors you can choose from, including the Swap Image behavior and the Open New Browser Window behavior covered in detail in the next two sections. The process of adding other behaviors is similar to these two, but each behavior has its quirks. The tips and tricks you find here can help you get started with behaviors, find out where the majority of Behaviors features are in the program, and how you match behaviors with triggers using the Behaviors panel.

Creating swaps with multiple images

Before you start creating a more complex page design with Dreamweaver's Swap Image behavior, first take a look at the finished page so you can see the result before you get into the details. Notice in Figure 10-3 that a collection of thumbnail images is on the right side of the page and a larger version of one of those images is displayed on the left side in the main area of the page.

Figure 10-3: When you use the Swap Image behavior, you can replace any or all the images on a page.

Notice in Figure 10-4 that when the page is displayed in a browser and I roll my cursor over another of the thumbnail images on the right, the larger image displayed on the left changes. With the Swap Image behavior, you can replace any or all the images on a page.

Follow these steps to use the Swap Image behavior:

1. **Create a page design with all the images you want displayed initially.**

   In the page design I created for these photos from India, the initial page design includes all thumbnail images positioned on the right, and the first of the big images displayed in the area on the left.

Figure 10-4: When you preview a behavior in a browser, you can see the effect of the Swap Image behavior when the cursor is rolled over an image.

You can use the Swap Image behavior to change images on any Web page no matter how the layout is created. In the design featured in this lesson, I used CSS to create a layout with separate `<div>` tags for each row of thumbnails on the right and another div tag for the bigger image on the left. These divs are positioned with CSS. (Find instructions for creating CSS layouts in Chapter 6.)

2. **Name your images in the Property inspector.**

   To target your images with JavaScript, which is how behaviors work, first give each image a unique ID. The image ID isn't the same as the image filename, although you can use the same or similar names. In this example, I gave each thumbnail image an ID of a letter, identifying the thumbnails in alphabetical order according to how I want them positioned. Thus, image *a* is the first image in the top-left row, image *b* is in the top right, and so on. You can name images anything you like as long as you don't use spaces or special characters. I find it helpful to use names that correspond to the image or its order. Using the same or similar IDs for your images as you use for the image filenames helps make it easier to match them when you create the behavior. For example, the filename for the thumbnail in the top-left row is `a_bridge.jpg`, and I gave the same image the ID of *a,* as shown in Figure 10-5. Each of the other thumbnails is similarly named and identified to make it easy to match them as I create the Swap Image effects.

Peeking at the JavaScript code

JavaScript is the code behind Dreamweaver behaviors. Writing JavaScript is more complex than writing HTML code, but not as difficult as writing in a programming language, such as C# or Java. (No, Java and JavaScript aren't the same.) Dreamweaver takes most of the challenge out of JavaScript by giving you a graphic interface that doesn't require you to write the complicated code yourself. When you use behaviors, Dreamweaver automatically writes the code for you behind the scenes.

To fully appreciate what Dreamweaver can do for you, you may want to switch to code view after setting up a behavior just to see the complex code required when you use JavaScript. If you don't like what you see, don't worry: Go back to design view and you can continue to let Dreamweaver take care of the code for you. (I just want you to see how lucky you are that Dreamweaver includes these features.)

In contrast, I'll replace the main image on the page with images that correspond to each of the thumbnails. I'll begin by inserting the main image of the boy getting his face painted, which I want to appear when the page is first loaded. I'll be replacing this image each time I set up a Swap Image for one of the thumbnails. Thus, naming this main image something simple and distinctive, such as `display_photo` or `main_photo`, makes it easier to keep track of which image I'm replacing each time.

Although Dreamweaver automatically assigns a name to each image you insert into a Web page, I find it easier to keep track when I set up the Swap Image behavior if I use names that describe the images or correspond to their order.

3. **Choose Window➪Behaviors.**

   The Behaviors panel opens. You can drag the Behavior panel elsewhere on the page, and you can expand it by dragging its bottom or side. You may also want to close any other open panels to make more room by clicking on the dark gray bar at the top of any panel.

4. **Select an image and choose the Swap Image behavior.**

   First click to select the image in the page that will serve as the trigger for the action. In this example, I'm using the thumbnail images as triggers, so I select them one at a time, starting with the `a_bridge.jpg` thumbnail. With the trigger image selected in the workspace, click the Add Behavior arrow in the Behaviors panel (the small arrow under the plus sign) to open the drop-down list of actions and then select the action you want to apply. In the example shown in Figure 10-6, I selected the Swap Image action, which opens the Swap Image dialog box.

Figure 10-5: In the top left of the Property inspector, enter an ID for each image.

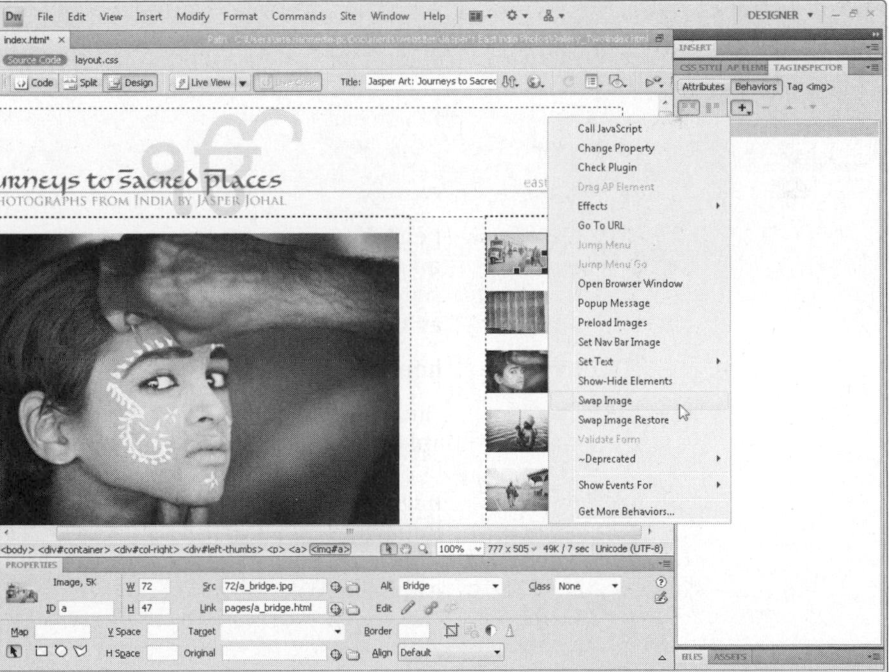

Figure 10-6: With a thumbnail image selected, use the drop-down list in the Behaviors panel to specify an action, such as Swap Image.

5. **Specify the images to swap.**

   a. **In the Swap Image dialog box, select the ID for the image that will be replaced.**

      In Figure 10-7, I selected the image with the ID `display-photo`.

   b. **Use the Browse button to select the image that will replace `display-photo`.**

      I selected the `a_bridge.jpg` image, which I carefully named to correspond to the matching thumbnail. Now when a user rolls a cursor over the `a_bridge` thumbnail image, the photo of the boy with the ID `display_photo` will be replaced with the bigger version of the `a_bridge` image.

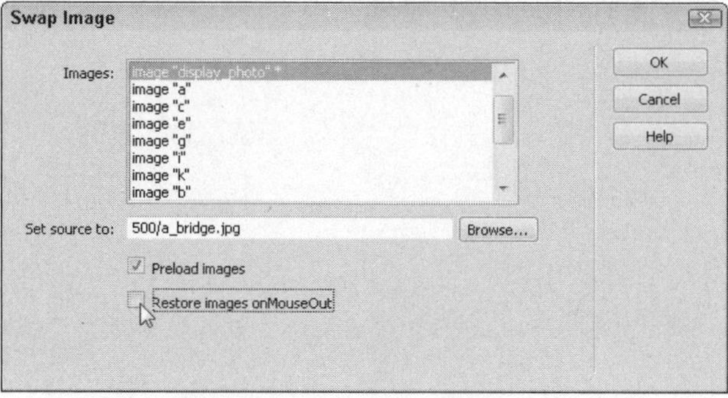

Figure 10-7: Use the Browse button to select the image you want to swap.

6. **At the bottom of the Swap Image dialog box, select Preload Images to instruct the browser to load all the images into the cache when the page is loaded.**

   If you don't select this option, there may be a delay when the image swap is used.

7. **Deselect the Restore Images OnMouseOut option if you wish.**

   The Restore Images OnMouseOut option means that when an event is completed (such as the mouse is moved off the triggering thumbnail), the original image is replaced. By default, Dreamweaver preselects this option for the Swap Image behavior, but in the example shown here, I deselect it because I found that replacing the original image each time I rolled the cursor over another thumbnail was distracting.

8. **After you specify all the settings for the behavior, click OK.**

   The new behavior appears in the Behaviors panel.

9. **Specify an event for the behavior.**

After the action is applied, you can go back and specify which event will trigger the action (as shown in Figure 10-8). By default, Dreamweaver applies the `OnMouseOver` event when you use the Swap Image action, but you can change that to any available event, such as `OnClick`, which requires that the user click the image to trigger the Swap Image action. In this example, I leave it set to `OnMouseOver`.

The list of Behaviors and Events varies depending on the element selected, the applied behavior, and the target browsers specified in the program. For more information about events and what each one accomplishes, see the "Choosing an event for a behavior" section, later in this chapter. For more on browser differences, see the sidebar "Specifying the target browser for behaviors."

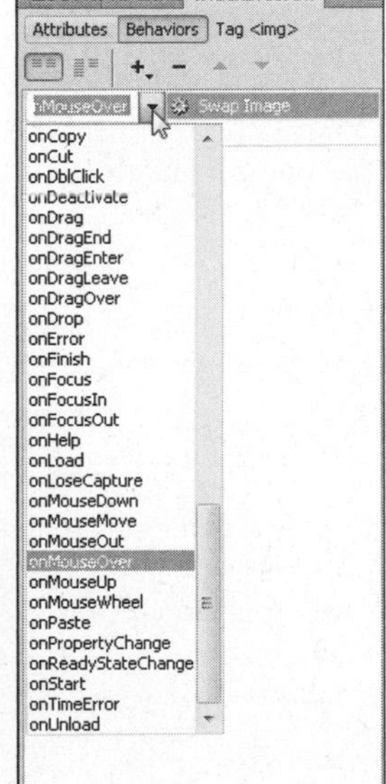

Figure 10-8: When you set up a behavior, you can specify any available action to trigger an event.

You can display or hide events by clicking the Show All Events icon in the top left of the Behaviors panel. Note that if you're using Windows, you also see a collection of events that begin with an <A> and are for elements that are linked.

10. **Apply additional behaviors.**

    To apply the Swap Image behavior to other images on a page, repeat Steps 5–7, clicking to select the image you want to serve as a trigger and then specifying the corresponding image that should be swapped. In this example, I selected each of the thumbnails in turn and set up a Swap Image behavior that replaced the `display_photo` image with the corresponding larger version of the image in the thumbnail.

For best display, make sure that the images that are swapped, such as the large photos shown in the main display area of this site, are all the same size.

11. **Test your work in a browser.**

    You can't see the effects of behaviors like this one until you click on the Live View button at the top of the workspace in Dreamweaver or preview your page in a browser, such as Firefox or Internet Explorer. (If you want to see this example in action, visit Jasper Johal's photo site at `www.EastIndia.com`.)

Using the Open Browser Window behavior

You can use behaviors in Dreamweaver to create many interactive features, such as opening a new browser window when someone clicks a link. As you can see in Figure 10-9, this is a great way to make supplemental information available without losing the original page a visitor was viewing. The Open Browser Window behavior enables you to specify the size of the new window and to display it over the existing window.

Choosing an event for a behavior

Events, in interactive Web-speak, are things a user does to trigger a behavior or an action in a Web page. Clicking an image is an event, as is loading a page into a browser, or pressing a key on the keyboard. Different browser versions support different events (the more recent the browser, the more events are available). Some events are available only for certain kinds of objects or behaviors. If an event can't be used with a selected element or behavior, it appears dimmed. This list describes the most common events:

- `onAbort`: Triggered when the user stops the browser from completely loading an image (for example, when a user clicks the browser's Stop button while an image is loading).
- `onBlur`: Triggered when the specified element stops being the focus of user interaction. For example, when a user clicks outside a text field after clicking in the text field, the browser generates an `onBlur` event for the text field. `onBlur` is the opposite of `onFocus`.
- `onChange`: Triggered when the user changes a value on the page, such as choosing an option from a pop-up list, or when the user changes the value of a text field and then clicks elsewhere on the page.
- `onClick`: Triggered when the user clicks an element, such as a link, a button, or an image.
- `onDblClick`: Triggered when the user double-clicks the specified element.
- `onError`: Triggered when a browser error occurs while a page or an image is

loading. This event can be caused, for example, when an image or a URL can't be found on the server.

- `onFocus`: Triggered when the specified element becomes the focus of user interaction. For example, clicking in or tabbing to a text field of a form generates an `onFocus` event.
- `onKeyDown`: Triggered as soon as the user presses any key on the keyboard. (The user doesn't have to release the key for this event to be generated.)
- `onKeyPress`: Triggered when the user presses and releases any key on the keyboard. This event is like a combination of the `onKeyDown` and `onKeyUp` events.
- `onKeyUp`: Triggered when the user releases a key on the keyboard after pressing it.
- `onLoad`: Triggered when an image or the entire page finishes loading.
- `onMouseDown`: Triggered when the user presses the mouse button. (The user doesn't have to release the mouse button to generate this event.)
- `onMouseMove`: Triggered when the user moves the mouse while pointing to the specified element and the pointer doesn't move away from the element (stays within its boundaries).
- `onMouseOut`: Triggered when the pointer moves off the specified element (usually a link).
- `onMouseOver`: Triggered when the mouse pointer moves over the specified element. Opposite of `onMouseOut`.
- `onMouseUp`: Triggered when a mouse button that's been pressed is released.
- `onMove`: Triggered when a window or frame is moved.
- `onReset`: Triggered when a form is reset to its default values, usually by clicking the Reset button.
- `onResize`: Triggered when the user resizes the browser window or a frame.
- `onScroll`: Triggered when the user scrolls up or down in the browser.
- `onSelect`: Triggered when the user selects text in a text field by highlighting it with the cursor.
- `onSubmit`: Triggered when the user submits a form, usually by clicking the Submit button.
- `onUnload`: Triggered when the user leaves the page, either by clicking to another page or by closing the browser window.

To add the Open Browser Window behavior to a selected image (or any other element) on a page, follow these steps:

1. **Create the page that will open in the new browser window.**

   For this example, I created a new blank HTML page and inserted a larger version of the image that corresponds to the thumbnail I'll be using as a trigger. The goal is that when a user clicks the trigger image, a browser window will open that is sized exactly to fit the larger image but much smaller than the full browser window.

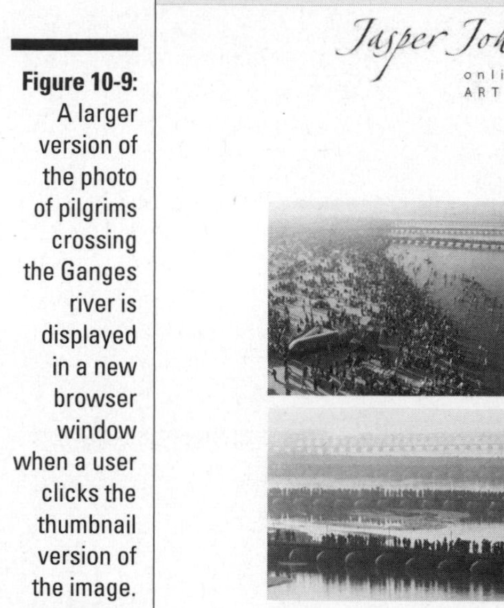

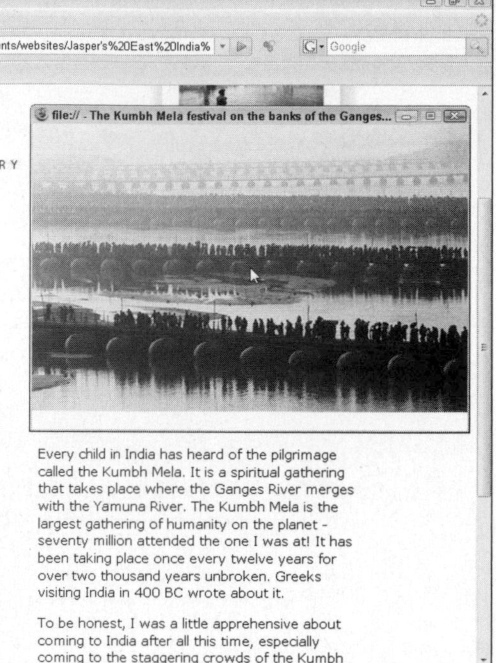

Figure 10-9: A larger version of the photo of pilgrims crossing the Ganges river is displayed in a new browser window when a user clicks the thumbnail version of the image.

When you name files that will be used in behaviors, such as a page that will open when the Open Browser Window behavior is used, avoid using slashes anywhere in a filename or numbers at the beginning of a filename (you can use numbers anywhere else in the name). You can use hyphens and underscores.

2. **Select the image, text, or other element you want to serve as the trigger for the action.**

   You can select any image, text, or layer on a page and apply a behavior to it the same way.

3. **Choose Window⇨Behaviors to open the Behaviors panel.**

4. **Click the plus sign (+) and choose the behavior you want from the drop-down list.**

   In this example, I selected the Open Browser Window behavior.

   If a behavior appears dimmed, it can't be associated with the selected element. For example, the Swap Image behavior can be applied only to an image, so it appears dimmed if you've selected text or another element.

5. **In the Open Browser Window dialog box, as shown in Figure 10-10, specify the settings.**

   You can set a number of options that control how the new browser window appears:

- **Use the Browse button to the right of the URL to Display box to select the page you want to open in the new browser window.** (You can also enter a URL in this box to open a page in another Web site.)
- **Set the window width and height to specify the size of the new browser window that will open.** In this example, I set the width to the exact size of the image and made the height 20 pixels larger to provide a little breathing room under the painting name.
- **Select the options Navigation Toolbar, Location Toolbar, Status Bar, Menu Bar, Scrollbars as Needed, or Resize Handles if you want the new browser window to include any of these features.** I selected Scrollbars as Needed in case my visitor's browser window is smaller than the size I specified for the photo, but I left all the others deselected because I want a clean, simple browser window without any menus or other features.
- **Name the new window, which is important if you want to target that same window to load other pages into it.**

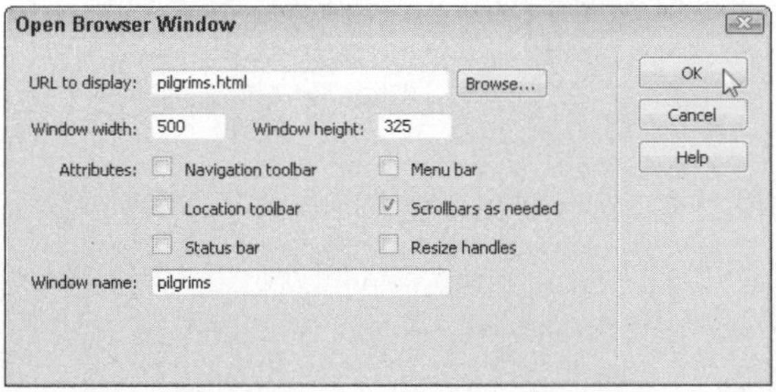

Open Browser Window

URL to display: pilgrims.html [Browse...]

Window width: 500 Window height: 325

Attributes: ☐ Navigation toolbar ☐ Menu bar
☐ Location toolbar ☑ Scrollbars as needed
☐ Status bar ☐ Resize handles

Window name: pilgrims

[OK] [Cancel] [Help]

Figure 10-10: Specify settings for the display of the window.

6. **After you specify all the settings for the behavior, click OK.**

   The new behavior appears in the Behaviors panel.

7. **To change the event that triggers your behavior, select the current event from the left side of the Behaviors panel.**

   In the Events drop-down list, select any available event to serve as the trigger for the behavior. For more information about events and what each one accomplishes, see the "Choosing an event for a behavior" section, later in this chapter.

8. **To test the action, choose File⇨Preview in Browser.**

   Click the image to test whether a new browser window opens.

Attaching Multiple Behaviors

You can attach multiple behaviors to the same element on a page (as long as they don't conflict, of course). For example, you can attach one action that's triggered when users click an image and another when they move their cursors over the image. You can also trigger the same action by using multiple events. For example, you can play the same sound when a user triggers any number of events.

To attach additional behaviors to an element, click the plus sign in the Behaviors panel and select another option from the pop-up list. Repeat this process as many times as you want.

Editing a Behavior

You can always go back and edit a behavior after you create it. You can choose a different event to trigger the behavior, choose a different action, or remove behaviors. You can also change behavior options after a behavior is applied.

To edit a behavior, follow these steps:

1. **Select an object with a behavior attached.**
2. **Choose Window⇨Behaviors to open the Behaviors panel.**

   Here are some options you can choose in the Behaviors panel:

   - **Change a triggering event:** Choose a different event in the Events drop-down list in the Behaviors panel.
   - **Remove a behavior:** Click the action in the Behaviors panel to select it and then click the minus sign at the top of the pane. The behavior disappears.
   - **Change parameters for an action:** Double-click the gear icon next to the action and change the parameters in the dialog box that opens.
   - **Change the order of actions when multiple actions are set:** Select an action and then click the Move Event Value Up or Move Event Value Down buttons to move the action to a different position in the list of actions.

Installing New Extensions for Behaviors

Even with all the cool features in Dreamweaver, a day will almost certainly come when you'll want to do things that Dreamweaver can't do with the features that shipped with the program. Fortunately, the programmers who created Dreamweaver made it possible for other programmers to add features with the Extension Manager. The result? You can add new functionality by adding extensions from a variety of third-party sources.

You can find extensions that do everything from adding highly customizable drop-down and fly-out menus to full-featured shopping cart systems. Keep in mind, however, that not all extensions are well supported and few come with good instructions. They're not all free, either. Some cost hundreds of dollars, but most are in the $20–$50 range. When you visit the Dreamweaver Exchange site, you find reviews and rankings to help you sort through the best options.

In the following steps, I explain how you find, download, and install a free Dreamweaver extension. Although how extensions work after they're installed can differ dramatically, the basic process of adding them to Dreamweaver is nearly the same.

1. **Visit the Dreamweaver Exchange site.**

   Get to the Dreamweaver Exchange site by

   - Choosing Get More Behaviors from the bottom of the Behaviors drop-down list in the Behaviors panel.
   - Visiting `www.adobe.com/exchange` and following the link to the Dreamweaver section.
   - Clicking the link in the bottom right of the Dreamweaver Welcome screen.

   Note: If you launch Dreamweaver and find a link to download an update for Dreamweaver instead of the link to the Exchange site, by all means download and install the update first. After you're finished, the update link is replaced by the link to the Exchange site.

2. **Sort through the many available extensions.**

   You'll find a wide range of extensions on the Dreamweaver Exchange site. You can search through extensions by category, keyword, and ranking options. Many of the extensions featured on the Exchange site include links to their creators' sites, where you'll often find even more extensions.

3. **Select an extension and review its features.**

   When you click a link to an extension on the Exchange site, you'll find more information about the extension, including system requirements and the version of Dreamweaver that the extension was designed for. In general, you can use extensions designed for earlier versions of Dreamweaver in more recent versions. Be aware, however, that extensions designed for later versions of Dreamweaver usually won't work in earlier versions of the program.

   Before you leave the extension's page, I highly recommend that you take the time to read the special instructions in the middle of the page.

Some extensions include important instructions, such as where you'll find the new feature in the Dreamweaver interface after it's installed and warnings that some of the functionality of an extension will work only when previewed on a live Web server (this is true for the random image extension, for example).

4. **To download an extension, click the Download button (for free extensions) or the Buy button next to the extension name and save the extension to your hard drive.**

5. **Install the new extension after it's downloaded by choosing Help➪Manage Extensions to open the installation dialog box.**

   Most extensions require that you close Dreamweaver before installation, and most install with the click of a button. Dreamweaver's Extension Manager launches automatically to install most extensions.

6. **In the Extension Manager dialog box, choose File➪Install Extension and then browse your drive to select the extension file you downloaded.**

   After the installation is complete, Dreamweaver displays instructions for using the extension. These are usually the same as the instructions included in the middle of the page on the Exchange site.

   Pay special attention to the part of the instructions that tells you where you'll find your newly installed extensions. Extensions may be added to menus, dialog boxes, and other parts of Dreamweaver depending on their functionality and how the programmer set them up, and it can be hard to find them if you don't know where to look.

7. **Launch Dreamweaver and find the new menu option, button, or other interface feature that controls your new extension.**

   In many cases, all you have to do is open an existing page or create a new page in Dreamweaver and then open the newly added dialog box or select the new option from a menu.

Adobe is constantly updating the Exchange site available by clicking on the Dreamweaver link at `www.adobe.com/exchange`. Visit it regularly to find new extensions you can download and install to enhance Dreamweaver's feature set.

Chapter 11

Showing Off with Multimedia

In This Chapter

- Understanding multimedia
- Creating Flash buttons and text within Dreamweaver
- Adding Flash files to Web pages
- Comparing audio and video formats
- Inserting multimedia files
- Introducing Java
- Linking to PDF files

Get your Web pages singing and dancing with multimedia. Audio, video, and animation are exploding on the Web and transforming static pages into rich multimedia experiences. You can use Dreamweaver to link to multimedia files, or you can insert audio, video, and other files so that they play within your pages. You can even control when and how they play for your users.

Not all Web sites warrant multimedia; if your goal is to provide information in the fastest way possible to the broadest audience, text is still generally the best option. If you want to provide a richer experience for your users, to *show* rather than just *tell,* or to entertain as well as inform, adding sound, video, and animation can help you share more information more vividly and even make you look more professional.

The most complicated aspect of multimedia on the Web is choosing the best format for your audience, which is why you'll find a primer on audio and video formats in this chapter. You can't create or edit multimedia files in Dreamweaver; but after your files are optimized and ready for the Internet, Dreamweaver makes it relatively easy to add them to your Web pages.

As you discover in this chapter, inserting video, audio, and Flash files is similar to adding image files to Web pages, but with many more options, such as settings that control how and when multimedia files play.

Understanding Multimedia Players

When you add sound, video, or any other kind of multimedia to a Web site, your visitors may need a special player (sometimes with an associated plug-in) to play or view your files.

Players are small programs that work alone or with a Web browser to add support for functions, such as playing sound, video, and animation files. Some of the best-known multimedia players are the Flash Player, Windows Media Player, RealNetworks RealPlayer, and Apple QuickTime.

The challenge is that not everyone on the Web uses the same player, and viewers must have the correct player to view your multimedia files. As a result, you need a strategy that helps visitors play your multimedia easily, such as the following ones:

- Many Web developers offer audio and video in two or three formats so users can choose the one that best fits the players they already have.
- Some developers also include the same multimedia files in different file sizes so that visitors with slower connection speeds don't have to wait as long. Optimizing multimedia for the Web works much as it does with images: The smaller the file size, the lower the quality but the faster the file downloads.
- Many Web developers also include information about how visitors can download and install the best player if they need it to view the files.

You can use Dreamweaver to insert or link to any type of multimedia file, but it's up to you to choose the format that's best for your audience. Although dozens of plug-ins are available for Web pages, Flash, Windows Media, and QuickTime are the most common on the Web today.

In general, I recommend that you avoid the more obscure players unless you're offering specialized content that users have a good reason to download, such as a three-dimensional game that requires a special program to run.

Working with Adobe Flash

Flash has clearly emerged as the favorite technology for creating animations and a wide variety of interactive features on the Web. You can even integrate sound and video into Flash, making it a common choice for combining formats.

Dreamweaver supports three different kinds of Flash files:

- **Flash files:** (extension `.swf`) The most versatile Flash format is the SWF file (pronounced SWIFF). Often referred to simply as *Flash files,* this format is sometimes called a Flash movie, even when it doesn't include video. Flash files with a .swf extension can include illustrations, photos, animation sequences, and video. In Dreamweaver, use the Insert⇨Media⇨SWF option for this format. You find detailed instructions for working with Flash files in the following section.
- **Flash video:** (extension `.flv`) As the name implies, Flash video is a video format, although it can also be used for audio files. To convert video into the Flash video format, you need the Flash Video Encoder. In Dreamweaver, use the Insert⇨Media⇨FLV option for this format. You find detailed instructions for working with `.flv` Flash files in the "Adding Flash audio and video files" section later in this chapter
- **Flash Paper:** Adobe's Flash Paper makes it easy to turn documents, such as Word files, into Flash files with the `.swf` extension. Flash Paper files are ideal for displaying documents on the Web. When you insert a Flash Paper file into a Web page, you can include a Flash control bar to add interactivity much as you would with any other Flash file format. In Dreamweaver, use the Insert⇨Media⇨Flash Paper option for this format. For instructions on how to make changes to Flash settings after you've inserted a Flash Paper file, see the "Settings Flash properties," section later in this chapter.

One thing that makes Flash files (with the `.swf` extension) so flexible and so fast on the Internet is that Flash uses *vector graphics* instead of *bitmaps.* Therefore, the graphics in Flash are based on mathematical descriptions *(vectors)* instead of dots *(bitmaps),* and those vector equations take up far less space than bit-mapped images. Vector graphics can also be scaled up or down in size without affecting the image quality or the size of the downloaded file. This capability to scale makes Flash ideally suited for the many different monitor sizes used by Web viewers as well as for the tiny displays on cell phones and other handheld devices. You can even project Flash graphics on a wall or movie screen without losing quality, although any photographs or video files integrated into a Flash file may lose quality or look distorted at higher or lower resolutions.

To create a Flash file, you need Adobe Flash or a similar program that supports the Flash format. Because Flash is an open standard, you can create Flash files with a variety of programs, including Adobe Illustrator, which has an Export to SWF option. If want to know how to create full-featured Flash files, check out *Adobe Flash CS4 For Dummies,* by Ellen Finkelstein and Gurdy Leete (Wiley Publishing, Inc.).

Flash is great overall but be aware of the important drawbacks:

- If you need printouts for some reason, Flash may not print as you would hope.

- Flash may cause accessibility problems. Screen readers and other specialized viewers can't read the text in a Flash file any better than they can read text in an image file. To make Flash files more accessible, include detailed alternative text.
- Text included in Flash files may not be read by search engines (although including alternative text can help with these limitations).
- Sites created entirely in Flash are harder to link to, especially if you want to link to a particular page within a site and not just to the front page of the site.

Inserting Flash SWF files

Flash files, often called Flash *movies,* use the `.swf` extension and can include animations, graphics, photos, and even video. Thanks to Dreamweaver, these files are relatively easy to insert into a Web page. In this section, I assume you have a completed Flash file (an animation or other Flash movie), and you want to add it to your Web page.

You insert a Flash file much as you insert an image file. But because Flash can do so much more than a still image, you have a variety of settings and options for controlling how your Flash file plays.

Before you start, make sure to save the Flash file you want to insert in the main folder for your Web site. I recommend creating a multimedia folder in your main Web site folder for audio and other multimedia files, just as most designers create an image folder for image files.

To add a Flash file to a Web site, open an existing page or create a new document and save the file. Then follow these steps:

1. **Click where you want the Flash file to appear on your Web page.**
2. **If it's not already open, choose Window⇨Insert and then use the drop-down list to select the Common Insert panel.**
3. **From the Media drop-down list on the Common Insert panel, choose the SWF Flash option (see Figure 11-1).**

   You can also choose Insert⇨Media⇨SWF. The Select File dialog box appears.
4. **Browse to locate the Flash file that you want to insert in your page and click to select the file.**
5. **If you have accessibility options turned on, you're prompted to add alternative text to describe the Flash file. Enter a description of the file and click OK.**

   The dialog box closes, and the Flash file is inserted into your document.

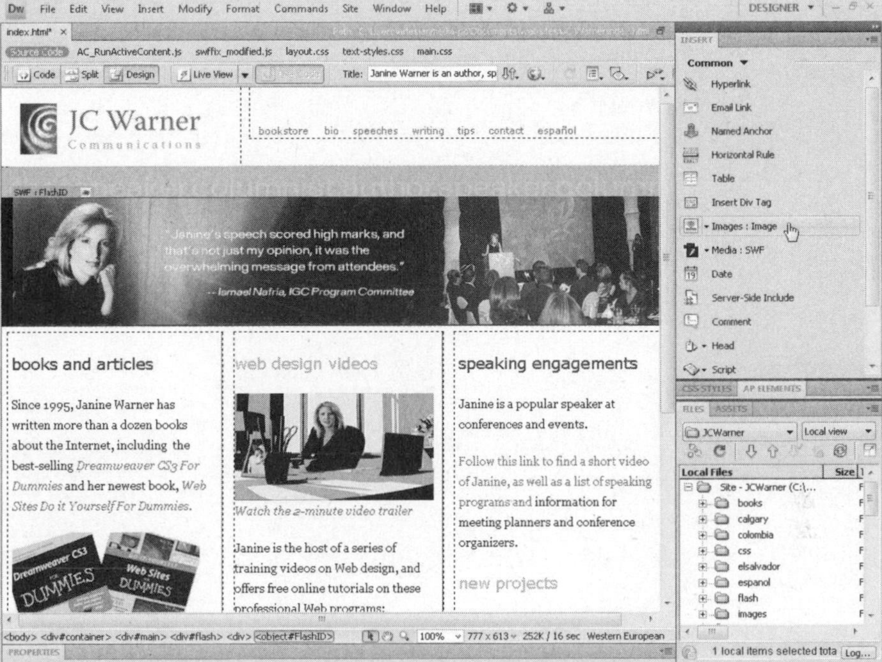

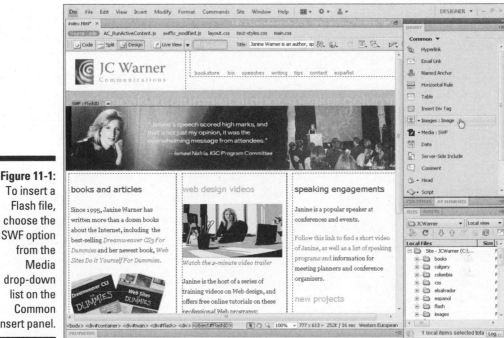

Figure 11-1: To insert a Flash file, choose the SWF option from the Media drop-down list on the Common Insert panel.

Dreamweaver displays Flash as a gray box with the dimensions of the Flash file. To display the Flash file, click to select it and then click the green Play button on the right side of the Property inspector. (In Figure 11-2, you see the Stop button because I've already clicked the Play button, which changed to the Stop button when the file began playing.) If you have the Flash player installed on your computer, the Flash file will also play when you preview the page in a browser.

Setting Flash properties

Like most HTML tags, the tags that link Flash and other multimedia files to Web pages have *attributes* (also called properties) that define how a file is displayed within a browser, controlling such actions as whether an animation plays automatically when a page is loaded or whether a visitor must click a link for the animation to begin. Dreamweaver automatically sets some of these options, such as the height and width of the Flash file, but you may want to specify others.

To display Flash attributes in the Property inspector, click to select the gray box that represents a Flash file after it's inserted into a Web page. The following describes the Flash options included in the Property inspector, as shown in Figure 11-2.

If you don't see all the options in the Property inspector, click the expander arrow in the lower-right corner to display the more advanced options.

- **ID field:** Use the text field in the upper-left corner of the Property inspector, just to the right of the F icon, to assign a name to the file. Dreamweaver automatically enters a name, such as FlashID1, or FlashID2. You can change this name to something that has more meaning; just don't use any spaces or special characters other than the dash or underscore. The name is important because it can be used to refer to the file in JavaScript.

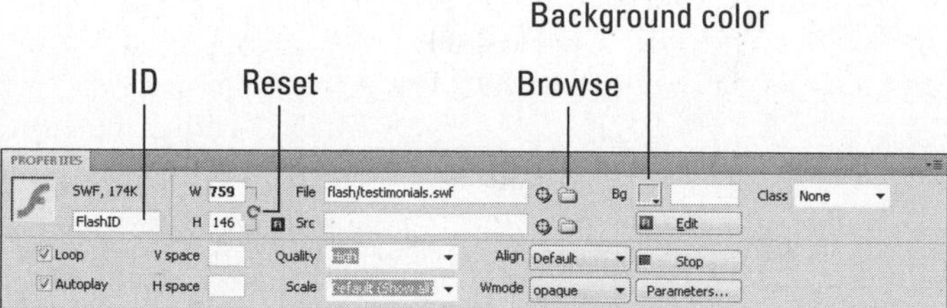

Figure 11-2: Select the Flash file to see these Flash Property inspector settings.

- **W (width):** Use this option to specify the width of the file. The file is measured in pixels.
- **H (height):** Use this option to specify the height of the file. The file is measured in pixels.
- **Reset Size:** (This icon is only visible if you have changed the size of a Flash file.) You can change the display size of a Flash file by clicking a corner and dragging it or by entering a number in the height or width fields. When the size of a Flash file has been altered, a small, circular icon appears just to the right of the height and width fields. Clicking this circular icon reverts the Flash file to its original size. You can resize Flash files, unlike images, video, and many other file types, without affecting image quality because they're vector-based. To keep the file proportionate, hold down the Shift key while you drag to resize the file.
- **File:** Dreamweaver automatically fills in this field when you insert a Flash file with the filename and path. You risk breaking the link to your flash file if you alter this field.
- **Src (source):** This text field enables you to identify the source file you used to create the `.swf` file inserted into a page. After this option is set, clicking the Edit button automatically opens the source file in Flash and provides a Done button to integrate changes back into Dreamweaver. Because the programs are integrated, any changes you make in Flash automatically reflect in Dreamweaver when you use this option.

- **Edit:** Click this button to open a Flash source file with the Adobe Flash program where you can edit it. Note that you can edit only the source Flash file. After saving the Flash file for Web use with the `.swf` extension, return to the original Flash file to edit it again.
- **Class:** Use this drop-down list to apply any class styles defined for the document.
- **Loop:** Selecting this box causes the Flash file to repeat (or *loop*). If you don't select this box, the Flash movie stops after it reaches the last frame.
- **Autoplay:** Selecting this box causes the Flash movie to play as soon as it downloads to the viewer's computer. If you don't select this box, whatever option you've set within the Flash file itself (such as `onMouseOver` or `onMouseDown`) is required to start the movie.
- **V Space (vertical space):** If you want blank space above or below the file, enter the number of pixels.
- **H Space (horizontal space):** If you want blank space on either side of the file, enter the number of pixels.
- **Quality:** This option enables you to prioritize the anti-aliasing options of your images versus the speed of playback. *Anti-aliasing,* which makes your files appear smoother, can slow down the rendering of each frame because the computer must first smooth the edges. The Quality parameter enables you to regulate how much the process is slowed by letting you set priorities based on the importance of appearance versus playback speed. You can choose from these Quality options:
    - **Low:** Anti-aliasing is never used. Playback speed has priority over appearance.
    - **High:** Anti-aliasing is always used. Appearance has priority over playback speed.
    - **Auto High:** With this option, playback is set to begin with anti-aliasing turned on. However, if the frame rate supported by the user's computer drops too low, anti-aliasing automatically turns off to improve playback speed. This option emphasizes playback speed and appearance equally at first but sacrifices appearance for the sake of playback speed, if necessary.
    - **Auto Low:** Playback begins with anti-aliasing turned off. If the Flash player detects that the processor can handle it, anti-aliasing is turned on. Use this option to emphasize speed at first but improve appearance whenever possible.
- **Scale:** Specify this option only if you change the file's original height and width size settings. The Scale parameter enables you to define how the Flash movie appears within those settings. The following options in the Scale drop-down list enable you to set preferences for how a scaled Flash movie appears within the window:

Finding Flash resources online

One of the best places to read more about creating Flash files is on the Internet, where a wide range of Web sites offers everything from predesigned Flash files you can easily customize to great ideas for getting the most from this award-winning technology. You may find these Web sites useful if you want to find out more about Flash:

- **Adobe** (`www.adobe.com`): You find loads of tips and tricks for creating and using Flash files (as well as many inspiring examples of Flash in action).
- **Swish** (`www.swishzone.com`): If you're looking for an alternative to Adobe Flash, Swish is a great little program that's more reasonably priced.
- **Flash Kit** (`www.flashkit.com`): You find a wide range of resources for Flash developers.
- **Flash Arcade** (`www.flasharcade.com`): This site has some of the best interactive games created in Flash.

  - **Default (show all):** This option enables the entire movie to appear in the specified area. The width and height proportions of the original movie are maintained and no distortion occurs, but borders may appear on two sides of the movie to fill the space.
  - **No Border:** This option enables you to scale a Flash movie to fill a specified area. No borders appear and the original aspect ratio is maintained, but some cropping may occur.
  - **Exact Fit:** The Flash movie is the exact width and height that are set, but the original aspect ratio may not be maintained and the movie may look squished.
- **Align:** This option controls the alignment of the file on the page. This setting works the same for plug-in files as for images.
- **Wmode:** Specify Window to display the flash file in a rectangular window on a Web page. Specify Opaque to hide everything behind a Flash file when you move or resize it using JavaScript. Specify Transparent to show the background of the HTML page though any transparent portions of the Flash file.
- **Play button:** Click the green Play button to play a Flash file in Dreamweaver. Note that when the Play button is activated, the button changes to Stop (refer to Figure 11-2).
- **Parameters:** This button provides access to a dialog box where you can enter parameters specific to your Flash files.

Using scripts to make Flash function better

When you insert Flash or other multimedia files with Dreamweaver CS4, the program creates a collection of JavaScript files that help the Flash file play properly. The files are named things like, `AC_RunActiveContent.js`, and are stored in a Scripts folder, which Dreamweaver automatically creates inside your root site folder. The first time Dreamweaver creates this file, a dialog box alerts you that you need to upload the script for your multimedia file to work properly. Make sure you include this script when you publish your site on your Web server.

If you don't include the script, your multimedia file may not play properly, or your visitors may be required to click the play button twice before the file begins to play.

Working with Video and Audio on the Web

As bandwidth has grown on the Web, the use of video files has grown more dramatically than almost any other multimedia file type. From YouTube to Google Video and MySpace to small personal Web sites, millions of video files are added to the Web every day. Adding a video file to a Web page with Dreamweaver is relatively easy, especially if you use the Flash video format described in the "Adding Flash audio and video files" section later in this chapter. If you use another video format, such as Windows Media Video or QuickTime, you find instructions for adding files in those formats in the following section, "Adding Audio and Video Files to Web Pages." You can specify video and audio settings, such as Autoplay, by changing setting parameters, an option that is a little more complicated if you use any format other than Flash video. You find instructions for managing these settings in Dreamweaver in the "Setting options for audio and video files," later in this chapter.

Instead of hosting your video on your own Web server, an alternative is to upload video files to the YouTube site and then include special code from the YouTube site in the HTML code of your Web pages so that the video plays within your pages, even though it's hosted on YouTube. Visit YouTube.com and follow their instructions for uploading video files. To learn how to add code from sites like YouTube to your own pages, visit my site at `www.DigitalFamily.com/dreamweaver` and read the tutorial on adding code from Google, YouTube, and other sites in Dreamweaver.

The first challenge to working with multimedia is choosing the right format and optimizing your video so it downloads quickly and still looks good. Optimizing video is beyond the scope of this book, but I've included some general information about video formats to help you make more informed decisions about the type of video files to add to your pages.

Unfortunately, no single video format works for everyone on the Web (although Flash video is gaining popularity fast). Most new computers come with preinstalled video and audio players that play the most common file formats. If you use a Windows computer, you probably have Windows Media Player on your computer. If you use a Mac, you have QuickTime. Both video players can handle multiple video formats, so anyone with a relatively new computer can likely view video in common formats.

Many people surf the Web in their offices, in libraries, and in other locations where unexpected sound can be jarring, disruptive, or worse. Always give people a warning before you play video or audio and always give users a way to turn audio off quickly when necessary.

Comparing popular video formats

You can convert video from one file format to another relatively easily with most video-editing programs. You can open a video in AVI (Audio Video Interleave) format in a program, such as Adobe Premier Elements (a good video editor for beginners), and then choose File⇨Export to convert it to any of a dozen formatting and compression options. For example, you could convert an AVI file to the Windows Media format with the compression setting for a 56K modem or into the QuickTime format with the compression setting for a cable modem. Editing video can get complicated, and optimizing video for the best quality with the fastest download time is both an art and a science, but the most basic process of converting a video file isn't difficult after you understand the conversion options. Because Flash video is increasingly popular and because a free trial version of the Flash video encoder is available on the Adobe.com Web site, I've included basic instructions for using the encoder in the section, "Converting video files into Flash format with the Flash video encoder," later in this chapter. (To download the encoder, visit `www.adobe.com/products/flash/flashpro/productinfo/encoder`.)

The following sections provide a brief description of the most common digital video formats, their file extensions, and a Web address where you can find out more about each option.

Flash video

You can create Flash videos with Adobe Flash. Because the Flash player is so popular on the Web, many developers consider Flash one of the best options available today.

File extension: `.flv`

Web site: `www.adobe.com`

Windows Media Video

Defined by Microsoft and popular on the PC, this video format supports streaming and plays with Windows Media Player as well as many other popular players.

File extension: `.wmv`

Web site: `www.microsoft.com/windows/windowsmedia`

RealVideo

RealNetworks designed the RealVideo file format to play in RealPlayer (available for Mac and PC). RealMedia provides optimization well suited to low-speed and high-speed connections but requires special software on your Web server for streaming.

File extension: `.rm`, `.rv`

Web site: `www.real.com`

QuickTime

The QuickTime player is built into the Macintosh operating system and is used by most Mac programs that include video or animation. QuickTime is a great format for video on the Web and supports streaming, but it's used primarily by those who favor Macs (although QuickTime files can be viewed on Windows computers as well).

File extension: `.qt`, `.mov`

Web site: `www.quicktime.com`

AVI

Created by Microsoft, AVI (Audio Video Interleave) is one the most common video formats on Windows computers and can play on most common video players. AVI is fine if you're viewing video on a CD or on your hard drive, where the file doesn't have to download, but you can't optimize AVI files well for use on the Internet. If your files are in AVI, convert them to one of the other formats before adding them to your Web site. Otherwise, you force your visitors to download unnecessarily large video files.

File extension: `.avi`

Web site: No one site about AVI exists, but you can find information if you search for *AVI* at `www.microsoft.com`

Streaming media plays faster

To *stream* multimedia means to play a file while it's downloading from the server. This is a valuable trick on the Web because video and audio files can take a long time to download. Here's how streaming works. When you click a link to a video file, your computer begins to download it from the server. If you're using a player that supports streaming, the video or audio file begins to play as soon as enough of the file downloads successfully to ensure an uninterrupted experience. If you don't use streaming, the entire file must download before playing. Although it can take the same amount of time to download the entire file, streaming can greatly reduce the time your visitors need to wait before they can start viewing a video online.

Comparing popular audio formats

Audio works much like video on the Web. You can link to a sound file or embed the file into your page; either way, your visitors need to have the right player to listen to the file. You find instructions for adding both audio and video files to your pages in the following section, "Adding Audio and Video Files to Web Pages."

The following sections provide a brief description of the most common digital audio formats, their file extensions, and a Web address where you can find out more about each option.

MP3

One of the most successful audio compression formats, MP3 supports streaming audio. Most music you can download from the Internet is in MP3 format, and it's clearly the first choice of many Web developers. MP3 files can be played by most popular multimedia players on the Web.

File extension: `.mp3`

Web site: `www.mp3.com`

Windows Audio

Microsoft's Windows Audio format supports streaming and can be played with Windows Media Player as well as many other popular players. It also offers digital rights management functionality.

File extension: `.wma`

Web site: `www.microsoft.com/windows/windowsmedia`

RealAudio

RealAudio, designed by RealNetworks, is a streaming file format that plays in RealPlayer (available for Mac and PC). RealAudio is especially popular among radio stations and entertainment sites.

File extension: `.ra`

Web site: `www.real.com`

WAV

The WAV file format is popular in digital media because it offers the highest sound quality possible. Audio files in this format are often too big for use on the Web, averaging 10MB for a minute of audio. (In comparison, an MP3 file that is five times longer can be less than one-third the size.) Although WAV files are commonly used on the Internet because of their nearly universal compatibility, I recommend that you convert WAV files (especially for long audio clips) to one of the other audio formats.

File extension: `.wav`

Web site: No official Web site exists for WAV files, but you can find some documentation at `www.microsoft.com` when you search for *WAV*.

Adding Audio and Video Files to Web Pages

Like other multimedia files, you can link to an audio or a video file or you can insert multimedia files into a page. Linking to a multimedia file is as easy as linking to any other file, as you see in the instructions that follow. Inserting an audio or a video file is a little more complicated, but it lets a visitor play the file without leaving the Web page. Inserting audio and video files is covered in this section. If you're using Flash video or audio, see the "Adding Flash audio and video files" section, later in this chapter.

Linking to audio and video files

To use Dreamweaver to link to a video file, an audio file, or another multimedia file, follow these steps:

1. **Click to select the text, image, or other element you want to use to create a link.**

   This works just like creating a link to another Web page (see Figure 11-3).

If you're linking to a video file, a good trick is to take a single still image from the video and insert that into your Web page. Then create a link from that image to the video file.

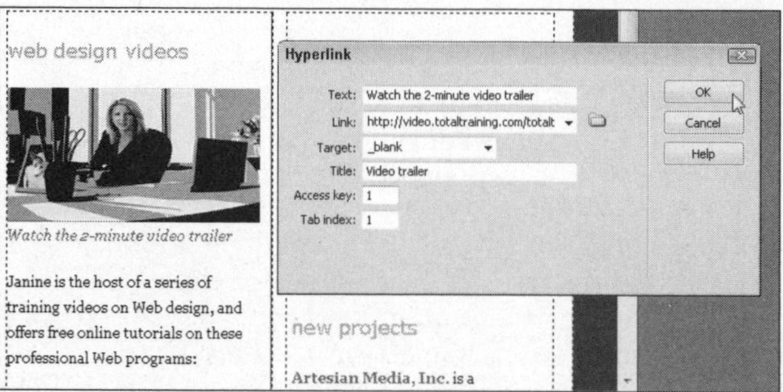

Figure 11-3: Link to an audio or a video file just as you'd create a link to another Web page.

2. **Choose Insert ⇨Hyperlink or click the Hyperlink icon in the Common Insert panel.**

   The Hyperlink dialog box opens, as shown in Figure 11-3.

   Alternatively, you can click the Browse button just to the right of the Link field in the Property inspector. (The Browse button looks like a small file folder.)

3. **Enter the text you want to serve as a link in the Text field.**

   If you selected a section of text on the page before opening the Hyperlink dialog box, that text automatically appears in the Text field.

4. **Enter the URL where the audio or video file is located.**

   Alternatively, click the Browse button (the small file folder icon) to the right of the Link field and browse your hard drive to find the video or audio file you want to link to.

   As with any other file you link to, make sure you've saved your audio or video files into your main Web site folder.

   Note that you can link to an audio or video file on another Web site, as I've done in the example shown in Figure 11-3, but you need to have the exact URL of the file's location.

5. **Click to select the file you want to link to and then click OK.**

   The dialog box closes, and the link is created automatically.

6. **(Optional) Choose _blank from the Target drop-down list if you want the video file to open in a new browser window or tab.**

7. **To specify Accessibility settings, enter a Title, Access Key, and Tab Index.**

8. **Click OK to add the hyperlink and to close the Hyperlink dialog box.**
9. **Click the Preview button (at the top of the work area) to open the page in a browser, where you can test the link to your multimedia file.**

   Dreamweaver launches your specified Web browser and displays the page. If you have the necessary player, the file downloads, your player launches, and your file automatically plays.

Many people like to have multimedia files, such as video, pop up in a new browser window. To do this, create an HTML file and embed your multimedia file in it. Then use the Open Browser Window behavior in Dreamweaver to create a pop-up window that displays your multimedia page. For more on how to work with Dreamweaver behaviors, see Chapter 10.

Inserting audio and video files

When you insert an audio or a video file into a Web page, you can set the file to play automatically when the page loads (as long as your visitor has the necessary player), or you can require that your visitors click the Play button first. Either way, when you insert an audio or a video file into a page, the file will play within the page instead of requiring that the video or audio player be opened separately.

To use Dreamweaver to embed an audio or a video file into a Web page, follow these steps:

1. **Click where you want the file to appear on your Web page.**

   If you're inserting a sound file, the play, pause, and stop controls appear wherever you insert the file. If you're inserting a video file, the first frame of the video appears where you insert the file.
2. **Select Common from the Insert panel, and in the Media drop-down list, choose Plugin (see Figure 11-4).**

   You can also choose Insert➪Media➪Plugin. The Select File dialog box appears.

   Use the Plugin option for all audio and video file types — except Flash video (`.flv`) files.
3. **Browse your hard drive to locate the sound or video file you want inserted in your page and then click to select it.**
4. **Click OK.**

   The dialog box closes, and the file is inserted automatically into the page. A small icon (resembling a puzzle piece) represents the file.

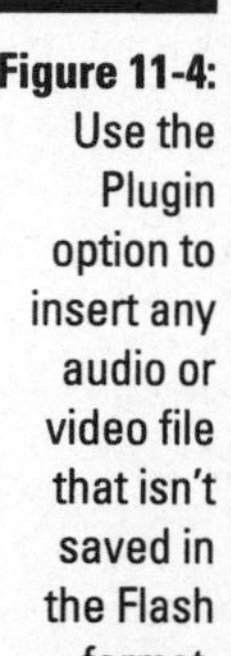

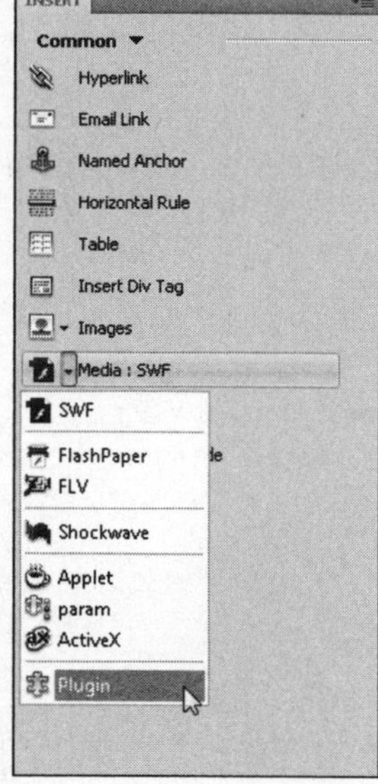

Figure 11-4: Use the Plugin option to insert any audio or video file that isn't saved in the Flash format.

When you add audio or video, Dreamweaver doesn't automatically determine the file size, so you need to add that information in the Property inspector after you insert the file. After you set the correct file size, the plug-in icon changes to reflect the specified size.

5. **Click the Plugin icon that represents the file in the Web page to display the file options in the Property inspector and specify your desired settings.**

   You find a description of each option in the next section, "Setting options for audio and video files."

6. **Click the Preview button (at the top of the work area) to open the page in a browser.**

   Dreamweaver doesn't include a Play button for audio and video files (unless they're in the Flash format). If you have the necessary player on your computer and you have the file set to Autoplay (the default setting), your file plays automatically when the page loads into the browser. To change video and audio settings that aren't included in the Property inspector, such as Autoplay, see the "Setting multimedia parameters" section later in this chapter.

Setting options for audio and video files

When you select an inserted multimedia file, such as a sound or a video file, the Property inspector displays the options for the file, as shown in Figure 11-5. Among these settings, the height and width are the most important.

Unlike image files or Flash files, Dreamweaver can't automatically detect the height and width of other audio or video formats, so it's important to set these options in the Property inspector. To determine the height and width of a video file, you may need to open the file in a video-editing program. For audio files, set the height and width based on the size required for the player you're using.

The following describes the multimedia options available from the Property inspector:

- **ID field:** Use the text field in the upper-left corner of the Property inspector, just to the right of the plug-in icon, if you want to assign a name to the file. If you leave this field blank, Dreamweaver doesn't enter a name automatically unless you are using a file in a Flash format. The name is important because it can be used to refer to the file in JavaScript.

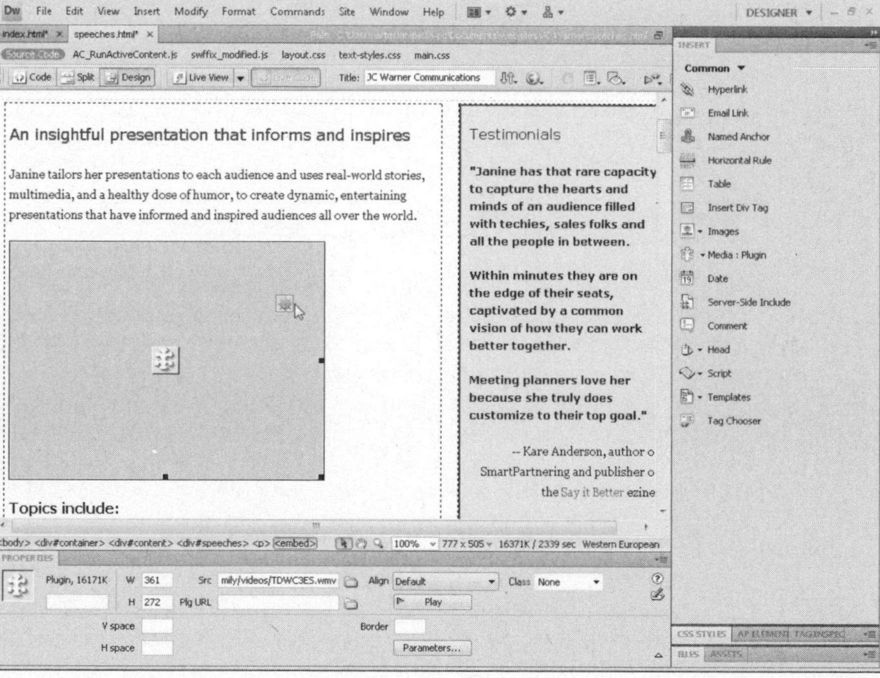

Figure 11-5: Select an audio or a video file in Dreamweaver, such as the Windows Media video shown here, to display the properties for the file in the Property inspector.

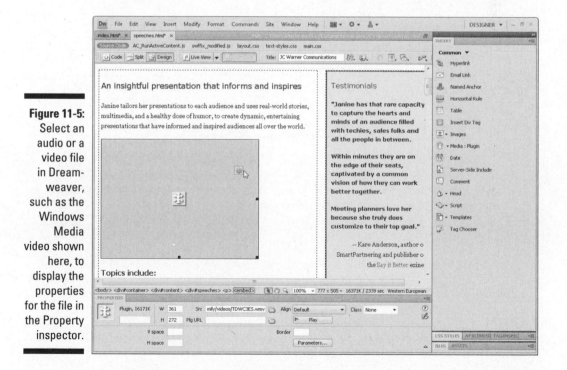

- **W (width) and H (height):** Specify the measurement of the file in pixels.
- **Src (source):** This option specifies the name and path to the file. You can type a filename or click the Browse button (which looks like a small yellow folder) to browse for the file. This field is filled in automatically when you embed the file.

- **Plg URL:** This option enables you to provide a URL where viewers can download the plug-in if they don't already have it.
- **Align:** This option enables you to specify how the element aligns on the page. Alignment works just as it does for images.
- **Play button:** Click the green Play button to preview the media file. The media plug-in must be installed in Dreamweaver (in the Configuration/ Plugins folder) for it to be previewed in Dreamweaver.
- **Class:** Use this drop-down list to apply any style sheets defined for the document.
- **V Space (vertical space):** If you want blank space above and below the plug-in, enter the number of pixels here.
- **H Space (horizontal space):** If you want blank space on either side of the plug-in, enter the number of pixels or use a percentage to specify a portion of the browser window's width.
- **Border:** This option specifies the width of the border around the file when it is displayed.
- **Parameters:** Click this button to access a dialog box where you can enter additional parameters specific to the type of multimedia file you inserted. For more information, see the following section.

Setting multimedia parameters

You can use parameters to control a wide range of multimedia options, such as whether a video file or an audio file starts playing as soon as a page is loaded. Setting parameters isn't intuitive, and Dreamweaver doesn't do the best job of helping with these settings. However, with some research on the options for the file type you're using and a little care in using the Parameters dialog box in Dreamweaver, you can have a lot more control over your multimedia files.

In fairness to the programmers who created Dreamweaver, it'd be hard to include all the parameters for all the possible multimedia file types in use on the Web today, but they could've included the common ones. Because they don't, I offer you this brief primer on using the parameters setting and a few common options for a few common file types. You also find Web addresses where you can find more complete lists of parameters for a few of the most popular audio and video formats.

In Figure 11-6, you see the Parameter dialog box with settings for a Windows Media Video file. The following steps outline how the process works:

1. **To access the Parameters dialog box, click to select the multimedia file in the Web page and then click the Parameters button in the Property inspector.**

The Parameters dialog box opens. The dialog is blank unless you have already entered parameters for the selected file.

2. **Use the plus sign (+) at the top of the dialog box to add a parameter; use the minus sign (–) to delete a selected parameter.**
3. **On the left side of the dialog box, enter the name of the parameter, such as** autoplay; **on the right side, enter the value you want, such as** false, **which I've entered in this example to prevent the Windows Video file from playing automatically.**

You can move from the name side of the Parameters dialog box to the value side using the tab key or by clicking to insert your cursor.

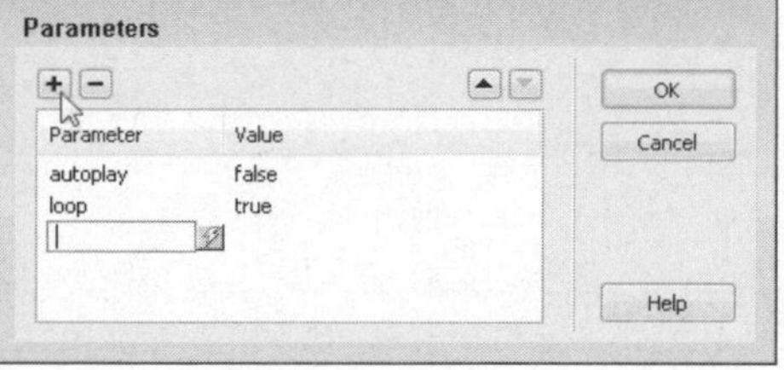

Figure 11-6: Add parameters for additional audio and video settings.

To help you get started with parameters, here are some of the most common and valuable parameters:

- **Autoplay (or Autostart, depending on the file type):** By default, when you add video or audio to an HTML file, most browsers play the file as soon as the page loads (except Firefox, which gives users more control). If you want to prevent your multimedia files from playing automatically in Internet Explorer and other browsers, set the Autoplay or Autostart parameter to `false`. Think of `true` and `false` as on and off when it comes to parameters.
- **Loop:** This parameter enables you to control whether a video file or an audio file loops, or continue to play over and over.
- **showControls:** This option makes it possible to hide the video or audio controls for a file.

Be careful about combining options like these. For example, if you set Autoplay to `false` and showControls to `false`, your visitor can never play your file. By default, the controls for most multimedia files are visible unless you set the showControls parameter to `false`.

Find more attributes for the Windows Media format at www.microsoft.com when you search for *WMV* attributes. For QuickTime attributes, visit www.apple.com and search for QuickTime attributes or go directly to www.apple.com/quicktime/tutorials/embed2.html. You'll find lots of great info about working with RealMedia files, including all the settings you could want for RealPlayer, at www.realnetworks.com/resources/samples/embedded.html.

Adding Flash audio and video files

Flash video is fast becoming the video format of choice among many designers. Video on the Web has been problematic for a long time because there are so many different formats, and you can never guarantee that everyone in your audience can view your videos in any one format.

But while the video players were fighting it out, Flash stepped in to provide an option that's increasingly well supported because so many people have the Flash Player and the player's such a small and easy download for those who don't have it.

Because Adobe owns both Flash and Dreamweaver, you find much better support for Flash files in Dreamweaver. An Insert dialog box makes it easy to set parameters for Flash. The Insert FLV dialog box is displayed in Figure 11-7. Dreamweaver can even automatically detect the size of Flash video files. You can also use Flash to create and insert audio files, displaying only the player (called a *skin* in Flash)

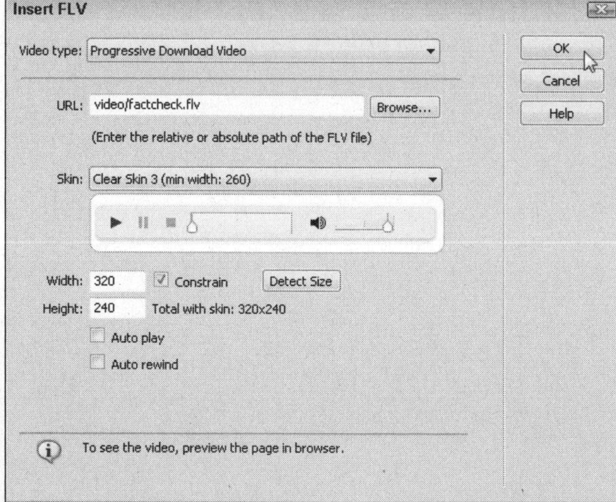

Figure 11-7: You can specify how a Flash video will be displayed in a Web page in the Insert FLV dialog box.

Follow these steps to insert a Flash video file into a Web page:

1. **Click where you want the file to appear on your Web page.**
2. **Select Common from the Insert panel, and from the Media drop-down list, choose FLV (refer to Figure 11-1).**

   You can also choose Insert➪Media➪FLV. The Insert FLV dialog box appears, as shown in Figure 11-7.
3. **At the top of the dialog box, specify Streaming or Progressive.**

   You must have a special server for streaming video. Check with your Internet hosting service or system administrator to find out whether your Web server supports streaming Flash files. If not, choose Progressive.
4. **Click the Browser button to the right of the URL field and browse to find the Flash FLV file you want to add to the page and Click OK.**

   Dreamweaver automatically adds the file name and path to your Flash file to the URL field.
5. **Choose a skin from the Skin drop-down list.**

   Dreamweaver calls the controls for a Flash file a *skin.* As you can see in Figure 11-7, a preview of the selected skin is displayed in the dialog box so you can better decide which one is best for your Flash file and your design. You can also create custom skins in Adobe Flash.
6. **Click the Detect Size button to insert the height and width of the inserted Flash file (if Dreamweaver hasn't already done so).**
7. **If you want the Flash video to play as soon as the page is loaded, select the Auto Play check box.**
8. **If you want the video to rewind after play is complete, select the Auto Rewind check box.**
9. **Click OK to insert the Flash file and close the dialog box.**

   The Flash file appears on the page, represented by a gray box that's the height and width of the file. To view the Flash video, preview the page in a Web browser.

When you insert a Flash video file and include a skin for the player, Dreamweaver creates a Flash file for the player with the `.swf` extension and saves the file in your root site folder. This Flash file contains the player controls and *must* be uploaded to your Web site when you publish the page with the Flash file for the player controls to work.

You can change the skin by clicking to select the inserted Flash file and using the Skin drop-down list in the Property inspector to select another option, as shown in Figure 11-8. Each time you choose a skin, Dreamweaver creates a new `.swf` file. You can delete any skins that aren't being used.

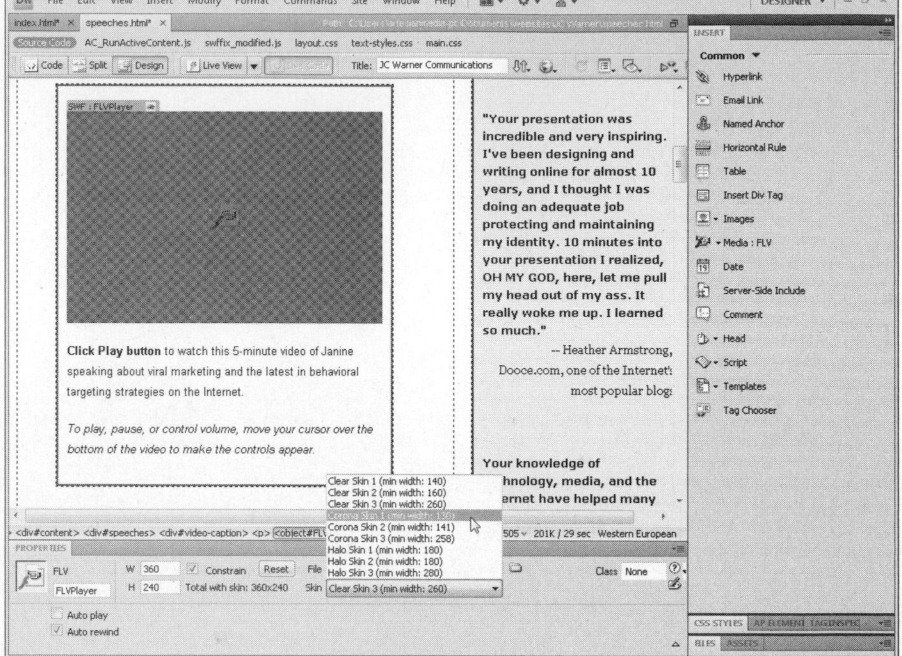

Figure 11-8: Use the Property inspector to alter the settings for a Flash video.

If you want to find out more about other Flash parameters, visit `www.adobe.com` and search for *setting Flash parameters.*

Converting video files into Flash format with the Flash video encoder

If you want to convert video from nearly any video format into the Flash video format, you can use the Flash video encoder. The following exercise walks you through the process of converting a video file into Flash video with the Flash video encoder. The Flash video encoder is included in the Adobe CS4 Creative Suite and can be downloaded at `www.adobe.com`.

1. **Launch the Flash video encoder, as shown in Figure 11-9.**
2. **Click the Add button to load a video into the encoder that you want to convert into a Flash video file.**

   In this example, I added a short video clip that was saved in the Windows Media Video (WMV) format, but you can add video in a variety of formats, including AVI and QuickTime. For best results, start with a video that hasn't already been compressed.

3. **Click the Settings button.**

   The Flash Video Encoding Settings dialog box opens, as shown in Figure 11-10.

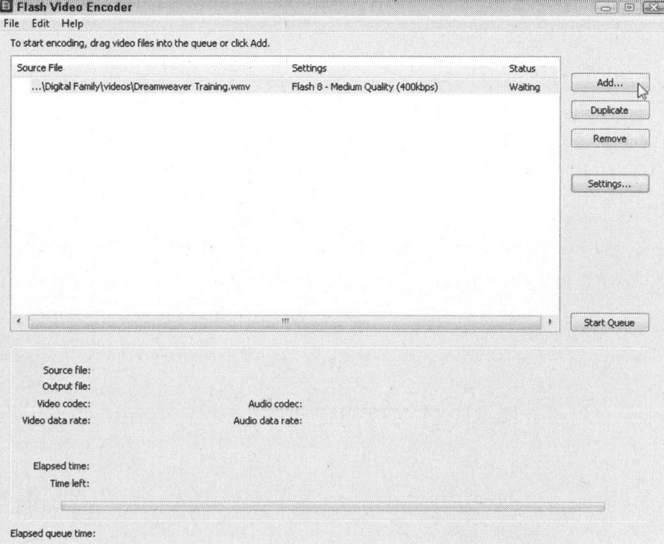

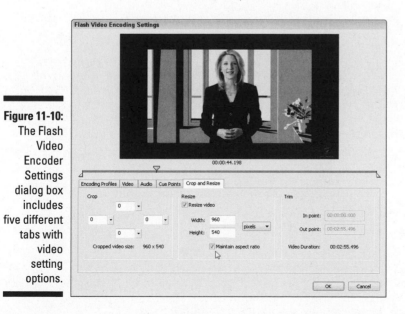

Figure 11-9: The Flash video encoder is designed to convert video in nearly any format into the Flash video format.

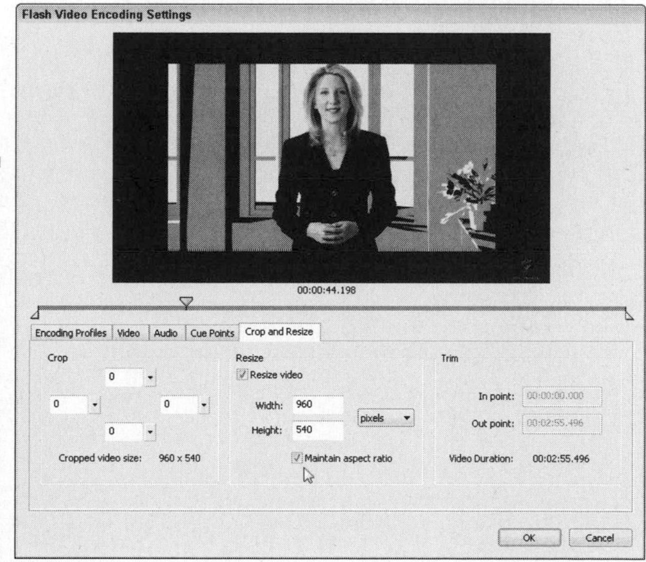

Figure 11-10: The Flash Video Encoder Settings dialog box includes five different tabs with video setting options.

4. **Click the Encoding Profiles tab and choose a Flash encoding profile.**

   The later the version of Flash, the better the encoding looks and the faster it plays, but here's the trade off: Not everyone has downloaded the latest version, so an earlier version may mean fewer visitors have to download the player to view your video. Because Flash is such a fast and easy program to download, the latest version is generally the best choice though.

5. **Click the Video tab and specify additional video settings.**

   a. **Make sure Encode Video is checked.** The video *codec* (which controls the compression of the video) is set automatically based on the Flash version you selected in the Encoding Profiles. Select Deinterlace only if you're encoding video that's interlaced, such as video captured from a television or VCR. Video that's already been encoded in a format like Windows Media doesn't need to be Deinterlaced.

   b. **Set Framerate to the lowest setting that will look good to achieve the fastest download time.** If you're encoding a video that has lots of action, you need a higher frame rate, ideally 24 or better, or your video will lose details and look fuzzy in places. If you're converting a video, such as a Windows Media file that's already been encoded, your best option is to choose Same as Source to leave the framerate unchanged.

   c. **Set the Quality to the lowest level that still looks good to get the fastest download times.** Use the slider under the preview window to move through the frames of the video to see the effects of your settings.

6. **Click the Audio tab to adjust audio settings.**

   Under the Audio tab, adjust the Data rate. Again the lower the number, the lower the quality but the faster the download. If your audio has only a single voice, you can set this quite low, and it'll still sound good. If your audio file has music, special sound effects, or other multifaceted audio, set the Data rate to at least 96 kbps (kilobits per second).

7. **Use the Cue Points tab and insert cues in the file that make it easier for someone using the file to jump to a particular section.**

8. **Use the Crop and Resize tab to make the file physically smaller or larger.**

   Note that trying to increase the file size of a video can result in a severe loss of quality.

9. **After the settings are complete, press OK.**

   The Flash Video Encoder Settings dialog box closes, returning you to the Flash video encoder.

10. **Click Start Queue to begin the encoding process.**

This process can take several minutes, even for a very short file. A small preview window in the bottom-right corner of the Flash video encoder enables you to watch the encoding process in action.

When the encoding process is complete, the Flash video encoder has created a copy of the video file in the FLV Flash video format.

Working with Java

Java is a programming language, similar to Basic, C, or C++, that you can use to create programs that run on a computer. What makes Java special is that it can run on any computer system and can display within a browser.

If you create a program in another programming language, you usually have to create one version for the Macintosh, another for the PC, and a third for Unix. But Java, created by Sun Microsystems, is platform-independent, so developers can use it to create almost any kind of program — even complex programs, such as a sophisticated game or even a word processing program — that works on any type of computer without the user having to customize the code for each platform.

Another advantage of Java is that the program (dubbed an *applet*) can run within a Web browser, allowing the program to interact with different elements of the page or with other pages on the Web. This capability has made Java popular on the Internet because it provides a way to add sophisticated capabilities to Web pages irrespective of the operating system the Web browser is running on. You can embed Java applets in Web pages, you can use Java to generate entire Web pages, or you can run Java applications separately after they download.

Inserting Java applets

To insert a Java applet in your Web page, follow these steps:

1. **Click where you want the applet to appear on your Web page.**
2. **Select Common from the Insert panel, if it isn't already selected. In the Media drop-down list on the Common Insert panel, choose Applet (refer to Figure 11-4).**

   Alternatively, you can choose Insert⇨Media⇨Applet. The Select File dialog box appears.
3. **Use the Browse button to locate the Java applet file you want to insert on the page.**
4. **Click to highlight the filename and then click OK to close the dialog box.**

Dreamweaver doesn't display applets in the Dreamweaver work area. Instead, you see an icon that represents the applet. To view the applet on your Web page (the only way to see the applet in action), preview the page in a browser that supports applets, such as Navigator 4.0 and later or Internet Explorer 4.0 and later.

5. **Click the Applet icon to open the Property inspector.**

   You can set many options in the Property inspector. If you want to know more about these options, read on.

Setting Java parameters and other options

Like other file formats that require plug-ins or advanced browser support, the display of Java applets can be controlled by specifying a number of options. If you select a Java applet in Dreamweaver, the Property inspector displays the following options:

- **Applet name:** Use this field in the upper-left corner if you want to type a name for your applet. Dreamweaver doesn't apply a name if you leave this field blank. This name identifies the applet for scripting.
- **W (width):** This option specifies the width of the applet. You can set the measurement in pixels or as a percentage of the browser window's width.
- **H (height):** This option specifies the height of the applet. You can set the measurement in pixels or as a percentage of the browser window's height.
- **Code:** Dreamweaver automatically enters the code when you insert the file. Code specifies the content file of the applet. You can type your own filename or click the folder icon to choose a file.
- **Base:** Automatically entered when you insert the file, Base identifies the folder that contains the applet.
- **Align:** This option determines how the object aligns on the page. Alignment works just as it does for images.
- **Alt:** This option enables you to specify an alternative file, such as an image, that appears if the viewer's browser doesn't support Java. That way, the user doesn't see a broken file icon. If you type text in this field, the viewer sees this text; Dreamweaver writes it into the code by using the `Alt` attribute of the `<applet>` tag. If you use the folder icon to select an image, the viewer sees an image; Dreamweaver automatically inserts an `<img>` tag within the `<applet>` and `</applet>` tags of the applet.
- **V Space (vertical space):** If you want blank space above or below the applet, enter the number of pixels here.

- **H Space (horizontal space):** If you want blank space on either side of the applet, enter the number of pixels here.
- **Parameters:** Click this button to access a dialog box in which you can enter additional parameters for the applet.
- **Class:** Use this drop-down list to access style sheets created with CSS (Cascading Style Sheets).

You can find lots more information in *Java For Dummies,* 4th Edition, by Barry Burd (Wiley Publishing, Inc.).

Linking to PDFs

Adobe's Portable Document Format (PDF) has become increasingly popular on the Internet, and with good reason. Now that Acrobat Reader is widely distributed and even built into more recent browser versions, you can assume that most of your audience can read files in PDF.

PDF is a great option for files that you want to make easy to download in their entirety to be saved on a hard drive, as well as documents that you want printed exactly as they're designed.

To add a PDF file to your Web site, simply copy the file into your main root folder and link to it as you'd link to any other Web page on your site. When you upload the page with the link to your PDF file, make sure to upload the PDF as well.

JavaScript is not Java

JavaScript is a scripting language; Java is a programming language. Despite the similarity in their names, the two have little in common. Although JavaScript is much more complex than HTML, it's much simpler than Java and has far fewer capabilities. Unlike Java, JavaScript can be written directly into HTML code to create interactive features, such as rollover effects. Dreamweaver uses JavaScript to create most of the features included in the Behaviors panel (covered in Chapter 10).

You can use Java to create more complex programming than you can create with JavaScript. Java programs, or *applets,* are usually small, self-contained programs that can run on any operating system. If you search the Web for Java applets, you're likely to find cool little clocks, converters, and other programs that you can download and add to your Web pages. You can use Java to create programs that work on both the Mac and PC, an advantage over other programming languages that makes Java especially well-suited to the multiplatform world of Web design.

Chapter 12

Forms Follow Function

In This Chapter

- Creating forms in HTML
- Creating radio buttons, check boxes, and text fields
- Adding drop-down lists, Submit/Reset buttons, and jump menus
- Connecting forms to CGI scripts
- Working with hidden fields

Forms follow function, to paraphrase the old saying. On the Web, many of the most advanced and interactive features you can add to a Web page require forms to collect information from users — information that can then be used in a variety of ways. Forms are commonly used to create guest books, contact forms, search engine entry fields, chat rooms, and discussion areas.

When you design a form, Dreamweaver makes it relatively easy to create check boxes, radio buttons, text boxes, and other common form elements. You'll also find options in Dreamweaver for specifying text box sizes, character limits, and other features. After you build your form, you may want to consider formatting options, such as CSS (Cascading Style Sheets), to make it look good.

But if you want your form to actually do something, you have to pair it with a program on your Web server. One of the most confusing aspects of working with HTML forms is that they don't do much until you've connected them to a script. Most forms are processed by Common Gateway Interface (CGI) scripts or some other program. These scripts can be written in different programming languages, including C, C#, Java, and Perl. CGI scripts are far more complex than simple HTML files, and even experienced Web designers often purchase third-party solutions or hire experienced programmers to develop CGI scripts for them, especially for complex features, such as discussion boards or shopping carts.

Fortunately for those who don't have a computer science degree or a huge budget for programmers, many free and low-priced scripts are available on the Web. Search the Internet for *CGI scripts* and you'll find an impressive collection of ready-to-use programs, many of them free. Be aware, however, that when you download a program, you could be creating a security risk for your server (so look for trustworthy scripts with good reviews and support).

You also have to know how to configure and install any script you download on your Web server, which may require special access. How you install a script on your server depends on how your server is set up. Unfortunately, in this book, I can't show you everything there is to know about working with all the different kinds of scripts available on the Web on all the different kinds of servers, but I do try to give you an idea of what's involved in working with CGI scripts and what you'll need to do in Dreamweaver to make sure your HTML form will work with a script.

The first part of this chapter includes instructions for creating the common elements in an HTML form, from radio buttons to text boxes. In the last part of the chapter, I include instructions for configuring a form to work with a common CGI that you can use to send the contents of a form to any specified e-mail address. The steps and features covered in the final exercise also help you with other kinds of CGI scripts.

You also need to create forms when you build dynamic Web sites using Dreamweaver's ColdFusion, ASP.NET, or PHP features. If you're creating a dynamic or database-driven site, use the features specific to those technologies, which are covered in Chapters 14 and 15. In this chapter, you find out how to create the HTML forms in Dreamweaver.

Creating HTML Forms

The basic elements of HTML forms — radio buttons, check boxes, and text areas, for example — are easy to create with Dreamweaver. The following steps walk you through creating an HTML form. Start with an open page — either a new page or an existing page to which you want to add a form:

1. **Choose Insert⇨Form⇨Form or click the Form icon on the Forms Insert bar.**

   The Forms Insert bar displays all the common form elements. An empty `<form>` tag is inserted in your document and is displayed as a rectangle outlined by a red dotted line like the one shown in the Document area in Figure 12-1. This dotted line defines the boundaries of a form in the HTML code.

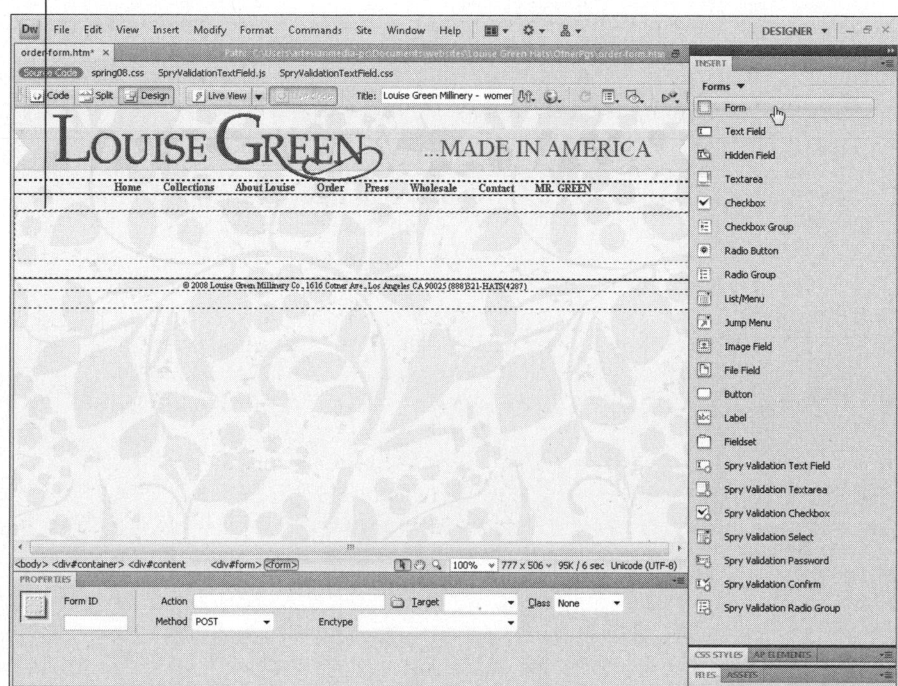

Figure 12-1: The Forms Insert bar provides easy access to all common form elements.

You can control the display of invisible elements, such as <form> tags. Choose Edit➪Preferences (Windows) or Dreamweaver➪Preferences (Mac). Then, in the Invisible Elements category, select or deselect the Form Delimiter box.

2. **Click the red outline to select the** <form> **tag and display the** <form> **tag options in the Property inspector (as shown in the bottom of Figure 12-1).**

3. **In the Form ID text box, type a name.**

   You can choose any name for this field as long as you don't use spaces, special characters, or punctuation. With your basic HTML form set up, you're ready to add elements to it, as explained in the following sections.

Before you begin filling your form with options, keep the following tips in mind:

- **The best way to get your form fields to line up nicely is to use CSS.** By creating styles that control the spacing and padding of form elements, you can make all your fields, buttons, and other elements line up neatly. Chapters 5 and 6 cover CSS.
- **After you design your form, your work isn't quite done; your form won't do anything unless you configure it to work with a script.** Although Dreamweaver doesn't provide any scripts, it does make linking your HTML forms to a script or database relatively easy. The section "Understanding How CGI Scripts Work" later in this chapter offers more details on making your form work with a script.

Most of the fields displayed in the Property inspector when the `<form>` tag options are displayed should be set based on the CGI script or other program that's used to collect and process the data from the form. You find instructions for filling in these fields in the "Configuring your form to work with a script" section, at the end of this chapter.

Making forms accessible

You can make your forms much easier to use and more accessible to all your visitors by using the label tag and other accessibility attributes with form items. Dreamweaver makes this easy by including an Input Tag Accessibility Attributes dialog box, as shown in the figure. For this dialog box to appear when you insert a form item, such as a radio button or a check box, you must have accessibility features turned on in Dreamweaver's Preference settings. To turn on these features, choose Edit⇨Preferences (Dreamweaver⇨Preferences on a Mac); in the Preferences dialog box, click the Accessibility category and select the Form Objects option.

With the accessibility options turned on, when you insert a form item (such as a radio button or a text box), the Input Tag Accessibility Attributes dialog box opens automatically. Use this dialog box to specify the following options:

- **ID:** Use the ID field to assign a name to a form element. You can leave this field blank, and Dreamweaver won't enter a name automatically. The name is important because it can be used to refer to the field in JavaScript. The ID is also used if you choose Attach Label Tag Using 'For' Attribute option under the Style options.
- **Label:** Enter a name that corresponds to the radio button or check box. This is the name that's read by a screen reader.
- **Style:** Check one of these three options to specify how the label should be included with the radio button or text box in the HTML code. The option Attach Label Tag Using 'For' Attribute is recommended as the best option for accessibility. If you choose this option, most browsers will associate a focus rectangle to the check box or radio button. This enables a user to select the check box and radio button by clicking anywhere in the text associated with it, instead of clicking precisely inside the check box or radio button.
- **Position**: Check the corresponding box to specify whether the label should appear before or after each form item.
- **Access Key:** This attribute enables you to create a keyboard shortcut for each of your form items. You can enter any letter in this field, and your users can select the form item by holding down the Alt key (Windows) or the Control key (Macintosh) and typing the letter you specify. For example, if you enter Q as the Access Key, visitors to your site who use a Windows computer could press Alt+Q to select the form item.
- **Tab Index:** By default, you can use the Tab key to move from one form field to another when you view a form on the Web. With the Tab Index, you can specify the order in which the Tab key progresses from one form item to another. This is especially helpful if you have links and other form items on a page, and you want the user to be able to tab through them in a specific order. To control the order, assign a number to each form.

Creating radio buttons and check boxes

Radio buttons and check boxes make filling in a form easy for viewers of your site. Rather than make users type a word, such as **yes** or **no,** you can provide radio buttons and check boxes so that users can simply click boxes or buttons.

What's the difference between radio buttons and check boxes? *Radio buttons* enable users to select only one option from a group. Thus, radio buttons are good for either/or options or situations in which you want users to make only one selection. *Check boxes,* on the other hand, enable users to make multiple choices, so they're good for choose-all-that-apply situations or for situations that require approval, such as "Check this box if . . ."

Creating radio buttons

To create radio buttons on a form, follow these steps:

1. **Click to place your cursor inside the boundary of the** `<form>` **tag where you want to add a radio button.**

If you haven't yet inserted the <form> tag, follow the steps in the section "Creating HTML Forms," earlier in this chapter.

2. **Click the Radio Button icon on the Forms Insert bar.**

   You can also choose Insert⇨Form⇨Radio Button. Either way, a radio button appears inside the form's red boundary line.

   If you have accessibility options turned on in Preferences, the Input Tag Accessibility Attributes dialog box opens. (See the sidebar "Making forms accessible," to find out more about these options.)

3. **Repeat Step 2 until you have the number of radio buttons you want.**
4. **Select one of the radio buttons on the form to reveal the radio button's properties in the Property inspector, as shown in Figure 12-2.**

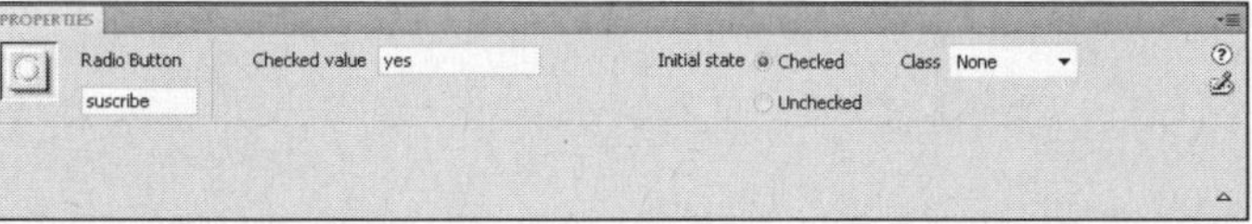

Figure 12-2: Radio button properties.

5. **In the Radio Button text box on the far left of the Property inspector, type a name.**

   All radio buttons in a group should have the same name so that the browser associates them with one another and prevents users from selecting more than one. If you want users to be able to choose more than one item from a list, use check boxes, as described in the following section.

6. **In the Checked Value text box, type a name.**

   Each radio button in a group should have a different Checked Value name so that it can be distinguished from the others. Naming radio buttons for the thing they represent is often a good practice; for example, *yes* when the choice is yes and *no* when it's no. If you're asking users about their favorite ice cream flavors, you might use as values the flavor each button represents. This name is usually included in the data you get back when the form is processed and returned to you (it can be returned in an e-mail message or sent directly to a database). How the data is returned depends on the CGI script or other programming used to process the form. If you're looking at the data later, interpreting it is easier if the name is something that makes sense to you.

7. **For the Initial State option, select Checked or Unchecked.**

These two options determine whether the radio button on your form appears already selected when the Web page loads. Select Checked if you want to preselect a choice. You should set only one radio button option to be preselected and remember that the user can always override this setting by selecting another radio button.

8. **Select the other radio buttons one by one in the main design area and repeat Steps 5–7 to specify the properties in the Property inspector for each one.**

If you want to create a series of radio buttons, you'll find some advantages to using the Radio Group button in the Insert Form panel. Dreamweaver automatically creates IDs for each radio button. If you want to change these IDs, you may find it easier to change them in Code view. You can split the screen between code and design views by clicking on the Split view button at the top of the workspace.

If you want to format your form with CSS styles, you can create tag styles for the form, radio button, and other tags, or you can create class styles and apply them to any or all of your tags using the Class drop-down list in the Property inspector, You find more information about creating and applying styles in Chapters 5 and 6.

If your form is complete, jump ahead to the "Finishing your form with Submit and Reset buttons" section, later in this chapter.

Creating check boxes

To create check boxes, follow these steps:

1. **Click to place your cursor inside the boundary of the `<form>` tag where you want to add a check box.**

   If you haven't yet inserted a `<form>` tag, follow the steps in the "Creating HTML Forms" section, earlier in this chapter.

2. **Click the Check Box icon on the Forms Insert bar.**

   You can also choose Insert⇨Form⇨Check Box.

   If you have accessibility options turned on in Preferences, the Input Tag Accessibility Attributes dialog box opens. (See the sidebar "Making forms accessible," to find out more about these options.)

3. **Repeat Step 2 to place as many check boxes as you want.**

4. **Select one of the check boxes on your form to reveal the check box properties in the Property inspector, as shown in Figure 12-3.**

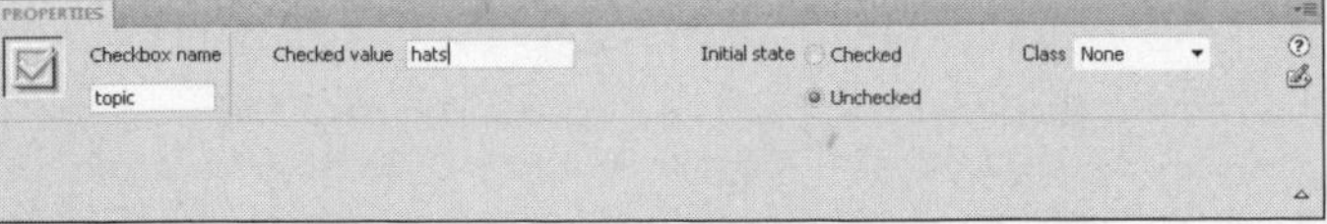

Figure 12-3: Check box properties.

5. **In the Checkbox Name text box, type a name.**

   Use a distinct name for each check box because users can select more than one check box, and you want to ensure that the information submitted is properly associated with each individual check box.

6. **In the Checked Value text box, type a name.**

   Each check box in a group should have a different Checked Value name so that the CGI script can distinguish it. Naming them for the things they represent is a good practice. As with radio buttons, the checked value is usually included in the data you get back when the form is processed and returned to you. If you're looking at the data later, interpreting it is easier if the name is something that makes sense to you.

7. **For the Initial State option, select Checked or Unchecked.**

   This option determines whether the check box appears already selected when the Web page loads. Select Checked if you want to preselect a choice. A user can always override this preselection by clicking the text box again to deselect it.

8. **Select the other check boxes one by one and repeat Steps 5–7 to set the properties in the Property inspector for each one.**

If you want to create a series of check boxes, you'll find some advantages to using the Checkbox Group button in the Insert Form panel.

If your form is complete, jump ahead to the "Finishing your form with Submit and Reset buttons" section, later in this chapter.

Adding text fields and text areas

When you want users to enter text, such as a name, an e-mail address, or a comment, use a text field. To insert text fields, follow these steps:

1. **Click to place your cursor inside the `<form>` tag where you want to add a text field.**

   If you haven't yet inserted a `<form>` tag, follow the steps in the "Creating HTML Forms" section, earlier in this chapter.

2. **Click the Text Field icon on the Forms Insert bar.**

   You can also choose Insert⇨Form⇨Text Field. A text field box appears.

   If you have accessibility options turned on in Preferences, the Input Tag Accessibility Attributes dialog box opens. (See the sidebar "Making forms accessible," to find out more about these options.)

3. **On the form, click to place your cursor next to the first text field and type a question or other text prompt.**

   For example, you may want to type **E-mail Address:** next to a text box where you want a user to enter an e-mail address.

4. **Select the text field on your form to reveal the Text Field properties in the Property inspector, as shown in Figure 12-4.**

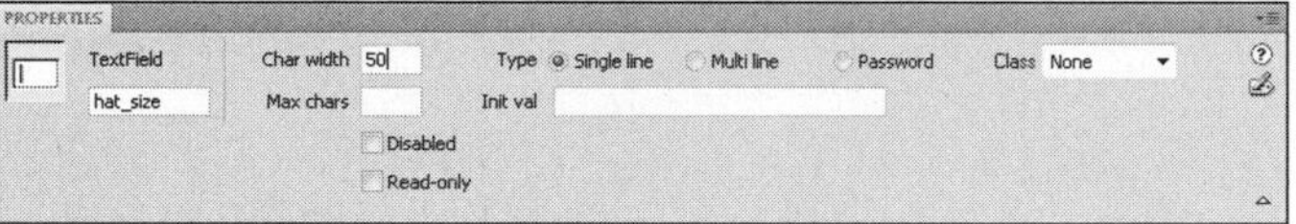

Figure 12-4: The Text Field option enables users to enter text.

5. **In the TextField text box, type a name.**

   Each text area on a form should have a different text field name so that the CGI script can distinguish it. Naming text areas for the things they represent is usually best, but don't use any spaces or special characters (other than the hyphen or underscore). In Figure 12-4, you can see that I named the text field *hat_size.* Many scripts return this name next to the contents of the text field a visitor enters at your Web site. If you're looking at the data later, you can more easily interpret it if the name corresponds to the choice.

6. **In the Char Width box, type the number of characters you want visible in the field.**

   This setting determines the width of the text field that appears on the page. In the example shown here, I've set the character width to 50 to create a text box that is more than wide enough for most e-mail addresses. How wide you make your text boxes depends on the amount of information you expect users to enter and the constraints of your design.

7. **In the Max Chars box, type the maximum number of characters you want to allow.**

   If you leave this field blank, users can type as many characters as they choose, even if they exceed the physical length of the text box specified in the Char Width field.

I usually limit the number of characters only if I want to maintain consistency in the data. For example, I like to limit the State field to a two-character abbreviation. Creating drop-down lists, which require users to make a selection rather than risking that they might make a typo, is an even better way to ensure consistent data. You find instructions for creating drop-downs in the exercise that follows.

You can set the Char Width field to be longer or shorter than the Max Chars field. If users type more characters than can appear in the text field, the text scrolls so that users can still see all the text they enter, even if it can't be displayed in the text field all at once.

8. **Next to Type, select one of the following options:**

   - **Single Line** creates a one-line text box, such as the kind I created for the hat size field shown in Figure 12-4.
   - **Multi Line** gives users space to enter text. (Note that if you select Multi Line, you also need to specify the number of lines you want the text area to cover by typing a number in the Num Lines field, which appears as an option when you choose Multi Line.)
   - **Password** is used if you're asking users to enter data that they might not want to display on-screen. This type of field causes entered data to appear as asterisks and disables copying from the field.

9. **Use the Class drop-down list to apply any class CSS styles that may be defined in the site.**

   You can create class styles for many purposes, including formatting form elements. You can read more about creating and applying class styles in Chapters 5 and 6.

10. **In the Init Val text box, type any text you want displayed when the form loads.**

    For example, you can include `Add comments here` on the form in the text field under Comments. Users can delete the Init Val text or leave it and add more text in the same text field.

11. **If you're creating a multiline text area, specify the Wrap options.**

    The Wrap field controls how the users' data is displayed if it exceeds the length of the text field. Selecting Off or Default prevents the users' text from wrapping to the next line. (Note this option is available only for multiline text boxes.)

12. **Select the other text areas one by one and repeat Steps 5–9 to set the properties in the Property inspector for each one.**

If your form is complete, jump ahead to the "Finishing your form with Submit and Reset buttons" section, later in this chapter.

Creating drop-down lists

When you want to give users a multiple-choice option but don't want to take up lots of space on the page, drop-down lists are an ideal solution. To create a drop-down list with Dreamweaver, follow these steps:

1. **Click to place your cursor inside the** `<form>` **tag where you want to add a drop-down list.**

   If you haven't yet created a `<form>` tag, follow the steps in the "Creating HTML Forms" section, earlier in this chapter.

2. **Click the List/Menu icon on the Forms Insert bar.**

   You can also choose Insert⇨Form⇨List/Menu. A drop-down list appears.

   If you have accessibility options turned on in Preferences, the Input Tag Accessibility Attributes dialog box opens. (See sidebar "Making forms accessible," to find out more about these options.)

3. **Click to place your cursor next to the List field and enter a question or other text prompt.**

   I typed **What state do you live in?**

4. **Select the field that represents the list on your page to reveal the List/ Menu properties in the Property inspector, as shown at the bottom of Figure 12-5.**

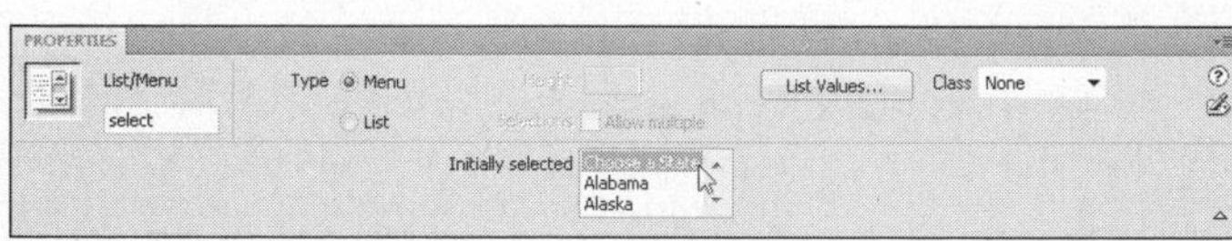

Figure 12-5: The List/ Menu option enables you to create a drop-down list.

5. **In the List/Menu text box, type a name.**

   Each list or menu on a form should have a different name so that you can differentiate the lists when the form data is returned.

6. **Next to Type, select the Menu or List option.**

   This step determines whether the form element is a drop-down list or a scrollable list. If you select List, you can specify the height and control of how many items are shown at a time. You can also specify whether a user can select more than one item. If you select Menu, these options aren't available.

Forms display differently in different browsers

Firefox, Netscape, Safari, and Microsoft Internet Explorer don't display text fields in forms equally. The differences vary depending on the version of the browser, but the general result is that a text field appears with different dimensions in one browser than in another. Slight differences also exist with color, scroll bars, and shape in the case of check boxes. Forms are also displayed differently on Macintosh and PC computers. Unfortunately, this problem has no perfect solution, but as long as your forms look okay in the browsers you consider most important, it isn't a problem that they display slightly differently in other browsers. For best results, test your pages on a variety of browsers and on both Macs and PCs, and be especially careful that form fields and other elements aren't cut off.

7. **Click the List Values button, in the upper right of the Property inspector.**

   The List Values dialog box appears, as shown in Figure 12-6.

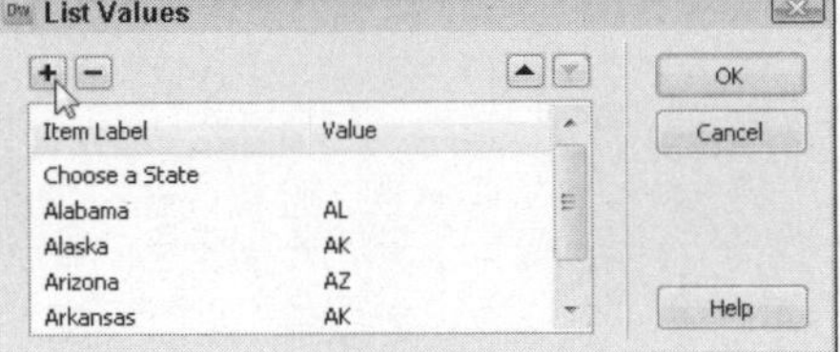

Figure 12-6: Create the options in the List form field.

8. **Enter the choices you want to make available.**

   Click the plus sign (+) to add an item label and then type the label text you want in the text box that appears in the dialog box. Item labels appear on the menu or list on the Web page in the order in which you enter them. Use the minus sign (–) to delete a selected option.

   Press the Tab key to move the cursor to the Value side of the dialog box, where you can enter a value. Values are optional, but if present, they're sent to the server instead of the label text. This provides a way of including information that you don't want to display on the drop-down list. For example, if you enter **Alabama** as a label on the left, you can enter the abbreviation **AL** as a value on the right. If you enter **Alaska** as a label, you can enter **AK** as a value, and so on. That way, you visitors can select from a list that displays the full name of each state, but your script can collect only the two-letter abbreviations. If you don't enter a value, the label is used as the submitted data when the form is processed.

The first label entered in the List Values dialog box is the only one that's displayed on the page until a user clicks the drop-down arrow. Thus, it's good practice to include an instruction in this space, such as Choose a State, as shown in the example in Figures 12-5 and 12-6.

9. **Click OK to close the dialog box.**

Finishing your form with Submit and Reset buttons

For your users to be able to send their completed forms to you, create a Submit button, which, when clicked, tells the user's browser to send the form to the CGI script or other program that processes the form. You may also want to add a Reset button, which enables users to erase any information they've entered if they want to start over.

Many developers don't use the Reset button because they find that it can be confusing to visitors (and annoying if it means they accidentally erase all the information they just entered). Because visitors can always leave a page before clicking the Submit button if they choose not to complete a form, the simplest way to avoid this problem is to avoid using a Reset button.

To create a Submit, Reset, or other button in Dreamweaver, follow these steps:

1. **Click to place your cursor inside the `<form>` tag where you want to add a button.**

   If you haven't yet inserted the `<form>` tag (which appears as a red dotted line around your form), follow the steps in the earlier section "Creating HTML Forms" before continuing with these steps. You might also want to enter at least one text field or other field option. There's not much point in having a Submit button if you don't provide any fields where a user can enter data to be submitted.

2. **Click the Button icon on the Forms Insert bar.**

   You can also choose Insert⇨Form⇨Button.

   If you have accessibility options turned on in Preferences, the Button Accessibility Attributes dialog box opens. (See sidebar "Making forms accessible," to find out more about these options.)

   A Submit button appears.

3. **Click to select the button.**

   The Property inspector changes to reveal the form button properties, as shown in Figure 12-7. You can change the button to a Reset button or other kind of button by altering the attributes in the Property inspector, as shown in the remaining steps.

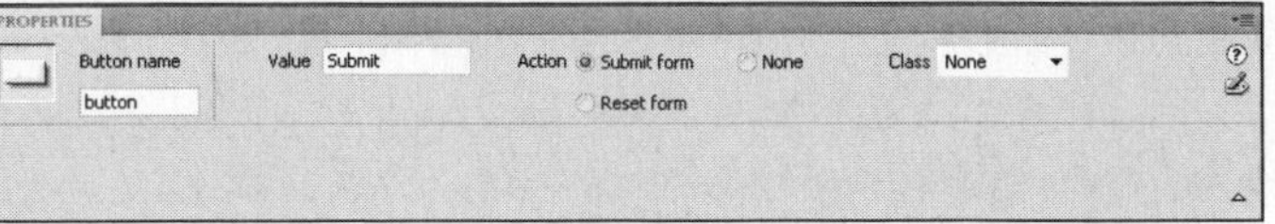

Figure 12-7: The form button properties.

4. **Next to Action, click the Submit Form or Reset Form option.**

   The Submit Form option invokes an action, such as sending user information to an e-mail address. The Reset Form option returns the page to the way it was when the page loaded. You can also select the None option, which creates a button that can be used for many purposes by combining it with a script.

5. **In the Value text box, type the text you want to display on the button.**

   You can type any text you want for the label, such as Search, Go, Clear, or Delete.

Clicking a Submit button in a form doesn't do much unless you've configured the form to work with a CGI script or other program to collect or process user-entered data.

Using jump menus

Many designers use jump menus as navigational elements because they can provide a list of links in a drop-down list without taking up lots of room on a Web page. You can also use a jump menu to launch an application or start an animation sequence.

To create a jump menu, follow these steps:

1. **Click to place your cursor inside the `<form>` tag where you want to add a jump menu.**

   Alternatively, you can create a jump menu anywhere on a page. If there is no form tag in place, Dreamweaver automatically adds one around the jump menu tag.

2. **Click the Jump Menu icon on the Forms Insert bar.**

   You can also choose Insert⇨Form⇨Jump Menu. The Insert Jump Menu dialog box opens.

3. **In the Text field, under Menu Items, type the name you want to display in the drop-down list.**

   Click the plus sign (+) to add more items. As you type items in the Text field, they appear in the Menu Items list, as shown in Figure 12-8.

4. **Click the Browse button to locate the page you want to link to or type the URL for the page in the When Selected, Go to URL field.**

   You can link to a local file or enter any URL to link to a page on another Web site, and you can use the Browse button to specify the URL you want to link to.

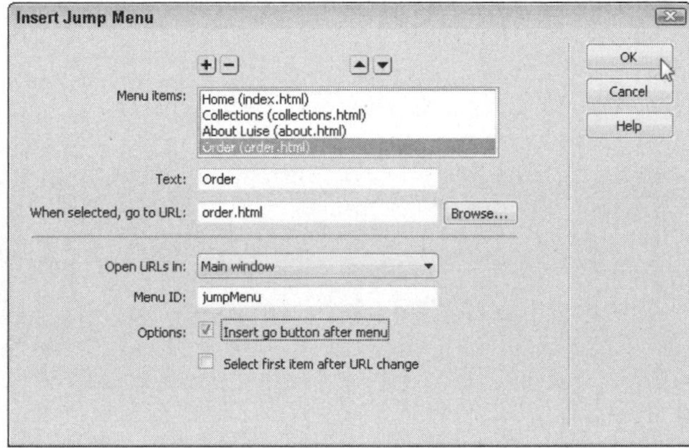

Figure 12-8: When you create a jump list, items you type in the Text field appear in the Menu Items list.

5. **If you're using frames, use the Open URLs In field to specify a target.**

   If you're not using frames, the default is Main Window. When the user selects an option, the new page replaces the page he or she is viewing. (I explain how to target links in frames in Chapter 8.)

6. **If you want to enter a unique identifier for this menu, use the Menu ID field.**

   This option can be useful if you have multiple jump menus on a page. You can use any name you want, but you can't use spaces, special characters, or punctuation.

7. **If you want to force users to click a button to activate the selection, select the Insert Go Button after Menu option.**

   If you don't add a Go button, the linked page loads as soon as the user makes a selection. The Go button works like a Submit button for the jump menu options.

Understanding How CGI Scripts Work

Common Gateway Interface (CGI) scripts are programs written in a programming language, such as Perl, Java, C++, ASP, or PHP. They work in tandem with your Web server to process the data submitted by a user. Think of CGI scripts as the engine behind an HTML form and many other automated features on a Web site. These scripts are much more complex to create than HTML pages, and these languages take much longer to figure out than HTML. CGI scripts reside and run on the server and are usually triggered by an action a user takes, such as clicking the Submit button on an HTML form.

A common scenario with a script may go like this:

1. A user loads a page, such as a guest book, fills out the HTML form, and clicks the Submit button.
2. The browser gathers all the data from the form and sends it to the Web server in a standard format.
3. The Web server takes the incoming data and hands it off to the CGI script, which unpacks the data and does something with it, such as placing the data in an e-mail message and sending the message to a specified e-mail address or adding the data to a Web page where guest book comments are posted.
4. The CGI script then sends instructions or a block of HTML back to the browser through the Web server to report on the outcome of the script and to complete any final actions, such as displaying a Thank You page.

Configuring your form to work with a script

After you create a form using the features covered in the previous sections of this chapter, configure the form to work with a CGI script or a program. To help you understand how this process works, I use the common `formmail.pl` script in the following exercise. This clever little script is designed to collect data entered into an HTML form and send it to a specified e-mail address. You can find out more about `formmail.pl` at `www.scriptarchive.com` (a great place to find lots of free CGI scripts).

Every script is different, and the details of how you install and configure each script depend on the program and how your server is set up.

If your service provider doesn't offer a form mail script, you can download and configure the script if you have the right access on your server and knowledge of how your server is configured. Ask your service provider for more information. If your service provider doesn't provide the interactive scripts you want, you may want to consider moving your site to a hosting service that does provide CGI scripts you can use.

The following exercise shows you how to use Dreamweaver with the `formmail.pl` script. This gives you a good introduction to how you'd set up any form to work with any script, but be aware that you may have to alter some of the steps to work with the program you're using:

1. **Select the `<form>` tag that surrounds your form by clicking anywhere on the red dotted line that represents the boundary of the `<form>` tag or by clicking the `<form>` tag in the tag selector at the bottom of the work area, as shown in Figure 12-9.**

   With the `<form>` tag selected, the Property inspector changes to feature the form tag options. ***Note:*** All HTML forms must be enclosed by the `<form>` tag. If your script doesn't have a `<form>` tag, add one around the entire contents of your form by following the steps in the "Creating HTML Forms" section found earlier in this chapter.

   To select the `<form>` tag in Dreamweaver, place your cursor anywhere in the body of your form and then use the tag selector at the bottom of the work area to select the `<form>` tag. Make sure you've selected the `<form>` tag and not just one of the form elements, such as the text box I created in this form for comments.

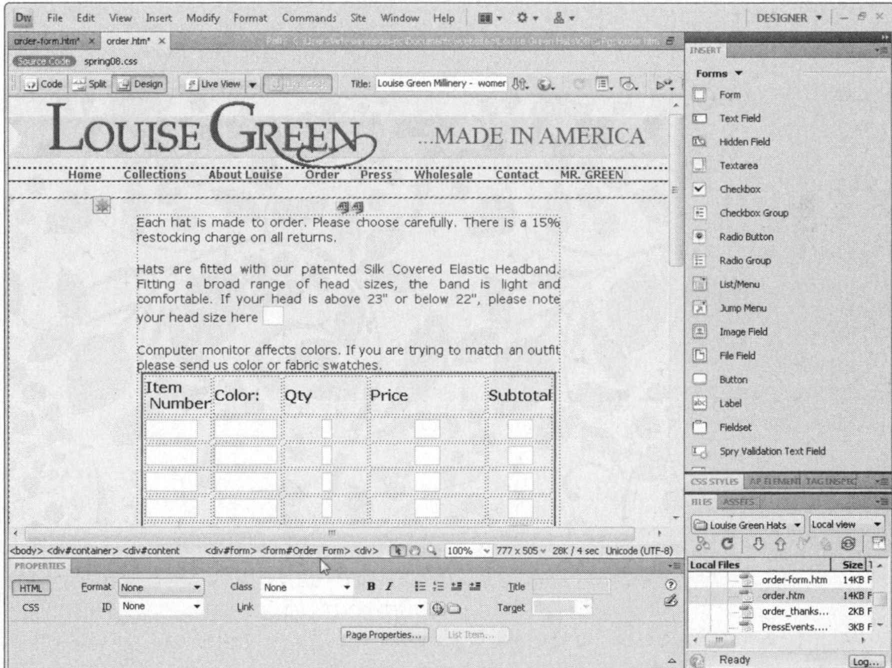

Figure 12-9: You can use the tag selector to select the <form> tag and display form properties in the Property inspector.

2. **In the Property inspector, give your form a name.**

   Dreamweaver automatically gives each form you create a distinct name (form1, form2, and so on), but I prefer to change the name to something that has more meaning, such as *contact* for this contact form. You can name your form whatever you like but don't use spaces or special characters.

3. **Specify the action for the form.**

   For the `formmail.pl` script used in this example (as well as many other scripts you might use), the action is simply the path to the script's location on your server. In Figure 12-10, you can see that I've entered the address `/cgi-bin/formmail.pl`. The address you enter depends on your service provider, but a common convention is to call the folder where CGI scripts are stored `cgi-bin`. The last part of the address (`formmail.pl`) is the name of the script. In this case, it's a Perl script, indicated by the `.pl` extension.

   You can only use the Browse button (the yellow folder icon in the Property inspector) to automatically enter an address in the Action field if you're working on a live server and Dreamweaver has identified the location of your script, or if you have the script on your local system in the same directory structure that exists on your server. In most cases, however, it's simplest just to ask your service provider or programmer for the address and type it in the Action field.

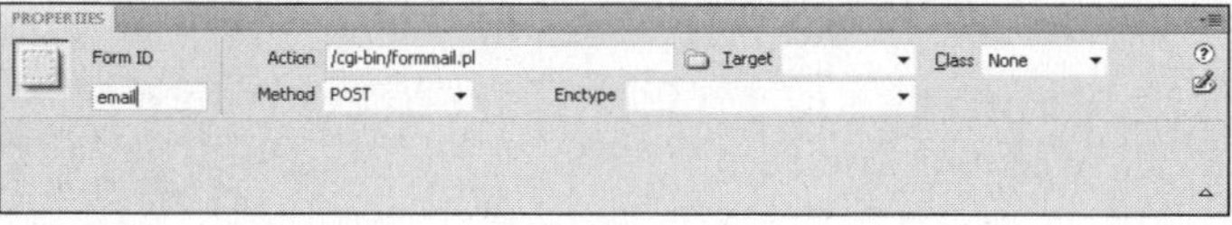

Figure 12-10: In the Action field, enter the path to the script.

4. **In the Method field, use the drop-down arrow to choose Get, Post, or Default.**

   Again, what you choose depends on your script, but Dreamweaver's default is Post. If you're using a script, such as `formmail`, which is featured in the final sections of this chapter, the best option is Post.

   The Get option is generally used for nondestructive, safe form transactions that may be repeated, such as a search engine. Transactions with the Get option are generally stored in the log files on a server and in a browser's history files, so this option isn't recommended for sensitive data, such as financial information. The Post option is generally used for transactions that occur only once, such as sending an e-mail with the data from a form, registering for a service, or unsubscribing to a newsletter. Post can also handle larger chunks of data than Get.

5. **Click the Target option to specify what the browser does when the submit action is completed.**

   If you choose _blank, the results page opens in a new browser window. If you leave this field blank, the browser window is simply replaced with the results page. A results page is usually a simple HTML page with a message, such as *Thanks for playing,* delivered when the Submit button is clicked.

6. **Use the Enctype field to specify how the data is formatted when it's returned (see Figure 12-11).**

   For example, if you're using a form mail script, the Enctype field determines how the text appears in your e-mail when the contents of the form are sent to you. By default, this field in blank.

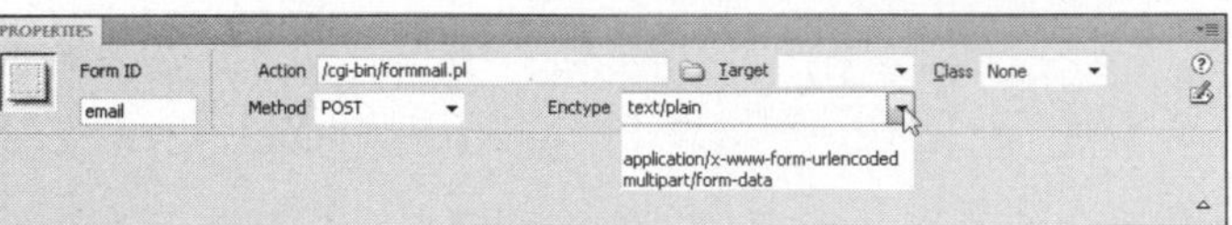

Figure 12-11: Enter a type in the Enctype field.

7. **Use the Class field at the far right of the Property inspector to apply a CSS style to the form.**

   In this example, I applied CSS to some of the elements in the form, such as the text, but not to the entire form.

That takes care of all the options in the Property inspector. You still need to insert a hidden form field into this form to make it work with the `formmail.pl` script, as shown in the next exercise.

Using hidden fields

Many scripts, including the `formmail.pl` script, require the use of hidden fields. Hidden fields are used for data you want associated with a form but not shown to visitors to a site, such as the e-mail address to which a form is sent when a visitor clicks the Submit button. To insert and use a hidden field, follow these steps:

1. **Click to place your cursor inside the `<form>` tag.**

   If you haven't yet inserted the `<form>` tag (which appears as a red dotted line around your form), follow the steps in the first exercise in the "Creating HTML Forms" section before continuing with this exercise.

   Even though the hidden field doesn't appear in the form area, make sure that it's inside the `<form>` tag before you add a hidden field. Placing your cursor at the top or bottom of the form area before inserting a hidden field is a good option because it makes the hidden field easier to find in the HTML code.

After the hidden field is inserted into the `<form>` tag, the Property inspector changes to feature the hidden field options.

2. **In the Property inspector, enter a name.**

   If you're using `formmai.pl`, you'd enter **recipient** as the name and the e-mail address where you want the form data sent as the value. You can even enter more than one e-mail address, separated by commas. So, for example, I could enter **janine@jcwarner.com, janine@digitalfamily.com** in the Value field, and the data from the form would be e-mailed to both these e-mail addresses when a user clicks the Submit button. See Figure 12-12.

Figure 12-12: The Hidden Field properties.

3. **Click to place your cursor inside the `<form>` tag and then click the Hidden Field icon in the Forms Insert Bar to add another hidden field to create a subject line.**

4. **In the Property inspector, enter the name** subject; **in the Value field, include a subject line you want inserted into the e-mail message automatically when a user submits the form.**

   In this example, I entered **Contact Information from DigitalFamily.com** as the value.

   You can add many other hidden fields to a form, depending on the script you're using and how much you want to customize the results.

That's it. Assuming all fields are filled in correctly and the `formmail.pl` (or a similar) script is properly installed and configured on your server, you should receive via e-mail any data a user enters into your form and submits.

There are so many reasons to create forms on the Web, but e-mailing the contents of a contact form is one of the most common. I hope this little exercise has helped to give you an idea of what you need to do to make your HTML forms interact with a CGI script on your server.

Remember, most service providers offer a collection of scripts you can use for common tasks, such as discussion boards and guest books. All you have to do is create the HTML part of the form and then specify the form fields to interact with the script on your server. Check the Web site of your Web hosting service for instructions specific to the scripts available on your server.

Chapter 13

Creating AJAX Features with Spry

In This Chapter

- Creating drop-down menus
- Creating collapsible and tabbed panels
- Working with Spry validation widgets

If you still think AJAX (Asynchronous JavaScript and XML) is just something you can use to clean the house, you're missing out on one of the greatest innovations in Web design. On the Internet, AJAX combines JavaScript and XML to create highly interactive features, such as drop-down menus and panels that can be opened and closed without reloading a Web page.

To make it easier to create these advanced features, Dreamweaver CS4 includes a collection of widgets known as the Spry Framework. Even if you don't know how to write JavaScript, XML, or CSS, you can use to Spry add AJAX features to your Web pages, such as drop-down menus (like the one shown in Figure 13-1), collapsible and tabbed panels, and form validation features, which I cover in this chapter.

Making Magic with AJAX

Web designers are all a buzz about AJAX because it makes it possible to create pages that are more interactive and faster to load than was possible with previous Web technologies. One of the biggest changes is the ability to add features that a Web page visitor can change without having to reload the entire page.

For example, at the highly popular iGoogle page of the Google search engine (available at `www.igoogle.com`), AJAX makes it possible to open and close it and to add and remove content boxes. Thanks to AJAX, Google users can

- Create highly customized pages that feature things like weather from their local area.

- Do things like delete the box that features CNN news headlines and replace it with headlines from another news source.
- Click and drag content boxes to change their location on the page.

Although iGoogle is a very advanced example of AJAX, it's a great example of what's possible.

Dreamweaver's Spry features are designed to make it easy to create some of these basic features, such as panels that open and close the way the weather content box on iGoogle opens or closes.

To save you from having to write the code for these kinds of features yourself, Dreamweaver includes a collection of widgets that instantly adds things like collapsible panels to your pages and combines them with editing tools that make it easy to customize them. To view the list of AJAX widgets available in Dreamweaver, open the Spry Insert panel by choosing Spry from the Insert panel drop-down menu shown in Figure 13-2.

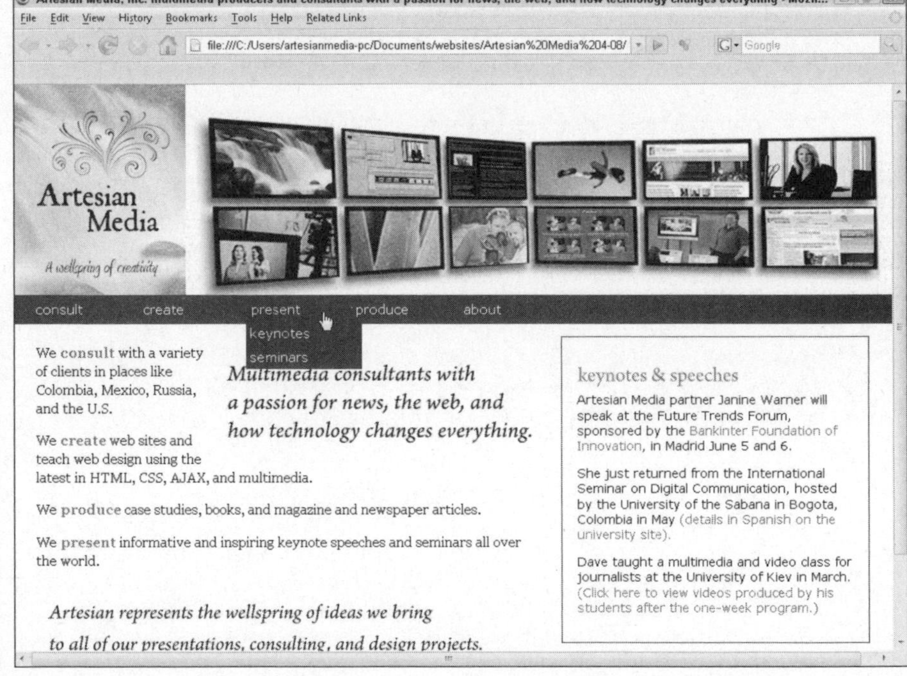

Figure 13-1: You can create drop-down menus like these with the Spry menu in Dreamweaver.

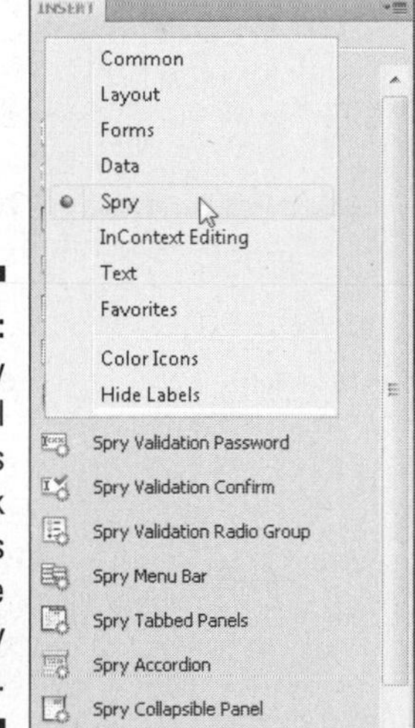

Figure 13-2: The Spry Insert panel provides quick access to the many Spry options.

Creating Drop-Down Menus with AJAX

An increasingly popular option for navigation bars, drop-down menus make it possible to provide a menu (or list) of links to the main sections of a Web site, with a secondary menu of links to the sub-categories within those sections. You can even create a third layer with the Spry Menu Bar widget.

With the Dreamweaver Spry Menu Bar, you can create menus that span horizontally or vertically. The process works the same for both. As you see in the following steps, you simply choose which way you want the menu to span when you insert it from the Spry menu.

To create a drop-down menu with the Spry Menu Bar widget, follow these steps:

1. **Place your cursor on a page where you want the menu to appear.**

   If you haven't already saved your page, make sure you save it before adding Spry features because Dreamweaver will prompt you with a warning message that you need to do so.

2. **Choose Insert⇨Spry⇨Spry Menu Bar.**

   Alternatively, you can click the Spry Menu Bar icon in the Spry Insert panel, (visible in Figure 13-3).

   The Spry Menu Bar dialog box appears, as shown in Figure 13-3.

3. **In the Spry Menu Bar dialog box, choose Horizontal or Vertical.**

   Horizontal creates a menu that drops down into a page; Vertical creates a menu that opens out to the right.

4. **Click OK.**

   A menu with four items and several sub-items is created and inserted into the page.

5. **Enter your own text for the menu items.**

   You can edit the text for the top-level items in the main workspace by simply clicking and dragging to select the generic text, such as Item1, and then typing to replace it.

   In general, it's best to make changes to menu bar items in the Property inspector, as described in the remaining steps of this exercise. To change formatting options, such as color, font face, and size, make changes to the style sheet rules, described in Step 14.

6. **Click the blue Menu Bar tab at the top left of the menu bar to display the settings in the Property inspector, as shown in Figure 13-3.**

   You find settings to add, remove, edit, and change the order of items and sub-items in the Property inspector.

Click the MenuBar tab

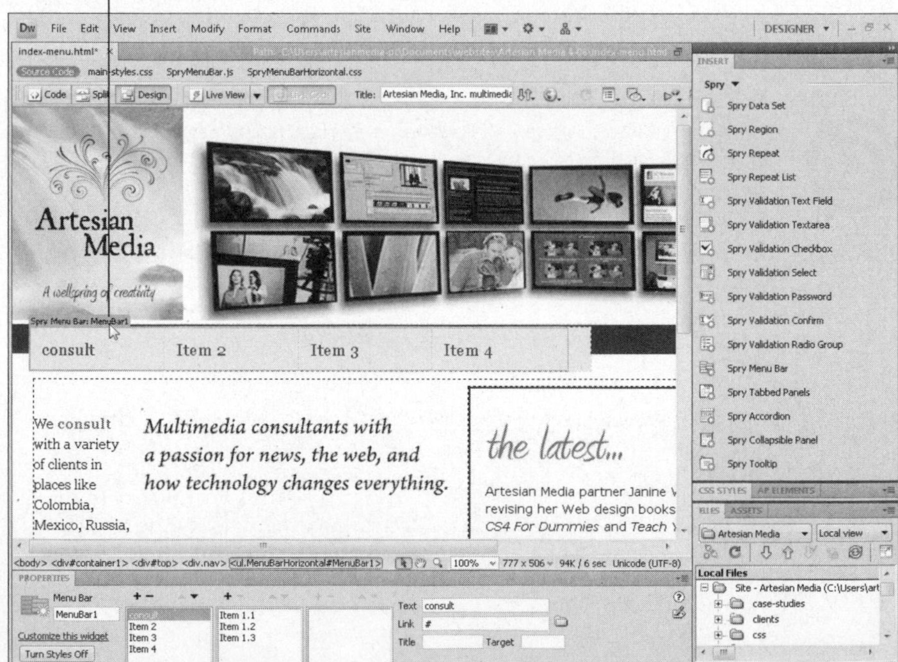

Figure 13-3: Click the blue Menu Bar tab to display the options in the Property inspector.

7. **To change the name of an item or subitem, click to select the item in the Property inspector and then type a new name in the Text field on the far-right side of the Property inspector, as shown in Figures 13-3 and 13-4.**

8. **To link a menu item, select the item name and enter a URL in the Link field or click the Browse button (which looks like a file folder), and select the page you want to link to (see Figure 13-4).**

9. **To remove an item, select it and then click the minus (–) sign at the top of the field in the Property inspector.**

   A deleted item is removed from the menu in the Property inspector as well as the main work area.

10. **To add an item, select the plus (+) sign at the top of the item field in the Property inspector.**

    When you add an item, it appears in the Property inspector menu as well as in the menu bar in the main work area. (See Step 11 for how to change an item name.)

11. **To add a sub-item, select the item you want the sub-item to appear under and then click the plus (+) sign in the item box to the right of the selected item (refer to Figure 13-3).**

12. **To change the order of items, click to select an item name and then use the arrows at the top of each item box.**

    Items move up and down the menu when you click the up or down arrows. Items appear in the Web page in the order they appear in the Property inspector.

13. **Choose File⇨Save to save the page, and when the Copy Dependent Files dialog box appears, click OK to automatically generate all the related files.**

    You must upload these files to your Web server when you upload the Web page for the Spry features to work.

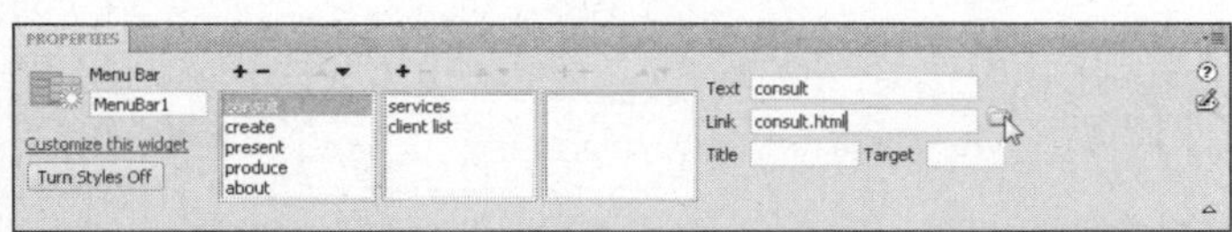

Figure 13-4: Edit any item selected in the Property inspector with the Text, Link, Title, and Target fields.

14. **To change the appearance of a drop-down menu, edit the corresponding CSS style rules.**

    CSS (Cascading Style Sheets) style rules determine the text size, font, background color, and other formatting features. When you create a menu bar, a collection of CSS styles are generated automatically and saved in an external CSS file dubbed `SpryMenuBarHorizontal.CSS` (for horizontal menus) or `SpryMenuBarVertical.CSS` (for vertical menus). You can access these styles through the CSS Styles panel, shown in Figure 13-5.

    Here are a few examples of how Spry menu bar styles can be edited:

    a. **To change the font size or face, double-click the style name `ul.MenuBarHorizontal` and alter the corresponding Type category settings.** In the example, shown here, I've changed the font size to 80 percent, which will make the text in the menu display at 80 percent of the size of the default text setting for the page.

    b. **You can remove or edit the border of a menu bar by editing the border settings in the style `ul.MenuBarHorizontal ul`.** (In the example shown here, I removed the border by simply deleting all of the settings for the border.)

    c. **You can change the text and background colors for the active links (effectively changing the colors of the menu bar when the page first loads) by changing the colors for the rule `ul.MenuBarHorizontal a`.**

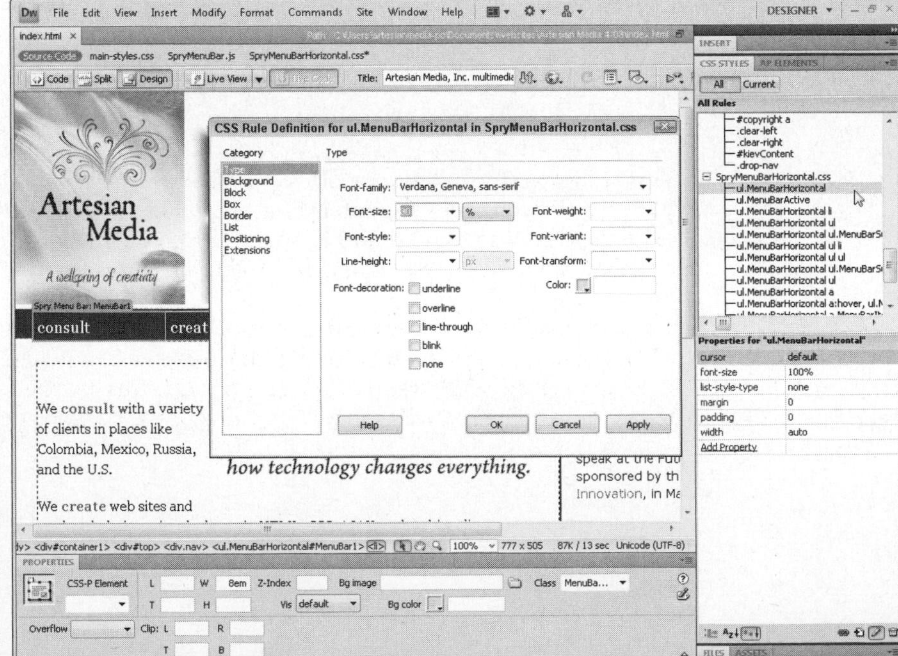

Figure 13-5: To change the appearance of a drop-down menu, edit the corresponding CSS styles.

To find other settings you may want to change, click to select each of the style names in the Spry Menu Bar style sheet and use the CSS Properties pane, in the lower half of the CSS Styles panel, to view the rules that have been defined for each style. By simply clicking through the collection of styles, you can identify each of the settings in a drop-down menu (or any other spry feature) and determine where you'll need to edit them to change the appearance of each element. You find more detailed instructions for creating and editing style rules in Chapters 5 and 6.

15. **Click the globe icon at the top of the workspace to preview your work in a browser.**

    Here you can see how the styles appear in the menu and test the drop-down effects and links.

    The example in Figure 13-6 is in the Firefox browser.

Creating Collapsible Panels

The Spry Collapsible Panel option makes it easy to add panels that can be opened or closed on a Web page. This AJAX feature enables you to make better use of the space on a page by making it easy to display more information in less space within a browser window.

In Figures 13-6, you can see how I used collapsible panels to contain the biography of each partner and consultant in a consulting firm. The result is that you can easily see the names of all the consultants on one page. To view a consultant's bio, a user need only click the tab at the top of the panel (where the consultant's name appears) and the panel opens instantly. In Figure 13-6 you can see that the bio for Designer Davi Cheng is open while the others on the page are all closed. The beauty of AJAX is that the page doesn't have to be reloaded for the panels to open or close. Click once on a tab and a panel opens instantly. If a user clicks the tab again, the panel closes. Collapsible panels can be used to display text and images. You can also include multimedia files in panels, such as audio, video, and Flash files.

When you create collapsible panels with the Spry menu in Dreamweaver, you can set the panels so that they're closed or opened when a page is first loaded. Because each panel is created separately, you can create a page that displays all panels open, all panels closed, or a mix of the two options.

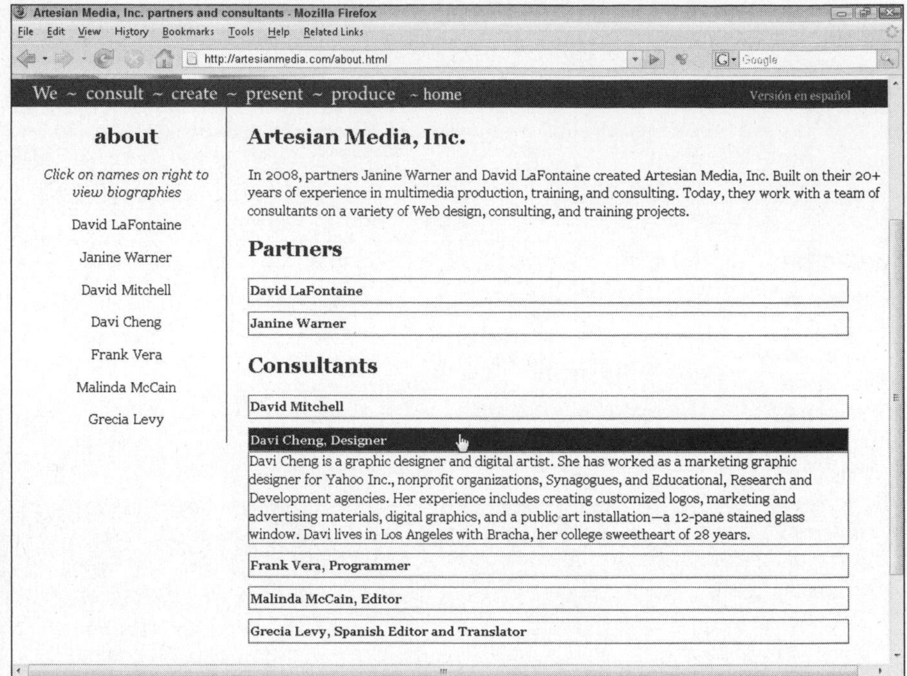

Figure 13-6: The collapsible panel in this menu is shown in the open position.

Follow these steps to create a collapsible panel:

1. **Place your cursor on a page where you want the collapsible panel to appear.**
2. **Choose Insert⇨Spry⇨Spry Collapsible Panel.**

   Alternatively, you can click the Spry Collapsible Panel icon in the Spry Insert panel, as shown in Figure 13-7.

   A Spry collapsible panel appears in the page, as shown in Figure 13-7.
3. **Click and drag to select the word Tab and replace it with the text you want to appear in the panel's Tab area.**

   By default, the text in the Tab area is bold, but you can change that by altering the corresponding CSS rule.
4. **Click to select the word Content in the main area of the panel and enter any text or images you want to display.**

   You can copy text into a panel by pasting it just as you'd paste text anywhere else on the page. Similarly, you insert images into panels just as you would anywhere else on a page by choosing Insert⇨Image and selecting the GIF, JPEG, or PNG file you want to display.

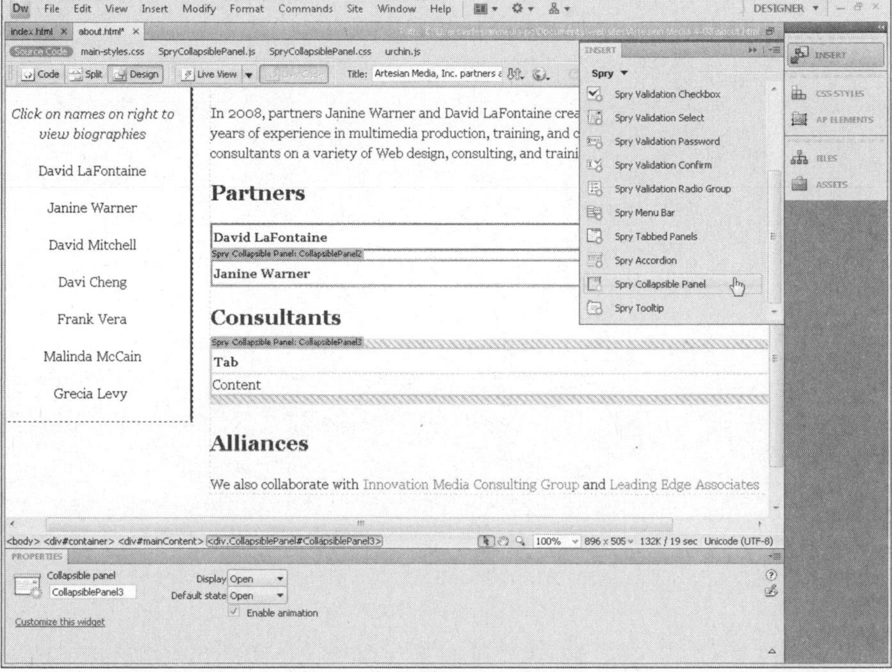

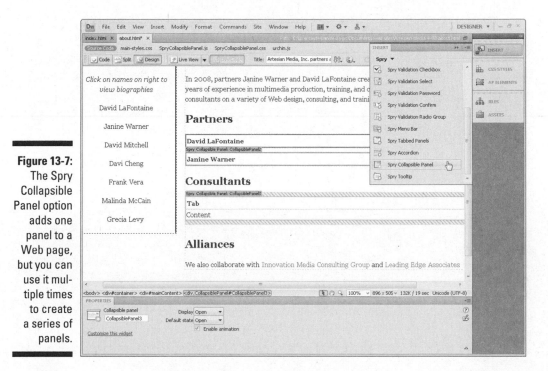

Figure 13-7: The Spry Collapsible Panel option adds one panel to a Web page, but you can use it multiple times to create a series of panels.

When you paste text into a panel, choose Edit➪Paste Special to choose the amount of formatting you want to preserve in the text you paste in Dreamweaver. Limiting the amount of formatting preserved can cut down on potential style conflicts.

5. **Click the blue Spry Collapsible Panel tab at the top of the panel to display panel settings in the Property inspector, as shown in Figure 13-7.**

   When you correctly click the blue tab, the settings immediately appear in the Property inspector, as shown in Figure 13-7. Click anywhere else on the page, and the inspector returns to its default settings.

6. **From the Display drop-down menu in the Property inspector, choose Closed.**

   The Closed option immediately closes the panel in the main workspace in Dreamweaver. This setting only affects the way the panel displays in the Dreamweaver workspace.

7. **From the Default State drop-down menu in the Property inspector, choose Closed.**

This setting controls how the panel displays in a Web browser. Choosing Closed means the panel is closed when the page loads. If you choose Open, the panel appears open when the page is loaded.

8. **Make sure the Enable Animation check box is selected if you want the panel to open and close when a user clicks the tab.**
9. **To change the appearance of the panel, such as the font face or color, edit the corresponding CSS rule.**

   For example, to edit the background color of the tab, or the font face, style, or color, select the `.CollapsiblePanelTab` style and alter the settings in the Properties panel in the lower half of the CSS Styles panel, as shown in Figure 13-8. Alternatively, you can double-click any style name to launch the CSS Rule Definition dialog box to make your changes there. You find more detailed instructions for creating and editing styles in Chapters 5 and 6.

10. **Choose File⇨Save to save the page, and when the Copy Dependent Files dialog box appears, click OK to automatically generate all the related files.**

   REMEMBER

   You must upload these files to your Web server when you upload the Web page for the Spry features to work.

11. **Click the globe icon at the top of the workspace to preview your work in a browser.**

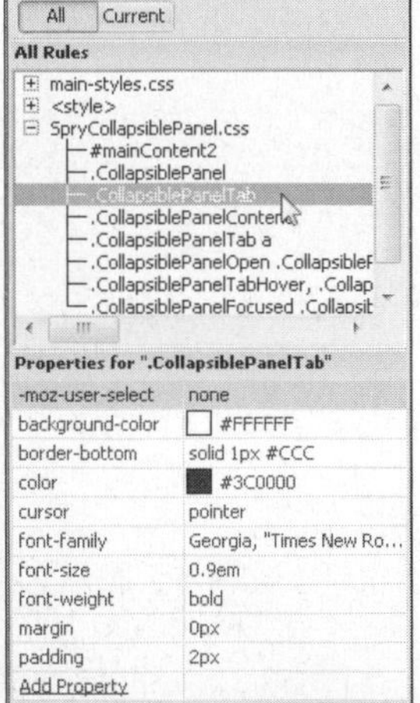

Figure 13-8: To alter the appearance of a Spry collapsible panel, edit the corresponding CSS rule.

Creating Tabbed Panels

The Spry Tabbed Panel option makes it easy to add a series of panels that display or hide content corresponding to a series of tabs, as shown in Figure 13-9. Similar to the collapsible panels, this AJAX feature lets you display more information in less space within a browser window.

Similar to the collapsible panels, tabbed panels can be used to display text, images, and multimedia.

When you create tabbed panels with the Spry menu in Dreamweaver, you can control the order of the tabs, effectively controlling what content appears when the page is first loaded.

Follow these steps to create a tabbed panel:

1. **Place your cursor on a page where you want the tabbed panel to appear.**
2. **Choose Insert⇨Spry⇨Spry Tabbed Panels.**

   Alternatively, you can click the Spry Tabbed Panels icon in the Spry Insert panel, as shown in Figure 13-10.

   A Spry tabbed panel appears on the page, as shown in Figure 13-10.

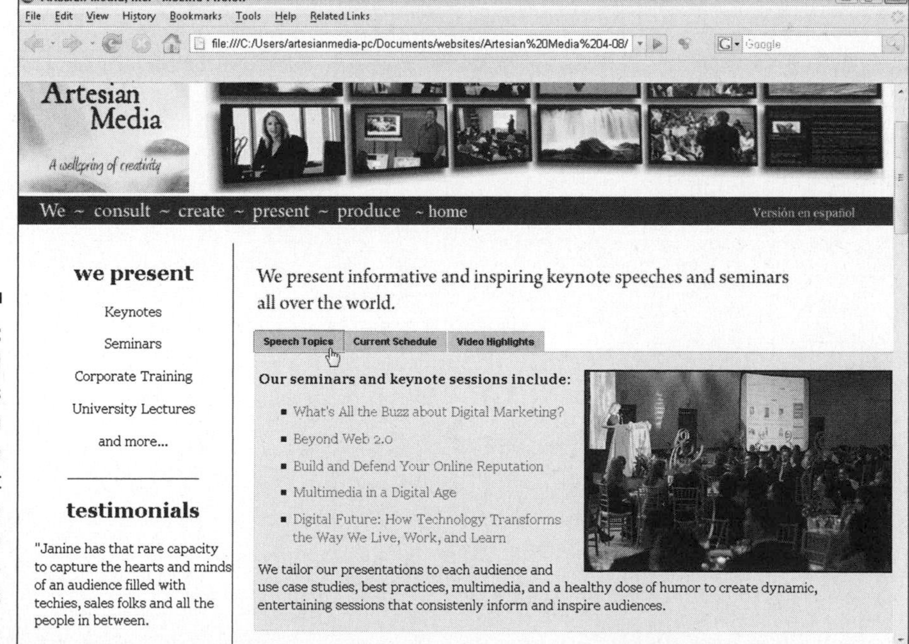

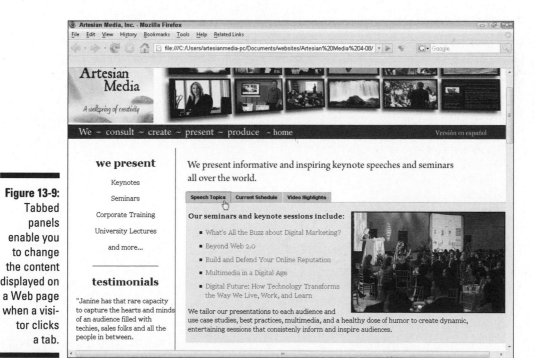

Figure 13-9: Tabbed panels enable you to change the content displayed on a Web page when a visitor clicks a tab.

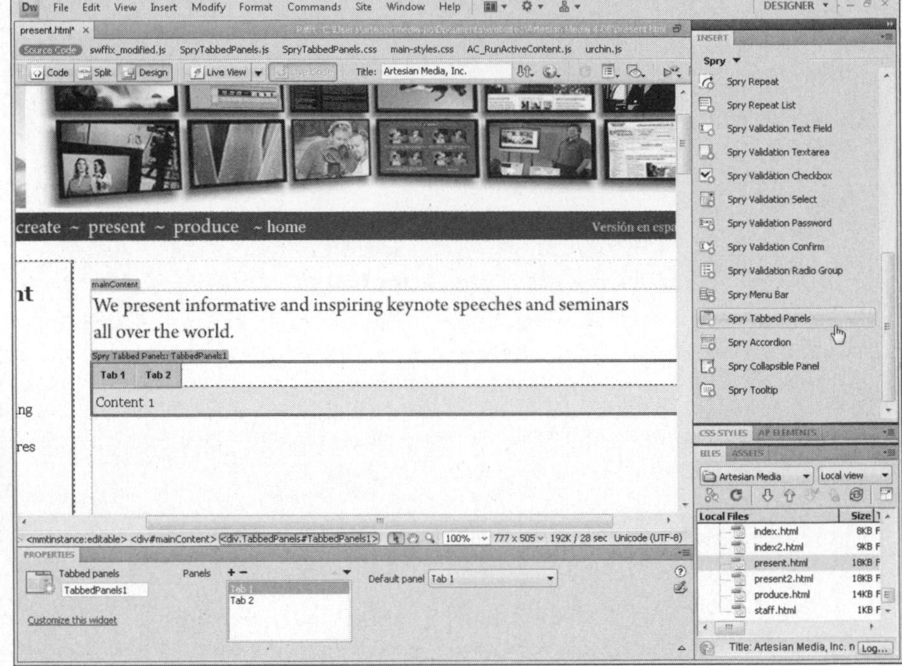

Figure 13-10: The Spry Tabbed Panel option adds a tabbed panel to a Web page.

3. **Click and drag to select the word Tab in the main workspace and replace it with the text you want to appear in the panel's Tab area.**

   You can edit the contents of the tabs only in the workspace, not in the Property inspector.

   By default, the text in the Tab area is bold and black, but you can change that by altering the corresponding CSS rule.

4. **Click the blue Spry Tabbed Panels tab at the top of the panel set to display the settings in the Property inspector, as shown in Figure 13-10.**

   When you correctly click the blue tab, the settings immediately appear in the Property inspector, as shown in Figure 13-9. Click anywhere else on the page, and the Property inspector returns to its default settings.

5. **To add tabs, click the plus (+) icon in the Property inspector, as shown in Figure 13-10.**

   New tabs appear in the workspace.

6. **To change the order of tabs, click to select the tab name in the Property inspector and then use the arrows in the Panels field to move the panel.**

Panel names move up and down the menu as the order is changed. Panels and their corresponding tabs appear in the Web page in the order they appear in the Property inspector.

7. **Use the Default Panel drop-down menu to choose the panel you want to display when the page is first loaded into a Web browser.**

   The drop-down menu corresponds to the names you give each tab in the workspace.

8. **To add content, select the word Content in the main area of any selected tab panel and enter text, images, or multimedia.**

   You can copy text into a panel by pasting it just as you'd paste text anywhere else on the page. Similarly, insert images into panels just as you would anywhere else on a page by choosing Insert⇨Image and then selecting the GIF, JPEG, or PNG file you want to display. You can also add multimedia, such as Flash video files. (Find instructions for adding multimedia to Web pages in Chapter 11.)

9. **To change the appearance of a tab or a panel, such as the font face or color, edit the corresponding CSS rule, shown in Figure 13-11.**

   For example, to edit the background color of the tabs, click to select the `.TabbedPanelsTab` style and alter the settings in the Properties panel in the lower half of the CSS Styles panel. Alternatively, you can double-click any style name to launch the CSS Rule Definition dialog box to make your changes there. You find more detailed instructions for creating and editing styles in Chapters 5 and 6.

   In tabbed panels styles, the tab background colors are controlled by two different styles — the `.TabbedPanelsTab` and the `.TabbedPanelsTabSelected` styles. As a result, you can specify a different background color and other formatting settings to distinguish the tab that's selected from the tabs that aren't selected.

10. **Choose File⇨Save to save the page, and when the Copy Dependent Files dialog box appears, click OK to automatically generate all the related files.**

    You must upload these files to your Web server when you upload the Web page for the Spry features to work.

11. **Click the globe icon at the top of the workspace to preview your work in a browser.**

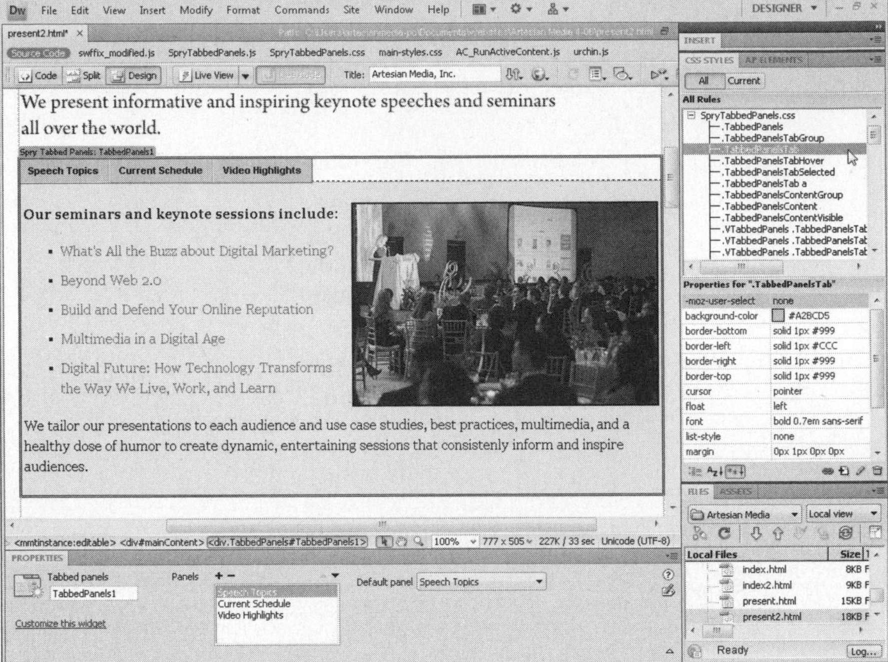

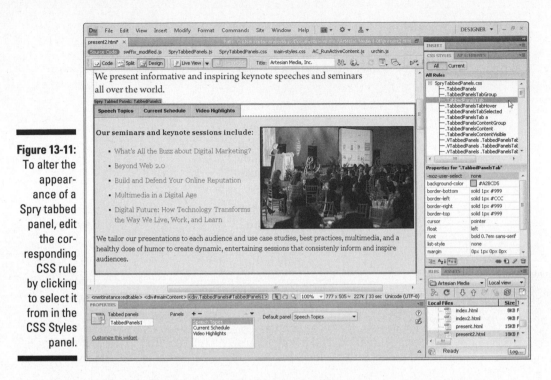

Figure 13-11: To alter the appearance of a Spry tabbed panel, edit the corresponding CSS rule by clicking to select it from in the CSS Styles panel.

Using Spry Validation Widgets

The Spry menu also includes a collection of validation widgets for validating data that visitors enter into forms on your site. For example, you can use the Text Field Validation widget to verify whether a visitor has filled in a specified minimum number of characters — a handy way to ensure that someone has filled in all the digits in a phone number or social security number. You can also add hints to a text field to provide additional instructions.

Similarly, you can use the Validation Checkbox widget to verify that a check box has been selected. This is common, for example, when you have a legal disclaimer or contract and want to ensure that a visitor selects the Accept box before progressing into another area of your site.

To use these widgets, first create an HTML form (find instructions for creating form elements in Chapter 12). Then you can add Spry validation, such as the Validation Checkbox, which I cover in this exercise.

To use the Spry Validation Checkbox Wizard to require that users select one or more check boxes on a Web page, follow these steps:

1. **Select the check box where you want to add Spry validation.**
2. **Choose Insert⇨Spry⇨Spry Validation Checkbox.**

   Alternatively, you can click the Spry Validation Checkbox icon in the Spry Insert panel.
3. **Specify validation requirements in the Property inspector.**

   When you add a validation widget to a form element, such as the check box shown in this example, the Property inspector automatically displays the properties for that validation option. If those properties aren't visible, click the blue Spry tab just above the form element to display them.
4. **To require that users select a check box, choose Required from the Preview States drop-down menu in the Property inspector, as shown in Figure 13-12.**

   Dreamweaver automatically adds Please Make a Selection, just to the right of the check box in the workspace. You can edit this text by selecting it in the workspace and typing any message you want, such as, **You must accept our policy to continue.**

   The validation message displays only if a visitor fails to select the check box before clicking the Submit button (which is labeled Send in Figure 13-12).

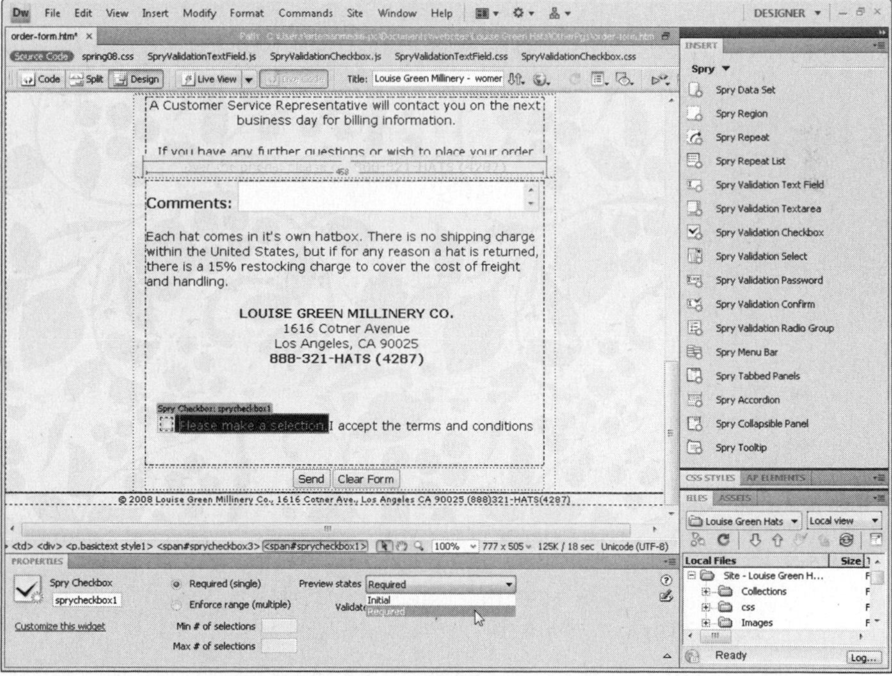

Figure 13-12: You can use the Checkbox Validation widget to require that visitors select a check box before continuing to another page in your site.

5. **Choose File⇨Save to save the page, and when the Copy Dependent Files dialog box appears, click OK to automatically generate all the related files.**

   For the Spry features work, you must upload these files to your Web server when you upload the Web page.

6. **Click the globe icon at the top of the workspace to preview your work in a browser where you can test the validation features.**

Part IV
Working with Dynamic Content

"Games are an important part of my Web site. They cause eye strain."

In this part . . .

The most sophisticated and technically complicated Web sites are created using databases to dynamically generate Web pages — ideal for content-heavy Web sites. Although creating a Web site with these advanced features is far more complex than using methods you find in earlier parts of this book, the rewards can be worth the trouble. In Chapters 14 and 15, you discover the benefits of creating a dynamic site, find out how to work with a database on the Web, and follow step-by-step instructions to build a simple database-driven site.

Chapter 14

Building a Dynamic Web Site: Getting Started

In This Chapter

- Defining a dynamic Web site
- Going over the basic terminology
- Choosing the dynamic development technology
- Setting up your computer for dynamic Web pages
- Creating a data connection

The most sophisticated Web sites on the Internet, such as Amazon.com or CNN.com, were created using complex programming and databases. Combining a database that records information about users with the capability to generate pages automatically is what enables Amazon to greet you by name when you return to its site, track your orders, and even make recommendations based on your previous purchases.

Static Web sites, which you can build using the instructions in the rest of this book, work well for many Web sites (including my own at `www.JCWarner.com`). But for anyone creating a really large, content-heavy site, such as a magazine or a newspaper Web site or large e-commerce sites where you need to track inventory and want users to be able to search through products, dynamic Web sites are a better choice.

Before you even start down this path, let me warn you of two things. First, creating a dynamic Web site is far, far more complex than creating the kinds of static page Web sites described in the earlier chapters of this book. Second, the most sophisticated sites on the Web, such as Amazon and CNN, use highly customized systems that require teams of very experienced programmers to create.

That said, Dreamweaver does include dynamic development features that you can use to create database-driven Web sites more easily than if you had to write all the code manually. In this chapter and Chapter 15, you find an introduction to these features and instructions for creating a basic, database-driven site.

A description of the more advanced Dreamweaver database features is beyond the scope of this book. If you want to use Dreamweaver's most advanced database features, find more information in *Dreamweaver CS4 All-in-One Desk Reference For Dummies,* by Sue Jenkins, Michele E. Davis, and Jon A. Phillips; or *Dreamweaver CS4 Bible,* by Joseph Lowery (Wiley Publishing, Inc.).

This chapter begins by introducing you to what people mean when they talk about dynamic Web sites and databases, and it explores the many ways in which, through a dynamic Web site, you can display and edit information contained in a database. You also discover what you need to have in place to create a dynamic Web site. In Chapter 15, you find step-by-step directions for creating various dynamic features for a simple real-world Web site.

Understanding the Dynamic Web Site

A *dynamic* Web site is connected to a *data source,* such as *a database,* which can deliver data to each Web site visitor based on his or her requests. Because data is delivered dynamically, it's possible to provide different content to each visitor on a Web site in response to actions or information gathered from a visitor.

A simple example of a dynamic Web site feature is a search engine:

1. You type what you want to find into a search field.
2. When you submit your request, that information is passed to a database.
3. The database then returns a list of instant results with information that's relevant (ideally, anyway!) to your search request. Thus information entered by a visitor results in a unique, dynamically-generated Web page with the results of the search.

The easiest way to add a simple search engine to a Web site (even a static-page site) is Google's free search engine, which lets you add advanced search features using Google's technology for free. Visit `www.google.com/coop/cse` for details.

Checking out dynamic site advantages

A dynamic Web site has many advantages beyond the ability to create a site-wide search. Suppose that you have a Web site where you sell 657 kinds of candy. Here's how a static versus a dynamic site might work:

- **On a *static* Web site,** you'd have to create 657 pages, one for each candy product. If you ever wanted to change the way those pages look, you'd have to change all 657 pages.
- **With a *dynamic* Web site,** you create just *one* page with the design for your candy products and then you add special code that dynamically pulls product name, image, description, and any other pertinent information from a database and displays it in that one page design each time a visitor requests one of the 657 kinds of candy.

When you compare the two, dynamic Web sites clearly offer advantages to site owners who have a lot of data, such as items for sale, to display in a consistent format:

- **A dynamic site saves lots of time** because you don't have to create all those individual pages.
- **Dynamic Web sites also enable you to make changes and updates with less effort.**
- **Dynamic sites enable you to display the same product information in different combinations in different page designs.** So, for example, you could create one page that displayed only the name and photo of each kind of candy and then another page that displayed all the product information, including a detailed description, pricing information, and so on.
- **Dynamic sites enable you to automatically create links between pages with related information so that visitors can drill down to find the details they want.** When you set up your dynamic site, you can create features that automatically set the links from the first page with many kinds of candy listed to the second, and when a visitor clicks the name of a type of candy, a page with all the details of that candy is generated dynamically and returned to the visitor.

  You can also use AJAX to link dynamic content, such as an XML file, to a Web page and display data dynamically. Either way, you store all your product information in a data source, such as a database or XML file, and then you use special code in the Web page to communicate with the data source, collect each product's information, and create a page on-the-fly as visitors request products (or any other kind of content).

Seeing a dynamic site in action

To better understand how dynamic sites work, here's an example of a dynamic Web site in action:

1. **Point your browser to** `www.poweryoga.com`**.**
2. **On the home page, hover your mouse over the About Yoga menu item and click Library of Articles.**

   On the Library of Articles page, you can see the headline and first paragraph of each of a series of articles about Yoga (see Figure 14-1).

   The Library of Articles page is generated dynamically by pulling just this first part of each story out of the database and displaying them in a specified order on this page.
3. **Click a headline and the browser displays a page that shows you the entire article, drawn from the same database.**

   When you view pages like this, keep in mind that there's really only one page design for all the articles linked from the library page. When you click a headline on the Library of Articles page, as shown in Figure 14-1, the system pulls the article from the database, inserts it into the page, and displays it in the Web browser.

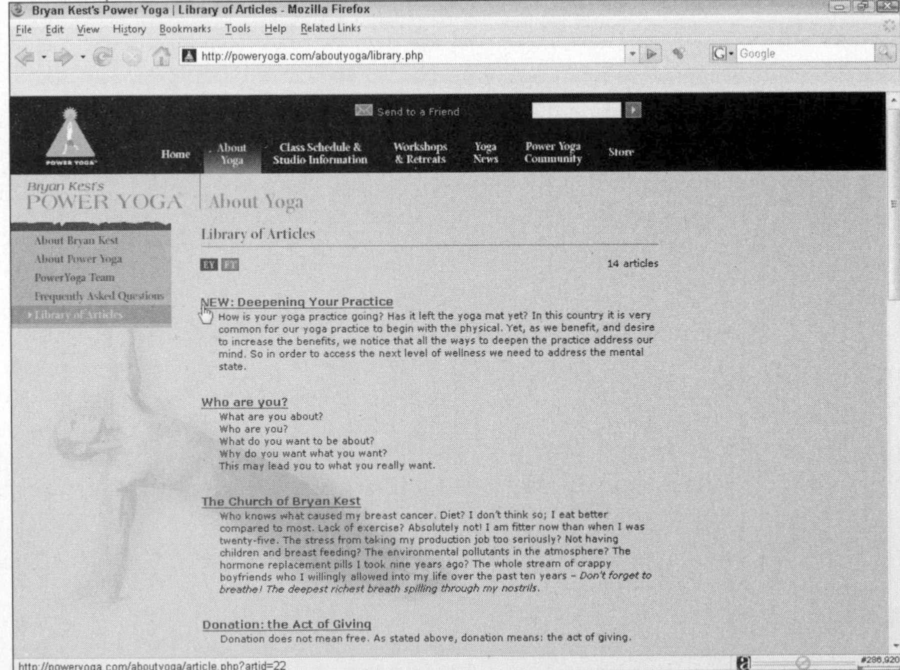

Figure 14-1: The PowerYoga.com Library of Articles page.

4. **Click the Back to Articles menu button or click the Back button in your browser to return to the Library of Articles page.**
5. **Click another headline, and the system pulls that article and displays it in the same article page.**

   Not only does this mean you only need one page for all the articles, it also means you only need one copy of each article. So, for example, if you find a typo in the headline on the Library of Articles page and you correct it in the database, the headline is corrected automatically on the Library of Articles page, as well as on the page that displays the entire article because it's the same headline, entered once in the database, and displayed as many times as it's requested on different pages of your site.

Creating Dynamic Sites: Key Concepts

One of the first things you need to understand about creating dynamic Web sites is that you need one program to create the data source (usually a database or an XML file) and then you need another program (or programming language, such as PHP or ASP.NET) to connect the data source to your Web pages. In the two sections that follow, you find a list of some of the most common database programs you might use, such as Access and MySQL, as well as a description of the five technologies Dreamweaver supports for creating dynamic sites: PHP, JSP, ASP, ASP.NET, and ColdFusion.

Understanding databases

First, you need to understand what a database is and how tables are structured. A *database* is a collection of information compiled in one or more *tables.* Each table has multiple *records* (or *rows*) organized in *fields* (or *columns*).

If this is all new to you, an analogy may help you appreciate how tables and columns work. Picture a mail-order catalog, such as the one used by the home furnishing store Pottery Barn. From the smallest element (the fields) to the largest element (the database), here's how the elements in this catalog fit into the parlance of a database:

- Consider that each product has an item number, a price, and a color. Think of each of those elements of a product as a *field.*
- Each product is a *record* in the database. A *record* in a database consists of one complete set of all fields.

- Taking it a step further, within the catalog, the various products are organized in categories, usually because they have something in common, such as all the fuzzy things that are designed for the floor might be in a rugs category whereas all the things with legs might go best in the furniture category (you get the idea). Think of each of the categories (furniture, rugs, and so on) as a *table* — a grouping of records from a database that have something in common.
- Think of the catalog itself as the *database,* which contains a collection of information about various products.

Okay, so that's a very simple description of a database, but it's important that you understand the way databases are structured because how a database is set up and how information is organized within tables and rows affects how you can organize that content on a Web page.

When I refer to a table in a database, I'm not talking about the same kind of table discussed in Chapter 7. HTML tables are used to format information, much as you'd use a spreadsheet program, such as Excel. Database tables aren't used for formatting; they're used for grouping and organizing content. Just to make things even more confusing, one of the few legitimate uses of HTML tables these days is for formatting the contents of a database when it's displayed on a Web page.

Databases can be created with a variety of different programs, including Microsoft Access, FileMaker Pro, SQL Server, MySQL, FoxPro, and Oracle. On the simpler side, Access is commonly used to create small databases (files with a `.mdb` extension) like the contact database featured in Chapter 15. Access is also commonly used to communicate with bigger databases, such as Microsoft SQL Server. At the other extreme, a site like Amazon.com, which has millions of products stored in a database, would probably use an Oracle database or an SQL Server.

To keep things simple in this introduction to dynamic sites, I created the database example used in Chapter 15 in Microsoft Access, but the basic concepts and the features in Dreamweaver are similar no matter which database application you use.

Choosing a dynamic development technology

After you have the data source covered (database or XML files), find a way for the Web site and the data source to communicate. That's where server technologies, such as PHP, come in.

Dreamweaver supports five server technologies (described in detail in the following sections):

- Active Server Pages (ASP)
- ASP.NET
- JavaServer Pages (JSP)
- ColdFusion
- PHP (which stands for PHP Hypertext Preprocessor — a recursive acronym, for you wordsmiths)

The examples in this book use ASP mostly because it's one of the simpler options to set up on your computer and it provides an easy place to start, but in essence, all five offer similar functionality. After you see how Dreamweaver works with ASP, you'll have a pretty good introduction to how Dreamweaver works with the other four options as well:

- They all provide the capability to generate HTML dynamically.
- They all can be used to connect your Web site to a database or other data source.
- With server-side code, they all can display information from a database and create HTML based on certain criteria, such as the actions or data entered by a visitor to your site.

I don't recommend any one technology over another. They all offer similar functionality with slight variations in speed and efficiency. One consideration that is important — make sure that your Web host supports whatever technology you choose. Not all Web servers are set up to handle all these technologies. The following descriptions are designed to help you make a more informed decision about which option best serves your needs.

ASP

Extension: `.asp`

Although ASP has been replaced by ASP.NET, it's still used by many active sites on the Web. ASP is a server technology built into the Windows 2003 Server, Windows 2000, Windows XP Professional, and Windows Vista at no additional cost. ASP can also be used with Microsoft IIS (Internet Information Services) or Personal Web Server, which is useful for building and testing on your local hard drive. ASP isn't a standalone programming language because much of the code you write for ASP pages is in VBScript or *JScript* (Microsoft's version of JavaScript). You can check out `www.4guysfromrolla.com` to find out more about ASP in what more closely resembles plain English.

For the examples in this book, I chose ASP, mostly because it's much easier to set up than any of the other technologies. After you see how the basics work with ASP, you can graduate to other options, such as PHP or ASP.NET. Consider the examples in this chapter and Chapter 15 as an introduction to dynamic site design. I don't want to throw you into the deep end (at least, not yet).

Warning: Even with ASP, which is a relatively simple option, the example steps in this chapter and Chapter 15 get a lot more technical than the earlier chapters in this book.

ASP.NET

Extension: `.aspx`

ASP.NET is Microsoft's replacement for ASP. ASP.NET isn't just a revision of ASP 3.0; it's a complete redesign of the language. Microsoft has done more than add new tags. The language is similar to traditional programming languages, such as C++, where code is compiled. This arrangement suggests that applications written in ASP.NET can run faster because Web servers work more efficiently with less coding overhead. However, ASP.NET isn't as verbose as ASP 3.0, so it's much harder for novice programmers to read. ASP.NET is a Microsoft technology, and you can find more information at `msdn.microsoft.com/asp.net` and `www.asp.net`.

ColdFusion

Extension: `.cfm`

ColdFusion, owned by Adobe, uses its own server and scripting language. ColdFusion is probably the easiest language to figure out how to use because it includes custom tags that also enable you to separate dynamic code from HTML, which makes it similar to JSP. Also like JSP, it's ultimately based on Java. But the many tags included in ColdFusion make it much easier and faster to use than technologies like Java or PHP. ColdFusion also includes built-in XML processing. You can read more about ColdFusion at `www.adobe.com/products/coldfusion`.

JavaServer Pages (JSP)

Extension: `.jsp`

JSP is from Sun Microsystems. Because its dynamic code is based on Java, you can run JSP pages on non-Microsoft Web servers. You can use JSP on Allaire JRun Server and IBM WebSphere. With JSP, you can create and keep the dynamic code separate from the HTML pages, or you can embed the JSP code into the page. Unless you're a hardcore programmer, however, this language isn't for you. JSP is horribly complex. You can find out more about JSP at `java.sun.com/products/jsp`.

PHP

Extension: `.php`

PHP is an open source technology so it's free, which has helped make it one of the most popular options for creating dynamic Web sites. PHP is often used with databases created with MySQL and many commercial Web hosting services provide MySQL and PHP support as part of their standard Web hosting services. PHP is native to UNIX-based servers. However, you can download Windows binaries from `www.php.net` to run *Apache* (a server software typically used with PHP) from any version of Windows as well as IIS (Internet Information Services) on NT, Windows 2000, Windows XP Professional, and Windows 2003 Server. You can even configure PHP to run on Personal Web Server (although doing so is tricky). The PHP scripting language is based on C, Perl, and Java. You can get more functionality with PHP right out of the box than you can with ASP. For example, virtually every ASP add-on that's on sale at `www.serverobjects.com` comes built-in or is available for free from `www.php.net`.

If you're working with PHP and MySQL, here's a great way to get a testing server set up on your local computer. The Webserver on a Stick (WOS) is available for free from `www.chsoftware.net/en/useware/wos/wos.htm`. According to the site: you can use this service to run a Web server based on Apache, MySQL and PHP from an USB Stick. Other writable media (your hard drive, flash drives, and so on) also work. You need to be running Windows.

Creating dynamic pages with AJAX (using Spry)

AJAX combines the power of Asynchronous JavaScript and XML to create dynamic features that can be changed in a Web browser without ever reloading the page from the Web server. The Adobe Spry Framework in Dreamweaver is designed to make it easier to create AJAX features. Spry *widgets* are ready-to-use, common Web page components that can be customized with CSS. Dreamweaver includes a collection of Spry widgets designed for creating advanced features, such as drop-down menus, collapsible panels, and tabbed panels. (All three features are covered in detail in Chapter 13.)

Spry can also be used to create pages that feature dynamically-generated content. For example, you can combine a Spry widget with a data source, such as an XML file. You can see some cool examples of Spry at `http://labs.adobe.com/technologies/spry/demos`.

Setting Up Your Computer to Serve Dynamic Web Pages

When you're creating dynamic sites, you can't just preview your dynamic pages the way you can preview the pages from *static* Web sites. Remember a static Web site is made up of individual pages, each of which must be altered and uploaded separately to a Web server, and each of which can be viewed separately in a Web browser. When you create a static site, you can easily preview your pages directly from your local hard drive. When your content is dynamic, previewing your pages isn't that simple because you need a Web server to process the page and create it dynamically before it can be displayed in a Web browser. Thus, you need to have Web server software on your local computer to view dynamic pages.

Fortunately, a number of servers can be installed for free and can be used to mimic the functions of the kind of Web server that will host your site when it's published online.

Web server is commonly used to describe both a piece of computer hardware on which a Web site is stored (usually a high-powered computer) and the software on that computer that provides the server functionality. To test your dynamic pages in Dreamweaver, you need Web server and application server software (although in some cases you can get both in one). If you can run Dreamweaver CS4, your personal computer should be more than powerful enough to act as a Web server.

In the sections that follow, I show you how to set up a simple Web server on a Windows computer and how to make a few other adjustments to your system so that you can preview your pages on your local computer.

To set up a Web server, you need server software. A *Web server* responds to requests from a Web browser by serving up Web pages based on those requests. You also need to set up an *application server,* which helps the Web server process specially marked Web pages. When the browser requests one of these pages, the Web server hands off the page to the application server, which processes the page before sending it to the browser. One of the advantages of working with ASP is that the IIS server, which I use in the examples in this chapter and the next, can handle both functions.

Don't skip these next two sections because you can't complete the example tasks that follow if you haven't first set up a local Web server and set the proper permissions on your local computer.

Setting up a local Web server

When you use ASP, you have a choice of Web server options. Both Microsoft IIS and Personal Web Server (PWS) work for testing your ASP pages and both can serve as a Web server and an application server. PWS runs with Windows XP and Windows Vista; you can install either from your Windows CD. If you have Windows 2000 Server, Windows XP Professional, or Windows Vista (Business, Enterprise, and Ultimate editions), IIS is part of the package. If you can't find your CD, you can download IIS or PWS for free from the Microsoft Web site.

IIS doesn't work on Windows XP or Vista Home editions. You must upgrade to use these advanced features.

If you're running an edition of Vista or Windows XP that supports IIS, all you have to do is make sure it's enabled by following these steps:

1. **Click the Start menu and choose Control Panel.**

2a. ***Vista:* Choose Programs to open the Programs and Features dialog box, and then choose Turn Windows Features On or Off from the left side of the dialog box.**

If you're prompted with a dialog box that states Windows Needs Your Permission to Continue, click Continue.

2b. ***XP:* Click the Add or Remove Programs option in the Control Panel and then click the Add/Remove Windows Components button on the left side of the Add or Remove Programs window.**

On XP, the Windows Components Wizard dialog box opens. On Vista, the Windows Features dialog box opens.

3a. ***XP and Vista:* Scroll down in the Windows Features dialog box until you find the Internet Information Services option (as shown on Vista in Figure 14-2) and select the check box.**

In the boxes under IIS, make sure that ASP and ASP.NET are checked.

3b. ***XP:* Scroll down in the Windows Components dialog box until you find the Internet Information Services option and select the check box.**

4a. ***Vista:* Click OK.**

4b. ***XP:* Click Next.**

A dialog box appears explaining that configuring the components can take several minutes. The dialog box closes automatically when the components are configured.

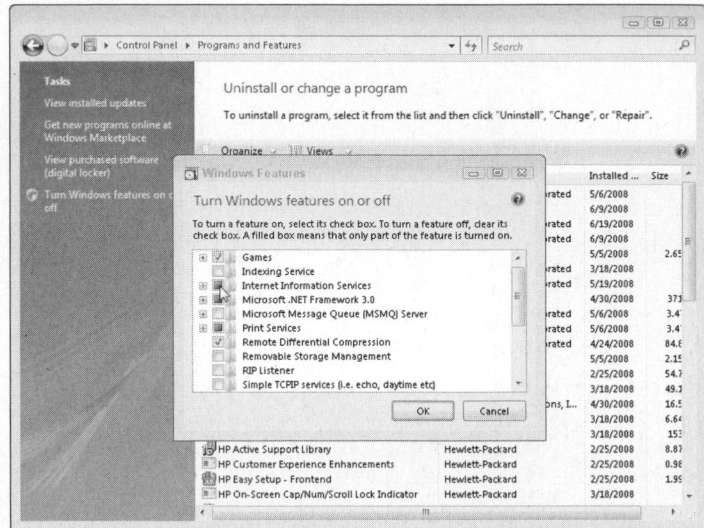

Figure 14-2: You can use Internet Information Services in Windows to test your dynamic Web pages on your local hard drive.

If you didn't install these components when you first installed your operating system, you may be prompted to insert your original Windows software disk (or the setup disk that came with your computer) so that these components can be added.

5. **Click to close the Programs and Features folder on Vista or the Add or Remove Programs window on XP.**

6. **To test to make sure that the IIS server is functioning properly, open a Web browser, such as Firefox, and enter the URL** `http://localhost`**.**

   If you're using Vista, the localhost page appears in the browser, as shown in Figure 14-3. Click a link in the language of your choice for more information about IIS.

   If you're using XP, a message appears in red in the Web browser stating, Your Web Service Is Now Running. This page also provides additional information about IIS.

If you don't have your Windows CD, you can download IIS from the Microsoft Web site and install it separately.

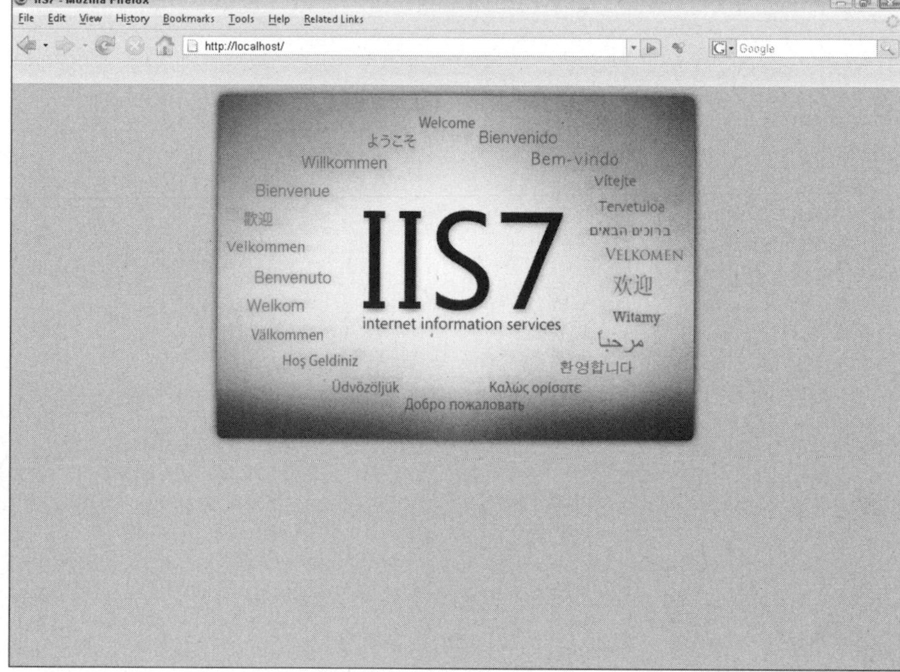

Figure 14-3: You can test your local server by entering http://localhost into a Web browser.

Setting up permission

The next challenge to getting your computer set up to build and test your database-driven site locally has to do with the way Windows handles permissions on a computer. Most Windows operating systems have security features that limit how computer users can access certain features or folders on your hard drive. If you're using a Windows operating system, your hard drive probably uses Microsoft's security-conscious New Technology File System (NTFS) format. For the database examples in the following chapters to work, make some changes to the permission settings on your computer.

You also want to copy or move your database and any other files you have ready for your Web site into a special wwwroot folder on your operating system. The Inetpub and wwwroot folders are created automatically when you install IIS. Changing permissions on these folders and copying your files into them before you set up your site is a relatively simple, and *very important* step, covered in the exercise that follows.

It's important that you store the database and the other files for your Web site in the wwwroot folder because this is what IIS considers the root level of your local Web server. You need your site in the wwwroot folder for your pages to preview properly in a Web browser on your hard drive. However, by default, Windows protects this folder, so before you can work on your site in this folder, you have to change the security settings.

Another important step in creating a database-driven site is, not surprisingly, that you have to create a database. How you create a database is way beyond the scope of this book. For the purposes of the following exercises and the ones in the following chapter, I created a simple contact database with Microsoft Access. If you don't yet have a database file and just want to follow along, you can download this database file (`contacts.mdb`) from my Web site at `www.digitalfamily.com/dwd`.

I created this file in Microsoft Access because it's an easy database program to use and one that many readers are likely to already have, but you don't need Access to use this file with Dreamweaver. You can't edit any of the contact names or other data in the database file without Access or a similar program, but you can use this file to follow along with the exercises in this chapter and Chapter 15 as you try Dreamweaver's database features.

Follow these steps to copy your files into the wwwroot folder and set up permissions in Windows:

1. **Choose Start⇨Computer.**

   The My Computer folder opens with a list of your hard drives.

2. **Double-click the C: drive, double-click the Inetpub folder, and then right-click the wwwroot folder and choose File⇨Properties.**

   The Properties dialog box appears.

3. **Click the Security tab and then click the Edit button.**

   The wwwroot Properties dialog box appears, as shown in Figure 14-4.

4. **Click the Edit button under the Group or User Names list.**

   The Permissions for wwwroot dialog box opens, as shown in Figure 14-5.

5. **Select Users (COMPUTER\Users) from the Group or User Names list.**

6. **In the Permission for Users box, select the Full Control Allow check box, as shown in Figure 14-5.**

   A check mark appears automatically in each of the check boxes in the dialog box.

7. **Click Apply, click OK, and click OK again to close these dialog boxes.**

8. **Create, copy, or move a folder into the wwwroot folder to serve as your main local root Web site folder.**

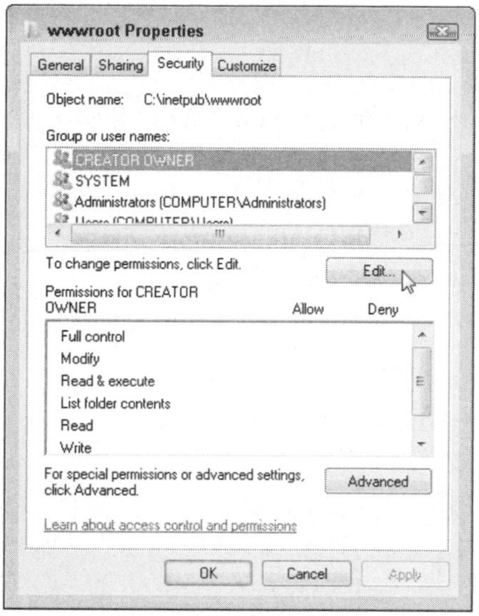

Figure 14-4: Before you can set up a data-base driven site in Windows using IIS, change the permission settings in the www-root folder properties dialog box under the Security tab.

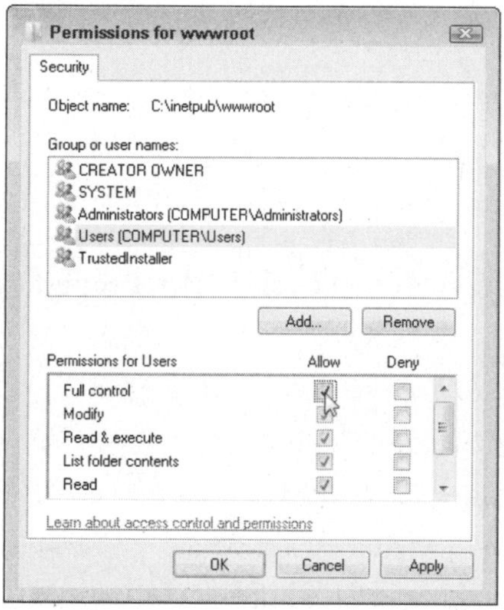

Figure 14-5: Set permis-sion to Full Control to enable access to the www-root folder.

As shown in Figure 14-6, I copied the myContacts folder into the www-root folder. The myContacts folder contains the `contacts.mdb` data-base file and an images folder. You can call your main site root folder anything you like, but it's best not to use spaces or special characters, and the files for your site need to be stored in this wwwroot folder for the local Web server to be able to display your dynamic pages on your hard drive.

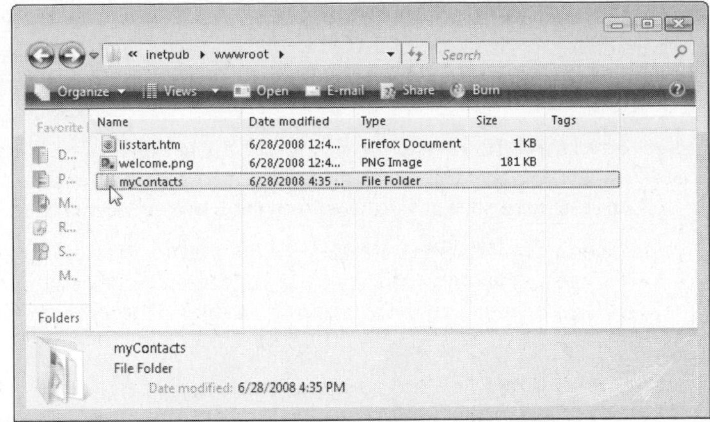

Figure 14-6: You need to store all the files for your Web site, including the database file, in your wwwroot folder.

Creating a Data Connection in Dreamweaver

Creating the data connection in Dreamweaver takes a few quick steps. Start by setting up your site's local information and remote site information and then establish a connection between the site and the data source.

In this example, I assume that you've completed the steps in the previous two sections, that you're running IIS on the same computer as Dreamweaver, that you've stored your data source in the wwwroot folder, and that you've changed permissions so that you can write to that folder on Windows. All these steps are crucial to your ability to set up a local connection, which I cover in this section.

To set up a dynamic site in Dreamweaver, follow these steps:

1. **Choose Site⇨New Site.**

   The Site Definition dialog box appears.

2. **Click the Advanced tab.**

   The Advanced window appears. If you prefer, you can use the Basic Wizard that steps you through the setup process, but I find it faster and easier to view all the options at once on the Advanced tab.

3. **In the Category box on the left, make sure that the Local Info category is selected.**

4. **In the Site Name text box, type a name for your site.**

   You can call your site whatever you like; this name is used only to help you keep track of your sites in Dreamweaver. Many people work on more than one Web site, and the name you enter here is the name you'll choose from the drop-down list in the Files panel or the Manage Sites dialog box. In the example shown in Figure 14-7, I named the new site `myContacts`.

5. **Click the Browse icon (which looks like a file folder) next to the Local Root Folder text box and browse your hard drive to locate the www-root folder where you saved the files for your dynamic site.**

   If you haven't copied the database and any other files you'll be using in your site into the wwwroot folder yet, exit the Site Definition dialog box, copy the files into the wwwroot folder, and start these steps over from the beginning.

6. **Specify the Default Images Folder by entering the location or using the Browse icon (which looks like a file folder) to locate it.**

   This works just like the previous step, you simply want to browse to the images folder and select it so that Dreamweaver can identify the location. You can create a new folder for your images when you select it, but again, this folder must be located within the wwwroot folder.

7. **For Links Relative To, choose Site root, as you see in Figure 14-7.**

   This setting controls how the path is set in links. When you're working with dynamic content, Site Root is the best option.

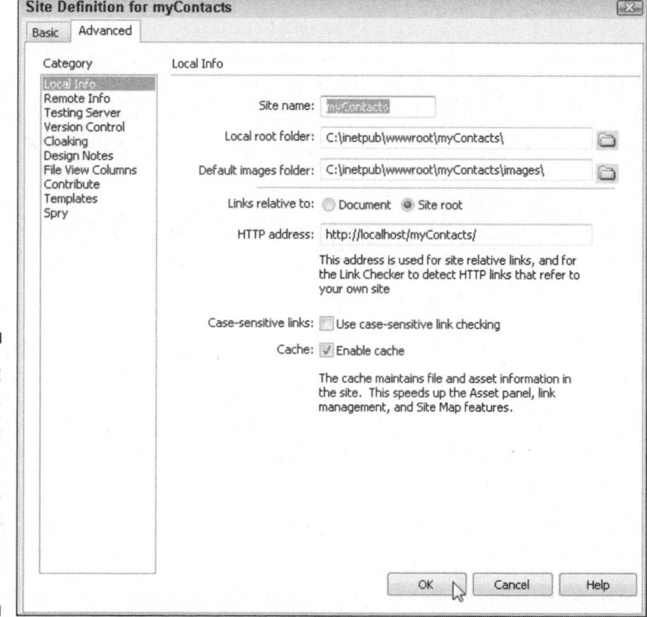

Figure 14-7: When working with dynamic content, set Links Relative To to Site Root.

8. **In the HTTP Address text box, type the URL of your local Web server.**

   On most computers, if you're using IIS, the local URL for the Web server is `http://localhost` followed by the name of your root site folder. In this example, you'd enter **http://localhost/myContacts**, as shown in Figure 14-7.

9. **Select the Enable Cache option.**

   Dreamweaver creates a local cache of your site to quickly reference the location of files in your site. The local cache speeds up many site management features of the program and takes only a few seconds to create.

10. **Click the Testing Server category on the left side of the dialog box, as shown in Figure 14-8.**

    The Testing Server options are opened in the Site Definition dialog box.

11. **From the Server Model drop-down list, choose the server technology you're using for your site.**

    In this example, I'm using ASP JavaScript, as shown in Figure 14-8. You'll find a complete list of the technologies supported by Dreamweaver in this drop-down list.

12. **From the Access drop-down list, choose Local/Network.**

    Again, I'm assuming that you're testing and developing your site on your local drive or on a local area network.

13. **Click the Browse button (which looks like a folder) and then locate and select the wwwroot folder.**

    If you're using a different server technology, such as ColdFusion, the root folder may be in a different location.

14. **Enter the URL for the local Web server in the URL Prefix field.**

    As shown in Figure 14-8, in this example, the URL is the same as the URL entered into the Local Info settings, `http://localhost/myContacts/`.

15. **Click OK to close the Site Definition dialog box and save your settings.**

    If the folder you selected as your local site folder already contains files or folders, they're automatically cached and all the files and folders in your site are displayed in the Files panel.

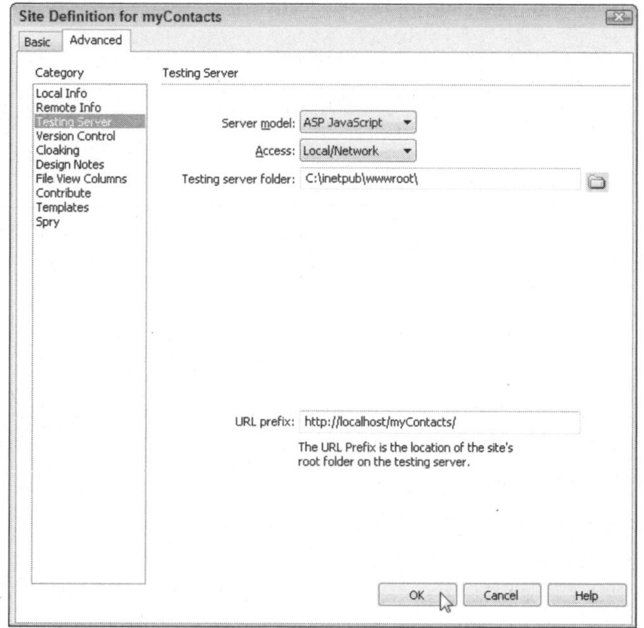

Figure 14-8: Specify the server model and other settings in the Testing Server category.

To establish a connection to a data source in Dreamweaver, make sure you've completed all the steps in the previous three sections and then follow these steps:

1. **Choose File➪New.**

   The New Document dialog box opens, as shown in Figure 14-9.

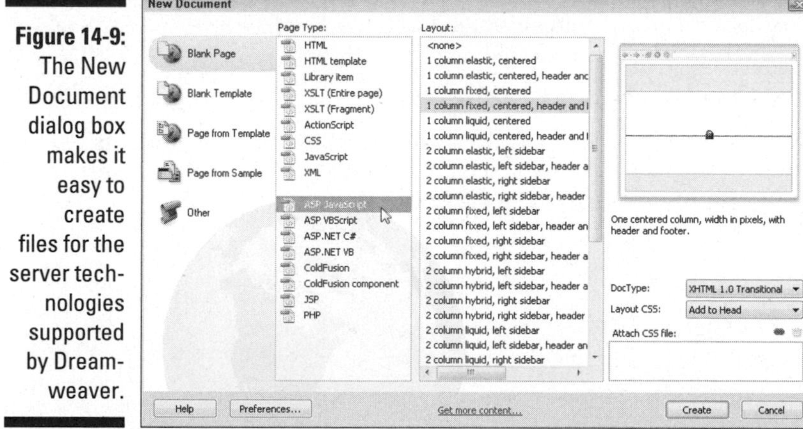

Figure 14-9: The New Document dialog box makes it easy to create files for the server technologies supported by Dreamweaver.

2. **Choose the Blank Page icon from the left.**
3. **In the Page Type list, click ASP JavaScript.**

   If you're working with a different server technology, such as ColdFusion, make sure you choose the corresponding page type.
4. **Under Layout, choose a layout option.**

   For this example, I choose the CSS Layout 1 Column Fixed, Centered, Header, and Footer.
5. **Click Create to automatically create a new page and close the New Document dialog box.**
6. **Choose File⇨Save, name the file, and save it in your root folder.**

   Because this will be the main page of my ASP site, I named the file `index.asp`.
7. **With your new page open, choose Window⇨Databases to open the Databases panel, as shown in Figure 14-10.**

   If the Databases panel is already open in the workspace, you can simply double-click to open the panel and then click the Databases tab.
8. **Click the plus sign (+) at the top of the Databases panel and select Custom Connection String from the list, as shown in Figure 14-10.**

   The Custom Connection String dialog box opens (see Figure 14-11).

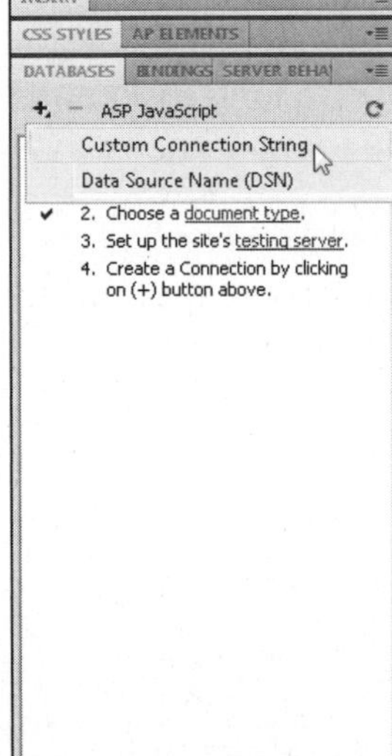

Figure 14-10: The Custom Connection String settings are available from the Databases panel.

9. **Enter the name for the new connection.**

   In this example, I entered **myContacts**. You can call the connection anything you like, but it's best not to use spaces or special characters in the name.

10. **Type the connection string (see Figure 14-11).**

    This part gets a little tricky depending on which technology you're using. If you're using ColdFusion, you can use the Browser button and simply locate the database file in your local root folder. ASP.NET has a similar feature, but with some of the technology options, such as ASP, which I'm using in this example, you need to type in the string manually based on the data source you're using and the location of your root folder.

    For this example, I'm using the Microsoft Access driver installed on my computer and an MS Access database at `c:\Inetpub\wwwroot\myContacts\contacts.mdb` with the appropriate permissions set in Windows. With this as the case, I typed the following into the box exactly as you see it here (make sure to include the space between Data and Source, the quote marks, and the semicolon at the end):

    ```
    "Provider=Microsoft.Jet.OLEDB.4.0;Data Source=c:\Inetpub\wwwroot\
             myContacts\contacts.mdb;"
    ```

    If you're using another database option, alter this string accordingly.

11. **Click the Test button.**

    A pop-up message appears, letting you know that the connection was made successfully, and your database is now listed in the Databases panel. If the connection isn't successful, review the string carefully for typos.

    When Dreamweaver creates the connect, it also creates a Connections folder, which is displayed in the Files panel. The Connections folder contains an ASP file with the connection information for the database. Again, if you're using another technology, this file has a different name and extension. Dreamweaver automatically references this file on any page you create that uses this database connection, saving you from inserting it every time.

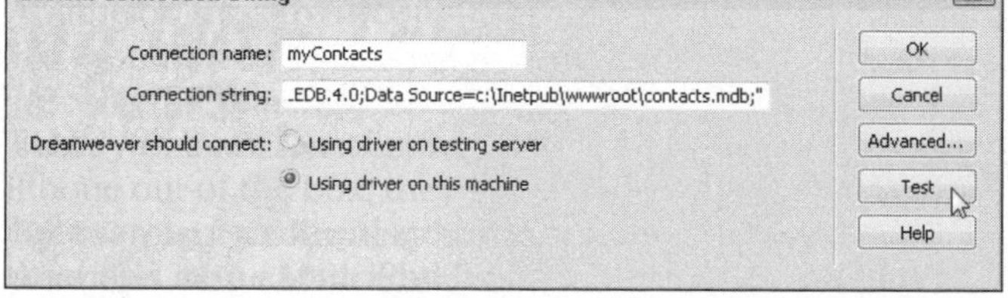

Figure 14-11: The Custom Connection String dialog box.

The ASP files in the Connections folder store necessary information that makes your page work correctly with the database. Make sure that you upload this folder when you upload your site files to the server. Also note that if your Web server is configured differently than your hard drive, you may need to adjust this connection string to work properly on your Web server. Check with your system administrator or hosting service about where database files need to be stored and how connection strings need to be set up on your server.

If your connection fails, check your Custom Connection String again and check the URL prefix for the application server. You can also check the Dreamweaver Help Index for other troubleshooting tips.

Now you're ready to build a dynamic Web site. In Chapters 15, you can start putting these great Dreamweaver features to use by adding content from this database to a Web page.

Setting up Dreamweaver for Mac users

Setting up a data connection on a Mac is a little more complicated because you can't run one of Dreamweaver's support Web servers or application servers locally unless you're running OS X; you must connect to a remote server. Ideally, you can connect your Mac to an NT server with permission to browse the Mac. After you're networked, make the data connection. Dreamweaver includes information in its Help files that specifically covers this process for Mac users.

OS X users can alternatively download Apache's HTTP server from `http://httpd.apache.org`.

Chapter 15

Bringing Data into the Mix

In This Chapter

- Taking a look at the panels
- Covering the recordset basics
- Getting dynamic with your data
- Creating master-detail page sets
- Looking at more ways to use database-driven sites

If you've never used the dynamic development capabilities of Dreamweaver, get familiar with the windows and inspectors covered at the beginning of this chapter before you start creating your first project. In the rest of this chapter, you find out how these elements work together to create a Web site with dynamic features.

For the purpose of illustration, I use a simple Contacts database file, created with Microsoft Access, that features information about a few people — names, addresses, and pictures. If your site features another type of data, such as product descriptions or articles, don't worry — you'll add product names and descriptions to a Web page in much the same way I add names and titles from this Contacts database. Consider this a simple introduction to Dreamweaver's dynamic site features and remember that you can use these same steps to create any kind of dynamic Web site.

Make sure your test server is running and, because this chapter assumes that you're using Internet Information Server (IIS) or Peer Web Services (PSW) for Windows, make sure that you save all the pages as ASP pages (`filename.asp`) so that the server parses the code correctly. If you haven't already set up the application server and established a connection to your database in Dreamweaver, go to Chapter 14 and follow the instructions for these crucial preliminary steps before you do the exercises in this chapter.

Exploring the Panels

In Dreamweaver, the most fundamental elements of creating a dynamic Web site are in the Application panel, which includes the Databases, Bindings, Components, and Server Behaviors panels. In this section, I introduce you to these panels to give you an overview of how these panels work together to help you create a dynamic site.

The Databases panel

The Databases panel lets you look at the databases on your application server. In the Databases panel, you can view your entire database structure within Dreamweaver — tables, fields, views, and stored procedures — without needing to use separate database software.

You can find the Databases panel by choosing Window⇨Databases.

In Figure 15-1, you see that a connection has been established to the Contacts database and that you can view all the fields in that database by clicking the plus (+) sign next to Contacts.

If you have not yet established a connection to a database, go to Chapter 14 where you find instructions for creating a connection with a Custom Connection String using the Databases panel.

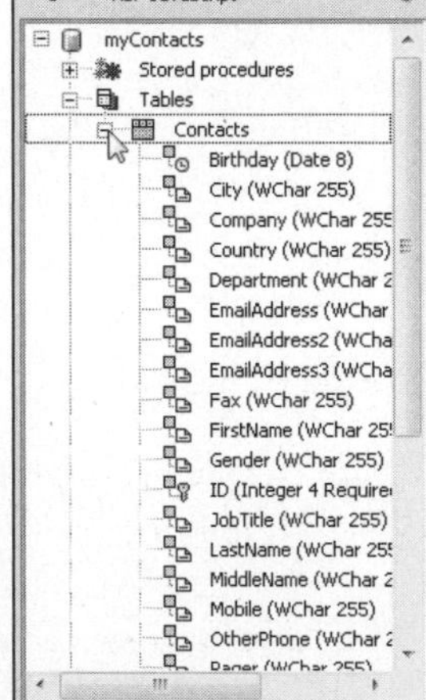

Figure 15-1: The Databases panel displaying the contents of the Contacts database.

The Bindings panel

The Bindings panel enables you to add and remove dynamic content data sources from your document. The number and kinds of available data sources can vary depending on whether you use ASP, JSP, or any other server technology. A *data source* is where you get information to use on your dynamic Web page. An example of a data source is a recordset from a database, which you explore further in the next few sections of this chapter. A *recordset* is used to hold a collection of data from a database. After you create a recordset, the data can be displayed on a Web page.

If you don't see the Bindings panel, you can open it by choosing Window➪Bindings.

With the Bindings panel, you can access data sources in several ways. You can find out what data source objects you have available by clicking the plus sign (+) in the Bindings panel to display the Add Bindings pop-up menu (see Figure 15-2).

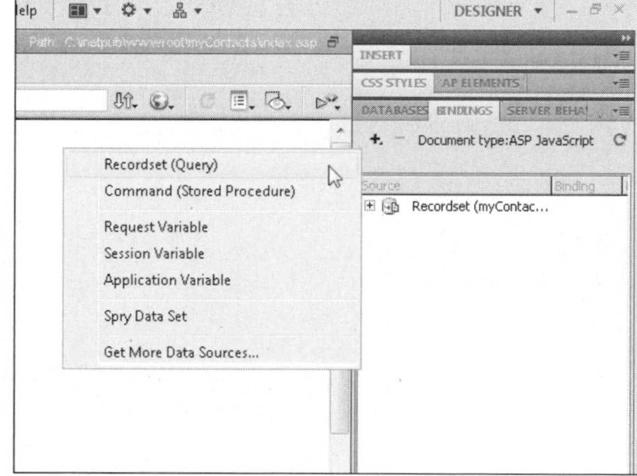

Figure 15-2: The Add Bindings panel and its pop-up menu.

The Add Bindings pop-up menu has the following options:

- **Recordset (Query):** A recordset stores data from your database for use on a page or set of pages. I explain recordsets in more detail later in this chapter.
- **Command (Stored Procedure):** *Commands,* or *stored procedures,* are reusable database items that contain SQL (Structured Query Language)

code and are commonly used to modify a database (insert, update, or delete records).

- **Request Variable:** Commonly used wherever a search is involved, a *request variable* carries information from one page to another. When you use a form to submit data to another page, a request variable is created.
- **Session Variable:** *Session variables* store and display information for the duration of a user's *session* (or visit). A different session is created on the server for each user and is kept in use either for a set period of time or until a specific action on the site terminates the session (such as a logging out).
- **Application Variable:** *Application variables* store and display information that must be present for all users and is constant throughout the lifetime of an application. These types of variables are commonly used for page counters or date and time counters. Application variables are available only for ASP and ColdFusion pages, not for PHP and JSP.
- **Spry Data Set:** *Spry data sets* link existing XML files to display with any of the various Spry widgets.
- **Get More Data Sources:** Use this option to open Dreamweaver Exchange in your browser. You can use Exchange to download extensions for Dreamweaver. You find instructions for downloading and installing extensions in Chapter 10.

The Server Behaviors panel

Server behaviors are server-side scripts that perform some type of action. Through the Server Behaviors panel, you can add server-side scripts, such as user authentication and record navigation, to your pages. Server behaviors available to you vary depending on the server technology you use.

You can get to the Server Behaviors panel by choosing Window⇨Server Behaviors.

You can view the available server behaviors by clicking the plus sign (+) in the Server Behaviors panel to get the Server Behaviors pop-up menu (see Figure 15-3).

The Server Behaviors pop-up menu has the following options:

- **Recordset (Query):** A *recordset* stores data from your database for use on a page or set of pages. I explain recordsets in more detail later in this chapter.
- **Command:** *Commands* are reusable database items that contain SQL code and are commonly used to modify a database (insert, update, or delete records).

- **Repeat Region:** This server object displays multiple records on a page. Repeat Region is most commonly used on HTML tables or HTML table rows. You can find out more about this behavior later in this chapter.
- **Recordset Paging:** If you have to display a large number of records and want them to appear a page at a time, this set of behaviors allows you to navigate from page to page or from record to record.
- **Show Region:** With this set of server behaviors, you can show or hide record navigation based on the records displayed. For instance, if you have Next and Previous links on the bottom of every page and your user is on the first page or first record of the recordset, you can set a behavior to display only the Next link. The same is true if the user is on the last page or record — you can set the behavior to hide the Next link and display only the Previous link.
- **Dynamic Text:** This option enables you to display information from your recordset anywhere on the page.
- **Go to Detail Page:** With this behavior, you can link each record in your repeated region to a detail page for that particular record. The behavior also tells the detail page which record's information to display.
- **Go to Related Page:** You can use this behavior to link a particular dynamic page to another page that contains related information, passing the parameters of the first page to the related page.

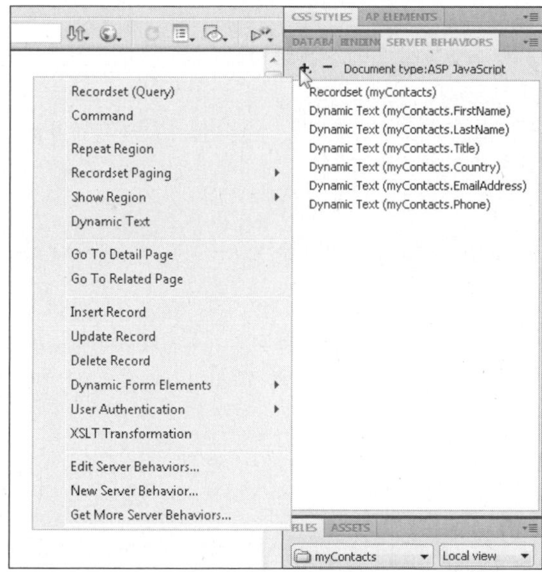

Figure 15-3: The Server Behaviors panel and its pop-up menu.

- **Insert Record:** Use this behavior on a page to add new records to a database via a Web browser.
- **Update Record:** Use this behavior on a page to update existing records in a database via a Web browser.
- **Delete Record:** Use this behavior on a page to permanently delete a record from a database via a Web browser.
- **Dynamic Form Elements:** This set of server behaviors turns text fields, list or menu fields, radio buttons, or check boxes into dynamic form elements, which you can set to retrieve and display particular information from a recordset.
- **User Authentication:** The User Authentication set of behaviors allows you to log in a user, log out a user, check a username against the information in your database, and restrict access to a page.
- **XSLT Transformation:** Extensible Stylesheet Language Transformation (XSLT) is a language that displays XML data on a Web page after transforming it into HTML.
- **Edit Server Behaviors:** Use this option to customize or remove existing server behaviors. Unless you're very comfortable with coding or SQL, I advise you to not mess with this option. (If you're curious about SQL, see *SQL For Dummies,* 6th Edition, by Allen G. Taylor; Wiley Publishing, Inc.)
- **New Server Behavior:** Use this option to create new server behaviors and add them to the list of existing behaviors. Again, this option is for more advanced users who are comfortable with coding.
- **Get More Server Behaviors:** Use this option to open Dreamweaver Exchange in your browser. You can use Exchange to download extensions for Dreamweaver. You find instructions for downloading and installing extensions in Chapter 10.

The Components panel

Components are reusable bits of code that you can create and insert directly into your pages. To open the Components panel, choose Window➪Components. In Dreamweaver, you can create components for JSP, ColdFusion, and ASP.NET pages to use (or *consume*) Web services, display information, or for any other use that you can imagine.

Creating a Recordset

A *recordset* holds data from your database for use on a page or set of pages. A *query* gathers information from a database to be used on a page, selecting only the records matching the fields and conditions of the particular query.

The queries for a recordset are built with SQL, but you don't need to know SQL to get the job done. Dreamweaver writes it all for you.

All you really need to understand is that you can't add data from your database to your Web pages until you've created a recordset.

Before you can create a recordset, you must first connect to a database. Chapter 14 includes instructions for creating a Custom Connection String, which you must do before you can create a recordset.

To define a recordset in Dreamweaver:

1. **Open the ASP page that will use the recordset.**
2. **In the Bindings panel, click the plus sign and select Recordset (Query).**

   You see the Recordset dialog box.
3. **In the Name box, enter a name for your recordset.**

   Usually, adding *rs* to the beginning of the name is recommended to distinguish it as a recordset in your code, but it isn't necessary. I used *myContacts,* as shown in Figure 15-4.
4. **In the Connection drop-down list, select your connection.**

   This list includes any data connections defined from the Databases panel. Chapter 14 explains how to create a connection.
5. **In the Table drop-down list, choose a database table where the data for your recordset will be collected.**

   You can select all the columns or only specific columns of data to be displayed.
6. **(Optional) If you want the available information to show only records that meet specific criteria, select a filter in the Filter area.**
7. **(Optional) If you want to change the sort order of the displayed records, use the Sort drop-down list to specify the field by which you want the records sorted (Name, Phone Number, and so on) and then specify Ascending or Descending.**

   If you want to tweak the results further and you feel comfortable working with SQL, you can click the Advanced button to edit the SQL statement directly.
8. **To test the connection to the database, click the Test button.**

   You can find the Databases panel by choosing Window➪Databases. To create more complicated recordsets, click the Advanced button and you can create SQL statements directly.

   If the test is successful, you see a window with the data in the recordset

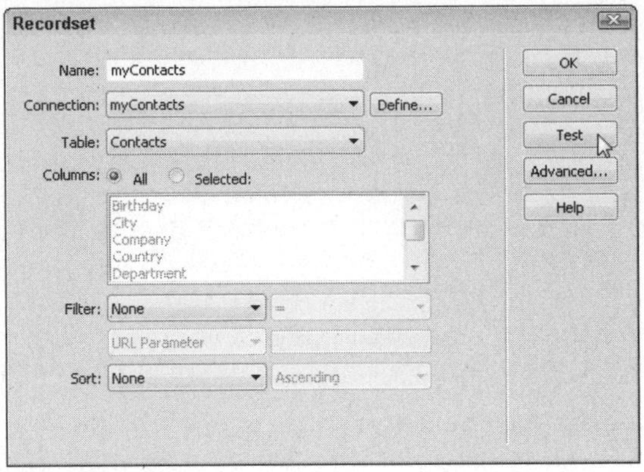

Figure 15-4: The Recordset dialog box.

9. **Click OK to close the Test screen.**
10. **Click OK to complete the Recordset dialog box.**

    The Bindings panel appears displaying the contents of the recordset. You can expand it by clicking the plus sign next to the recordset, as shown in Figure 15-5.

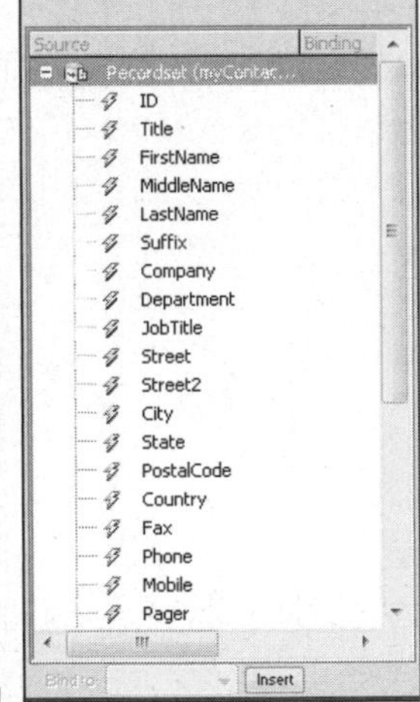

Figure 15-5: The myContacts recordset appears in the Bindings panel.

Using a Recordset on Your Page

After you create a recordset, you can place the information on your page as you want. For this example, I designed a basic page with a table that has room to list the name, title, country, e-mail address, and phone number of each contact in the database. In Figure 15-6, you see my simple page with headings across the top of the table, but no content displayed in the table cells.

After you set up the document the way you want it, you can drag and drop each data source from the recordset to the place on the page where you want the data displayed. To add data from the recordset to your Web page, follow these steps:

1. **From the Bindings panel, select your first data source, such as First Name, and drag it onto your page, dropping it where you want it to go.**

   The name of the dynamic text appears inside curly brackets, as shown in Figure 15-7.

   You can format dynamic text just as you would format any other text on the page.

2. **Test the result by clicking the Live View button.**

   The first record of your database appears in place of the dynamic text, as shown in Figure 15-8.

To display more than just the first record in a Web page, define and repeat a region, which you find out how to do in the next sections.

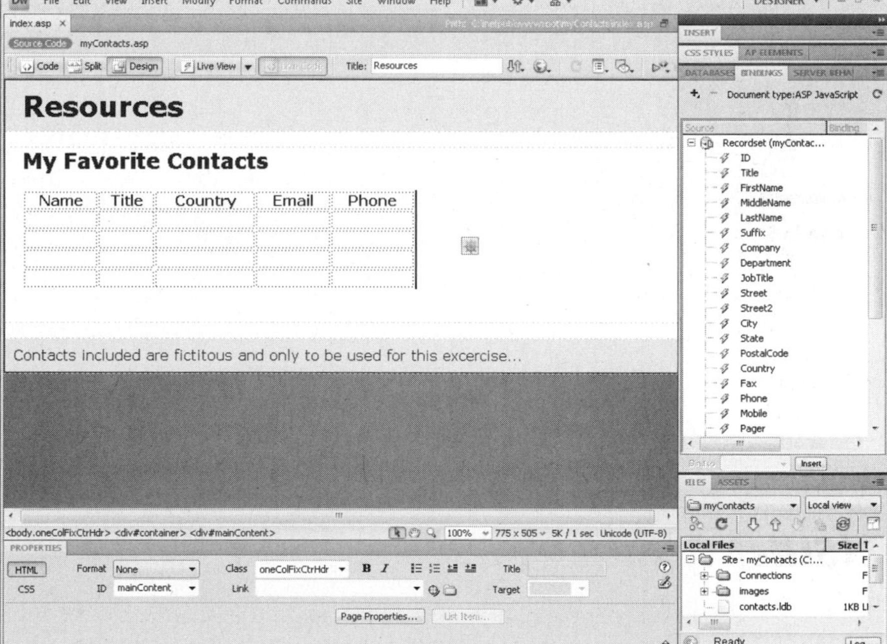

Figure 15-6: I created a page using CSS to create the layout and a Table to display the data with the contact information from my database.

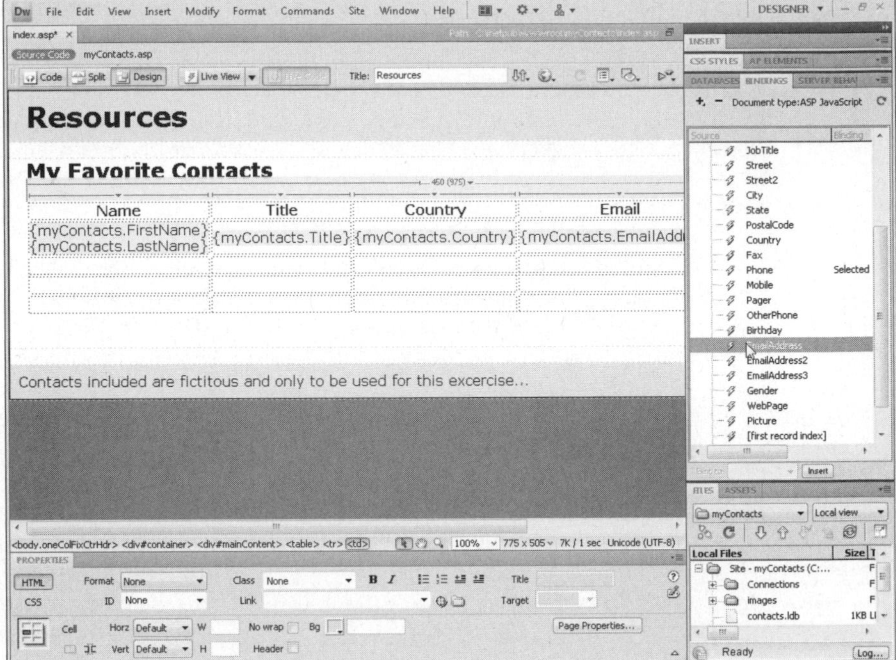

Figure 15-7: The dynamic text is inserted and formatted.

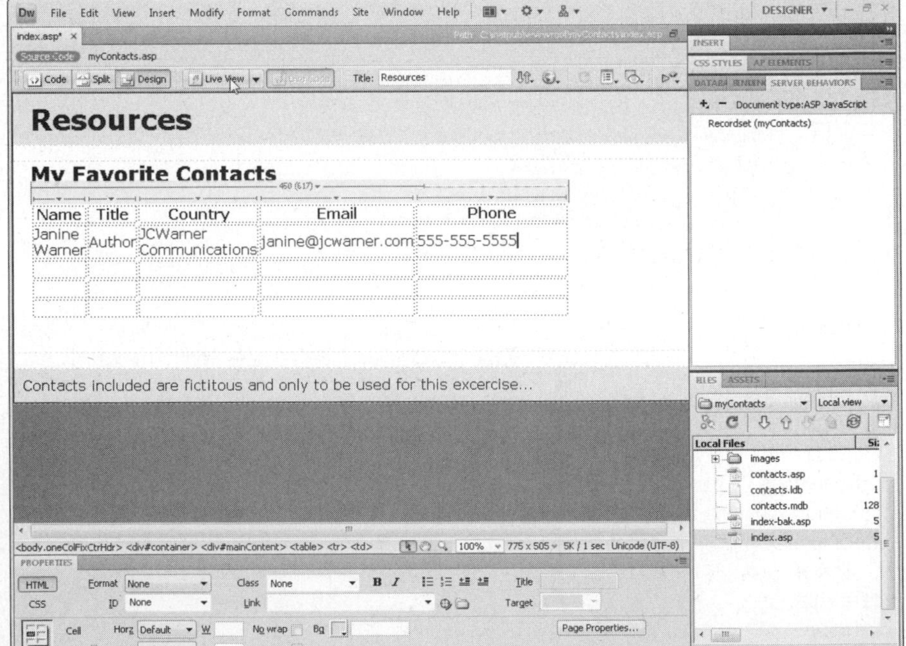

Figure 15-8: The information from the first record in your database replaces the data source code.

Repeating a Region

One of the greatest advantages of creating a dynamic site like this is the ability to display any combination of content from more than one record at a time on a page. You can do this by applying a server behavior to your region. *Server behaviors* are code blocks that let you add dynamic capabilities to your Web site.

A *region* is any area of a page that displays information from a database on your page. After you define your region, you can apply a Repeat Region server behavior, which causes that area to be written to the page over and over, displaying every record, or as many records as you tell it to on as many pages as needed to display all the contents of the database (or whatever subset of the database you want displayed). The Repeat Region is most commonly used on HTML tables or table rows.

To add a Repeat Region server behavior to your page:

1. **Select the area on your page that you want to define as a region.**
2. **Click the Server Behaviors panel, click the plus sign (+), and select Repeat Region from the menu that appears (see Figure 15-9).**

   The Repeat Region dialog box appears (see Figure 15-10).

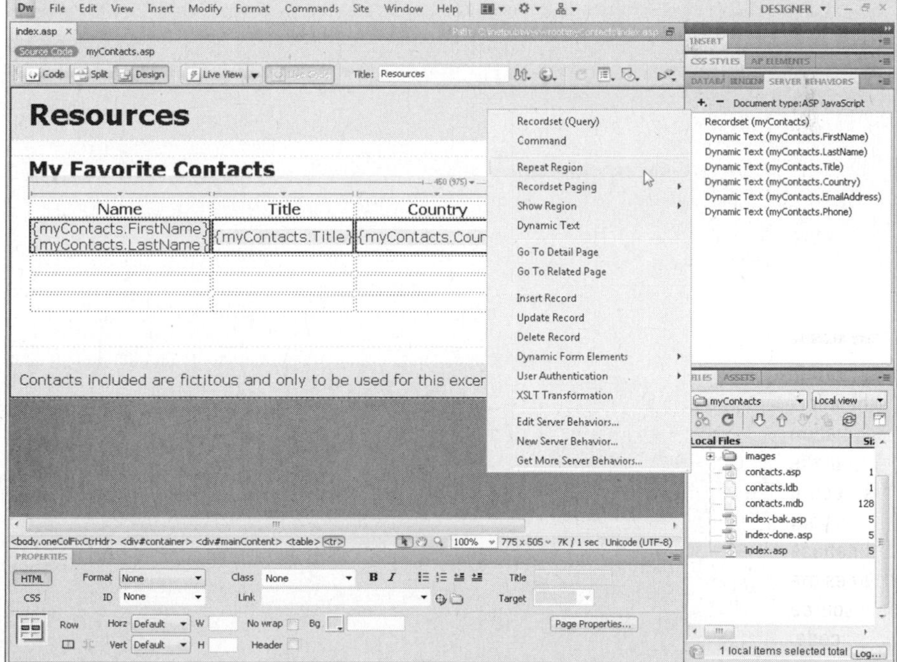

Figure 15-9: To define a region, choose the Repeat Region option from the Server Behaviors panel.

3. **Select the number of records that you want to appear on the page and then click OK (see Figure 15-10).**

   In this example, I chose to have ten records displayed on the page. If you follow the steps in the section "Adding Navigation to a Dynamic Page," later in this chapter, you can set up your pages to automatically display any number of records per page and then to automatically link to the next and previous pages as pages are created until all the records in the database are displayed.

4. **Click the Live View button to see the results.**

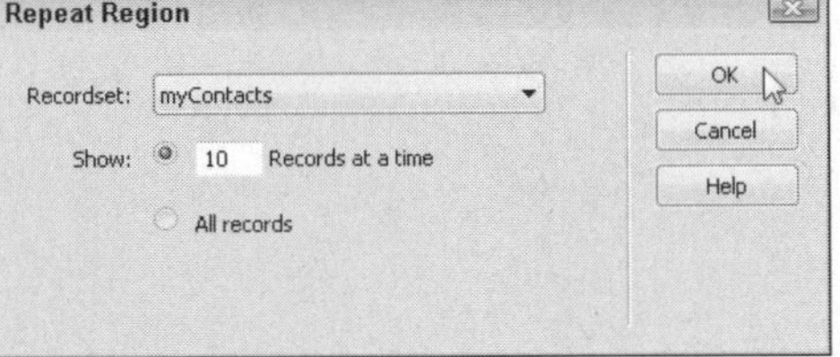

Figure 15-10: The Repeat Region dialog box.

Adding a Dynamic Image

If your database only contains text, the preceding section covers all that you need to do to display content on your pages. But if you're like most Web designers, you probably want to include photos of the people in your Contacts database or images of each product. To do that, you need to do a little prep work and then bind an image to a recordset so that you can add it to the page.

Preparing to add an image

Before you bind an image so you can add it dynamically, take care of these preliminary steps:

1. **Make sure that you have a field for each record in your database that lists the actual path of the image for that record.**

   For example, if your images reside in an images folder, one level above your dynamic page, enter the following in the image field in your database: **images/*imagename.gif***, remembering to replace the *imagename.gif* part with the actual filename for each image.

2. **Make sure your images are in your site root folder in your wwwroot folder or, if you're testing your work on a remote server, make sure that you've uploaded the images to the root folder on the server.**

3. **Place a placeholder image in the spot where you want an image to appear for all the records.**

You can use any of the images in your image folder as a placeholder or choose Insert➪Image Object➪Image Placeholder to use the built-in image placeholder.

Binding the image

After you insert the placeholder image, you can bind images in two easy ways — with the Bindings panel or the Property inspector.

Follow these steps to bind images with the Bindings panel:

1. **Select your placeholder image in the open document.**
2. **Click the plus sign (+) to expand your recordset. (On a Mac, click the triangle.)**
3. **Select the Picture field in your recordset that contains the name of the image file.**
4. **Click the Bind button at the bottom of the Bindings panel.**

   The image changes to a tree with a lightning bolt along its side, and the Src field is automatically filled in the Property inspector.

After an image is bound, the Bind button changes to the Unbind button, as shown in Figure 15-11.

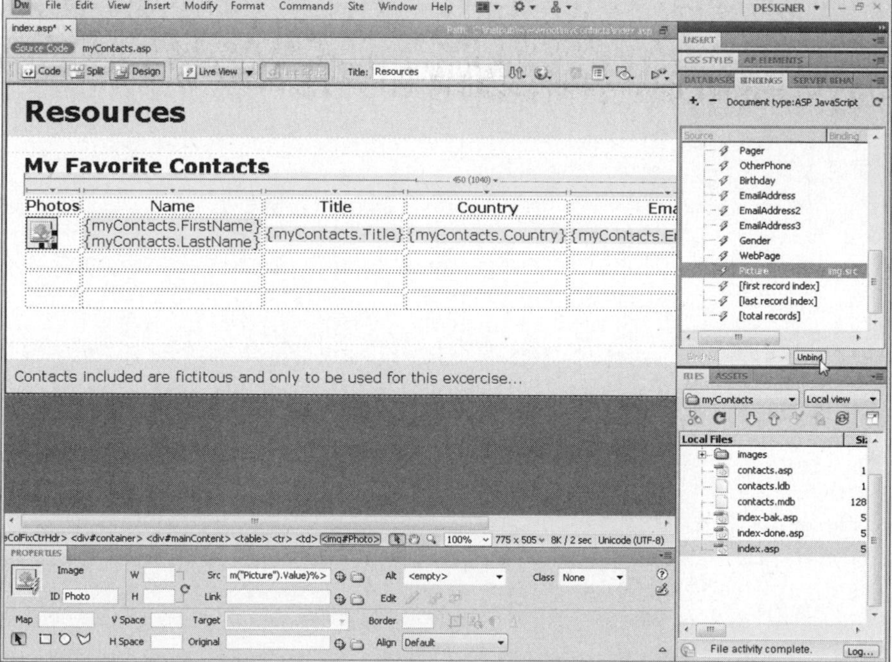

Figure 15-11: Use the Bindings panel to bind an image field to an image placeholder in your Web page.

Follow these steps to bind images with the Property inspector:

1. **Click to select the placeholder image in the open document.**
2. **In the Property inspector, click the Browse button (which looks like a folder) next to the Src field.**

   The Select Image Source dialog box appears.
3. **At the very top of the Select File Name From section, click the radio button to select the Data Sources option, as shown in Figure 15-12.**

   The Recordset appears in the Field area (see Figure 15-12).
4. **Click to select the field that contains your image information.**

   Dreamweaver automatically fills in the URL field at the bottom of the Select Image Source dialog box.
5. **Click OK.**

   The image changes to a tree with a lightning bolt along its side, and the Src field is automatically filled in the Property inspector.

After performing either of these two methods to bind your images to the page, click the Live View button to check the results and the images, which are displayed in Dreamweaver.

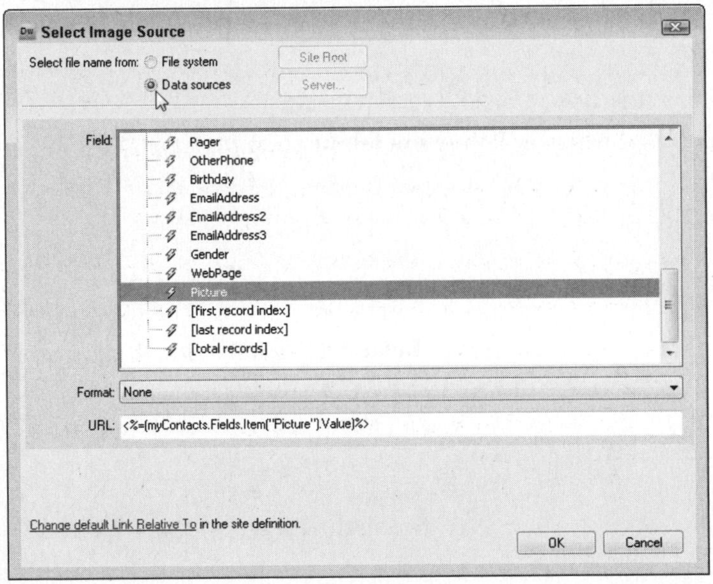

Figure 15-12: The Select Image Source dialog box.

Adding Navigation to a Dynamic Page

If your database contains many records, you'll likely want to show only a few records per page so that you don't overwhelm the user. You'll probably also want to create a series of pages, linked together, so that it's easy for visitors to view all the records by clicking through a series of pages.

To help you easily automate the creation of a series of pages like this, the Server Behaviors panel includes features you can use to add navigation to your pages so that visitors can move forward or backward through all the pages that display the records from your database.

The first step is to set up a Repeat Region, which I cover in the section, "Repeating a Region," earlier in this chapter. Add navigation only if you've set up the Repeat Region and you want have enough data to warrant creating multiple pages with navigation that will help users move through multiple pages. Assuming you have more records than you want on each page, you can add button images or text links at the bottom of each page to provide navigation, such as Previous Page and Next Page links. With the buttons in place, you can activate them by using the Server Behaviors panel.

To add Next and Previous links, follow these steps:

1. **Add text with the words you want to use for your links to the page with the Repeat Regions.**

   For this example, I simply typed in text, separated by the tilde button, like this: First ~ Previous ~ Next ~ Last, as shown in Figure 15-13.

2. **Click the Server Behaviors tab to open the Server Behaviors panel.**

   Alternatively, you can open the Server Behaviors panel by choosing Window➪Server Behaviors from the main menu.

3. **Click and drag to select the text you want to serve as a link.**

   In this example, as shown in Figure 15-13, I've selected Previous.

4. **At the top of the Server Behaviors panel, click the plus sign (+) and select Recordset Paging from the menu.**

5. **From the Recordset Paging submenu, choose the appropriate navigation option.**

   In the example shown in Figure 15-13, you can see that I've selected the text Previous and am applying the Recordset Paging option, Move to Previous Record.

   The Move to Record dialog box appears and, in most cases, you can just click OK because Dreamweaver automatically fills in the fields based on the option you selected.

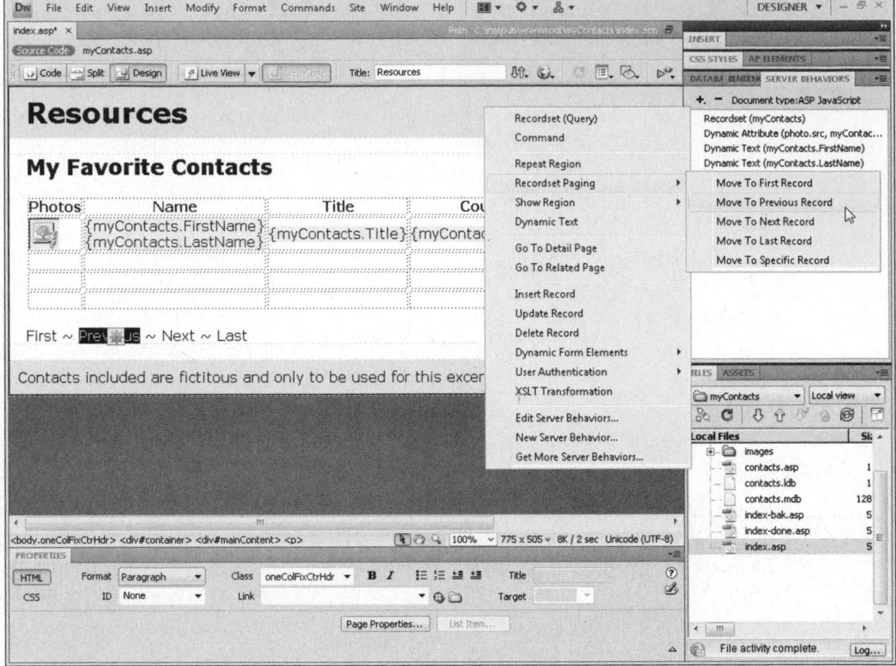

Figure 15-13: For each link option, select Recordset Paging and choose the corresponding navigation option.

6. **Follow Steps 1–5 for each navigation link.**

7. **Choose File⇨Preview in Browser to test the links.**

   Assuming you have your test server set up properly (see Chapter 14 for instructions), the page displays in a browser with the dynamic content and links in place, and you can page through your records.

That's a pretty nifty trick. Did you notice that on the first page, the Previous Page button or link still appears, even though there's no previous page? Not to worry — a server behavior tells the navigation button when to show up:

1. **Click the Previous Page button in the Document window to select it.**

2. **Click the plus sign (+) in the Server Behaviors panel and then choose Show Region from the menu.**

3. **If you're working with the Previous Page button, choose Show Region if Not First Record. If you're working with the Next Page button, choose Show Region if Not Last Record.**

   The Show Region dialog box appears. The Move to Record dialog box appears and, in most cases, you can just click OK because Dreamweaver automatically fills in the fields based on the option you selected.

4. **Choose File⇨Preview in Browser to display your pages and test these new dynamic features.**

   Notice that now when you're on the first page of records, the Previous Page button doesn't appear; when you're on the last page, the Next Page button doesn't appear.

Now that you know how to add navigation to your recordsets, you can get fancy and add buttons to go to the first or last record. So if you have, say, 100 pages of records, you can jump from page 1 to page 100 without clicking Previous Page or Next Page through countless other pages of records. The server behaviors for those two are Move to Record⇨Move to First Record and Move to Record⇨Move to Last Record. Useful stuff to know.

Creating a Master-Detail Page Set

A *master* page displays a list of records and a link for each record. When a user clicks a particular link, a detail page appears with more information about that record.

Here are the two types of master pages:

- **A list of records determined by you:** Users can't alter the list of records on this page; they can only click to view more information about those records displayed.
- **A dynamically-created master page:** A good example of this type of master page is a search results page that appears when a user performs a search for specific records.

A *detail* page is the page that appears when a user clicks a particular link from a master page. This page can either display more information about a record (such as providing a more detailed description of a product in an online catalog), or it can be set up for administrative purposes to provide a way for users to update or delete a record.

Systems like these that enable users to add or remove records are great ways to make it easy for many people to update a Web site, but they're generally restricted to users who have been given password access to a protected section of a site.

Creating a master-detail page requires just a few clicks of the mouse. Using the functions described earlier in this chapter, create a page that you will use to list all your contacts, and name it something like `contacts.asp`. This is your master page. Next, create the page you use as the detail page in the same way and call it something like `contactDetails.asp`. Now you're ready to create the master-detail page set:

1. **Open the `contacts.asp` page you created as the master page and choose Insert➪Data Objects➪Master Detail Page Set.**

   The Insert Master-Detail Page Set dialog box opens (see Figure 15-14). The top part of the dialog box is where you define the properties of the master page. The bottom part is where you define the detail page.

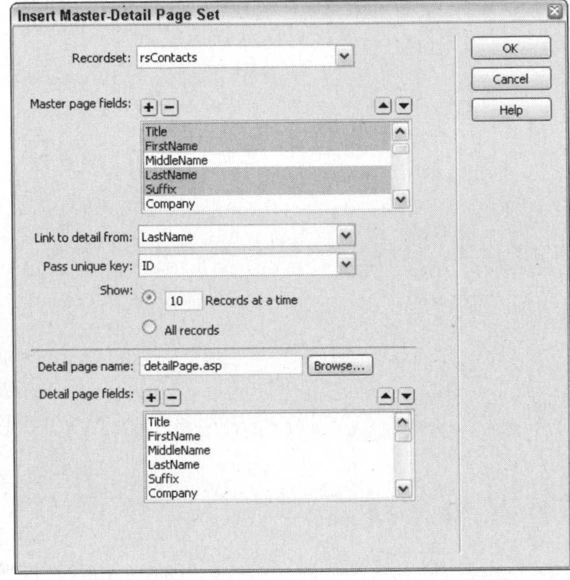

Figure 15-14: The Insert Master-Detail Page Set dialog box.

2. **In the Recordset drop-down list, select the recordset that you use for your master page.**
3. **Next to Master Page Fields, use the plus sign (+) and minus sign (–), respectively, to add or remove fields from the master page.**
4. **Select the field from which you want to provide a link to the detail page for each record.**

   For example, if you list a bunch of contacts, you can use each contact's name as a link to its detail.

5. **In the Pass Unique Key drop-down list, the default is usually correct; if it isn't, select the unique identifier that you want to pass on to the detail page.**
6. **Select the number of records you want to show at one time on the master page.**

   Showing only a partial listing is okay because you can add navigation to view more records.

7. **In the Detail Page Name box, type the filename for the detail page or click the Browse button to search for the file.**
8. **Just as with the Master Page Fields section, use the plus and minus signs (respectively) to add or remove fields that you want or don't want to appear on the detail page.**
9. **Click OK.**

Dreamweaver automatically adds all the necessary recordset information and SQL code for you to begin using your master-detail page set. Everything from navigation to record status is in there.

After you create the master and detail pages, you may want to rearrange and format the fields. (Dreamweaver just plops the stuff onto the pages, creating a generic look.) For example, you can change the column labels to text that has more meaning and is friendlier to your visitors. You can also format the font, color, and size as well as add padding to the table cells and change the order of the columns.

More Ways to Use Database-Driven Sites

This chapter and Chapter 14 were designed to give you a basic introduction to what's involved with creating dynamic Web sites and the range of features you'll find in Dreamweaver that can help make it easier to create dynamic Web pages.

If you've spent much time on the Web, you know there are many other ways to create pages with dynamic data, from shopping carts to blogging tools. Yep, that's right; the same basic concepts illustrated in these two chapters are used to create programs like TypePad or WordPress for blogging or to create elaborate e-commerce sites.

Creating such advanced dynamic features requires far more instruction and experience than I can provide in this book about Dreamweaver, but you should know that you can go far beyond what I've covered here in the world of Web development.

You should also know that you don't need to reinvent the wheel, as they say. Many of the most common dynamic site features, such as shopping carts, can be purchased, or rented, from people and companies who have spent far more time building them than you've probably spent reading this book.

Before you attempt to create your own shopping cart, for example, you might want to consider creating a Web store at Amazon.com and simply linking it to the site you've created in Dreamweaver. Similarly, Google now offers a simple Google Checkout button as well as a more elaborate shopping system. You'll find many other shopping cart and e-commerce systems with just a little searching on the Web.

Similarly, if you want to set up and manage an online publication and expect to have many writers and editors, you may want to consider purchasing a good content management system (CMS). Every blogging program is essentially a CMS, but you'll find content management systems that range from the attractive price of free (for example, `www.drupal.org`), to prices that might surprise you because you can literally spend more than seven figures on a customized, high-end CMS, the likes of which publications like *The New York Times* rely on.

If you're excited about creating your own dynamic Web site, I encourage you to keep learning because there's so much you can do with Dreamweaver. I also want to make sure you know that you can turn to lots of places to find high-end features, such as shopping cards, without creating them all yourself. To help you keep up with the ever-changing range of options out there, I've created a resource guide on my Web site, which I update regularly with cool programs, services, and such. You'll find my resource list as well as many other tips and tutorials at `www.DigitalFamily.com/dreamweaver`.

Part V
The Part of Tens

The 5th Wave By Rich Tennant

In this part . . .

The Part of Tens features Chapter 16 with ten great online resources to help you register a domain name, protect your e-mail address from spammers, and add advanced features to your Web pages, such as detailed traffic tracking and e-commerce features. In Chapter 17, you find ten timesaving tips to help you get the most out of Dreamweaver.

Chapter 16

Ten Resources You May Need

In This Chapter

- Finding domain registration services
- Protecting your e-mail address
- Highlighting your links with pop-ups
- Selling stuff on the Web and tracking your traffic
- Surveying your site visitors
- Creating templates and keeping up with Web standards
- Using Adobe.com and Favicon

Although Dreamweaver is a wonderful tool for creating Web sites, it can't handle everything you need to put a site online. For example, you can't register a domain name using Dreamweaver, and when you're ready to publish your site, you'll need a Web server. I added this chapter to offer you a handy list of resources that can help you finish your site when you need to go beyond the features in Dreamweaver.

Registering a Domain Name

The address for your Web site is its *domain name.* The domain name is what visitors need to know to find your Web site. For example, you can visit my Digital Family Web site at `DigitalFamily.com`.

Even before you start building your Web site, I recommend that you register your own domain name. The process is simple, painless, and costs less than $10 per year, but it can take from a few hours to a few days for the domain registration process to be completed.

You can register any domain name that hasn't already been taken by someone else, and for free you can check to see whether a domain name is already taken. Just visit any domain registrar, such as `www.godaddy.com` or `1and1.com`, and enter the domain name you want into the search field on the main page of the registrar's site. If the name you want is no longer available, most registration services will give you a list of recommended alternatives.

Most domain registration services also provide Web hosting services, but you don't have to host your site at the same place where you register the name. You can set up a Web server anywhere you want and then use the domain management settings at your domain registration services to point your name to the server where your Web site is hosted.

When you enter a domain name into a Web browser, everything before the extension (the `.com`, `.net`, or `.org` part) can be written in uppercase or lowercase, and it will work just fine. However, if you want to go to a specific page within a Web site, such as `www.DigitalFamily.com/videos`, the text that comes after the extension is often case sensitive. Because the part before the `.com` doesn't matter, I find it easier to recognize domain names when they're written with capital letters. So, for example, I use `www.DigitalFamily.com` on my business cards instead of `www.digitalfamily.com`.

Protecting Your E-mail Address from Spammers

Spammers gather millions of e-mail addresses from Web sites every day by collecting e-mail addresses from links on Web pages. It's common practice for Web designers to include an e-mail link to make it easy for visitors to contact them. Unfortunately, those simple e-mail links make it even easier for spammers to gather e-mail addresses automatically.

To help counter this problem, the programmers at AddressMunger.com have come up with a special way of "hiding" e-mail addresses from the automated bots that spammers use. When you add this special code to your Web pages and use AddressMunger to create the e-mail links on your Web pages, your visitors can still e-mail you easily, but spammer's can't read your e-mail address. It's an easy way to cut down on all that spam in your inbox.

Highlighting Links with Pop-Ups

This innovative online service creates a small pop-up preview of any page you link to on your site, like you see in Figure 16-1. You simply sign up (for free) at Snap.com and use their online tool to generate special code you can copy and paste into the code in your Web pages.

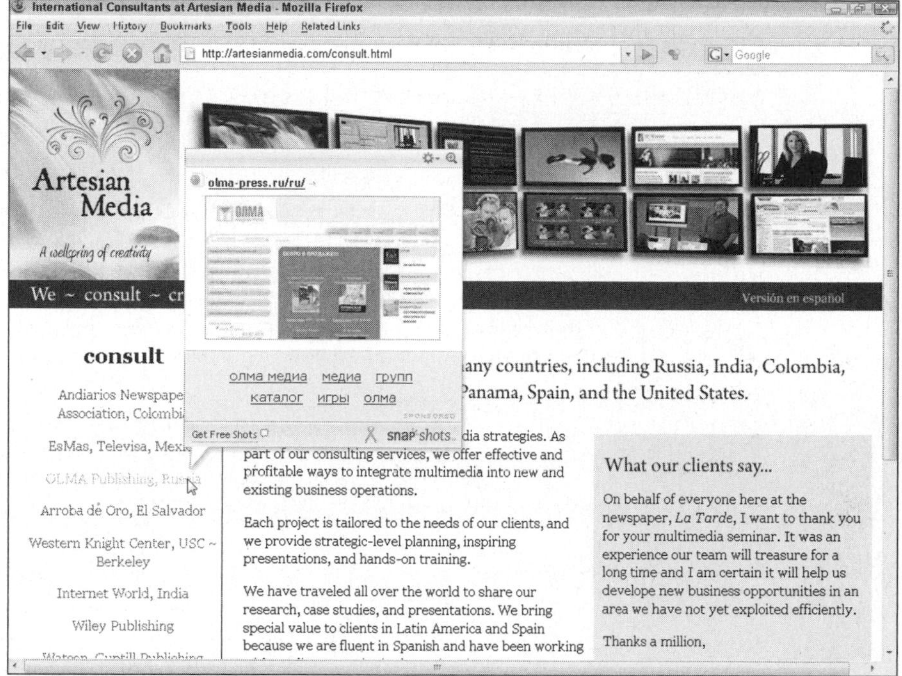

Figure 16-1: You can create links with pop-up previews with Snap.com.

With Snap.com's unique pop-ups, anytime your visitors roll their cursors over a link, a small pop-up window appears with a preview that displays the page or site that you've linked to from your site. It's a great way to give visitors a little more information as they peruse your pages and to highlight the links on your site.

Selling Stuff on the Web

You can sell things online in many ways. As a general rule, I recommend that you start simple and add more complex and expensive options after you know that you'll make money with your site.

At the simple end of the spectrum, you can add a purchase button with the services offered at `www.PayPal.com` or `checkout.google.com`. Moving up in complexity and price, you can create a shopping system at `smallbusiness.yahoo.com/ecommerce`. If you want a more custom solution and the ability to create your own shopping cart, check out the powerful, highly customizable Dreamweaver-compatible programs at `www.WebAssist.com` or `www.cartweaver.com`.

Keeping Track of Traffic

Most Web hosting services provide basic log reports and traffic information, but if you want to know for sure how people are finding your Web site and what they're doing after they get there, consider using a service like Google Analytics, `StatCounter.com` or `WebSTAT.com`.

To use any of these services, set up an account and copy a bit of code from the site into your Web pages. (It's a simple copy-and-paste procedure you can do with code view in Dreamweaver.) StatCounter and WebSTAT then use that bit of code to track your traffic.

Visit any of the three services I mention in this section for a demo and a sample report with all the different kinds of information you can collect, including what search terms someone used to find your site through a search engine. Studying how people use your Web site is one of the best ways to determine how you should continue to develop your content and your design.

If you need instructions for how to copy and paste code from a site like StatCounter or Google Adsense, see the tutorial on my Web site at `www.DigitalFamily.com/dreamweaver`.

Surveying Your Visitors

Want to know what your visitors really think? Ask them. You can create a free, online survey at `SurveyMonkey.com` and link to it from your Web site. SurveyMonkey makes it easy to create the survey using a Web browser and then automatically tallies the results and presents them in a series of reports and pie charts. It's a great way to impress your board of directors at the next annual meeting.

Saving Time with Templates

If you want more predesigned templates than the ones included in Dreamweaver, use one of the many third-party companies that create and (usually) sell their templates over the Web.

Visit `www.dreamweaver-templates.org` for a long list of sites that offer templates for free or for a fee. Just download and open them in Dreamweaver, and you can start building your Web site around these professionally created templates in no time.

Keeping Up with Web Standards at W3.org

If you want to keep up with the latest developments in Web design and make sure you're following standards, there is no better place than `W3.org`, the official Web site of the organization that sets Web standards. You'll find loads of information on this nonprofit site, including the full specification for HTML, CSS, and much more. You can also test your Web pages by entering the URL into the CSS validator at `jigsaw.w3.org/css-validator`, or the MarkUp validator at `validator.w3.org`.

Extending Dreamweaver at Adobe.com

Visit the Dreamweaver Exchange Site at `www.adobe.com/cfusion/exchange/` to find a vast collection of extensions you can use to add behaviors and other features to Dreamweaver. It's easy to install them using the Extensions Manager, which I cover in Chapter 10.

While you're at the site, check out Adobe's growing collection of tutorials, updates, and resources, including the new CSS section, where you'll find the latest in CSS tips, tricks, and workarounds at `www.adobe.com/devnet/dreamweaver`.

Dressing Up the Address Bar with a Favicon

Have you ever wondered how some sites add a custom graphic to the address bar at the top of browsers like Internet Explorer? Google adds a capital *G,* Adobe adds its logo, and you can add an image, too. But first you have to get the image in the right format.

To convert an image into a Favicon, visit `Favicon.com`, where you can upload a graphic and have it converted for free. Then just add that image to the root level of your main site folder, and it automatically displays in the address bar of a browser.

Chapter 17

Ten Timesaving Tips

In This Chapter

- Design for your audience
- Create a consistent design
- Follow the three clicks rule
- Get a head start on your designs
- Split the view
- Design in a flash
- Find functional fonts
- Keep frequently used items handy
- Be prepared for fast updates
- Back it up

All good Web sites grow and evolve. If you start with a strong design and pay close attention to some basic rules about interface, navigation, and style, you'll have a better foundation to build on. The following design ideas and Dreamweaver tips can help you save time as you create Web sites that look great for all your visitors.

Design for Your Audience

No matter how technically sophisticated a Web site is or how great the writing, most people notice the design first. Make sure that you leave plenty of time and budget to develop an appropriate and attractive design for your Web site. The right design is one that best suits your audience — and that may or may not mean lots of fancy graphics and animations.

Think about whom you want to attract to your Web site before you develop the design. A gaming Web site geared toward teenagers should look very different from a Web site with gardening tips for the semiretired or an online investment site for busy professionals.

A great way to find ideas is to visit other sites designed for your target market, even if they don't offer the same content, products, or services. As you consider design ideas, keep in mind your audience's time constraints, attention span, and goals. If you're creating a site for busy professionals, you may want to include a search engine and lists of links that make it easy to go directly to key information. If you're designing an entertainment destination, your audience may be willing to wait a little longer for animation, video, and other interactive features.

Create a Consistent Design

Most Web sites work best and are easiest to navigate when they follow a consistent design theme. Case in point: Most readers take for granted that books don't change their design from page to page, and that newspapers don't change headline fonts and logos from day to day. Indeed, many people would argue that when users say something is "intuitive to use," what they really mean is that it's familiar. Consistency is one of the primary tools used in design to help readers find a site familiar and make it easy to follow a story or a series of navigation elements.

When you lay out Web pages, keep in mind that you want viewers to instantly understand which pieces of information are related to each other and how to move from one area of a Web site to another. Distinguish different kinds of information with the following:

- **Design:** Make sure that similar elements follow the same design parameters, such as type style, banner size, and page background color. Streamlining the number of design elements can also make your site more user-friendly: If you use too many different elements on any single page or even on the same Web site, you risk confusing your viewers.

  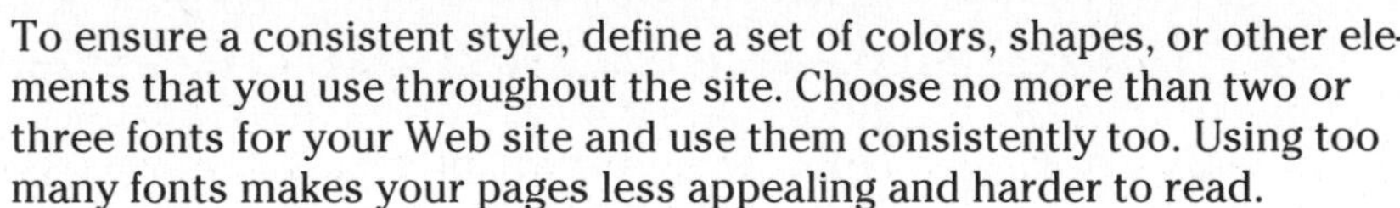

  To ensure a consistent style, define a set of colors, shapes, or other elements that you use throughout the site. Choose no more than two or three fonts for your Web site and use them consistently too. Using too many fonts makes your pages less appealing and harder to read.

  Use a new font, color, or other contrasting element only when you want to call attention to something special. A little surprise here and there can keep your Web site alive.

- **Location:** Keep related items close to one another and be consistent about where you locate similar elements. For example, a menu of links should appear in the same place on all your pages to make it easier for visitors to quickly find their way around your site.

- **Prominence:** Give elements of similar importance the same weight on a page. For example, the most important headline on each page should be formatted with the same size and style.

This type of organization makes following information visually much easier.

Follow the Three Clicks Rule

The three clicks rule states that no important piece of information should ever be more than three clicks away from anywhere else on your Web site. The most important information should be even closer at hand. Some information, such as contact information, should never be more than one click away. You can make finding information easy for viewers by creating a *site map* (with links to all or most of the pages in your site) and a *navigation bar* — a set of links to all the main sections on your site.

Get a Head Start on Your Designs

Dreamweaver features many predesigned templates, including a collection of CSS designs you can edit to create two-column, three-column, and other popular CSS layouts.

When you create a file in Dreamweaver (such as by choosing File➪New), the New Document window offers you many ways to create a predesigned page, including the following:

- **Template pages:** Choose the Template Page category to open a list of templates types. The options are ASP JavaScript, ASP VBScript, ASP.Net C#, ASP.Net VB, ColdFusion, HTML, JSP, and PHP. Note that all these formats except HTML require programming and require the most advanced features of Dreamweaver. You find more about these options and how they can be used to create database-driven Web sites in Chapters 14 and 15.
- **Layout designs for frames:** If you're going to use frames, get a head start with one of Dreamweaver's many predesigned framesets. Because these templates can save you so much time, they're a "must use" feature if you're creating a site that uses frames.
- **CSS-designed pages:** Choose from any of the predesigned layouts included in the New Document window under Layout when you create a new file.
- **Regular template designs:** Choose Page Designs to open a list of basic HTML templates. Although they may seem simple by comparison, these are well-designed pages that can help you get a static Web site up and running with a lot less effort than creating it from scratch.

Split the View

If you like to switch back and forth between the HTML source code and design view in Dreamweaver, you'll appreciate the option to split the window so that you can view both the source code and the page design at the same time. To split the window, choose View➪Code and Design or click the Split View button, located just under the Insert bar at the top of the workspace.

Dreamweaver's source code has helpful color coding and tagging features, similar to those in HTML editors such as HomeSite and BBEdit. Notice as you're working that if you select an image, text, or another element on a page in design view, it is automatically highlighted in code view, a useful feature that makes it easier to find your place in the raw code.

Design in a Flash

Flash rocks! Adobe has made Flash better than ever by providing enhanced integration with Dreamweaver, Photoshop, and Fireworks. Flash is a vector-based design and animation program and the tool used to create some of the coolest Web sites on the Net today. Flash makes it possible to create fast-loading images and complex animations that dynamically adjust to fit any screen size. Now that the vast majority of Web surfers have the Flash plug-in, Flash has become a standard for video and animations, and Dreamweaver makes inserting Flash video and animation files easier than ever.

Just choose Insert➪Media, select a Flash option from the list (SWF, Flash Paper, or FLV), use the dialog box to customize the Flash file, and save it to your Web site. You find detailed instructions for inserting Flash files into Web pages in Chapter 11.

Find Functional Fonts

Designers get so excited when they find out that they can use any font on a Web page. In reality, your viewers must still have the font on their computers for the font to appear. The more common the font, the more likely it is to appear the way you intend. If you want to use a more unusual font, go for it — just be sure that you also include alternatives. The Dreamweaver font list already includes collections of common fonts, and you can create your own font list by choosing Format➪Font➪Edit Font List.

In an effort to make text easier to read on the Web, Adobe and Microsoft have both created fonts especially suited to computer screens. To find out more, visit their Web sites at www.adobe.com and www.microsoft.com, respectively, and search for Web fonts.

Keep Frequently Used Items Handy

Ever wish you could keep all your favorite Dreamweaver features in one convenient place? You can! Just customize the Favorites collection in the Insert panel. To get started, follow these steps:

1. **Launch Dreamweaver, and choose Window➪Insert to open the Common Insert panel.**

   The Insert panel includes several sections, including Layout, Forms, HTML, and Favorites.

2. **Click the arrow in the Insert panel and choose Favorites from the drop-down list.**

   The Favorites option is at the end of the Insert panel drop-down list.

3. **To customize the Favorites panel with all your favorite feature icons, right-click (or Control+click on a Mac) and choose Customize Favorites.**

Use the Favorites Insert panel as a convenient way to keep all your favorite features handy. You can even change it for special projects that require a collection of program features.

Be Prepared for Fast Updates

The Web provides a powerful vehicle for businesses and nonprofit organizations to present their side of any story and get the word out quickly when tragic events, bad press, and other crises arise. But don't wait for an emergency to find out whether you're prepared to add new information to your Web site quickly, and don't fool yourself into thinking that just because you don't manage a daily Internet newspaper, you don't have to worry about speedy updates.

With a little planning and key systems set up in advance, you can be prepared for events that require timely information — whether an international crisis stops air travel, a flood closes your nonprofit, or an embarrassing event makes your CEO cringe and demand that the real story be told as soon as possible.

Most organizations develop Web sites that are updated on a weekly, monthly, or even annual basis. More sophisticated sites may link to databases that track inventory or update product listings in real time, but even high-end sites are often ill prepared to update special information quickly.

Here are a few precautions you can take to be prepared for timely updates on your site:

- **Make sure you can send new information to your Web site quickly.** Many Web sites are designed with testing systems that safeguard against careless mistakes, but these systems can add hours, or even days, to the time it takes to add new information to your Web site. Work with your technical staff or consultants to make sure you can update your site quickly if necessary. This may require creating a new section that you can update independently from the rest of the site or that can override the regular update system.
- **Make updating important sections of your site easy.** Consider building or buying a content management system that uses Web-based forms to post new information to your site. Such a system can be designed to change or add information to a Web page as easily as filling out an online order form. You need an experienced programmer to develop a form-based update system. Many Web consultants offer this kind of service for a reasonable fee. This method works, for example, if you're a real estate agent and need to change listings or if you have a calendar of events. Include password protection so that you control access to the form. As an added advantage, a form enables you to make updates from any computer connected to the Internet, so you can update your Web site even if you can't get back into your office.
- **Identify and train key staff to update the site.** With the right systems in place, you don't need to have much technical experience to make simple updates to a site, but your staff needs some instruction and regular reminders. Make sure you also develop a schedule for retraining to ensure that no one forgets emergency procedures. Your most serious emergency could happen tomorrow or may not happen for years to come — you never know — but being prepared pays off in the end.

Back It Up

Make sure you have a system in place to back up your Web site. Always keep a copy of all the files on your server in a separate location and update it regularly to make sure you have the latest version of your site backed up at all times. Even the best Internet service providers sometimes have technical problems, so keep a backup of your site where you have easy access to it and can get it back online quickly if something deletes any or all the files you have on the server.

Also keep a backup of your original source files, such as Photoshop images. For example, when you develop images for the Web, you usually start in a program such as Photoshop, creating a high-resolution image that may include layers and other elements. Before the image goes on your Web site, those layers get flattened and the image gets compressed or reduced and converted into a GIF or a JPEG. If you ever want to go back and alter that image, you'll want the original source file before it was compressed and the layers were flattened. Whether you create your own images or you hire a professional designer, make sure you develop a system for saving all these original elements and make sure you get the original files from the designer, if possible, so that you have them if you ever need to alter an image later.

Index

Symbols

•A•

•B•

•E•

•F•

•G•

•H•

•M•

•N•

•O•

•Q•

•R•

T

• U •

• V •

•W•

USINESS, CAREERS & PERSONAL FINANCE

:counting For Dummies, 4th Edition*
8-0-470-24600-9

okkeeping Workbook For Dummies†
8-0-470-16983-4

mmodities For Dummies
8-0-470-04928-0

ing Business in China For Dummies
8-0-470-04929-7

E-Mail Marketing For Dummies
978-0-470-19087-6

Job Interviews For Dummies, 3rd Edition*†
978-0-470-17748-8

Personal Finance Workbook For Dummies*†
978-0-470-09933-9

Real Estate License Exams For Dummies
978-0-7645-7623-2

Six Sigma For Dummies
978-0-7645-6798-8

Small Business Kit For Dummies, 2nd Edition*†
978-0-7645-5984-6

Telephone Sales For Dummies
978-0-470-16836-3

USINESS PRODUCTIVITY & MICROSOFT OFFICE

cess 2007 For Dummies
8-0-470-03649-5

cel 2007 For Dummies
8-0-470-03737-9

fice 2007 For Dummies
-0-470-00923-9

tlook 2007 For Dummies
-0-470-03830-7

PowerPoint 2007 For Dummies
978-0-470-04059-1

Project 2007 For Dummies
978-0-470-03651-8

QuickBooks 2008 For Dummies
978-0-470-18470-7

Quicken 2008 For Dummies
978-0-470-17473-9

Salesforce.com For Dummies, 2nd Edition
978-0-470-04893-1

Word 2007 For Dummies
978-0-470-03658-7

UCATION, HISTORY, REFERENCE & TEST PREPARATION

rican American History For Dummies
-0-7645-5469-8

ebra For Dummies
-0-7645-5325-7

ebra Workbook For Dummies
-0-7645-8467-1

History For Dummies
-0-470-09910-0

ASVAB For Dummies, 2nd Edition
978-0-470-10671-6

British Military History For Dummies
978-0-470-03213-8

Calculus For Dummies
978-0-7645-2498-1

Canadian History For Dummies, 2nd Edition
978-0-470-83656-9

Geometry Workbook For Dummies
978-0-471-79940-5

The SAT I For Dummies, 6th Edition
978-0-7645-7193-0

Series 7 Exam For Dummies
978-0-470-09932-2

World History For Dummies
978-0-7645-5242-7

OD, GARDEN, HOBBIES & HOME

dge For Dummies, 2nd Edition
-0-471-92426-5

n Collecting For Dummies, 2nd Edition
-0-470-22275-1

king Basics For Dummies, 3rd Edition
-0-7645-7206-7

Drawing For Dummies
978-0-7645-5476-6

Etiquette For Dummies, 2nd Edition
978-0-470-10672-3

Gardening Basics For Dummies*†
978-0-470-03749-2

Knitting Patterns For Dummies
978-0-470-04556-5

Living Gluten-Free For Dummies†
978-0-471-77383-2

Painting Do-It-Yourself For Dummies
978-0-470-17533-0

ALTH, SELF HELP, PARENTING & PETS

ger Management For Dummies
-0-470-03715-7

ciety & Depression Workbook Dummies
-0-7645-9793-0

ting For Dummies, 2nd Edition
-0-7645-4149-0

Training For Dummies, 2nd Edition
0-7645-8418-3

Horseback Riding For Dummies
978-0-470-09719-9

Infertility For Dummies†
978-0-470-11518-3

Meditation For Dummies with CD-ROM, 2nd Edition
978-0-471-77774-8

Post-Traumatic Stress Disorder For Dummies
978-0-470-04922-8

Puppies For Dummies, 2nd Edition
978-0-470-03717-1

Thyroid For Dummies, 2nd Edition†
978-0-471-78755-6

Type 1 Diabetes For Dummies*†
978-0-470-17811-9

parate Canadian edition also available
parate U.K. edition also available

able wherever books are sold. For more information or to order direct: U.S. customers visit www.dummies.com or call 1-877-762-2974. ustomers visit www.wileyeurope.com or call (0) 1243 843291. Canadian customers visit www.wiley.ca or call 1-800-567-4797.

INTERNET & DIGITAL MEDIA

AdWords For Dummies
978-0-470-15252-2

Blogging For Dummies, 2nd Edition
978-0-470-23017-6

Digital Photography All-in-One Desk Reference For Dummies, 3rd Edition
978-0-470-03743-0

Digital Photography For Dummies, 5th Edition
978-0-7645-9802-9

Digital SLR Cameras & Photography For Dummies, 2nd Edition
978-0-470-14927-0

eBay Business All-in-One Desk Reference For Dummies
978-0-7645-8438-1

eBay For Dummies, 5th Edition*
978-0-470-04529-9

eBay Listings That Sell For Dummies
978-0-471-78912-3

Facebook For Dummies
978-0-470-26273-3

The Internet For Dummies, 11th Edition
978-0-470-12174-0

Investing Online For Dummies, 5th Edition
978-0-7645-8456-5

iPod & iTunes For Dummies, 5th Editi
978-0-470-17474-6

MySpace For Dummies
978-0-470-09529-4

Podcasting For Dummies
978-0-471-74898-4

Search Engine Optimization For Dummies, 2nd Edition
978-0-471-97998-2

Second Life For Dummies
978-0-470-18025-9

Starting an eBay Business For Dummi 3rd Edition†
978-0-470-14924-9

GRAPHICS, DESIGN & WEB DEVELOPMENT

Adobe Creative Suite 3 Design Premium All-in-One Desk Reference For Dummies
978-0-470-11724-8

Adobe Web Suite CS3 All-in-One Desk Reference For Dummies
978-0-470-12099-6

AutoCAD 2008 For Dummies
978-0-470-11650-0

Building a Web Site For Dummies, 3rd Edition
978-0-470-14928-7

Creating Web Pages All-in-One Desk Reference For Dummies, 3rd Edition
978-0-470-09629-1

Creating Web Pages For Dummies, 8th Edition
978-0-470-08030-6

Dreamweaver CS3 For Dummies
978-0-470-11490-2

Flash CS3 For Dummies
978-0-470-12100-9

Google SketchUp For Dummies
978-0-470-13744-4

InDesign CS3 For Dummies
978-0-470-11865-8

Photoshop CS3 All-in-One Desk Reference For Dummies
978-0-470-11195-6

Photoshop CS3 For Dummies
978-0-470-11193-2

Photoshop Elements 5 For Dummie
978-0-470-09810-3

SolidWorks For Dummies
978-0-7645-9555-4

Visio 2007 For Dummies
978-0-470-08983-5

Web Design For Dummies, 2nd Edit
978-0-471-78117-2

Web Sites Do-It-Yourself For Dumm
978-0-470-16903-2

Web Stores Do-It-Yourself For Dumm
978-0-470-17443-2

LANGUAGES, RELIGION & SPIRITUALITY

Arabic For Dummies
978-0-471-77270-5

Chinese For Dummies, Audio Set
978-0-470-12766-7

French For Dummies
978-0-7645-5193-2

German For Dummies
978-0-7645-5195-6

Hebrew For Dummies
978-0-7645-5489-6

Ingles Para Dummies
978-0-7645-5427-8

Italian For Dummies, Audio Set
978-0-470-09586-7

Italian Verbs For Dummies
978-0-471-77389-4

Japanese For Dummies
978-0-7645-5429-2

Latin For Dummies
978-0-7645-5431-5

Portuguese For Dummies
978-0-471-78738-9

Russian For Dummies
978-0-471-78001-4

Spanish Phrases For Dummies
978-0-7645-7204-3

Spanish For Dummies
978-0-7645-5194-9

Spanish For Dummies, Audio Set
978-0-470-09585-0

The Bible For Dummies
978-0-7645-5296-0

Catholicism For Dummies
978-0-7645-5391-2

The Historical Jesus For Dummies
978-0-470-16785-4

Islam For Dummies
978-0-7645-5503-9

Spirituality For Dummies, 2nd Edition
978-0-470-19142-2

NETWORKING AND PROGRAMMING

ASP.NET 3.5 For Dummies
978-0-470-19592-5

C# 2008 For Dummies
978-0-470-19109-5

Hacking For Dummies, 2nd Edition
978-0-470-05235-8

Home Networking For Dummies, 4th Edition
978-0-470-11806-1

Java For Dummies, 4th Edition
978-0-470-08716-9

Microsoft® SQL Server™ 2008 All-in-One Desk Reference For Dummies
978-0-470-17954-3

Networking All-in-One Desk Reference For Dummies, 2nd Edition
978-0-7645-9939-2

Networking For Dummies, 8th Edition
978-0-470-05620-2

SharePoint 2007 For Dummies
978-0-470-09941-4

Wireless Home Networking For Dummies, 2nd Edition
978-0-471-74940-0

PERATING SYSTEMS & COMPUTER BASICS

lac For Dummies, 5th Edition
'8-0-7645-8458-9

aptops For Dummies, 2nd Edition
'8-0-470-05432-1

nux For Dummies, 8th Edition
'8-0-470-11649-4

acBook For Dummies
'8-0-470-04859-7

ac OS X Leopard All-in-One esk Reference For Dummies
8-0-470-05434-5

Mac OS X Leopard For Dummies
978-0-470-05433-8

Macs For Dummies, 9th Edition
978-0-470-04849-8

PCs For Dummies, 11th Edition
978-0-470-13728-4

Windows® Home Server For Dummies
978-0-470-18592-6

Windows Server 2008 For Dummies
978-0-470-18043-3

Windows Vista All-in-One Desk Reference For Dummies
978-0-471-74941-7

Windows Vista For Dummies
978-0-471-75421-3

Windows Vista Security For Dummies
978-0-470-11805-4

PORTS, FITNESS & MUSIC

oaching Hockey For Dummies
8-0-470-83685-9

oaching Soccer For Dummies
8-0-471-77381-8

tness For Dummies, 3rd Edition
3-0-7645-7851-9

otball For Dummies, 3rd Edition
3-0-470-12536-6

GarageBand For Dummies
978-0-7645-7323-1

Golf For Dummies, 3rd Edition
978-0-471-76871-5

Guitar For Dummies, 2nd Edition
978-0-7645-9904-0

Home Recording For Musicians For Dummies, 2nd Edition
978-0-7645-8884-6

iPod & iTunes For Dummies, 5th Edition
978-0-470-17474-6

Music Theory For Dummies
978-0-7645-7838-0

Stretching For Dummies
978-0-470-06741-3

Get smart @ dummies.com®

- **Find a full list of Dummies titles**
- **Look into loads of FREE on-site articles**
- **Sign up for FREE eTips e-mailed to you weekly**
- **See what other products carry the Dummies name**
- **Shop directly from the Dummies bookstore**
- **Enter to win new prizes every month!**

parate Canadian edition also available
parate U.K. edition also available

able wherever books are sold. For more information or to order direct: U.S. customers visit www.dummies.com or call 1-877-762-2974. customers visit www.wileyeurope.com or call (0) 1243 843291. Canadian customers visit www.wiley.ca or call 1-800-567-4797.